Skoda
Favorit
Owners
Workshop
Manual

Andrew Hamlin

Models covered
Skoda Favorit 135 & 136 Hatchback models,
including special/limited editions;
1289 cc (carburettor) engine

Covers major features of Estate, Van and Pick-up models
Does not cover single-point fuel injection models

ABCDE
FGHIJ
KLMNO
PQ

Haynes Publishing Group
Sparkford Nr Yeovil
Somerset BA22 7JJ England

Haynes Publications, Inc
861 Lawrence Drive
Newbury Park
California 91320 USA

Acknowledgements

Thanks are due to Champion Spark Plug, who supplied the illustrations showing spark plug conditions, to Holt Lloyd Limited who supplied the illustrations showing bodywork repair, and to Duckhams Oils, who provided lubrication data. Thanks are also due to Garland Motors, Nr. Salisbury, Wilts., who provided valuable technical assistance, to Sykes-Pickavant Limited, who provided some of the workshop tools, and to all those people at Sparkford who helped in the production of this manual.

Technical authors who contributed to this project include Jeremy Churchill, Ian Coomber and Mark Coombs.

A book in the **Haynes Owners Workshop Manual Series**

Printed by J. H. Haynes & Co. Ltd., Sparkford, Nr Yeovil, Somerset BA22 7JJ, England

ISBN 1 85010 801 3

British Library Cataloguing in Publication Data
A catalogue record for this book is available from the British Library.

We take great pride in the accuracy of information given in this manual, but vehicle manufacturers make alterations and design changes during the production run of a particular vehicle of which they do not inform us. No liability can be accepted by the authors or publishers for loss, damage or injury caused by any errors in, or omissions from, the information given.

Restoring and Preserving our Motoring Heritage

Few people can have had the luck to realise their dreams to quite the same extent and in such a remarkable fashion as John Haynes, Founder and Chairman of the Haynes Publishing Group.

Since 1965 his unique approach to workshop manual publishing has proved so successful that millions of Haynes Manuals are now sold every year throughout the world, covering literally thousands of different makes and models of cars, vans and motorcycles.

A continuing passion for cars and motoring led to the founding in 1985 of a Charitable Trust dedicated to the restoration and preservation of our motoring heritage. To inaugurate the new Museum, John Haynes donated virtually his entire private collection of 52 cars.

Now with an unrivalled international collection of over 210 veteran, vintage and classic cars and motorcycles, the Haynes Motor Museum in Somerset is well on the way to becoming one of the most interesting Motor Museums in the world.

A 70 seat video cinema, a cafe and an extensive motoring bookshop, together with a specially constructed one kilometre motor circuit, make a visit to the Haynes Motor Museum a truly unforgettable experience.

Every vehicle in the museum is preserved in as near as possible mint condition and each car is run every six months on the motor circuit.

Enjoy the picnic area set amongst the rolling Somerset hills. Peer through the William Morris workshop windows at cars being restored, and browse through the extensive displays of fascinating motoring memorabilia.

From the 1903 Oldsmobile through such classics as an MG Midget to the mighty 'E' Type Jaguar, Lamborghini, Ferrari Berlinetta Boxer, and Graham Hill's Lola Cosworth, there is something for everyone, young and old alike, at this Somerset Museum.

Haynes Motor Museum

Situated mid-way between London and Penzance, the Haynes Motor Museum is located just off the A303 at Sparkford, Somerset (home of the Haynes Manual) and is open to the public 7 days a week all year round, except Christmas Day and Boxing Day.

Contents

Page

Preliminary sections
Acknowledgements **2**
About this manual **5**
Introduction to the Skoda Favorit **5**
General dimensions and weights **6**
Jacking, towing and wheel changing **7**
Buying spare parts and vehicle identification numbers **9**
Safety first! **10**
General repair procedures **12**
Tools and working facilities **13**
Booster battery (jump) starting **17**
Conversion factors **18**
Fault diagnosis **19**
MOT test checks **24**

Chapter 1 Routine maintenance and servicing **28**
Lubricants, fluids and capacities **30**
Maintenance schedule **31**
Maintenance procedures **36**

Chapter 2 Engine **50**
Part A: In-car engine repair procedures **53**
Part B: Engine removal and general engine overhaul procedures ... **67**

Chapter 3 Cooling, heating and ventilation systems **85**

Chapter 4 Fuel and exhaust systems **95**

Chapter 5 Ignition system **110**

Chapter 6 Clutch **117**

Chapter 7 Transmission **122**

Chapter 8 Driveshafts **130**

Chapter 9 Braking system **135**

Chapter 10 Suspension and steering **158**

Chapter 11 Bodywork and fittings **180**

Chapter 12 Electrical system **197**

Wiring diagrams **220**

Index **224**

Spark plug condition and bodywork repair colour pages between pages 32 and 33

Skoda Favorit 136 LX Hatchback

Skoda Favorit Forum Estate

About this manual

Its aim

The aim of this manual is to help you get the best value from your vehicle. It can do so in several ways. It can help you decide what work must be done (even should you choose to get it done by a garage), provide information on routine maintenance and servicing, and give a logical course of action and diagnosis when random faults occur. However, it is hoped that you will use the manual by tackling the work yourself. On simpler jobs it may even be quicker than booking the vehicle into a garage and going there twice, to leave and collect it. Perhaps most important, a lot of money can be saved by avoiding the costs a garage must charge to cover its labour and overheads.

The manual has drawings and descriptions to show the function of the various components so that their layout can be understood. Then the tasks are described and photographed in a clear step-by-step sequence.

Its arrangement

The manual is divided into Chapters, each covering a logical sub-division of the vehicle. The Chapters are each divided into Sections, numbered with single figures, eg 5; the Sections are divided into paragraphs, or into sub-sections and paragraphs.

It is freely illustrated, especially in those parts where there is a detailed sequence of operations to be carried out. There are two forms of illustration: figures and photographs. The figures are numbered in sequence with decimal numbers, according to their position in the Chapter – eg Fig. 6.4 is the fourth drawing/illustration in Chapter 6. Photographs carry the same number (either individually or in related groups) as the Section and paragraph to which they relate.

There is an alphabetical index at the back of the manual, as well as a contents list at the front. Each Chapter is also preceded by its own individual contents list.

References to the 'left' or 'right' of the vehicle are in the sense of a person in the driver's seat facing forward.

Unless otherwise stated, nuts and bolts are removed by turning anti-clockwise, and tightened by turning clockwise.

Vehicle manufacturers continually make changes to specifications and recommendations, and these, when notified, are incorporated into our manuals at the earliest opportunity.

We take great pride in the accuracy of information given in this manual, but vehicle manufacturers make alterations and design changes during the production run of a particular vehicle of which they do not inform us. No liability can be accepted by the authors or publishers for loss, damage or injury caused by any errors in, or omissions from, the information given.

Project vehicles

The main project vehicle used in the preparation of this manual, and appearing in many of the photographic sequences, was a Skoda Favorit 136 LX.

Introduction to the Skoda Favorit

The Skoda Favorit covered in this manual was first launched onto the UK market in the summer of 1989. The introduction of the Favorit saw the Czechoslovakian manufacturer moving away from its traditional rear-engined, rear-wheel-drive layout to their first-ever front-engined, front-wheel-drive layout.

The 1289 cc overhead valve engine is similar to that used in previous Skoda models, but has been updated and modified to include an aluminium alloy cylinder head, and to enable it to be mounted transversely and run on unleaded fuels. The five-speed gearbox is fitted to the left-hand end of the engine, and the resulting assembly drives the front wheels through unequal-length driveshafts.

The suspension at the front is of the MacPherson strut type, with coil springs and telescopic shock absorbers. Rear suspension incorporates trailing arms, a torsion beam, coil springs and telescopic shock absorbers.

Braking is by discs at the front and drums at the rear, utilising a dual-circuit hydraulic system.

The Bertone-styled body is available in five-door Hatchback, Estate, Van and Pick-up versions, all with a range of fittings and interior trim dependent on model designation.

General dimensions and weights

Dimensions

Overall length:
Hatchback and Freeway Van	3815 mm
Estate and Freeway Plus Van	4160 mm
Pick-up	4065 mm
Overall width	1620 mm

Overall height:
Hatchback and Freeway Van	1415 mm
Estate and Freeway Plus Van	1425 mm
Pick-up	1430 mm
Wheelbase	2450 mm

Front track:
With steel wheels	1400 mm
With alloy wheels	1415 mm

Rear track:
With steel wheels	1365 mm
With alloy wheels	1380 mm
Turning circle	10.5 metres

Weights

Kerb weight:
136 Forum, L Hatchback	875 kg
136 LX, LS Hatchback	895 kg
136 Forum, L Estate	920 kg
136 LX, LS Estate	930 kg
Freeway Van	875 kg
Freeway Plus Van	920 kg
Foreman Pick-up	860 kg

Maximum gross vehicle weight:
Hatchback and Freeway Van	1325 kg
Estate and Freeway Plus Van	1370 kg
Pick-up	1360 kg
Maximum roof rack load	50 kg

Maximum towing weight:
Braked trailer	750 kg
Unbraked trailer	400 kg
Maximum towing hitch downward load	50 kg

Jacking, towing and wheel changing

Changing a wheel

Wheel changing should only be carried out with the car on firm, level ground; obviously, it is not possible to choose where you'll have a puncture, but if the car can safely be moved to a suitable location, this is to be recommended. Before changing a wheel, apply the handbrake firmly; for additional security, the car could be left in gear, but remember to disengage the gear before starting up. Place chocks (any blocks of wood, bricks or stones lying around will do) at the front and rear of the roadwheel diagonally opposite the one to be changed. Remove the spare wheel, jack and wheelbrace from under the luggage compartment floor. Remove the wheel trim (if necessary for access to the bolts) and loosen the wheel bolts slightly with the wheelbrace provided (photo).

Make sure that the ground beneath the jack base is firm and level, then locate the jack head in the jacking point nearest to the wheel to be changed, and slowly raise the jack (photo). For additional safety, it is worthwhile sliding the spare wheel under the side of the car, close to the jack, while the car is raised. When the spare wheel is required, put the punctured wheel under the car in its place. This will reduce the risk of personal injury (and of damage to the car), should the car slip off the jack.

When the wheel is clear of the ground, remove the bolts and lift off the wheel. Check that the threads and the wheel-to-hub mating surfaces are clean and undamaged, and that the inside of the spare wheel is clean. The threads may be cleaned with a brass wire brush if rusty. Apply a thin smear of copper-based anti-seize compound (such as Holts Copaslip) to the threads and roadwheel-to-hub mating surfaces, to prevent the formation of corrosion. *Obviously, you are not likely to be able to do anything about this at the roadside, but it is worthwhile attending to it as soon as possible once the car is running again, or changing a wheel may be even more difficult next time!*

Fit the spare wheel (and trim where applicable), and tighten the bolts securely, but not yet fully while the car is still raised. If you put the punctured wheel under the car, remove it now and lower the car to the ground. Tighten the bolts fully, working in progressive stages and in a diagonal sequence, to the specified torque wrench setting if possible (photo).

Before driving off, **check the spare tyre pressure** (Chapter 1), and remember to take the car out of gear (if applicable) before starting up. Remove the chocks, and stow the jack, tools and punctured wheel. If a new roadwheel has been fitted, have it balanced as soon as possible. If the roadwheel bolts were tightened using the car's wheelbrace, check as soon as possible that they are tightened to the specified torque wrench setting (see Chapter 1 or 10).

Jacking

When jacking up the vehicle to carry out repair or maintenance tasks, position the jack under the body sill jacking points as follows.

If the front of the vehicle is to be raised, use the front jacking points to raise the vehicle in stages, jacking one side at a time and then supporting it while the opposite side is raised.

To raise the rear of the vehicle, use the rear jacking points to raise the vehicle in stages, jacking one side at a time and then supporting it while the opposite side is raised.

To raise the side of the vehicle, use the side jacking points to raise the vehicle in stages, jacking the front end first and then supporting it while the rear is raised.

When raising the car using a trolley or workshop jack, use a suitably-shaped wooden block placed between the jack head and the body sill to avoid damaging the sill. Support the car using axle stands or sturdy

Slacken the roadwheel nuts with the wheelbrace provided

Jack positioned in jacking point

Tighten roadwheel bolts to specified torque setting

Front towing eye

Rear towing eye – for towing light vehicles only

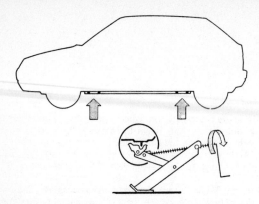 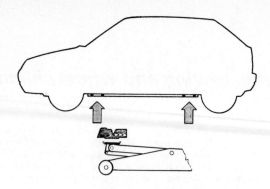

Front and rear jacking point locations under the body sills

blocks positioned under a load-bearing area of the chassis near to the jacking point. **Never** work under, around or near a raised vehicle unless it is adequately supported in at least two places with axle stands or suitable sturdy blocks.

Never raise or support the vehicle under a suspension component or the engine/transmission.

Towing

The vehicle may be towed for breakdown recovery purposes only, using the towing eyes positioned at the front and rear of the vehicle. These eyes are only intended for towing, and must not be used for lifting the vehicle either directly or indirectly (photos).

Buying spare parts and vehicle identification numbers

Buying spare parts

Spare parts are available from many sources; for example, Skoda garages, other garages and accessory shops, and motor factors. Our advice regarding spare part sources is as follows.

Officially-appointed Skoda garages – This is the best source for parts which are peculiar to your vehicle, and are not generally available (eg complete cylinder heads, internal gearbox components, badges, interior trim etc). It is also the only place at which you should buy parts if the vehicle is still under warranty. To be sure of obtaining the correct parts, it will be necessary to give the storeman your vehicle's VIN (vehicle identification number), and if possible, take the old parts along for positive identification. Many parts are available under a factory exchange scheme – any parts returned should always be clean. It obviously makes good sense to go straight to the specialists on your vehicle for this type of part, as they are best equipped to supply you.

Other garages and accessory shops – These are often very good places to buy materials and components needed for the maintenance of your vehicle (eg oil filters, spark plugs, bulbs, drivebelts, oils and greases, touch-up paint, filler paste, etc). They also sell general accessories, usually have convenient opening hours, charge lower prices and can often be found not far from home.

Motor factors – Good factors will stock all the more important components which wear out comparatively quickly (eg exhaust systems, brake pads, seals and hydraulic parts, clutch components, bearing shells, pistons, valves etc). Motor factors will often provide new or reconditioned components on a part exchange basis – this can save a considerable amount of money.

Vehicle identification numbers

Modifications are a continuing and unpublicised process in vehicle manufacture, quite apart from major model changes. Spare parts manuals and lists are compiled upon a numerical basis, the individual vehicle identification numbers being essential to correct identification of the component concerned.

When ordering spare parts, always give as much information as possible. Quote the vehicle model, year of manufacture, body and engine numbers as appropriate.

The *vehicle identification plate* is located on the bonnet lock platform. It gives the VIN (vehicle identification number) and vehicle weight information (photo).

The *chassis number* is located on the right-hand front suspension turret, and is sometimes repeated on the bonnet lock platform (photo).

The *engine number* is stamped on the cylinder block, just above the timing chain cover (photo).

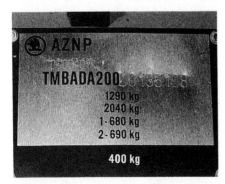

Vehicle identification plate on bonnet lock platform

Chassis number location on right-hand front suspension turret

Engine number location on cylinder block

Safety first!

However enthusiastic you may be about getting on with the job in hand, do take the time to ensure that your safety is not put at risk. A moment's lack of attention can result in an accident, as can failure to observe certain elementary precautions. There will always be new ways of having accidents, and the following points do not pretend to be a comprehensive list of all dangers; they are intended rather to make you aware of the risks and to encourage a safety-conscious approach to all work you carry out on your vehicle.

Essential DOs and DON'Ts

DON'T rely on a single jack when working underneath the vehicle. Always use reliable additional means of support, such as axle stands, securely placed under a structural part of the vehicle that you know will not give way.

DON'T attempt to loosen or tighten high-torque nuts (eg wheel hub nuts) while the vehicle is on a jack; it may be pulled off.

DON'T start the engine without first ascertaining that the transmission is in neutral (or 'Park' where applicable) and the handbrake applied.

DON'T suddenly remove the filler cap from a hot cooling system – cover it with a cloth and release the pressure gradually first, or you may get scalded by escaping coolant.

DON'T attempt to drain oil, automatic transmission fluid, or coolant until you are sure it has cooled sufficiently to avoid scalding you.

DON'T grasp any part of the engine, exhaust or catalytic converter without first ascertaining that it is sufficiently cool to avoid burning you.

DON'T allow brake fluid or antifreeze to contact vehicle paintwork.

DON'T syphon toxic liquids such as fuel, brake fluid or antifreeze by mouth, or allow them to remain on your skin.

DON'T inhale dust – it may be injurious to health (see *Asbestos* below).

DON'T allow any spilt oil or grease to remain on the floor – wipe it up straight away, before someone slips on it.

DON'T use ill-fitting spanners or other tools which may slip and cause injury.

DON'T attempt to lift a heavy component which may be beyond your capability – get assistance.

DON'T rush to finish a job, or take unverified short cuts.

DON'T allow children or animals in or around an unattended vehicle.

DON'T park vehicles with catalytic converters over combustible materials such as dry grass, oily rags, etc if the engine has recently been run. As catalytic converters reach extremely high temperatures, any such materials in close proximity may ignite.

DON'T run vehicles equipped with catalytic converters without the exhaust system heat shields fitted.

DO wear eye protection when using power tools such as an electric drill, sander, bench grinder, etc., and when working under the vehicle.

DO use a barrier cream on your hands prior to undertaking dirty jobs – it will protect your skin from infection as well as making the dirt easier to remove afterwards; but make sure your hands aren't left slippery. Note that long term contact with used engine oil can be a health hazard.

DO keep loose clothing (cuffs, tie, etc.,) and long hair well out of the way of moving mechanical parts.

DO remove rings, wristwatch, etc., before working on the vehicle – especially the electrical system.

DO ensure that any lifting tackle or jacking equipment used has a safe working load rating adequate for the job, and is used precisely as recommended by the manufacturer.

DO keep your work area tidy – it is only too easy to fall over articles left lying around.

DO get someone to check periodically that all is well when working alone on the vehicle.

DO carry out work in a logical sequence and check that everything is correctly assembled and tightened afterwards.

DO remember that your vehicle's safety affects that of yourself and others. If in doubt on any point, get specialist advice.

IF, in spite of following these precautions, you are unfortunate enough to injure yourself, seek medical attention as soon as possible.

Asbestos

Certain friction, insulating, sealing, and other products – such as brake linings, brake bands, clutch linings, gaskets, etc. – contain asbestos. *Extreme care must be taken to avoid inhalation of dust from such products since it is hazardous to health.* If in doubt, assume that they *do* contain asbestos.

Fire

Remember at all times that petrol is highly flammable. Never smoke, or have any kind of naked flame around, when working on the vehicle. But the risk does not end there – a spark caused by an electrical short-circuit, by two metal surfaces contacting each other, by careless use of tools, or even by static electricity built up in your body under certain conditions, can ignite petrol vapour, which in a confined space is highly explosive. The vapour produced by spilling oil or hydraulic fluid onto hot metal, such as an exhaust manifold, can also be flammable or explosive.

Whenever possible disconnect the battery earth terminal before working on any part of the fuel or electrical system, and never risk spilling fuel on to a hot engine or exhaust. Catalytic converters run at extremely high temperatures, and consequently can be an additional fire hazard. Observe the precautions outlined elsewhere in this section.

It is recommended that a fire extinguisher of a type suitable for fuel and electrical fires is kept handy in the garage or workplace at all times. Ideally a suitable extinguisher should also be carried in the vehicle. Never try to extinguish a fuel or electrical fire with water. If a vehicle fire does occur, take note of the remarks below about hydrofluoric acid.

Note: *Any reference to a 'torch' appearing in this manual should always be taken to mean a hand-held battery-operated electric light or flashlight. It does NOT mean a welding/gas torch or blowlamp.*

Hydrofluoric acid

Hydrofluoric acid is extremely corrosive. It is formed when certain types of synthetic rubber, which may be found in O-rings, oil seals, brake hydraulic system seals, fuel hoses, etc., are exposed to temperatures above 400°C. The obvious circumstance in which this could happen on a vehicle is in the case of a fire. The rubber does not burn, but changes into a charred or sticky substance which contains the acid. *Once formed, the acid remains dangerous for years. If it gets onto the skin, it may be necessary to amputate the limb concerned.*

When dealing with a vehicle which has suffered a fire, or with components salvaged from such a vehicle, always wear protective gloves and discard them carefully after use. Bear this in mind if obtaining components from a car breaker.

Fumes

Certain fumes are highly toxic and can quickly cause unconsciousness and even death if inhaled to any extent, especially if inhalation takes place through a lighted cigarette or pipe. Petrol vapour comes into this category, as do the vapours from certain solvents such as trichloroethylene. Any draining or pouring of such volatile fluids should be done in a well-ventilated area.

When using cleaning fluids and solvents, read the instructions carefully. Never use materials from unmarked containers – they may give off poisonous vapours.

Never run the engine of a motor vehicle in an enclosed space such as a garage. Exhaust fumes contain carbon monoxide which is extremely poisonous; if you need to run the engine, always do so in the open air or at least have the rear of the vehicle outside the workplace. Although vehicles fitted with catalytic converters have greatly reduced toxic exhaust emissions, the above precautions should still be observed.

If you are fortunate enough to have the use of an inspection pit, never drain or pour petrol, and never run the engine, while the vehicle is standing over it; the fumes, being heavier than air, will concentrate in the pit with possibly lethal results.

The battery

Batteries which are sealed for life require special precautions which are normally outlined on a label attached to the battery. Such precautions are primarily related to situations involving battery charging and jump starting from another vehicle.

With a conventional battery, never cause a spark, or allow a naked light, in close proximity to it. It will normally be giving off a certain amount of hydrogen gas, which is highly explosive.

Whenever possible disconnect the battery earth terminal before working on the fuel or electrical systems.

If possible, loosen the filler plugs or cover when charging the battery from an external source. Do not charge at an excessive rate or the battery may burst. Special care should be taken with the use of high charge-rate boost chargers to prevent the battery from overheating.

Take care when topping up and when carrying the battery. The acid electrolyte, even when diluted, is very corrosive and should not be allowed to contact clothing, eyes or skin.

Always wear eye protection when cleaning the battery to prevent the caustic deposits from entering your eyes.

The vehicle electrical system

Take care when making alterations or repairs to the vehicle wiring. Electrical faults are the commonest cause of vehicle fires. Make sure that any accessories are wired correctly, using an appropriately-rated fuse and wire of adequate current-carrying capacity. When possible, avoid the use of 'piggy-back' or self-splicing connectors to power additional electrical equipment from existing feeds; make up a new feed with its own fuse instead.

When considering the current which a new circuit will have to handle, do not overlook the switch, especially when planning to use an existing switch to control additional components – for instance, if spotlights are to be fed via the main lighting switch. For preference, a relay should be used to switch heavy currents. If in doubt, consult an auto electrical specialist.

Any wire which passes through a body panel or bulkhead must be protected from chafing with a grommet or similar device. A wire which is allowed to chafe bare against the bodywork will cause a short-circuit and possibly a fire.

Mains electricity and electrical equipment

When using an electric power tool, inspection light, diagnostic equipment, etc., which works from the mains, always ensure that the appliance is correctly connected to its plug and that, where necessary, it is properly earthed. Do not use such appliances in damp conditions and, again, beware of creating a spark or applying excessive heat in the vicinity of fuel or fuel vapour. Also ensure that the appliances meet the relevant national safety standards.

Ignition HT voltage

A severe electric shock can result from touching certain parts of the ignition system, such as the HT leads, when the engine is running or being cranked, particularly if components are damp or the insulation is defective. Where an electronic ignition system is fitted, the HT voltage is much higher and could prove fatal, especially to wearers of cardiac pacemakers.

Jacking and vehicle support

The jack provided with the vehicle is designed primarily for emergency wheel changing, and its use for servicing and overhaul work on the vehicle is best avoided. Instead, a more substantial workshop jack (trolley jack or similar) should be used. Whichever type is employed, it is essential that additional safety support is provided by means of axle stands designed for this purpose. Never use makeshift means such as wooden blocks or piles of house bricks, as these can easily topple or, in the case of bricks, disintegrate under the weight of the vehicle. Further information on the correct positioning of the jack and axle stands is provided in the *Jacking, towing and wheel changing* section.

If removal of the wheels is not required, the use of drive-on ramps is recommended. Caution should be exercised to ensure that they are correctly aligned with the wheels, and that the vehicle is not driven too far along them so that it promptly falls off the other ends or tips the ramps.

General repair procedures

Whenever servicing, repair or overhaul work is carried out on the vehicle or its components, it is necessary to observe the following procedures and instructions. This will assist in carrying out the operation efficiently and to a professional standard of workmanship.

Joint mating faces and gaskets

When separating components at their mating faces, never insert screwdrivers or similar implements into the joint between the faces in order to prise them apart. This can cause severe damage which results in oil leaks, coolant leaks, etc., upon reassembly. Separation is usually achieved by tapping along the joint with a soft-faced hammer in order to break the seal. However, note that this method may not be suitable where dowels are used for component location.

Where a gasket is used between the mating faces of two components, ensure that it is renewed on reassembly and fit it dry unless otherwise stated in the repair procedure. Make sure that the mating faces are clean and dry with all traces of old gasket removed. When cleaning a joint face, use a tool which is not likely to score or damage the face, and remove any burrs or nicks with an oilstone or fine file.

Make sure that tapped holes are cleaned with a pipe cleaner and keep them free of jointing compound, if this is being used, unless specifically instructed otherwise.

Ensure that all orifices, channels or pipes are clear and blow through them, preferably using compressed air.

Oil seals

Oil seals can be removed by levering them out with a wide flat-bladed screwdriver or similar implement. Alternatively, a number of self-tapping screws may be screwed into the seal and these used as a purchase for pliers or some similar device in order to pull the seal free.

Whenever an oil seal is removed from its working location, either individually or as part of an assembly, it should be renewed.

The very fine sealing lip of the seal is easily damaged and will not seal if the surface it contacts is not completely clean and free from scratches, nicks or grooves. If the original sealing surface of the component cannot be restored, and the manufacturer has not made provision for slight relocation of the seal relative to the sealing surface, the component should be renewed.

Protect the lips of the seal from any surface which may damage them in the course of fitting. Use tape or a conical sleeve where possible. Lubricate the seal lips with oil before fitting and, on dual-lipped seals, fill the space between the lips with grease.

Unless otherwise stated, oil seals must be fitted with their sealing lips toward the lubricant to be sealed.

Use a tubular drift or block of wood of the appropriate size to install the seal and, if the seal housing is shouldered, drive the seal down to the shoulder. If the seal housing is unshouldered, the seal should be fitted with its face flush with the housing top face (unless otherwise instructed).

Screw threads and fastenings

Seized nuts, bolts and screws are quite a common occurrence where corrosion has set in, and the use of penetrating oil or releasing fluid will often overcome this problem if the offending item is soaked for a while before attempting to release it. The use of an impact driver may also provide a means of releasing such stubborn fastening devices when used in conjunction with the appropriate screwdriver bit or socket. If none of these methods works, it may be necessary to resort to the careful application of heat, or the use of a hacksaw or nut splitter device.

Studs are usually removed by locking two nuts together on the threaded part and then using a spanner on the lower nut to unscrew the stud. Studs or bolts which have broken off below the surface of the component in which they are mounted can sometimes be removed using a proprietary stud extractor. Always ensure that a blind tapped hole is completely free from oil, grease, water or other fluid before installing the bolt or stud. Failure to do this could cause the housing to crack due to the hydraulic action of the bolt or stud as it is screwed in.

When tightening a castellated nut to accept a split pin, tighten the nut to the specified torque, where applicable, and then tighten further to the next split pin hole. Never slacken the nut to align the split pin hole unless stated in the repair procedure.

When checking or retightening a nut or bolt to a specified torque setting, slacken the nut or bolt by a quarter of a turn, and then retighten to the specified setting. However, this should not be attempted where angular tightening has been used.

For some screw fastenings, notably cylinder head bolts or nuts, torque wrench settings are no longer specified for the latter stages of tightening, 'angle-tightening' being called up instead. Typically, a fairly low torque wrench setting will be applied to the bolts/nuts in the correct sequence, followed by one or more stages of tightening through specified angles.

Locknuts, locktabs and washers

Any fastening which will rotate against a component or housing in the course of tightening should always have a washer between it and the relevant component or housing.

Spring or split washers should always be renewed when they are used to lock a critical component such as a big-end bearing retaining bolt or nut. Locktabs which are folded over to retain a nut or bolt should always be renewed.

Self-locking nuts can be re-used in non-critical areas, providing resistance can be felt when the locking portion passes over the bolt or stud thread. However, it should be noted that self-locking stiffnuts tend to lose their effectiveness after long periods of use, and in such cases should be renewed as a matter of course.

Split pins must always be replaced with new ones of the correct size for the hole.

When thread-locking compound is found on the threads of a fastener which is to be re-used, it should be cleaned off with a wire brush and solvent, and fresh compound applied on reassembly.

Special tools

Some repair procedures in this manual entail the use of special tools such as a press, two or three-legged pullers, spring compressors, etc. Wherever possible, suitable readily available alternatives to the manufacturer's special tools are described, and are shown in use. In some instances, where no alternative is possible, it has been necessary to resort to the use of a manufacturer's tool and this has been done for reasons of safety as well as the efficient completion of the repair operation. Unless you are highly skilled and have a thorough understanding of the procedures described, never attempt to bypass the use of any special tool when the procedure described specifies its use. Not only is there a very great risk of personal injury, but expensive damage could be caused to the components involved.

Environmental considerations

When disposing of used engine oil, brake fluid, antifreeze, etc., give due consideration to any detrimental environmental effects. Do not, for instance, pour any of the above liquids down drains into the general sewage system or onto the ground to soak away. Many local council refuse tips provide a facility for waste oil disposal as do some garages. If none of these facilities are available, consult your local Environmental Health Department for further advice.

With the universal tightening-up of legislation regarding the emission of environmentally harmful substances from motor vehicles, most current vehicles have tamperproof devices fitted to the main adjustment points of the fuel system. These devices are primarily designed to prevent unqualified persons from adjusting the fuel/air mixture with the chance of a consequent increase in toxic emissions. If such devices are encountered during servicing or overhaul, they should, wherever possible, be renewed or refitted in accordance with the vehicle manufacturer's requirements or current legislation.

Tools and working facilities

Introduction

A selection of good tools is a fundamental requirement for anyone contemplating the maintenance and repair of a motor vehicle. For the owner who does not possess any, their purchase will prove a considerable expense, offsetting some of the savings made by doing-it-yourself. However, provided that the tools purchased meet the relevant national safety standards and are of good quality, they will last for many years and prove an extremely worthwhile investment.

To help the average owner to decide which tools are needed to carry out the various tasks detailed in this manual, we have compiled three lists of tools under the following headings: *Maintenance and minor repair, Repair and overhaul*, and *Special*. Newcomers to practical mechanics should start off with the *Maintenance and minor repair* tool kit and confine themselves to the simpler jobs around the vehicle. Then, as confidence and experience grow, more difficult tasks can be undertaken, with extra tools being purchased as, and when, they are needed. In this way, a *Maintenance and minor repair* tool kit can be built up into a *Repair and overhaul* tool kit over a considerable period of time without any major cash outlays. The experienced do-it-yourselfer will have a tool kit good enough for most repair and overhaul procedures and will add tools from the *Special* category when it is felt that the expense is justified by the amount of use to which these tools will be put.

Maintenance and minor repair tool kit

The tools given in this list should be considered as a minimum requirement if routine maintenance, servicing and minor repair operations are to be undertaken. We recommend the purchase of combination spanners (ring one end, open-ended the other); although more expensive than open-ended ones, they do give the advantages of both types of spanner.

Combination spanners:
  Metric – 8, 9, 10, 11, 12, 13, 14, 15, 17 & 19 mm
Adjustable spanner – 35 mm jaw (approx)
Engine sump/gearbox/drain plug key (where applicable)
Spark plug spanner (with rubber insert)
Spark plug gap adjustment tool
Set of feeler gauges
Brake bleed nipple spanner
Screwdrivers:
  Flat-bladed – approx 100 mm long x 6 mm dia
  Cross-bladed – approx 100 mm long x 6 mm dia
Combination pliers
Hacksaw (junior)
Tyre pump
Tyre pressure gauge
Oil can
Oil filter removal tool
Fine emery cloth
Wire brush (small)
Funnel (medium size)

Repair and overhaul tool kit

These tools are virtually essential for anyone undertaking any major repairs to a motor vehicle, and are additional to those given in the *Maintenance and minor repair* list. Included in this list is a comprehensive set of sockets. Although these are expensive, they will be found invaluable as they are so versatile – particularly if various drives are included in the set. We recommend the half-inch square-drive type, as this can be used with most proprietary torque wrenches. If you cannot afford a socket set, even bought piecemeal, then inexpensive tubular box spanners are a useful alternative.

The tools in this list will occasionally need to be supplemented by tools from the *Special* list.

Sockets (or box spanners) to cover range in previous list
Reversible ratchet drive (for use with sockets) (photo)
Extension piece, 250 mm (for use with sockets)
Universal joint (for use with sockets)
Torque wrench (for use with sockets)
Self-locking grips
Ball pein hammer
Soft-faced mallet (plastic/aluminium or rubber)

Sockets and reversible ratchet drive

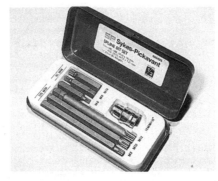

Spline bit set

Spline key set

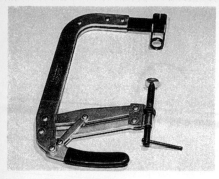

Valve spring compressor

Piston ring compressor

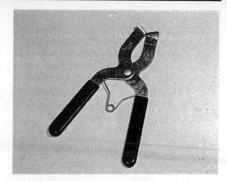

Piston ring removal/installation tool

Cylinder bore hone

Three-legged hub and bearing puller

Micrometer set

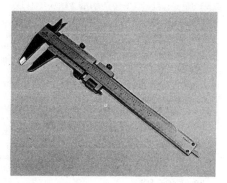

Vernier calipers

Dial test indicator and magnetic stand

Screwdrivers:
  Flat-bladed – long & sturdy, short (chubby), and narrow (electrician's) types
  Cross-bladed – long & sturdy, and short (chubby) types
Pliers:
  Long-nosed
  Side cutters (electrician's)
  Circlip (internal and external)
Cold chisel – 25 mm
Scriber
Scraper
Centre-punch
Pin punch
Hacksaw
Brake hose clamp
Brake/clutch bleeding kit

Selection of twist drills
Steel rule/straight-edge
Allen keys (inc. splined/Torx type) (photos)
Selection of files
Wire brush
Axle stands
Jack (strong trolley or hydraulic type)
Light with extension lead

Special tools

The tools in this list are those which are not used regularly, are expensive to buy, or which need to be used in accordance with their manufacturers' instructions. Unless relatively difficult mechanical jobs are undertaken frequently, it will not be economic to buy many of these tools. Where this is the case, you could consider clubbing together with

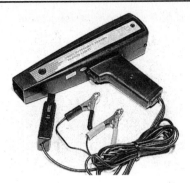

Stroboscopic timing light

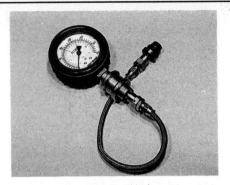

Compression testing gauge

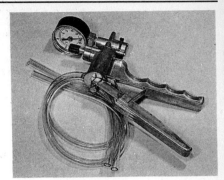

Vacuum pump and gauge

Clutch plate alignment set

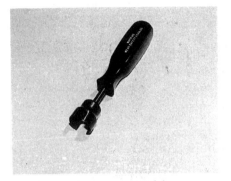

Brake shoe steady spring cup removal tool

Bush and bearing removal/installation set

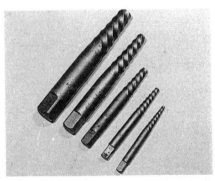

Stud extractor set

Tap and die set

friends (or joining a motorists' club) to make a joint purchase, or borrowing the tools against a deposit from a local garage or tool hire specialist. It is worth noting that many of the larger DIY superstores now carry a large range of special tools for hire at modest rates.

The following list contains only those tools and instruments freely available to the public, and not those special tools produced by the vehicle manufacturer specifically for its dealer network. You will find occasional references to these manufacturers' special tools in the text of this manual. Generally, an alternative method of doing the job without the vehicle manufacturers' special tool is given. However, sometimes there is no alternative to using them. Where this is the case and the relevant tool cannot be bought or borrowed, you will have to entrust the work to a franchised garage.

Valve spring compressor (photo)
Valve grinding tool
Piston ring compressor (photo)
Piston ring removal/installation tool (photo)
Cylinder bore hone (photo)
Balljoint separator
Coil spring compressors
Two/three-legged hub and bearing puller (photo)
Impact screwdriver
Micrometer and/or vernier calipers (photos)
Dial test indicator/gauge (photo)
Stroboscopic timing light (photo)
Dwell angle meter/tachometer
Universal electrical multi-meter
Cylinder compression gauge (photo)
Hand-operated vacuum pump and gauge (photo)
Clutch plate alignment set (photo)
Brake shoe steady spring cup removal tool (photo)
Bush and bearing removal/installation set (photo)
Stud extractors (photo)
Tap and die set (photo)
Lifting tackle
Trolley jack

Buying tools

For practically all tools, a tool factor is the best source since he will have a very comprehensive range compared with the average garage or accessory shop. Having said that, accessory shops often offer excellent quality tools at discount prices, so it pays to shop around.

Remember, you don't have to buy the most expensive items on the shelf, but it is always advisable to steer clear of the very cheap tools. There are plenty of good tools around at reasonable prices, but always aim to purchase items which meet the relevant national safety standards. If in doubt, ask the proprietor or manager of the shop for advice before making a purchase.

Care and maintenance of tools

Having purchased a reasonable tool kit, it is necessary to keep the tools in a clean and serviceable condition. After use, always wipe off any dirt, grease and metal particles using a clean, dry cloth, before putting the tools away. Never leave them lying around after they have been used. A simple tool rack on the garage or workshop wall for items such as screwdrivers and pliers is a good idea. Store all normal spanners and sockets in a metal box. Any measuring instruments, gauges, meters, etc., must be carefully stored where they cannot be damaged or become rusty.

Take a little care when tools are used. Hammer heads inevitably become marked and screwdrivers lose the keen edge on their blades from time to time. A little timely attention with emery cloth or a file will soon restore items like this to a good serviceable finish.

Working facilities

Not to be forgotten when discussing tools is the workshop itself. If anything more than routine maintenance is to be carried out, some form of suitable working area becomes essential.

It is appreciated that many an owner-mechanic is forced by circumstances to remove an engine or similar item without the benefit of a garage or workshop. Having done this, any repairs should always be done under the cover of a roof.

Wherever possible, any dismantling should be done on a clean, flat workbench or table at a suitable working height.

Any workbench needs a vice; one with a jaw opening of 100 mm is suitable for most jobs. As mentioned previously, some clean dry storage space is also required for tools, as well as for any lubricants, cleaning fluids, touch-up paints and so on, which become necessary.

Another item which may be required, and which has a much more general usage, is an electric drill with a chuck capacity of at least 8 mm. This, together with a good range of twist drills, is virtually essential for fitting accessories.

Last, but not least, always keep a supply of old newspapers and clean, lint-free rags available, and try to keep any working area as clean as possible.

Spanner jaw gap and bolt size comparison table

Jaw gap – in (mm)	Spanner size	Bolt size
0.197 (5.00)	5 mm	M 2.5
0.216 (5.50)	5.5 mm	M 3
0.218 (5.53)	$\frac{7}{32}$ in AF	
0.236 (6.00)	6 mm	M 3.5
0.250 (6.35)	$\frac{1}{4}$ in AF	
0.275 (7.00)	7 mm	M 4
0.281 (7.14)	$\frac{9}{32}$ in AF	
0.312 (7.92)	$\frac{5}{16}$ in AF	
0.315 (8.00)	8 mm	M 5
0.343 (8.71)	$\frac{11}{32}$ in AF	
0.375 (9.52)	$\frac{3}{8}$ in AF	
0.394 (10.00)	10 mm	M 6
0.406 (10.32)	$\frac{13}{32}$ in AF	
0.433 (11.00)	11 mm	M 7
0.437 (11.09)	$\frac{7}{16}$ in AF	$\frac{1}{4}$ in SAE
0.468 (11.88)	$\frac{15}{32}$ in AF	
0.500 (12.70)	$\frac{1}{2}$ in AF	$\frac{5}{16}$ in SAE
0.512 (13.00)	13 mm	M8
0.562 (14.27)	$\frac{9}{16}$ in AF	$\frac{3}{8}$ in SAE
0.593 (15.06)	$\frac{19}{32}$ in AF	
0.625 (15.87)	$\frac{5}{8}$ in AF	$\frac{7}{16}$ in SAE
0.669 (17.00)	17 mm	M 10
0.687 (17.44)	$\frac{11}{16}$ in AF	
0.709 (19.00)	19 mm	M 12
0.750 (19.05)	$\frac{3}{4}$ in AF	$\frac{1}{2}$ in SAE
0.781 (19.83)	$\frac{25}{32}$ in AF	
0.812 (20.62)	$\frac{13}{16}$ in AF	
0.866 (22.00)	22 mm	M 14
0.875 (22.25)	$\frac{7}{8}$ in AF	$\frac{9}{16}$ in SAE
0.937 (23.79)	$\frac{15}{16}$ in AF	$\frac{5}{8}$ in SAE
0.945 (24.00)	24 mm	M 16
0.968 (24.58)	$\frac{31}{32}$ in AF	
1.000 (25.40)	1 in AF	$1\frac{1}{16}$ in SAE
1.062 (26.97)	$1\frac{1}{16}$ in AF	$\frac{3}{4}$ in SAE
1.063 (27.00)	27 mm	M 18
1.125 (28.57)	$1\frac{1}{8}$ in AF	
1.182 (30.00)	30 mm	M 20
1.187 (30.14)	$1\frac{3}{16}$ in AF	
1.250 (31.75)	$1\frac{1}{4}$ in AF	$\frac{7}{8}$ in SAE
1.260 (32.00)	32 mm	M 22
1.312 (33.32)	$1\frac{5}{16}$ in AF	
1.375 (34.92)	$1\frac{3}{8}$ in AF	
1.418 (36.00)	36 mm	M 24
1.437 (36.49)	$1\frac{7}{16}$ in AF	1 in SAE
1.500 (38.10)	$1\frac{1}{2}$ in AF	
1.615 (41.00)	41 mm	M 27

Booster battery (jump) starting

When jump starting a vehicle using a booster battery, observe the following precautions.

(a) Before connecting the booster battery, make sure that the ignition is switched off.
(b) Ensure that all electrical equipment (lights, heater, wipers, etc.) is switched off.
(c) Make sure that the booster battery is the same voltage as the discharged one in the vehicle.
(d) If the battery is being jump started from the battery in another vehicle, the two vehicles MUST NOT TOUCH each other.
(e) Make sure that the transmission is in Neutral (manual gearbox) or Park (automatic transmission).

Connect one jump lead between the positive (+) terminals of the two batteries. Connect the other jump lead first to the negative (-) terminal of the booster battery, and then to a good earthing point on the vehicle to be started, such as a bolt or bracket on the engine block, at least 45 cm from the battery if possible. Make sure that the jump leads will not come into contact with the fan, drivebelts or other moving parts of the engine.

Start the engine using the booster battery, then with the engine running at idle speed, disconnect the jump leads in the reverse order of connection.

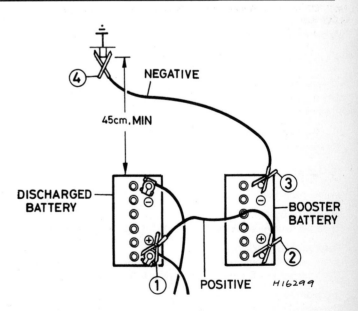

Jump start lead connections for negative-earth vehicles – connect leads in order shown

Conversion factors

Length (distance)

Inches (in)	X	25.4	= Millimetres (mm)	X	0.0394	= Inches (in)
Feet (ft)	X	0.305	= Metres (m)	X	3.281	= Feet (ft)
Miles	X	1.609	= Kilometres (km)	X	0.621	= Miles

Volume (capacity)

Cubic inches (cu in; in^3)	X	16.387	= Cubic centimetres (cc; cm^3)	X	0.061	= Cubic inches (cu in; in^3)
Imperial pints (Imp pt)	X	0.568	= Litres (l)	X	1.76	= Imperial pints (Imp pt)
Imperial quarts (Imp qt)	X	1.137	= Litres (l)	X	0.88	= Imperial quarts (Imp qt)
Imperial quarts (Imp qt)	X	1.201	= US quarts (US qt)	X	0.833	= Imperial quarts (Imp qt)
US quarts (US qt)	X	0.946	= Litres (l)	X	1.057	= US quarts (US qt)
Imperial gallons (Imp gal)	X	4.546	= Litres (l)	X	0.22	= Imperial gallons (Imp gal)
Imperial gallons (Imp gal)	X	1.201	= US gallons (US gal)	X	0.833	= Imperial gallons (Imp gal)
US gallons (US gal)	X	3.785	= Litres (l)	X	0.264	= US gallons (US gal)

Mass (weight)

Ounces (oz)	X	28.35	= Grams (g)	X	0.035	= Ounces (oz)
Pounds (lb)	X	0.454	= Kilograms (kg)	X	2.205	= Pounds (lb)

Force

Ounces-force (ozf; oz)	X	0.278	= Newtons (N)	X	3.6	= Ounces-force (ozf; oz)
Pounds-force (lbf; lb)	X	4.448	= Newtons (N)	X	0.225	= Pounds-force (lbf; lb)
Newtons (N)	X	0.1	= Kilograms-force (kgf; kg)	X	9.81	= Newtons (N)

Pressure

Pounds-force per square inch (psi; lbf/in^2; lb/in^2)	X	0.070	= Kilograms-force per square centimetre (kgf/cm^2; kg/cm^2)	X	14.223	= Pounds-force per square inch (psi; lbf/in^2; lb/in^2)
Pounds-force per square inch (psi; lbf/in^2; lb/in^2)	X	0.068	= Atmospheres (atm)	X	14.696	= Pounds-force per square inch (psi; lbf/in^2; lb/in^2)
Pounds-force per square inch (psi; lbf/in^2; lb/in^2)	X	0.069	= Bars	X	14.5	= Pounds-force per square inch (psi; lbf/in^2; lb/in^2)
Pounds-force per square inch (psi; lbf/in^2; lb/in^2)	X	6.895	= Kilopascals (kPa)	X	0.145	= Pounds-force per square inch (psi; lbf/in^2; lb/in^2)
Kilopascals (kPa)	X	0.01	= Kilograms-force per square centimetre (kgf/cm^2; kg/cm^2)	X	98.1	= Kilopascals (kPa)
Millibar (mbar)	X	100	= Pascals (Pa)	X	0.01	= Millibar (mbar)
Millibar (mbar)	X	0.0145	= Pounds-force per square inch (psi; lbf/in^2; lb/in^2)	X	68.947	= Millibar (mbar)
Millibar (mbar)	X	0.75	= Millimetres of mercury (mmHg)	X	1.333	= Millibar (mbar)
Millibar (mbar)	X	0.401	= Inches of water (inH$_2$O)	X	2.491	= Millibar (mbar)
Millimetres of mercury (mmHg)	X	0.535	= Inches of water (inH$_2$O)	X	1.868	= Millimetres of mercury (mmHg)
Inches of water (inH$_2$O)	X	0.036	= Pounds-force per square inch (psi; lbf/in^2; lb/in^2)	X	27.68	= Inches of water (inH$_2$O)

Torque (moment of force)

Pounds-force inches (lbf in; lb in)	X	1.152	= Kilograms-force centimetre (kgf cm; kg cm)	X	0.868	= Pounds-force inches (lbf in; lb in)
Pounds-force inches (lbf in; lb in)	X	0.113	= Newton metres (Nm)	X	8.85	= Pounds-force inches (lbf in; lb in)
Pounds-force inches (lbf in; lb in)	X	0.083	= Pounds-force feet (lbf ft; lb ft)	X	12	= Pounds-force inches (lbf in; lb in)
Pounds-force feet (lbf ft; lb ft)	X	0.138	= Kilograms-force metres (kgf m; kg m)	X	7.233	= Pounds-force feet (lbf ft; lb ft)
Pounds-force feet (lbf ft; lb ft)	X	1.356	= Newton metres (Nm)	X	0.738	= Pounds-force feet (lbf ft; lb ft)
Newton metres (Nm)	X	0.102	= Kilograms-force metres (kgf m; kg m)	X	9.804	= Newton metres (Nm)

Power

Horsepower (hp)	X	745.7	= Watts (W)	X	0.0013	= Horsepower (hp)

Velocity (speed)

Miles per hour (miles/hr; mph)	X	1.609	= Kilometres per hour (km/hr; kph)	X	0.621	= Miles per hour (miles/hr; mph)

Fuel consumption

Miles per gallon, Imperial (mpg)	X	0.354	= Kilometres per litre (km/l)	X	2.825	= Miles per gallon, Imperial (mpg)
Miles per gallon, US (mpg)	X	0.425	= Kilometres per litre (km/l)	X	2.352	= Miles per gallon, US (mpg)

Temperature

Degrees Fahrenheit = (°C x 1.8) + 32

Degrees Celsius (Degrees Centigrade; °C) = (°F – 32) x 0.56

* It is common practice to convert from miles per gallon (mpg) to litres/100 kilometres (l/100km), where mpg (Imperial) x l/100 km = 282 and mpg (US) x l/100 km = 235

Fault diagnosis

Contents

Engine 1
Engine fails to rotate when attempting to start
Engine rotates but will not start
Engine difficult to start when cold
Engine difficult to start when hot
Starter motor noisy or excessively rough in engagement
Engine starts but stops immediately
Engine idles erratically
Engine misfires at idle speed
Engine misfires throughout the driving speed range
Engine hesitates on acceleration
Engine stalls
Engine lacks power
Engine backfires
Oil pressure warning light illuminated with engine running
Engine runs-on after switching off
Engine noises

Cooling system 2
Overheating
Overcooling
External coolant leakage
Internal coolant leakage
Corrosion

Fuel and exhaust systems 3
Excessive fuel consumption
Fuel leakage and/or fuel odour
Excessive noise or fumes from exhaust system

Clutch 4
Pedal travels to floor – no pressure or very little resistance
Clutch fails to disengage (unable to select gears)
Clutch slips (engine speed increases with no increase in vehicle speed)
Judder as clutch is engaged
Noise when depressing or releasing clutch pedal

Transmission 5
Noisy in neutral with engine running

Noisy in one particular gear
Difficulty engaging gears
Jumps out of gear
Vibration
Lubricant leaks

Driveshafts 6
Clicking or knocking noise on turns (at slow speed on full-lock)
Vibration when accelerating or decelerating

Braking system 7
Vehicle pulls to one side under braking
Noise (grinding or high-pitched squeal) when brakes applied
Excessive brake pedal travel
Brake pedal feels spongy when depressed
Excessive brake pedal effort required to stop vehicle
Judder felt through brake pedal or steering wheel when braking
Brakes binding
Rear wheels locking under normal braking

Suspension and steering systems 8
Vehicle pulls to one side
Wheel wobble and vibration
Excessive pitching and/or rolling around corners or during braking
Wandering or general instability
Excessively-stiff steering
Excessive play in steering
Tyre wear excessive

Electrical system 9
Battery will not hold a charge for more than a few days
Ignition warning light remains illuminated with engine running
Ignition warning light fails to come on
Lights inoperative
Instrument readings inaccurate or erratic
Horn inoperative or unsatisfactory in operation
Windscreen/tailgate wipers inoperative or unsatisfactory in operation
Windscreen/tailgate washers inoperative or unsatisfactory in operation

Introduction

The vehicle owner who does his or her own maintenance according to the recommended service schedules should not have to use this section of the manual very often. Modern component reliability is such that, provided those items subject to wear or deterioration are inspected or renewed at the specified intervals, sudden failure is comparatively rare. Faults do not usually just happen as a result of sudden failure, but develop over a period of time. Major mechanical failures in particular are usually preceded by characteristic symptoms over hundreds or even thousands of miles. Those components which do occasionally fail without warning are often small and easily carried in the vehicle.

With any fault finding, the first step is to decide where to begin investigations. Sometimes this is obvious, but on other occasions a little detective work will be necessary. The owner who makes half a dozen haphazard adjustments or replacements may be successful in curing a fault (or its symptoms), but will be none the wiser if the fault recurs and ultimately may have spent more time and money than was necessary. A calm and logical approach will be found to be more satisfactory in the long run. Always take into account any warning signs or abnormalities that may have been noticed in the period preceding the fault – power loss, high or low gauge readings, unusual smells, etc. – and remember that failure of components such as fuses or spark plugs may only be pointers to some underlying fault.

The pages which follow provide an easy reference guide to the more common problems which may occur during the operation of the vehicle. These problems and their possible causes are grouped under headings denoting various components or systems, such as Engine, Cooling system, etc. The Chapter and/or Section which deals with the problem is also shown in brackets. Whatever the fault, certain basic principles apply. These are as follows:

Verify the fault. This is simply a matter of being sure that you know what the symptoms are before starting work. This is particularly important if you are investigating a fault for someone else who may not have described it very accurately.

Don't overlook the obvious. For example, if the vehicle won't start, is there petrol in the tank? (Don't take anyone else's word on this particular point, and don't trust the fuel gauge either!) If an electrical fault is indicated, look for loose or broken wires before digging out the test gear.

Cure the disease, not the symptom. Substituting a flat battery with a fully charged one will get you off the hard shoulder, but if the underlying cause is not attended to, the new battery will go the same way. Similarly, changing oil-fouled spark plugs for a new set will get you moving again, but remember that the reason for the fouling (if it wasn't simply an incorrect grade of plug) will have to be established and corrected.

Don't take anything for granted. Particularly, don't forget that a 'new' component may itself be defective (especially if it's been rattling around in the boot for months), and don't leave components out of a fault diagnosis sequence just because they are new or recently fitted. When you do finally diagnose a difficult fault, you'll probably realise that all the evidence was there from the start.

1   Engine

Engine fails to rotate when attempting to start
- Battery terminal connections loose or corroded (Chapter 1).
- Battery discharged or faulty (Chapter 1 or 12).
- Broken, loose or disconnected wiring in the starting circuit (Chapter 12).
- Defective starter solenoid or switch (Chapter 12).
- Defective starter motor (Chapter 12).
- Flywheel ring gear or starter pinion teeth loose or broken (Chapter 2 or 12).
- Engine earth strap broken or disconnected (Chapter 2 or 12).

Engine rotates but will not start
- Fuel tank empty.
- Battery discharged (engine rotates slowly) (Chapter 12).
- Battery terminal connections loose or corroded (Chapter 1).
- Ignition components damp or damaged (Chapter 1 or 5).
- Broken, loose or disconnected wiring in the ignition circuit (Chapter 1 or 5).
- Worn, faulty or incorrectly-gapped spark plugs (Chapter 1).
- Choke mechanism sticking, incorrectly adjusted, or faulty (Chapter 4).
- Major mechanical failure (eg camshaft drive) (Chapter 2).

Engine difficult to start when cold
- Battery discharged (Chapter 12).
- Battery terminal connections loose or corroded (Chapter 1).
- Worn, faulty or incorrectly-gapped spark plugs (Chapter 1).
- Choke mechanism sticking, incorrectly adjusted, or faulty (Chapter 4).
- Other ignition system fault (Chapter 1 and 5).
- Low cylinder compressions (Chapter 2).

Engine difficult to start when hot
- Air cleaner filter element dirty or clogged (Chapter 1).
- Choke mechanism sticking, incorrectly adjusted, or faulty (Chapter 4).
- Carburettor float chamber flooding (Chapter 4).
- Low cylinder compressions (Chapter 2).

Starter motor noisy or excessively rough in engagement
- Flywheel ring gear or starter pinion teeth loose or broken (Chapter 2 or 12).
- Starter motor mounting bolts loose or missing (Chapter 12).
- Starter motor internal components worn or damaged (Chapter 12).

Engine starts but stops immediately
- Insufficient fuel reaching carburettor (Chapter 4).
- Loose or faulty electrical connections in the ignition circuit (Chapter 1 or 5).
- Vacuum leak at the carburettor or inlet manifold (Chapter 4).
- Blocked carburettor jet(s) or internal passages (Chapter 4).

Engine idles erratically
- Incorrectly-adjusted idle speed and/or mixture settings (Chapter 1).
- Air cleaner filter element clogged (Chapter 1).
- Vacuum leak at the carburettor, inlet manifold or associated hoses (Chapter 4).
- Worn, faulty or incorrectly-gapped spark plugs (Chapter 1).
- Incorrectly-adjusted valve clearances (Chapter 1).
- Uneven or low cylinder compressions (Chapter 2).
- Camshaft lobes worn (Chapter 2).
- Excessively-worn timing chain (Chapter 2).

Engine misfires at idle speed
- Worn, faulty or incorrectly-gapped spark plugs (Chapter 1).
- Faulty spark plug HT leads (Chapter 1).
- Incorrectly-adjusted idle mixture setting (Chapter 1).
- Incorrect ignition timing (Chapter 1).
- Vacuum leak at the carburettor, inlet manifold or associated hoses (Chapter 4).
- Distributor cap cracked or tracking internally (Chapter 1).

- Incorrectly-adjusted valve clearances (Chapter 1).
- Uneven or low cylinder compressions (Chapter 2).
- Disconnected, leaking or perished crankcase ventilation hoses (Chapter 1 or 4).

Engine misfires throughout the driving speed range
- Blocked carburettor jet(s) or internal passages (Chapter 4).
- Carburettor incorrectly adjusted or worn (Chapter 1 or 4).
- Fuel filter choked (Chapter 1).
- Fuel pump faulty or delivery pressure low (Chapter 4).
- Fuel tank vent blocked or fuel pipes restricted (Chapter 4).
- Vacuum leak at the carburettor, inlet manifold or associated hoses (Chapter 4).
- Worn, faulty or incorrectly-gapped spark plugs (Chapter 1).
- Faulty spark plug HT leads (Chapter 1).
- Distributor cap cracked or tracking internally (Chapter 1).
- Faulty ignition coil (Chapter 5).
- Uneven or low cylinder compressions (Chapter 2).

Engine hesitates on acceleration
- Worn, faulty or incorrectly-gapped spark plugs (Chapter 1).
- Carburettor accelerator pump faulty (Chapter 4).
- Blocked carburettor jets or internal passages (Chapter 4).
- Vacuum leak at the carburettor, inlet manifold or associated hoses (Chapter 4).
- Carburettor incorrectly adjusted or worn (Chapter 1 or 4).

Engine stalls
- Incorrectly-adjusted idle speed and/or mixture settings (Chapter 1).
- Blocked carburettor jet(s) or internal passages (Chapter 4).
- Vacuum leak at the carburettor, inlet manifold or associated hoses (Chapter 4).
- Fuel filter choked (Chapter 1).
- Fuel pump faulty or delivery pressure low (Chapter 4).
- Fuel tank vent blocked or fuel pipes restricted (Chapter 4).

Engine lacks power
- Incorrect ignition timing (Chapter 1).
- Carburettor incorrectly adjusted or worn (Chapter 1 or 4).
- Timing chain incorrectly fitted (Chapter 2).
- Fuel filter choked (Chapter 1).
- Fuel pump faulty or delivery pressure low (Chapter 4).
- Uneven or low cylinder compressions (Chapter 2).
- Worn, faulty or incorrectly-gapped spark plugs (Chapter 1).
- Vacuum leak at the carburettor, inlet manifold or associated hoses (Chapter 4).
- Brakes binding (Chapter 1 or 9).
- Clutch slipping (Chapter 6).

Engine backfires
- Ignition timing incorrect (Chapter 1).
- Timing chain incorrectly fitted (Chapter 2).
- Carburettor incorrectly adjusted or worn (Chapter 1 or 4).
- Vacuum leak at the carburettor, inlet manifold or associated hoses (Chapter 4).

Oil pressure warning light illuminated with engine running
- Low oil level or incorrect grade (Chapter 1).
- Faulty oil pressure transmitter (sender) unit (Chapter 2).
- Worn engine bearings and/or oil pump (Chapter 2).
- High engine operating temperature (Chapter 3).
- Oil pump pressure relief valve defective (Chapter 2).
- Oil pump pick-up strainer clogged (Chapter 2).

Engine runs-on after switching off
- Idle speed excessively high (Chapter 1).
- Excessive carbon build-up in engine (Chapter 2).
- High engine operating temperature (Chapter 3).

Engine noises
Pre-ignition (pinking) or knocking during acceleration or under load
- Ignition timing incorrect (Chapter 1).
- Incorrect grade of fuel (Chapter 4).
- Vacuum leak at the carburettor, inlet manifold or associated hoses (Chapter 4).

- Excessive carbon build-up in engine (Chapter 2).
- Worn or damaged distributor or other ignition system component (Chapter 1 or 5).
- Carburettor incorrectly adjusted or worn (Chapter 1 or 4).

Whistling or wheezing noises
- Leaking inlet manifold or carburettor gasket (Chapter 4).
- Leaking exhaust manifold gasket or pipe-to-manifold joint (Chapter 1 or 4).
- Leaking vacuum hose (Chapter 4, 5 or 9).
- Blowing cylinder head gasket (Chapter 2).

Tapping or rattling noises
- Incorrect valve clearances (Chapter 1).
- Worn valve gear or camshaft (Chapter 2).
- Worn timing chain (Chapter 2).
- Ancillary component fault (water pump, alternator, etc.) (Chapter 3 or 12).

Knocking or thumping noises
- Worn big-end bearings (regular heavy knocking, perhaps less under load) (Chapter 2).
- Worn main bearings (rumbling and knocking, perhaps worsening under load) (Chapter 2).
- Piston slap (most noticeable when cold) (Chapter 2).
- Ancillary component fault (alternator, water pump, etc.) (Chapter 3 or 12).

2   Cooling system

Overheating
- Insufficient coolant in system (Chapter 1).
- Thermostat faulty (Chapter 3).
- Radiator fins blocked or grille restricted (Chapter 1 or 3).
- Electric cooling fan or thermostatic switch faulty (Chapter 3).
- Pressure cap faulty (Chapter 1).
- Water pump drivebelt worn, or incorrectly adjusted (Chapter 1).
- Ignition timing incorrect (Chapter 1).
- Inaccurate temperature gauge sender unit (Chapter 3).
- Air-lock in cooling system (Chapter 1).

Overcooling
- Thermostat faulty (Chapter 3).
- Inaccurate temperature gauge sender unit (Chapter 3).

External coolant leakage
- Deteriorated or damaged hoses or hose clips (Chapter 1).
- Radiator core or heater matrix leaking (Chapter 1 or 3).
- Pressure cap faulty (Chapter 1).
- Water pump seal leaking (Chapter 3).
- Boiling due to overheating (Chapter 3).
- Core plug leaking (Chapter 2).

Internal coolant leakage
- Leaking cylinder head gasket (Chapter 2).
- Cracked cylinder head or cylinder bore (Chapter 2).

Corrosion
- Infrequent draining and flushing (Chapter 1).
- Incorrect antifreeze mixture or inappropriate type of antifreeze (Chapter 1).

3   Fuel and exhaust systems

Excessive fuel consumption
- Air cleaner filter element dirty or clogged (Chapter 1).
- Carburettor incorrectly adjusted or worn (Chapter 1 or 4).
- Choke incorrectly adjusted or choke sticking (Chapter 4).
- Ignition timing incorrect (Chapter 1).
- Tyres underinflated (Chapter 1).

Fuel leakage and/or fuel odour
- Damaged or corroded fuel tank, pipes or connections (Chapter 1).
- Carburettor float chamber flooding (Chapter 4).

Excessive noise or fumes from exhaust system
- Leaking exhaust system or manifold joints (Chapter 1 or 4).
- Leaking, corroded or damaged silencers or pipe (Chapter 1).
- Broken mountings causing body or suspension contact (Chapter 1).

4   Clutch

Pedal travels to floor – no pressure or very little resistance
- Broken clutch cable (Chapter 6).
- Incorrect clutch adjustment (Chapter 1).
- Broken clutch release bearing or fork (Chapter 6).
- Broken diaphragm spring in clutch pressure plate (Chapter 6).

Clutch fails to disengage (unable to select gears)
- Incorrect clutch adjustment (Chapter 1).
- Clutch disc sticking on gearbox input shaft splines (Chapter 6).
- Clutch disc sticking to flywheel or pressure plate (Chapter 6).
- Faulty pressure plate assembly (Chapter 6).
- Clutch release mechanism worn or incorrectly assembled (Chapter 6).

Clutch slips (engine speed increases with no increase in vehicle speed)
- Incorrect clutch adjustment (Chapter 1).
- Clutch disc linings excessively worn (Chapter 6).
- Clutch disc linings contaminated with oil or grease (Chapter 6).
- Faulty pressure plate or weak diaphragm spring (Chapter 6).

Judder as clutch is engaged
- Clutch disc linings contaminated with oil or grease (Chapter 6).
- Clutch disc linings excessively worn (Chapter 6).
- Clutch cable sticking or frayed (Chapter 1).
- Faulty or distorted pressure plate or diaphragm spring (Chapter 6).
- Worn or loose engine or gearbox mountings (Chapter 2).
- Clutch disc hub or gearbox input shaft splines worn (Chapter 6 or 7).

Noise when depressing or releasing clutch pedal
- Worn clutch release bearing (Chapter 6).
- Clutch pedal bushes dry or worn (Chapter 1 or 6).
- Faulty pressure plate assembly (Chapter 6).
- Pressure plate diaphragm spring broken (Chapter 6).
- Broken clutch disc cushioning springs (Chapter 6).

5   Transmission

Noisy in neutral with engine running
- Input shaft bearings worn (noise apparent with clutch pedal released, but not when depressed) (Chapter 7).*
- Clutch release bearing worn (noise apparent with clutch pedal depressed, possibly less when released) (Chapter 6).

Noisy in one particular gear
- Worn, damaged or chipped gear teeth (Chapter 7).*

Difficulty engaging gears
- Clutch fault (Chapter 6).
- Worn or damaged gear linkage (Chapter 7).
- Incorrectly-adjusted gear linkage (Chapter 7).*
- Worn synchroniser units (Chapter 7).*

Jumps out of gear
- Worn or damaged gear linkage (Chapter 7).
- Incorrectly-adjusted gear linkage (Chapter 7).*
- Worn synchroniser units (Chapter 7).*
- Worn selector forks (Chapter 7).*

Vibration
- Lack of oil (Chapter 1).
- Worn bearings (Chapter 7).*

Lubricant leaks
- Leaking differential output oil seal (Chapter 7).*
- Leaking housing joint (Chapter 7).*
- Leaking input shaft oil seal (Chapter 7).

Although the corrective action necessary to remedy the symptoms described is beyond the scope of the home mechanic, the above information should be helpful in isolating the cause of the condition so that the owner can communicate clearly with a professional mechanic.

6   Driveshafts

Clicking or knocking noise on turns (at slow speed on full-lock)
- Lack of constant velocity joint lubricant (Chapter 8).
- Worn outer constant velocity joint (Chapter 8).

Vibration when accelerating or decelerating
- Worn inner constant velocity joint (Chapter 8).
- Bent or distorted driveshaft (Chapter 8).

7   Braking system

Note: *Before assuming that a brake problem exists, make sure that the tyres are in good condition and correctly inflated, that the front wheel alignment is correct, and that the vehicle is not unevenly loaded.*

Vehicle pulls to one side under braking
- Worn, defective, damaged or contaminated front or rear brake pads/shoes on one side (Chapter 1).
- Seized or partially-seized front brake caliper piston or rear wheel cylinder (Chapter 1 or 9).
- A mixture of brake pad/shoe lining materials fitted between sides (Chapter 1).
- Brake caliper mounting bolts loose (Chapter 1 or 9).
- Rear brake backplate mounting bolts loose (Chapter 1 or 9).
- Worn or damaged steering or suspension components (Chapter 10).

Noise (grinding or high-pitched squeal) when brakes applied
- Brake pad or shoe friction lining material worn down to metal backing (Chapter 1).
- Excessive corrosion of brake disc or drum. (May be apparent after the vehicle has been standing for some time (Chapter 1).
- Foreign object (stone chipping, etc.) trapped between brake disc and splash shield (Chapter 1).

Excessive brake pedal travel
- Inoperative rear brake self-adjust mechanism (Chapter 9).
- Faulty master cylinder (Chapter 9).
- Air in hydraulic system (Chapter 9).
- Faulty vacuum servo unit (Chapter 9).

Brake pedal feels spongy when depressed
- Air in hydraulic system (Chapter 9).
- Deteriorated flexible rubber brake hoses (Chapter 1 or 9).
- Master cylinder mounting nuts loose (Chapter 9).
- Faulty master cylinder (Chapter 9).

Excessive brake pedal effort required to stop vehicle
- Faulty vacuum servo unit (Chapter 9).
- Disconnected, damaged or insecure brake servo vacuum hose (Chapter 1 or 9).
- Primary or secondary hydraulic circuit failure (Chapter 9).
- Seized brake caliper or wheel cylinder piston(s) (Chapter 1 or 9).
- Brake pads or brake shoes incorrectly fitted (Chapter 1 or 9).
- Incorrect grade of brake pads or brake shoes fitted (Chapter 1 or 9).
- Brake pads or brake shoe linings contaminated (Chapter 1).

Judder felt through brake pedal or steering wheel when braking
- Excessive run-out or distortion of front discs or rear drums (Chapter 9).
- Brake pad or brake shoe linings worn (Chapter 1).
- Brake caliper or rear brake backplate mounting bolts loose (Chapter 9).
- Wear in suspension or steering components or mountings (Chapter 10).

Brakes binding
- Seized brake caliper or wheel cylinder piston(s) (Chapter 9).
- Incorrectly-adjusted handbrake mechanism or linkage (Chapter 1).
- Faulty master cylinder (Chapter 9).

Rear wheels locking under normal braking
- Rear brake shoe linings contaminated (Chapter 1).
- Faulty brake pressure-regulating valve (Chapter 9).

8   Suspension and steering systems

Note: *Before diagnosing suspension or steering faults, be sure that the trouble is not due to incorrect tyre pressures, mixtures of tyre types or binding brakes.*

Vehicle pulls to one side
- Defective tyre (Chapter 1).
- Excessive wear in suspension or steering components (Chapter 10).
- Incorrect front wheel alignment (Chapter 10).
- Accident damage to steering or suspension components (Chapter 10).

Wheel wobble and vibration
- Front roadwheels out of balance (vibration felt mainly through the steering wheel) (Chapter 10).
- Rear roadwheels out of balance (vibration felt throughout the vehicle) (Chapter 10).
- Roadwheels damaged or distorted (Chapter 1).
- Faulty or damaged tyre (Chapter 1).
- Worn steering or suspension joints, bushes or components (Chapter 10).
- Wheel bolts loose (Chapter 1).

Excessive pitching and/or rolling around corners or during braking
- Defective shock absorbers (Chapter 10).
- Broken or weak coil spring and/or suspension component (Chapter 10).

Wandering or general instability
- Incorrect front wheel alignment (Chapter 10).
- Worn steering or suspension joints, bushes or components (Chapter 10).
- Roadwheels out of balance (Chapter 1).
- Faulty or damaged tyre (Chapter 1).
- Wheel bolts loose (Chapter 1).
- Defective shock absorbers (Chapter 10).

Excessively-stiff steering
- Lack of steering gear lubricant (Chapter 10).
- Seized track rod balljoint or suspension balljoint (Chapter 10).
- Incorrect front wheel alignment (Chapter 10).
- Steering rack or column bent or damaged (Chapter 10).

Excessive play in steering
- Worn steering column universal joint(s) or intermediate coupling (Chapter 10).
- Worn steering track rod balljoints (Chapter 10).
- Worn rack-and-pinion steering gear (Chapter 10).
- Worn steering or suspension joints, bushes or components (Chapter 10).

Tyre wear excessive
Tyres worn on inside or outside edges
- Tyres underinflated (wear on both edges) (Chapter 1).
- Incorrect camber or castor angles (wear on one edge only) (Chapter 10).
- Worn steering or suspension joints, bushes or components (Chapter 10).
- Excessively-hard cornering.
- Accident damage.

Tyre treads exhibit feathered edges
- Incorrect toe setting (Chapter 10).

Tyres worn in centre of tread
- Tyres overinflated (Chapter 1).

Tyres worn on inside and outside edges
- Tyres underinflated (Chapter 1).

Tyres worn unevenly
- Tyres out of balance (Chapter 1).
- Excessive wheel or tyre run-out (Chapter 1).
- Worn shock absorbers (Chapter 10).
- Faulty tyre (Chapter 1).

9 Electrical system

Note: *For problems associated with the starting system, refer to the faults listed under 'Engine' earlier in this Section.*

Battery will not hold a charge for more than a few days
- Battery defective internally (Chapter 1 or 12).
- Battery electrolyte level low (Chapter 1).
- Battery terminal connections loose or corroded (Chapter 1).
- Alternator drivebelt worn or incorrectly adjusted (Chapter 1).
- Alternator not charging at correct output (Chapter 12).
- Alternator or voltage regulator faulty (Chapter 12).
- Short-circuit causing continual battery drain (Chapter 12).

Ignition warning light remains illuminated with engine running
- Alternator drivebelt broken, worn, or incorrectly adjusted (Chapter 1).
- Alternator brushes worn, sticking, or dirty (Chapter 12).
- Alternator brush springs weak or broken (Chapter 12).
- Internal fault in alternator or voltage regulator (Chapter 12).
- Broken, disconnected, or loose wiring in charging circuit (Chapter 12).

Ignition warning light fails to come on
- Warning light bulb blown (Chapter 12).
- Broken, disconnected, or loose wiring in warning light circuit (Chapter 12).
- Alternator faulty (Chapter 12).

Lights inoperative
- Bulb blown (Chapter 12).
- Corrosion of bulb or bulbholder contacts (Chapter 12).
- Blown fuse (Chapter 12).
- Faulty relay (Chapter 12).
- Broken, loose, or disconnected wiring (Chapter 12).
- Faulty switch (Chapter 12).

Instrument readings inaccurate or erratic
Instrument readings increase with engine speed
- Faulty voltage regulator (Chapter 12).

Fuel or temperature gauge give no reading
- Faulty gauge sender unit (Chapter 3 or 4).
- Wiring open-circuit (Chapter 12).
- Faulty gauge (Chapter 12).

Fuel or temperature gauges give continuous maximum reading
- Faulty gauge sender unit (Chapter 3 or 4).
- Wiring short-circuit (Chapter 12).
- Faulty gauge (Chapter 12).

Horn inoperative or unsatisfactory in operation
Horn operates all the time
- Horn push either earthed or stuck down (Chapter 12).
- Horn cable to horn push earthed (Chapter 12).

Horn fails to operate
- Blown fuse (Chapter 12).
- Cable or cable connections loose, broken or disconnected (Chapter 12).
- Faulty horn (Chapter 12).

Horn emits intermittent or unsatisfactory sound
- Cable connections loose (Chapter 12).
- Horn mountings loose (Chapter 12).
- Faulty horn (Chapter 12).

Windscreen/tailgate wipers inoperative or unsatisfactory in operation
Wipers fail to operate, or operate very slowly
- Wiper blades stuck to screen, or linkage seized or binding (Chapter 1 or 12).
- Blown fuse (Chapter 12).
- Cable or cable connections loose, broken or disconnected (Chapter 12).
- Faulty relay (Chapter 12).
- Faulty wiper motor (Chapter 12).

Wiper blades sweep over too large or too small an area of the glass
- Wiper arms incorrectly positioned on spindles (Chapter 12).
- Excessive wear of wiper linkage (Chapter 12).
- Wiper motor or linkage mountings loose or insecure (Chapter 12).

Wiper blades fail to clean the glass effectively
- Wiper blade rubbers worn or perished (Chapter 1).
- Wiper arm tension springs broken, or arm pivots seized (Chapter 12).
- Insufficient windscreen washer additive to adequately remove road film (Chapter 1).

Windscreen/tailgate washers inoperative or unsatisfactory in operation
One or more washer jets inoperative
- Blocked washer jet (Chapter 12).
- Disconnected, kinked or restricted fluid hose (Chapter 12).
- Insufficient fluid in washer reservoir (Chapter 1).

Washer pump fails to operate
- Broken or disconnected wiring or connections (Chapter 12).
- Blown fuse (Chapter 12).
- Faulty washer switch (Chapter 12).
- Faulty washer pump (Chapter 12).

Washer pump runs for some time before fluid is emitted from jets
- Faulty one-way valve in fluid supply hose (Chapter 12).

MOT test checks

Introduction

Motor vehicle testing has been compulsory in Great Britain since 1960, when the Motor Vehicle (Tests) Regulations were first introduced. At that time, testing was only applicable to vehicles ten years old or older, and the test itself only covered lighting equipment, braking systems and steering gear. Current vehicle testing is far more extensive and, in the case of private vehicles, is now an annual inspection commencing three years after the date of first registration. Test standards are becoming increasingly stringent; for details of changes, consult the latest edition of the MOT Inspection Manual (available from HMSO or bookshops).

This section is intended as a guide to getting your vehicle through the MOT test. It lists all the relevant testable items, how to check them yourself, and what is likely to cause the vehicle to fail. Obviously it will not be possible to examine the vehicle to the same standard as the professional MOT tester, who will be highly experienced in this work and will have all the necessary equipment available. However, working through the following checks will provide a good indication as to the condition of the vehicle, and will enable you to identify any problem areas before submitting the vehicle for the test. Where a component is found to need repair or renewal, reference should be made to the appropriate Chapter in the manual, where further information will be found.

The following checks have been sub-divided into four categories as follows.

(a) Checks carried out from the driver's seat.
(b) Checks carried out with the vehicle on the ground.
(c) Checks carried out with the vehicle raised and with the wheels free to rotate.
(d) Exhaust emission checks.

In most cases, the help of an assistant will be necessary to carry out these checks thoroughly.

Checks carried out from the driver's seat

Handbrake (Chapter 1 or 9)

Test the operation of the handbrake by pulling on the lever until the handbrake is in the normal fully-applied position. Ensure that the travel of the lever (the number of clicks of the ratchet) is not excessive before full resistance of the braking mechanism is felt. If so, this would indicate incorrect adjustment of the rear brakes, or incorrectly-adjusted handbrake cables.

With the handbrake fully applied, tap the lever sideways, and make sure that it does not release, which would indicate wear in the ratchet and pawl. Release the handbrake, and move the lever from side to side to check for excessive wear in the pivot bearing. Check the security of the lever mountings, and make sure that there is no corrosion of any part of the body structure within 30 cm of the lever mounting. If the lever mountings cannot be readily seen from inside the vehicle, carry out this check later when working underneath.

Footbrake (Chapter 1 or 9)

Check that the brake pedal is sound, without visible defects such as excessive wear of the pivot bushes or broken or damaged pedal pad. Check also for signs of fluid leaks on the pedal, floor or carpets, which would indicate failed seals in the brake master cylinder.

Depress the brake pedal slowly at first, then rapidly until sustained pressure can be held. Maintain this pressure and check that the pedal does not creep down to the floor which would again indicate problems with the master cylinder. Release the pedal, wait a few seconds then depress it once until firm resistance is felt. Check that this resistance occurs near the top of the pedal travel. If the pedal travels nearly to the floor before firm resistance is felt, this would indicate incorrect brake adjustment resulting in 'insufficient reserve travel' of the footbrake. If firm resistance cannot be felt, ie the pedal feels spongy, this would indicate that air is present in the hydraulic system, which will necessitate complete bleeding of the system.

Check that the servo unit is operating correctly by depressing the brake pedal several times to exhaust the vacuum. Keep the pedal depressed and start the engine. As soon as the engine starts, the brake pedal resistance will be felt to alter. If this is not the case, there may be a leak from the brake servo vacuum hose, or the servo unit itself may be faulty.

Steering wheel and column (Chapter 10)

Examine the steering wheel for fractures or looseness of the hub, spokes or rim. Move the steering wheel from side to side and then up and down, in relation to the steering column. Check that the steering wheel is not loose on the column, indicating wear in the column splines or a loose steering wheel retaining nut. Continue moving the steering wheel as before, but also turn it slightly from left to right. Check that there is no abnormal movement of the steering wheel, indicating excessive wear in the column upper support bearing, universal joint(s) or flexible coupling.

Windscreen and mirrors (Chapter 11)

The windscreen must be free of cracks or other damage which will seriously interfere with the driver's field of view, or which will prevent the windscreen wipers from operating properly. Small stone chips are acceptable. Any stickers, dangling toys or similar items must also be clear of the field of view.

Rear view mirrors must be secure, intact and capable of being adjusted. The nearside (passenger side) door mirror is not included in the test unless the interior mirror cannot be used – for instance, in the case of a van with blacked-out rear windows.

Seat belts and seats (Chapter 11)

Note: *The following checks are applicable to all seat belts, front and rear. Front seat belts must be of a type that will restrain the upper part of the body; lap belts are not acceptable. Various combinations of seat belt types are acceptable at the rear.*

Carefully examine the seat belt webbing for cuts, or any signs of serious fraying or deterioration. If the seat belt is of the retractable type, pull the belt all the way out and examine the full extent of the webbing.

Fasten and unfasten the belt, ensuring that the locking mechanism holds securely and releases properly when intended. If the belt is of the retractable type, check also that the retracting mechanism operates correctly when the belt is released.

Check the security of all seat belt mountings and attachments which are accessible, without removing any trim or other components, from inside the vehicle (photo). Any serious corrosion, fracture or distortion of the body structure within 30 cm of any mounting point will cause the vehicle to fail. Certain anchorages will not be accessible or even visible from inside the vehicle; in this instance, further checks should be carried out later, when working underneath. If any part of the seat belt mechanism is attached to the front seat, then the seat mountings are treated as anchorages and must also comply as above.

The front seats themselves must be securely attached so that they cannot move unexpectedly, and the backrests must lock in the upright position.

Doors (Chapter 11)

Both front doors must be able to be opened and closed from outside and inside, and must latch securely when closed. In the case of a pick-up, the tailgate must be securely attached and capable of being securely fastened.

Electrical equipment (Chapter 12)

Switch on the ignition and operate the horn. The horn must operate, and produce a clear sound audible to other road users. Note that a gong, siren or two-tone horn fitted as an alternative to the manufacturer's original equipment is not acceptable.

Check the operation of the windscreen washers and wipers. The washers must operate with adequate flow and pressure, and with the jets adjusted so that the liquid strikes the windscreen near the top of the glass.

Operate the windscreen wipers in conjunction with the washers, and check that the blades cover their designed sweep of the windscreen without smearing. The blades must effectively clean the glass so that the driver has an adequate view of the road ahead, and to the front nearside and offside of the vehicle. If the screen smears or does not clean adequately, it is advisable to renew the wiper blades before the MOT test.

Depress the footbrake with the ignition switched on, and have your assistant check that both rear stop-lights operate, and are extinguished when the footbrake is released. If one stop-light fails to operate, it is likely that a bulb has blown or there is a poor electrical contact at, or near, the bulbholder. If both stop-lights fail to operate, check for a blown fuse, faulty stop-light switch or possibly two blown bulbs. If the lights stay on when the brake pedal is released, it is possible that the switch is at fault.

Checks carried out with the vehicle on the ground

Vehicle identification

Front and rear number plates must be in good condition, securely fitted and easily read. Letters and numbers must be correctly spaced, with the gap between the group of numbers and the group of letters at least double the gap between adjacent numbers and letters.

The vehicle identification number on the plate under the bonnet must be legible. It will be checked during the test as part of the measures taken to prevent the fraudulent acquisition of certificates.

Electrical equipment (Chapter 12)

Switch on the sidelights, and check that both front and rear sidelights and the number plate lights are illuminated, and that the lenses and reflectors are secure and undamaged. This is particularly important at the rear, where a cracked or damaged lens would allow a white light to show to the rear, which is unacceptable. Note in addition that any lens which is excessively dirty, either inside or out, such that the light intensity is reduced, could also constitute a fail.

Switch on the headlights, and check that both dipped beam and main beam units are operating correctly and at the same light intensity. If either headlight shows signs of dimness, this is usually attributable to a poor earth connection or severely-corroded internal reflector. Inspect the headlight lenses for cracks or stone damage. Any damage to the headlight lens will normally constitute a fail, but this is very much down to the tester's discretion. Bear in mind that with all light units, they must operate correctly when first switched on. It is not acceptable to tap a light unit to make it operate.

The headlights must not only be aligned so as not to dazzle other road users when switched to dipped beam, but also so as to provide adequate illumination of the road. This can only be accurately checked using optical beam setting equipment so if you have any doubts about the headlight alignment, it is advisable to have this professionally checked and if necessary reset, before the MOT test.

With the ignition switched on, operate the direction indicators and check that they show amber lights to the front and to the rear, that they flash at the rate of between one and two flashes per second and that the 'tell-tale' on the instrument panel also functions. Operation of the sidelights and stop-lights must not affect the indicators – if it does, the cause is usually a bad earth at the rear light cluster. Similarly check the operation of the hazard warning lights, which must work with the ignition on and off. Examine the lenses for cracks or damage as described previously.

Check the operation of the rear foglight(s). The test only concerns itself with the statutorily required foglight, which is the one on the offside. The light must be secure, and emit a steady red light. The warning light on the instrument panel or in the switch must also work.

Footbrake (Chapter 1 or 9)

From within the engine compartment, examine the brake pipes for signs of leaks, corrosion, insecurity, chafing or other damage, and check the master cylinder and servo unit for leaks, security of their mountings or excessive corrosion in the vicinity of the mountings. The master cylinder reservoir must be secure; if it is of the translucent type, the fluid level must be between the upper and lower level markings.

Turn the steering as necessary so that the right-hand front brake flexible hose can be examined. Inspect the hose carefully for any sign of cracks or deterioration of the rubber. This will be most noticeable if the hose is bent in half, and is particularly common where the rubber portion enters the metal end fitting (photo). Turn the steering onto full-left then full-right lock, and ensure that the hose does not contact the wheel, tyre, or any part of the steering or suspension mechanism. While your assistant depresses the brake pedal firmly, check the hose for any bulges or fluid leaks under pressure. Now repeat these checks on the left-hand front hose. Should any damage or deterioration be noticed, renew the hose.

Steering mechanism and suspension (Chapter 10)

Have your assistant turn the steering wheel from side to side slightly, up to the point where the steering gear just begins to transmit this movement to the roadwheels. Check for excessive free play between the steering wheel and the steering gear, which would indicate wear in the steering column joints, wear or insecurity of the steering column-to-steering gear coupling, or insecurity, incorrect adjustment, or wear in the steering gear itself. Generally speaking, free play greater than 1.3 cm for vehicles with rack-and-pinion type steering or 7.6 cm for vehicles with steering box mechanisms, should be considered excessive.

Have your assistant turn the steering wheel more vigorously in each direction, up to the point where the roadwheels just begin to turn. As this is done, carry out a complete examination of all the steering joints, linkages, fittings and attachments. Any component that shows signs of wear, damage, distortion, or insecurity should be renewed or attended to accordingly. On vehicles equipped with power steering, also check that the power steering pump is secure, that the pump drivebelt is in satisfactory condition and correctly adjusted, that there are no fluid leaks or damaged hoses, and that the system operates correctly. Additional checks can be carried out later with the vehicle raised, when there will be greater working clearance underneath.

Check that the vehicle is standing level, and at approximately the correct ride height. Ensure that there is sufficient clearance between the suspension components and the bump stops to allow full suspension travel over bumps.

Shock absorbers (Chapter 10)

Depress each corner of the vehicle in turn, and then release it. If the shock absorbers are in good condition, the corner of the vehicle will rise and then settle in its normal position. If there is no noticeable damping effect from the shock absorber, and the vehicle continues to rise and fall, then the shock absorber is defective and the vehicle will fail. A shock absorber which has seized will also cause the vehicle to fail.

Exhaust system (Chapter 1 or 4)

Start the engine, and with your assistant holding a rag over the tailpipe, check the entire system for leaks which will appear as a rhythmic fluffing or hissing sound at the source of the leak. Check the effectiveness of the silencer by ensuring that the noise produced is of a level to be expected from a vehicle of similar type. Providing that the system is structurally sound, it is acceptable to cure a leak using a proprietary exhaust system repair kit or similar method.

Check the security of all seat belt mountings

Check the flexible brake hoses for cracks or deterioration

Examine the steering rack rubber gaiters for condition and security

Checks carried out with the vehicle raised and with the wheels free to rotate

Jack up the front and rear of the vehicle, and securely support it on axle stands positioned at suitable load-bearing points under the vehicle structure. Position the stands clear of the suspension assemblies, ensuring that the wheels are clear of the ground and that the steering can be turned onto full-right and full-left lock.

Steering mechanism (Chapter 10)

Examine the steering rack rubber gaiters for signs of splits, lubricant leakage or insecurity of the retaining clips (photo). If power steering is fitted, check for signs of deterioration, damage, chafing or leakage of the fluid hoses, pipes or connections. Also check for excessive stiffness or binding of the steering, a missing split pin or locking device, or any severe corrosion of the body structure within 30 cm of any steering component attachment point.

Have your assistant turn the steering onto full-left then full-right lock. Check that the steering turns smoothly without undue tightness or roughness, and that no part of the steering mechanism, including a wheel or tyre, fouls any brake flexible or rigid hose or pipe, or any part of the body structure.

On vehicles with four-wheel steering, similar considerations apply to the rear wheel steering linkages. However, it is permissible for a rear wheel steering system to be inoperative, provided that the rear wheels are secured in the straight-ahead position and that the front wheel steering system is operating effectively.

Front and rear suspension and wheel bearings (Chapter 1 or 10)

Starting at the front right-hand side of the vehicle, grasp the roadwheel at the 3 o'clock and 9 o'clock positions, and shake it vigorously. Check for any free play at the wheel bearings, suspension balljoints, or suspension mountings, pivots and attachments. Check also for any serious deterioration of the rubber or metal casing of any mounting bushes, or any distortion, deformation or severe corrosion of any components. Look for missing split pins, tab washers or other locking devices on any mounting or attachment, or any severe corrosion of the vehicle structure within 30 cm of any suspension component attachment point.

If any excess free play is suspected at a component pivot point, this can be confirmed by using a large screwdriver or similar tool to lever between the mounting and the component attachment. This will confirm whether the wear is in the pivot bush, its retaining bolt or in the mounting itself (the bolt holes can often become elongated).

Now grasp the wheel at the 12 o'clock and 6 o'clock positions, shake it vigorously and repeat the previous inspection (photo). Rotate the wheel, and check for roughness or tightness of the front wheel bearing such that imminent failure of the bearing is indicated.

Carry out all the above checks at the other front wheel, and then at both rear wheels.

Roadsprings and shock absorbers (Chapter 10)

On vehicles with strut type suspension units, examine the strut assembly for signs of serious fluid leakage, corrosion or severe pitting of the piston rod, or damage to the casing (photo). Check also for security of the mounting points.

If coil springs are fitted, check that the spring ends locate correctly in their spring seats, that there is no severe corrosion of the spring, and that it is not cracked, broken or in any way damaged.

If the vehicle is fitted with leaf springs, check that all leaves are intact, that the axle is securely attached to each spring, and that there is no wear or deterioration of the spring eye mountings, bushes, or shackles.

The same general checks apply to vehicles fitted with other suspension types, such as torsion bars, hydraulic displacer units, etc. In all cases, ensure that all mountings and attachments are secure, that there are no signs of excessive wear, corrosion, cracking, deformation or damage to any component or bush, and that there are no fluid leaks or damaged hoses or pipes (hydraulic types).

Inspect the shock absorbers for signs of serious fluid leakage. (Slight seepage of fluid is normal for some types of shock absorber, and is not a reason for failing.) Check for excessive wear of the mounting bushes or attachments, or damage to the body of the unit.

Driveshafts (Chapter 8)

With the steering turned onto full lock, rotate each front wheel in turn and inspect the constant velocity joint gaiters for splits or damage (photo). Also check the gaiter is securely attached to its respective housings by clips or other methods of retention.

Continue turning the wheel, and check that each driveshaft is straight with no sign of damage.

Braking system (Chapter 1 or 9)

If possible, without dismantling, check for wear of the brake pads and the condition of the discs. Ensure that the friction lining material has not worn excessively, and that the discs are not fractured, pitted, scored or worn excessively.

Carefully examine all the rigid brake pipes underneath the vehicle, and the flexible hoses at the rear. Check the pipes for signs of excessive corrosion, chafing or insecurity, and the flexible hoses for signs of bulging under pressure, chafing, splits or deterioration (photo).

Look for signs of hydraulic fluid leaks at the brake calipers or on the brake backplates, indicating failed hydraulic seals in the components concerned.

Slowly spin each wheel, while your assistant depresses the footbrake then releases it. Ensure that each brake is operating, and that the wheel is free to rotate when the pedal is released. It is not possible to test brake efficiency without special equipment, but (traffic and local conditions permitting) a road test can be carried out to check that the vehicle pulls up in a straight line.

Examine the handbrake mechanism, and check for signs of frayed or broken cables, excessive corrosion, or wear or insecurity of the linkage. Have your assistant operate the handbrake, while you check that the mechanism works on each relevant wheel and releases fully without binding.

Fuel and exhaust systems (Chapter 1 or 4)

Inspect the fuel tank, fuel pipes, hoses and unions (including the unions at the pump, filter and carburettor). All components must be secure and free from leaks. The fuel filler cap must also be secure and of an appropriate type.

Examine the exhaust system over its entire length checking for any damaged, broken or missing mountings, security of the pipe retaining clamps and condition of the system with regard to rust and corrosion (photo).

Wheels and tyres (Chapter 1 or 10)

Carefully examine each tyre in turn, on both the inner and outer walls and over the whole of the tread area, and check for signs of cuts, tears, lumps, bulges, and for separation of the tread and exposure of the ply or cord due to wear or other damage. Check also that the tyre bead is correctly seated on the wheel rim, and that the tyre valve is sound and properly seated. Spin the wheel, and check that it is not excessively distorted or damaged, particularly at the bead rim.

Check that the tyres are of the correct size for the vehicle, and that they are of the same size and type on each axle. (Having a 'space saver' spare tyre in use is not acceptable.) The tyres should also be inflated to the specified pressures.

Using a suitable gauge, check the tyre tread depth. The current legal requirement states that the tread pattern must be visible over the whole tread area, and must be of a minimum depth of 1.6 mm over at least three-quarters of the tread width. It is acceptable for some wear of the inside or outside edges of the tyre to be apparent, but this wear must be in one even circumferential band, and the tread must be visible. Any excessive wear of this nature may indicate incorrect front wheel alignment, which should be checked before the tyre becomes excessively worn. See the appropriate Chapters for further information on tyre wear patterns and front wheel alignment.

Body corrosion

Check the condition of the entire vehicle structure for signs of corrosion in any load-bearing areas. For the purpose of the MOT test, all chassis box sections, side sills, crossmembers, pillars, suspension, steering, braking system and seat belt mountings and anchorages should all be considered as load-bearing areas. As a general guide, any corrosion which has seriously reduced the metal thickness of a load-bearing area to weaken it, is likely to cause the vehicle to fail. Should corrosion of this nature be encountered, professional repairs are likely to be needed.

Body damage or corrosion which causes sharp or otherwise dangerous edges to be exposed will also cause the vehicle to fail.

Shake the roadwheel vigorously to check for excess play in the wheel bearings and suspension components

Check shock absorbers for signs of damage or leakage

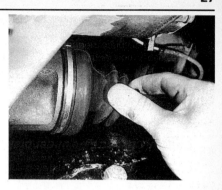

Inspect the constant velocity joint gaiters for splits or damage

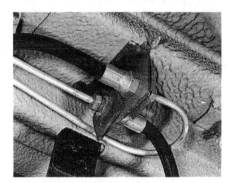

Check rigid brake pipes for security, damage or corrosion

Check the condition of exhaust system mountings

Exhaust emission checks

Have the engine at normal operating temperature, and make sure that the preliminary conditions for checking idle speed and mixture (ignition system in good order, air filter element clean, etc.) have been met.

Before any measurements are carried out, raise the engine speed to around 2500 rpm, and hold it at this speed for 20 seconds. Allow the engine speed to return to idle, and watch for smoke emissions from the exhaust tailpipe. If the idle speed is obviously much too high, or if dense blue or clearly-visible black smoke comes from the tailpipe for more than 5 seconds, the vehicle will fail. As a rule of thumb, blue smoke signifies oil being burnt (worn valve stem oil seals, valve guides, piston rings or bores), while black smoke signifies unburnt fuel (dirty air cleaner element, mixture extremely rich, or other carburettor or fuel injection system fault).

If the idle speed and smoke emission are satisfactory, an exhaust gas analyser capable of measuring carbon monoxide (CO) and hydrocarbons (HC) is now needed. The following paragraphs assume that such an instrument can be hired or borrowed – it is unlikely to be economic for the home mechanic to buy one. Alternatively, a local garage may agree to perform the check for a small fee.

CO emissions (mixture)

Current MOT regulations specify a maximum CO level at idle of 4.5% for vehicles first used after August 1983. The CO level specified by the vehicle maker is well inside this limit.

If the CO level cannot be reduced far enough to pass the test (and assuming that the fuel and ignition systems are otherwise in good condition) it is probable that the carburettor is badly worn, or that there is some problem in the fuel injection system. On carburettors with an automatic choke, it may be that the choke is not releasing as it should.

It is possible for the CO level to be within the specified maximum for MOT purposes but well above the maximum specified by the manufacturer. The tester is entitled to draw attention to this, but it is not in itself a reason for failing the vehicle.

HC emissions

With the CO emissions within limits, HC emissions must be no more than 1200 ppm (parts per million). If the vehicle fails this test at idle, it can be re-tested at around 2000 rpm; if the HC level is then 1200 ppm or less, this counts as a pass.

Excessive HC emissions can be caused by oil being burnt, but they are more likely to be due to unburnt fuel. Possible reasons include:

(a) *Spark plugs in poor condition or incorrectly gapped.*
(b) *Ignition timing incorrect.*
(c) *Valve clearances incorrect.*
(d) *Engine compression low.*

Note that excessive HC levels in the exhaust gas can cause premature failure of the catalytic converter (when fitted).

Chapter 1 Routine maintenance and servicing

Contents

Lubricants, fluids and capacities
Maintenance schedule
Maintenance procedures
Bodywork 10
Braking system.. 8
Clutch 5
Cooling, heating and ventilation systems.................... 2
Driveshafts 7
Electrical system 11
Engine 1
Fuel and exhaust systems 3
Ignition system.. 4
Suspension and steering.. 9
Transmission... 6

Specifications

Engine
Valve clearances:
    Inlet .... 0.2 mm
    Exhaust .... 0.2 mm
Oil filter type.. Champion C130

Cooling system
Antifreeze properties – 50% antifreeze (by volume):
    Commences freezing .... −36°C
    Frozen solid.. −48°C

Fuel system
Idle speed.. 800 ± 50 rpm
Idle mixture CO content .... 1.0% ± 0.5%
Fuel octane requirement....................................... 97 RON leaded (ie 4-star) or 95 RON unleaded (ie unleaded Premium)

Fuel filter element type:
    1989 to January 1992...................................... Champion type not available
    January 1992 onwards .... Champion L101
Air filter element type....................................... Champion W110

Ignition system
Firing order 1–3–4–2
Location of No 1 cylinder .... Crankshaft pulley end
Direction of crankshaft rotation.............................. Clockwise
Direction of distributor rotor arm rotation .... Clockwise
Ignition timing:
    Stroboscopic at idle speed (vacuum hose disconnected):
        135 engines .... 2° ± 2° BTDC at 750 rpm
        136 engines .... 5° ± 2° BTDC at 750 rpm
Spark plugs:
    Type:
        135 engines .... Champion RC7YCC (flat seat, washer type)
        136 engines .... Champion S7YCC (taper seat type)
    Electrode gap .... 0.8 mm
Ignition (HT) leads type .... Champion LS05 (boxed set)

Clutch
Pedal height adjustment .... Level with, or up to 10 mm below, brake pedal

Braking system
Minimum front brake pad lining thickness .... 2.0 mm
Minimum rear brake shoe lining thickness .... 1.0 mm
Handbrake adjustment:
    Roadwheels bind.. 4 notches
    Roadwheels lock .... 5 to 8 notches

Tyre pressures – tyres cold

	Front	Rear
Hatchback:		
Up to half-laden	1.9 bars (28 lbf/in²)	1.8 bars (26 lbf/in²)
Fully laden	2.1 bars (30 lbf/in²)	2.0 bars (29 lbf/in²)
Estate and Van:		
Up to half-laden	1.9 bars (28 lbf/in²)	1.8 bars (26 lbf/in²)
Fully laden	2.1 bars (30 lbf/in²)	2.1 bars (30 lbf/in²)
Pick-up:		
Up to half-laden	1.9 bars (28 lbf/in²)	1.8 bars (26 lbf/in²)
Fully laden	2.1 bars (30 lbf/in²)	2.3 bars (33 lbf/in²)

Electrical system
Alternator drivebelt deflection .... 10 to 15 mm at 2 kg pressure
Wiper blade type (front) .... Champion X-4503
Wiper blade type (rear) .... Champion X-3303

Torque wrench settings

	Nm	lbf ft
Spark plugs:		
With flat seat, washer (136 engines)	24 to 30	18 to 22
With taper seat (135 engines)	13 to 20	10 to 15
Engine oil drain plug	49 to 65	36 to 48
Engine coolant drain screw	15 to 25	11 to 18
Alternator pivot and clamp bolts:		
M8	16 to 24	12 to 18
M10	28 to 42	21 to 31
Roadwheel bolts	60 to 90	44 to 66

Lubricants, fluids and capacities

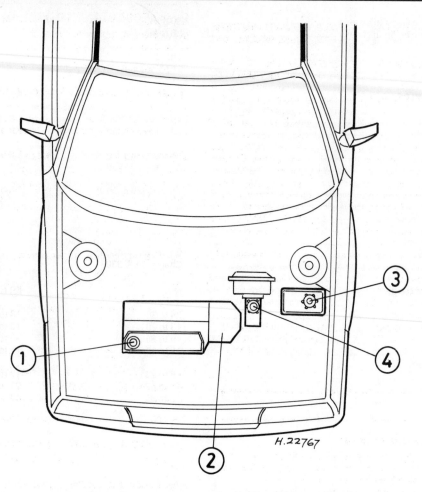

H.22767

Lubricants and fluids

Component or system	Lubricant type/specification	Duckhams recommendation
1 Engine	SAE 15W/40 Multigrade engine oil, to API SG	Duckhams QXR or Hypergrade
2 Transmission	Gear oil, viscosity SAE 80EP	Duckhams Hypoid 80S
3 Cooling system	Ethylene glycol-based antifreeze with corrosion inhibitors	Duckhams Universal Antifreeze and Summer Coolant
4 Braking system	Hydraulic fluid to SAE J1703	Duckhams Universal Brake and Clutch Fluid
Steering rack	Gear oil, viscosity SAE 90EP	Duckhams Hypoid 90S – to be used in a cleaned, grease-free unit only
General greasing	Multi-purpose lithium-based grease	Duckhams LB10 grease

Capacities

Engine oil	4.0 litres (+ 0.6 litres with optional oil cooler)
Cooling system	6.0 litres
Fuel tank	47 litres
Transmission	2.4 litres
Washer system reservoir	3.5 litres

Maintenance schedule

Introduction

This Chapter is designed to help the DIY owner maintain the Skoda Favorit with the goals of maximum economy, safety, reliability and performance in mind.

On the following pages is a master maintenance schedule, listing the servicing requirements, and the intervals at which they should be carried out as recommended by the manufacturers. The operations are listed in the order in which the work can be most conveniently undertaken. For example, all the operations that are performed from within the engine compartment are grouped together, as are all those that require the vehicle to be raised and supported for access to the suspension and underbody. Alongside each operation in the schedule is a reference which directs the user to the Sections in this Chapter covering maintenance procedures or to other Chapters in the Manual, where the operations are described and illustrated in greater detail. Specifications for all the maintenance operations, together with a list of lubricants, fluids and capacities are provided at the beginning of this Chapter. Refer to the accompanying photographs of the engine compartment and the underbody of the vehicle for the locations of the various components.

Servicing your car in accordance with the mileage/time maintenance schedule using step-by-step procedures will result in a planned maintenance programme that should produce a long and reliable service life. Bear in mind that it is a comprehensive plan, so maintaining some items but not others at the specified intervals will not produce the same results.

The first step in this maintenance programme is to prepare yourself before the actual work begins. Read through all the procedures to be undertaken then obtain all the parts, lubricants and any additional tools needed.

Daily

Operations internal and external

Check under the vehicle for signs of fluid leaks on the ground
Visually examine the tyres for tread depth, wear or damage (Section 9)
Check and if necessaryadjust the tyre pressures (Section 9)
Check the operation of all lights, direction indicators, wipers and washers (Section 11)

Operations in the engine compartment

Check the engine oil level (Section 1)
Check the engine coolant level (Section 2)
Check the washer fluid level (Section 11)

Every 250 miles (400 km) or weekly

Carry out the daily checks, then check the following:

Operations in the engine compartment

Check the brake fluid level (Section 8)

Every 1000 miles (1500 km) or monthly – whichever comes first

Carry out the daily and weekly checks, then check the following:

Operations internal and external

Check the operation of all locks, hinges and latch mechanisms (Section 10)

Operations in the engine compartment

Check the battery electrolyte level (Section 11)

Every 6000 miles (10 000 km) or 6 months – whichever comes first

In addition to all the items listed previously, carry out the following:

Operations internal and external

Check the clutch cable adjustment (Section 5)
Check the wiper blade rubbers (Section 11)
Check the front wheel alignment and steering angles (Chapter 10)

Operations with the vehicle raised and supported

Check the braking system flexible hoses and metal pipes (Section 8)
Check the driveshaft constant velocity joint rubber gaiters (Section 7)
Check the steering gear rubber gaiters (Section 9)
Check the suspension and steering joints and attachments (Section 9)
Check the condition of the exhaust system (Section 3)
Adjust and lubricate the handbrake linkage (Section 8)

Operations in the engine compartment

Check and adjust the valve clearances (Section 1)
Check and adjust alternator drivebelt (Section 11)
Renew the engine oil and filter (Section 1)
Check and adjust the idle speed and CO level (Section 3)
Lubricate the distributor (Section 4)

Every 12 000 miles (20 000 km) or 12 months – whichever comes first

In addition to all the items listed previously, carry out the following:

Operations internal and external

Check and adjust headlight alignment (Chapter 12)

Operations with the vehicle raised and supported

Check and adjust the rear wheel bearings (Section 9)
Check the condition of the shock absorbers (Section 9)
Check the front and rear brake pads/linings (Section 8)

Operations in the engine compartment

Renew the air cleaner filter element (Section 3)*
Renew the fuel filter element – vehicles up to January 1992 (Section 3)
Renew the spark plugs (Section 4)
Check the transmission oil level (Section 6)
Renew the brake fluid (Section 8)
*If the vehicle is operated in predominately dusty conditions, the air cleaner filter element should be renewed every 6000 miles/10 000 km or 6 months – whichever comes first.

Every 24 000 miles (40 000 km) or 24 months – whichever comes first

In addition to all the items listed under the 12 000 mile service heading, carry out the following:

Operations internal and external

Lubricate the wiper linkages (Chapter 12)

Operations in the engine compartment

Renew the transmission oil (Section 6)
Drain, flush and refill the cooling system, renewing the antifreeze (Section 2)

Operations with the vehicle raised and supported

Renew the rubber seals on the brake calipers and master cylinder (Chapter 9)

Every 30 000 miles (50 000 km) or 30 months – whichever comes first

Operations in the engine compartment

Renew the fuel filter element – vehicles from January 1992 onwards (Section 3)

Every 60 000 miles (100 000 km) or 60 months – whichever occurs first

In addition to all the items listed under the 12 000 mile service heading, carry out the following:

Operations with the vehicle raised and supported

Renew all flexible brake hoses (Chapter 9)
Renew the rubber seals in the braking system pressure-regulating valve(s) (Chapter 9)
Renew the rubber gaiters on the driveshafts (Chapter 8)
Renew the rubber gaiters on the steering gear (Chapter 10)
Renew the dust covers on the suspension joints (Chapter 10)
Check the vacuum servo unit operation (Section 8)

Are your plugs trying to tell you something?

Normal.
Grey-brown deposits, lightly coated core nose. Plugs ideally suited to engine, and engine in good condition.

Heavy Deposits.
A build up of crusty deposits, light-grey sandy colour in appearance.
Fault: Often caused by worn valve guides, excessive use of upper cylinder lubricant, or idling for long periods.

Lead Glazing.
Plug insulator firing tip appears yellow or green/yellow and shiny in appearance.
Fault: Often caused by incorrect carburation, excessive idling followed by sharp acceleration. Also check ignition timing.

Carbon fouling.
Dry, black, sooty deposits.
Fault: over-rich fuel mixture.
Check: carburettor mixture settings, float level, choke operation, air filter.

Oil fouling.
Wet, oily deposits. Fault: worn bores/piston rings or valve guides; sometimes occurs (temporarily) during running-in period.

Overheating.
Electrodes have glazed appearance, core nose very white – few deposits. Fault: plug overheating. Check: plug value, ignition timing, fuel octane rating (too low) and fuel mixture (too weak).

Electrode damage.
Electrodes burned away; core nose has burned, glazed appearance. Fault: pre-ignition. Check: for correct heat range and as for 'overheating'.

Split core nose.
(May appear initially as a crack). Fault: detonation or wrong gap-setting technique. Check: ignition timing, cooling system, fuel mixture (too weak).

WHY DOUBLE COPPER IS BETTER FOR YOUR ENGINE.

Unique Trapezoidal Copper Cored Earth Electrode — 50% Larger Spark Area — Copper Cored Centre Electrode

Champion Double Copper plugs are the first in the world to have copper core in both centre <u>and</u> earth electrode. This innovative design means that they run cooler by up to 100°C – giving greater efficiency and longer life. These double copper cores transfer heat away from the tip of the plug faster and more efficiently. Therefore, Double Copper runs at cooler temperatures than conventional plugs giving improved acceleration response and high speed performance with no fear of pre-ignition.

Champion Double Copper plugs also feature a unique trapezoidal earth electrode giving a 50% increase in spark area. This, together with the double copper cores, offers greatly reduced electrode wear, so the spark stays stronger for longer.

 FASTER COLD STARTING

 FOR UNLEADED OR LEADED FUEL

 ELECTRODES UP TO 100°C COOLER

 BETTER ACCELERATION RESPONSE

 LOWER EMISSIONS

 50% BIGGER SPARK AREA

 THE LONGER LIFE PLUG

Plug Tips/Hot and Cold.
Spark plugs must operate within well-defined temperature limits to avoid cold fouling at one extreme and overheating at the other.
Champion and the car manufacturers work out the best plugs for an engine to give optimum performance under all conditions, from freezing cold starts to sustained high speed motorway cruising.
Plugs are often referred to as hot or cold. With Champion, the higher the number on its body, the hotter the plug, and the lower the number the cooler the plug.

Plug Cleaning
Modern plug design and materials mean that Champion no longer recommends periodic plug cleaning. Certainly don't clean your plugs with a wire brush as this can cause metal conductive paths across the nose of the insulator so impairing its performance and resulting in loss of acceleration and reduced m.p.g.
However, if plugs are removed, always carefully clean the area where the plug seats in the cylinder head as grit and dirt can sometimes cause gas leakage.
Also wipe any traces of oil or grease from plug leads as this may lead to arcing.

1

This photographic sequence shows the steps taken to repair the dent and paintwork damage shown above. In general, the procedure for repairing a hole will be similar; where there are substantial differences, the procedure is clearly described and shown in a separate photograph.

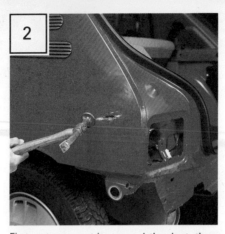

2

First remove any trim around the dent, then hammer out the dent where access is possible. This will minimise filling. Here, after the large dent has been hammered out, the damaged area is being made slightly concave.

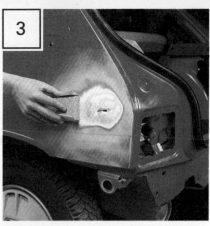

3

Next, remove all paint from the damaged area by rubbing with coarse abrasive paper or using a power drill fitted with a wire brush or abrasive pad. 'Feather' the edge of the boundary with good paintwork using a finer grade of abrasive paper.

4

Where there are holes or other damage, the sheet metal should be cut away before proceeding further. The damaged area and any signs of rust should be treated with Turtle Wax Hi-Tech Rust Eater, which will also inhibit further rust formation.

5

For a large dent or hole mix Holts Body Plus Resin and Hardener according to the manufacturer's instructions and apply around the edge of the repair area. Press Glass Fibre Matting over the repair area and leave for 20-30 minutes to harden. Then ...

5A

... brush more Holts Body Plus Resin and Hardener onto the matting and leave to harden. Repeat the sequence with two or three layers of matting, checking that the final layer is lower than the surrounding area. Apply Holts Body Plus Filler Paste as shown in Step 5B.

5B

For a medium dent, mix Holts Body Plus Filler Paste and Hardener according to the manufacturer's instructions and apply it with a flexible applicator. Apply thin layers of filler at 20-minute intervals, until the filler surface is slightly proud of the surrounding bodywork.

5C

For small dents and scratches use Holts No Mix Filler Paste straight from the tube. Apply it according to the instructions in thin layers, using the spatula provided. It will harden in minutes if applied outdoors and may then be used as its own knifing putty.

6

Use a plane or file for initial shaping. Then, using progressively finer grades of wet-and-dry paper, wrapped round a sanding block, and copious amounts of clean water, rub down the filler until glass smooth. 'Feather' the edges of adjoining paintwork.

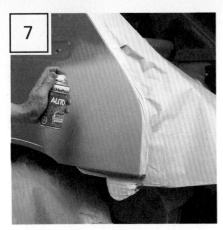

Protect adjoining areas before spraying the whole repair area and at least one inch of the surrounding sound paintwork with Holts Dupli-Color primer.

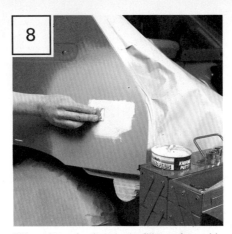

Fill any imperfections in the filler surface with a small amount of Holts Body Plus Knifing Putty. Using plenty of clean water, rub down the surface with a fine grade wet-and-dry paper – 400 grade is recommended – until it is really smooth.

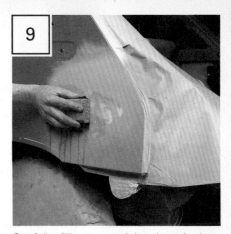

Carefully fill any remaining imperfections with knifing putty before applying the last coat of primer. Then rub down the surface with Holts Body Plus Rubbing Compound to ensure a really smooth surface.

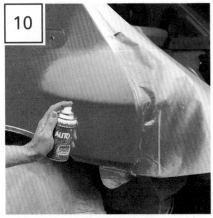

Protect surrounding areas from overspray before applying the topcoat in several thin layers. Agitate Holts Dupli-Color aerosol thoroughly. Start at the repair centre, spraying outwards with a side-to-side motion.

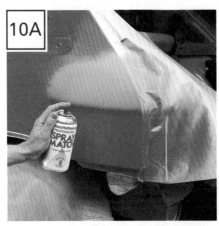

If the exact colour is not available off the shelf, local Holts Professional Spraymatch Centres will custom fill an aerosol to match perfectly.

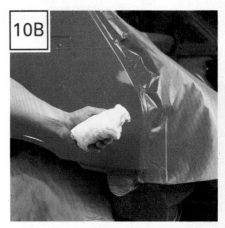

To identify whether a lacquer finish is required, rub a painted unrepaired part of the body with wax and a clean cloth.

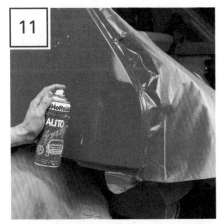

If *no* traces of paint appear on the cloth, spray Holts Dupli-Color clear lacquer over the repaired area to achieve the correct gloss level.

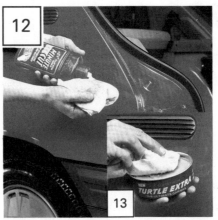

The paint will take about two weeks to harden fully. After this time it can be 'cut' with a mild cutting compound such as Turtle Wax Minute Cut prior to polishing with a final coating of Turtle Wax Extra.

When carrying out bodywork repairs, remember that the quality of the finished job is proportional to the time and effort expended.

Engine compartment component locations (air cleaner removed)

1   Carburettor
2   Engine oil level dipstick
3   Thermostat housing
4   Fuel pump
5   Engine oil filler cap
6   Brake vacuum servo unit

7   Brake system fluid reservoir
    filler cap
8   Starter motor
9   Radiator cooling fan
10 Alternator
11 VIN plate

12 Ignition control unit
13 Ignition coil
14 Suspension turret
15 Windscreen wiper motor
16 Ventilation system air inlet
17 Battery

18 Battery negative terminal
19 Battery positive terminal
20 Cooling system expansion
    tank and filler cap
21 Washer system reservoir
22 Distributor

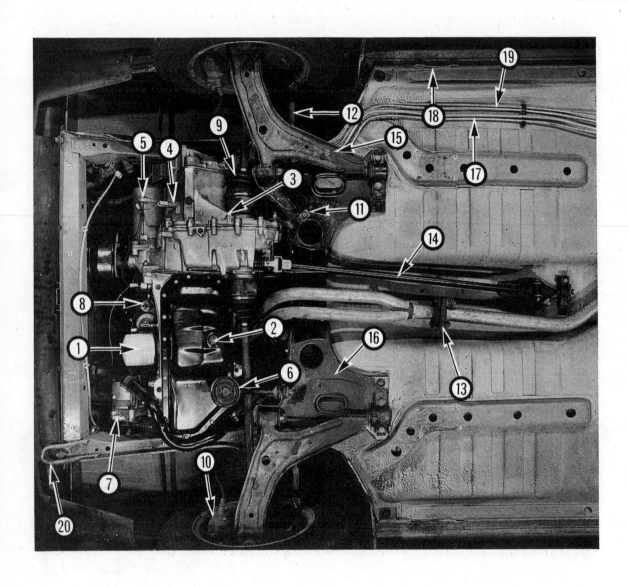

Front underbody view

1   Engine oil filter
2   Engine oil drain plug
3   Transmission oil drain plug
4   Reversing light switch
5   Starter motor
6   Engine mounting

7   Alternator
8   Fuel filter
9   Inboard constant velocity joint
    gaiter
10 Brake caliper
11 Engine-to-chassis earthing strap

12 Steering gear track rod
13 Exhaust flexible joint
14 Gearchange linkage
15 Front suspension lower
    arm

16 Front suspension
    subframe
17 Fuel feed and return pipes
18 Front jacking points
19 Brake pipes
20 Front towing eye

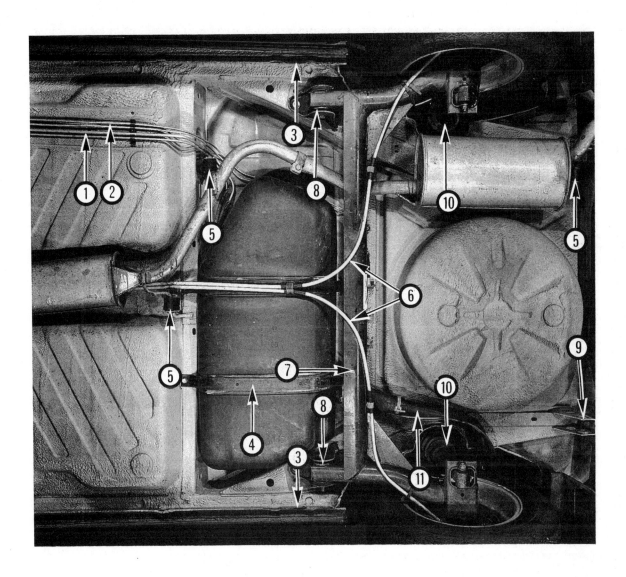

Rear underbody view

1 Fuel feed and return pipes	5 Exhaust system rubber	7 Rear suspension torsion	9 Rear towing eye
2 Brake pipes	mountings	beam axle	10 Rear suspension spring and
3 Rear jacking points	6 Handbrake cables	8 Rear suspension torsion	strut unit
4 Fuel tank retaining strap		beam axle pivot points	11 Fuel tank filler pipe

Maintenance procedures

1 Engine

Engine oil level check

1   The engine oil level is checked with a dipstick that extends through a tube and into the sump at the bottom of the engine. The dipstick is located on the left-hand rear side of the engine, fairly close to the thermostat.

2   The oil level should be checked with the vehicle standing on level ground and before it is driven, or at least 5 minutes after the engine has been switched off. If the oil is checked immediately after driving the vehicle, some of the oil will remain in the upper engine components and oil galleries, resulting in an inaccurate reading on the dipstick.

3   Withdraw the dipstick from the tube and wipe all the oil from the end with a clean rag or paper towel. Insert the clean dipstick back into the tube as far as it will go, then withdraw it once more. Note the oil level on the end of the dipstick. Add oil as necessary until the level is between the upper (MAX) mark and lower (MIN) mark on the dipstick (photo). Note that approximately 1 litre of oil will be required to raise the level from the lower mark to the upper mark.

4   Always maintain the level between the two dipstick marks. If the level is allowed to fall below the lower mark, oil starvation may result which could lead to severe engine damage. If the engine is overfilled by adding too much oil, this may result in oil-fouled spark plugs, oil leaks or oil seal failures.

5   Oil is added to the engine after removing the filler cap on the rocker cover (photo). An oil can spout or funnel may help to reduce spillage. Always use the correct grade and type of oil as shown in 'Lubricants fluids and capacities'.

Engine oil and filter renewal

6   Frequent oil and filter changes are the most important preventative maintenance procedures that can be undertaken by the DIY owner. As engine oil ages, it becomes diluted and contaminated, which leads to premature engine wear.

7   Before starting this procedure, gather together all the necessary tools and materials (photo). Also make sure that you have plenty of clean rags and newspapers handy to mop up any spills. Ideally, the engine oil should be warm as it will drain better and more built-up sludge will be removed with it. Take care however not to touch the exhaust or any other hot parts of the engine when working under the vehicle. To avoid any possibility of scalding and to protect yourself from possible skin irritants and other harmful contaminants in used engine oils, it is advisable to wear non-permeable gloves when carrying out this work. Access to the underside of the vehicle will be greatly improved if it can be raised on a lift, driven onto ramps or jacked up and supported on axle stands. Whichever method is chosen, make sure that the vehicle remains level, or if it is at an angle, that the drain plug (located on the underside of the sump) is at the lowest point.

8   Firstly, remove the full-width undershield by unscrewing the six retaining bolts (photo).

9   Using a spanner or preferably a suitable socket and bar, slacken the drain plug about half a turn. Position the draining container under the drain plug, then remove the plug completely. If possible, try to keep the plug pressed into the sump while unscrewing it by hand the last couple of turns. As the plug releases from the threads, move it away sharply so the stream of oil issuing from the sump runs into the container, not up your sleeve! (photo).

10   Allow some time for the old oil to drain, noting that it may be necessary to reposition the container as the oil flow slows to a trickle.

11   After all the oil has drained, wipe off the drain plug with a clean rag and, if necessary, renew the sealing washer. Clean the area around the drain plug opening and refit the plug. Tighten the plug securely, preferably to the specified torque using a torque wrench.

12   Move the container into position under the oil filter which is located on the side of the cylinder block, below the fuel pump.

13   Using an oil filter removal tool, slacken the filter initially then unscrew it by hand the rest of the way (photo). Empty the oil in the old filter into the container.

14   Use a clean rag to remove all oil, dirt and sludge from the filter sealing area on the engine. Check the old filter to make sure that the rubber sealing ring hasn't stuck to the engine. If it has, carefully remove it.

15   Apply a light coating of clean engine oil to the sealing ring on the new filter (photo), then screw it into position on the engine. Tighten the filter firmly by hand only – do not use any tools.

16   Remove the old oil and all tools from under the vehicle and refit the undershield then (if applicable) lower the vehicle to the ground.

17   Remove the oil filler cap and fill the engine, using the correct grade and type of oil, as described earlier in this Section. Pour in half the specified quantity of oil first, then wait a few minutes for the oil to fall to the sump. Continue adding oil a small quantity at a time until the level is up to the lower mark on the dipstick. Adding a further 1 litre will bring the level up to the upper mark on the dipstick.

18   Start the engine and run it for a few minutes while checking for leaks around the oil filter seal and the sump drain plug.

19   Switch off the engine and wait a few minutes for the oil to settle in the sump once more. With the new oil circulated and the filter now completely full, recheck the level on the dipstick and add more oil as necessary.

20   Dispose of the used engine oil safely with reference to 'General repair procedures' in the preliminary Sections of this Manual.

Valve clearance adjustment

21   Obtaining the correct rocker arm/valve stem clearances is vitally important to the performance of the engine. If the clearances are too loose, the valves will open later and close earlier than was intended, and in turn reduce the efficiency of the engine. If, on the other hand, the clearances are too tight, there is a danger that, when the stems and pushrods expand with heat, they will not allow the valves to close fully, which will cause loss of compression and lead to burning of the valve head and valve seat.

22   The valve clearance adjustments should be made with the engine cold. Disconnect the crankcase breather hose and remove the rocker cover (Chapter 2). It may be advantageous to remove the spark plugs at this stage, to enable the crankshaft to be rotated with the minimum of effort.

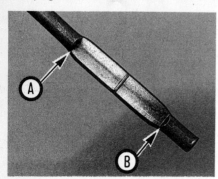

1.3 Engine oil dipstick MAX (A) and MIN (B) marks

1.5 Use only good quality oil of the specified type when topping-up the engine

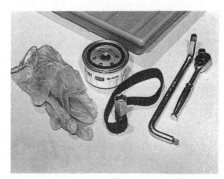

1.7 Tools and materials for engine oil and filter renewal

1.8 Undershield retaining bolts (arrowed)

1.9 Draining the engine oil

1.13 Using an oil filter removal tool to slacken the filter

1.15 Applying a light coating of clean oil to the sealing ring before fitting the new filter

1.24 Adjusting a valve clearance

23   It is important that the clearance is set when the tappet of the valve being adjusted is on the heel of the cam (ie opposite the peak). This can be done by numbering the valves from left to right and carrying out the adjustments in the following order, which also avoids the crankshaft being rotated more than necessary.

Valve fully open	Check and adjust
Valve No 8	*Valve No 1 (Ex)*
Valve No 6	*Valve No 3 (In)*
Valve No 4	*Valve No 5 (Ex)*
Valve No 7	*Valve No 2 (In)*
Valve No 1	*Valve No 8 (Ex)*
Valve No 3	*Valve No 6 (In)*
Valve No 5	*Valve No 4 (Ex)*
Valve No 2	*Valve No 7 (In)*

24   The correct valve clearance is given in the Specifications at the beginning of this Chapter. It is obtained by slackening the hexagonal locknut with a spanner while holding the ball-pin against rotation with a screwdriver. Insert a feeler gauge of thickness equal to the specified valve clearance between the valve stem head and the rocker arm and adjust the ball-pin until the feeler gauge is a tight sliding fit (photo). Then, still holding the ball-pin in the correct position, tighten the locknut and recheck. Turn the engine as necessary and repeat this procedure on the remaining valves.
25   Refit the rocker cover and crankcase breather hose, and if applicable, the spark plugs.

General engine checks

26   Visually inspect the engine joint faces, gaskets and seals for any signs of water or oil leaks. Pay particular attention to the areas around the rocker cover, cylinder head, oil filter and sump joint faces. Bear in mind that over a period of time some very slight seepage from these areas is to be expected – what you are really looking for is any indication of a serious leak. Should a leak be found, renew the offending gasket or oil seal by referring to the appropriate Chapters in this Manual.
27   Also check the security and condition of all the engine related pipes and hoses, particularly the crankcase breather hose from the rocker cover. Ensure that all cable ties or securing clips are in place and

in good condition. Clips which are broken or missing can lead to chafing of the hoses, pipes or wiring which could cause more serious problems in the future.

2   Cooling, heating and ventilation systems

Coolant level check

Warning: *DO NOT attempt to remove the expansion tank pressure cap when the engine is hot, as there is a very great risk of scalding.*

1   All vehicles covered by this manual are equipped with a sealed cooling system. A translucent expansion tank located on the left-hand side of the engine compartment, between the washer system reservoir and the suspension turret, is connected by hoses to the cooling system. As engine temperature increases, the coolant expands and travels through the hose to the expansion tank. As the engine cools, the coolant is automatically drawn back into the system to maintain the correct level.
2   The coolant level in the expansion tank should be checked regularly, preferably when the engine is cold. The level in the tank varies with the temperature of the engine. When the engine is cold, the coolant level should be between the MAX and MIN marks on the side of the tank (photo).
3   If topping-up is necessary, wait until the engine is cold, then turn the pressure cap on the expansion tank anti-clockwise until a hissing sound is heard; wait until the hissing ceases, indicating that all pressure is released, then slowly unscrew the filler cap until it can be removed. If more hissing sounds are heard, wait until they have stopped until unscrewing the cap. At all times keep well away from the filler opening.
4   Add a mixture of water and antifreeze (see below) through the expansion tank filler neck until the coolant is up to the level mark (photo). Refit the cap, turning it clockwise as far as it will go to secure.
5   With a sealed type cooling system, the addition of coolant should only be necessary at very infrequent intervals. If frequent topping-up is required, it is likely there is a leak in the system. Check the radiator, all

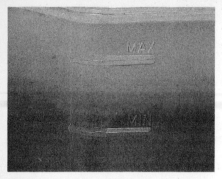

2.2 Coolant level must be maintained between expansion tank MAX and MIN marks

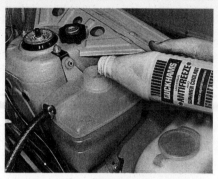

2.4 Use only the specified coolant mixture to top-up the cooling system

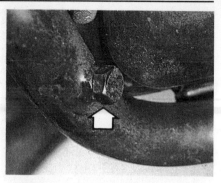

2.7 Cooling system drain plug (arrowed)

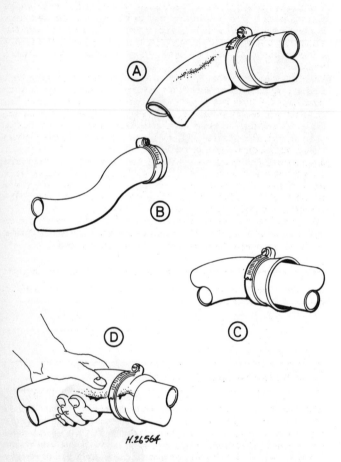

H.26564

Fig. 1.1 Coolant hose inspection (Sec 2)

A   Check hose for chafed or burned areas; these may lead to sudden and costly failure

B   A soft hose indicates inside deterioration, leading to contamination of the cooling system and clogging of the radiator

C   A hardened hose can fail at any time; tightening the clamps will not seal the joint or prevent leaks

D   A swollen hose or one with oil-soaked ends indicates contamination from oil or grease. Cracks and breaks can be easily seen by squeezing the hose

hoses and joint faces for any sign of staining or actual wetness, and rectify as necessary. If no leaks can be found, it is advisable to have the pressure cap and the entire system pressure-tested by a dealer or suitably-equipped garage, as this will often show up a small leak not previously visible.

Coolant draining

Warning: *Wait until the engine is cold before starting this procedure. Do not allow antifreeze to come in contact with your skin or painted surfaces of the vehicle. Rinse off spills immediately with plenty of water. Never leave antifreeze lying around in an open container, or in a puddle in the driveway or on the garage floor. Children and pets are attracted by its sweet smell, but antifreeze is fatal if ingested.*

6   To drain the system, remove the expansion tank filler cap as described above, then move the heater air temperature control to the maximum-heat position.

7   Remove the undershield (Section 1, paragraph 8) and place a large drain tray under the front of the vehicle. Unscrew the drain plug, which can be found on the underside of the metal pipe that connects the radiator bottom hose to the water pump, direct as much of the escaping coolant as possible into the tray (photo).

System flushing

8   With time, the cooling system may gradually lose its efficiency due to the radiator having become choked with rust, scale deposits from the water and other sediment. To minimise this (as well as using only good quality antifreeze and clean soft water) the system should be flushed as follows whenever the coolant is renewed.

9   With the system drained, refit the drain plug and undershield and refill with fresh clean water.

10   Refit the expansion tank filler cap, start the engine and allow it to warm up to normal operating temperature. Then stop it and (after allowing it to cool down completely) drain the system again. Repeat as necessary until only clean water is seen to emerge, then refill finally with the specified coolant mixture.

11   If the specified coolant mixture has been used and renewed at the

2.12 Radiator bottom hose removal

specified intervals, the above procedure will be sufficient to keep clean the system for a very long time. If, however, the system has been neglected, a more thorough operation will be required, as follows.

12   Firstly drain the coolant, this time by removing the radiator bottom hose from the radiator, then remove the radiator top hose from the thermostat housing (photo). Insert a garden hose into the top hose, and allow water to circulate through the radiator until it runs clear from the bottom outlet.

13   To flush the engine, insert the garden hose into the thermostat housing, and allow water to circulate through the engine until it runs clear from the bottom hose. If, after a reasonable period, the water still does not run clear, the system should be flushed with a good proprietary cleaning agent, such as Holts Radflush or Holts Speedflush.

14   In severe cases of contamination, reverse-flushing of the radiator may be necessary. To do this, remove the radiator (Chapter 3), invert it and insert a garden hose into the bottom outlet. Continue flushing until clean water runs from the top hose connection. A similar procedure can be adopted to flush the heater matrix.

Coolant filling

15   With the cooling system drained and flushed, refit the drain plug (or bottom hose, if appropriate) and ensure that all other disturbed unions have been correctly re-secured.

16   Prepare a sufficient quantity of the specified coolant mixture (see below); allow for surplus, so as to have a reserve supply for topping-up.

17   Fill the system slowly, so that any trapped air may escape through the expansion tank, until the correct level is achieved.

18   Start the engine and run it at no more than idle speed until it has reached normal operating temperature and the radiator cooling fan has cut in. At all times keep well away from the filler opening, as small amounts of coolant may be ejected from it as trapped air is forced out of the system.

19   Stop the engine and allow it to cool down, then top-up the coolant to the correct level. Refit the filler cap and wash off any spilt coolant from the engine compartment and bodywork.

20   After refilling, always check carefully all components of the system (but especially those disturbed during draining and flushing) for signs of coolant leak; fresh antifreeze has a searching action, which will rapidly expose any weak points in the system.

Note: *If, after draining and refilling the system, symptoms of overheating are found which did not occur previously, then the fault is almost certainly due to trapped air at some point in the system causing an air-lock and thus restricting the flow of coolant; usually the air is trapped because the system was refilled too quickly. In most cases the air-locks can be released by squeezing or tapping the coolant hoses with the filler cap removed.*

Antifreeze mixture

21   The antifreeze should always be renewed at the specified intervals. This is necessary not only to maintain the antifreeze properties, but also to prevent corrosion which would otherwise occur as the corrosion inhibitors become progressively less effective.

22   Always use an ethylene-glycol based antifreeze which is suitable for use in mixed-metal cooling systems. The quantity of antifreeze and levels of protection are indicated in the Specifications. To give the recommended 50% concentration, 3 litres of antifreeze must be mixed with 3 litres of clean, soft water; this should provide enough to refill the

complete system, but it is best to make up a larger amount so that a supply is available for subsequent topping-up.

23   Before filling with antifreeze the system should be drained, preferably flushed and all hoses checked for condition and security.

24   After filling with antifreeze, a label should be attached to the radiator or expansion tank stating the type and concentration of antifreeze used and the date installed. Any subsequent topping-up should be made with the same type and concentration of antifreeze.

25   Do not use engine antifreeze in the washer system, as it will cause damage to the vehicle paintwork. A screenwash additive such as Turtle Wax High Tech Screen Wash should be added to the washer system in the recommended quantities stated on the bottle.

General cooling system checks

26   The engine should be cold for the cooling system checks, so perform the following procedure before driving the vehicle or after it has been shut off for at least three hours.

27   Remove the expansion tank filler cap (see above) and clean it thoroughly inside and out with a rag. Also clean the filler neck on the expansion tank. The presence of rust or corrosion in the filler neck indicates that the coolant should be changed. The coolant inside the expansion tank should be relatively clean and transparent. If it is rust-coloured, drain and flush the system and refill with a fresh coolant mixture.

28   Carefully check the radiator hoses and heater hoses along their entire length. Renew any hose which is cracked, swollen or deteriorated. Cracks will show up better if the hose is squeezed. Pay close attention to the hose clips that secure the hoses to the cooling system components. Hose clips can pinch and puncture hoses, resulting in cooling system leaks. If wire type hose clips are used, it may be a good idea to replace them with screw-type clips.

29   Inspect all the cooling system components (hoses, joint faces, etc.) for leaks. A leak in the cooling system will usually show up as white-or rust-coloured deposits on the area adjoining the leak. Where any problems of this nature are found on system components, renew the component or gasket with reference to Chapter 3.

30   Clean the front of the radiator with a soft brush to remove all insects, leaves, etc., embedded in the radiator fins. Be extremely careful not to damage the radiator fins or cut your fingers on them.

Water pump drivebelt check, adjustment and renewal

31   See *'Alternator drivebelt check, adjustment and renewal'*, in Section 11 of this Chapter.

---

3   Fuel and exhaust systems

Warning: *Certain procedures in this Section require the removal of fuel lines and connections, which may result in some fuel spillage. Before carrying out any operation on the fuel system, refer to the precautions given in 'Safety first!' at the beginning of this manual, and follow them implicitly. Petrol is a highly-dangerous and volatile liquid, and the precautions necessary when handling it cannot be overstressed.*

3.1A Release the air cleaner assembly cover retaining clips ...

3.1B ... then remove the bolts and lift off the cover

3.3 Ensure the new filter element is correctly seated on reassembly

3.6 Renewing the fuel filter (models up to January 1992)

3.14 Adjusting the idle speed

3.16 Adjusting the CO level

Air cleaner filter element renewal

1   Remove the clips securing the air cleaner assembly cover, then undo the retaining bolts and carefully lift the cover from the assembly (photos). If the assembly is dislodged, lift it carefully and check that none of the vacuum pipes, hoses or wiring (as applicable) connected to its underside have become damaged or dislodged.

2   Lift out the air cleaner filter element and discard it. Wipe clean the inside of the assembly and the cover with a lint-free cloth, then check that there is no foreign matter visible either in the air cleaner intake duct or in the inlet tract.

3   Place the new element in the air cleaner assembly, ensure that it is correctly seated and place the cover back onto the assembly (photo). Refit the retaining bolts and the clips.

Fuel filter renewal

Vehicles up to January 1992

4   The fuel filter is part of the fuel pump and is located inside the settler bowl. Before commencing work, place a suitable container under the vehicle and wads of rags around the fuel pump to catch any spilled fuel.

5   Remove the settler bowl by unscrewing the retaining clip nut, taking care that the bowl does not fall to the ground, then carefully lift the settler bowl away from the body of the fuel pump. Pour any residual petrol from the bowl into the container under the vehicle.

6   Remove the filter from the settler bowl and discard it. Clean the inside and outside of the bowl with a clean cloth and then place a new filter in the bowl (photo).

7   Refitting of the settler bowl is the reversal of the above procedure.

Vehicles from January 1992

8   The fuel filter is of the in-line type and is located in the fuel supply line just before the fuel pump.

9   The filter is removed by undoing the clamps at its inlet and outlet ports, and then pulling the filter from the fuel pipes.

10   Fitting the new filter is the reverse of the removal procedure, ensuring that the arrow on the body of the filter points towards the fuel pump.

Idle speed and mixture adjustment

11   Before beginning any form of carburettor adjustment, always check the following first.

(a)   Check that the ignition timing is set accurately (Section 4).
(b)   Check that the spark plugs are in good condition and correctly gapped (Section 4).
(c)   Check that the throttle cable is correctly adjusted (Chapter 4).
(d)   Check that the air cleaner filter element is clean and in good condition.
(e)   Check that there are no leaks in the induction system.
(f)   Check that there are no leaks in the exhaust system.
(g)   Check that all electric equipment is switched off.
(h)   Check that the valve clearances are correct (Section 1).

12   Take the vehicle on a journey of sufficient length to warm it up to normal operating temperature. **Note:** *Adjustment should be completed within two minutes of return, without stopping the engine. If this cannot be achieved, or if the radiator electric cooling fan operates, wait for the cooling fan to stop and clear any excess fuel from the inlet manifold by increasing the engine speed two or three times to between 2000 and 3000 rpm, then allowing it to idle again.*

13   If the vehicle is not equipped with a tachometer, connect one following its manufacturer's instructions. Note the idle speed, comparing it with that specified.

14   The idle speed adjustment screw can be found on the left-hand rear side of the carburettor (as viewed from above). It is the lower of the two long adjustment screws, and bears directly onto the throttle linkage (photo). Turn the screw as necessary to obtain the correct speed.

15   The idle mixture is set at the factory, and should in theory require no further adjustment. If, due to a change in engine characteristics (carbon build-up, bore wear, etc.) or after a major carburettor overhaul, the mixture becomes incorrect, it can be reset. Note, however, that an exhaust gas analyser (CO meter) will be required to check the mixture and set it with the required level of accuracy. If a suitable instrument is not available, the vehicle must be taken to a Skoda dealer for the work to be carried out.

16   If an exhaust gas analyser is available, follow its manufacturer's instructions to check the CO level. If adjustment is required, it is made by turning the mixture control screw, which is set in the deep recess directly beneath the idle speed adjustment screw (photo). Turn the screw by very small increments until the specified CO level is reached.

17   When adjustments are complete, disconnect any test equipment and refit any components removed for access.

General fuel system checks

18   The fuel system is most easily checked with the vehicle raised on a hoist or suitably supported on axle stands so the components underneath are readily visible and accessible.

19   If the smell of petrol is noticed while driving or after the vehicle has been parked in the sun, the system should be thoroughly inspected immediately.

20   Remove the petrol tank filler cap and check for damage, corrosion and an unbroken sealing imprint on the gasket. Renew the cap if necessary.

21   With the vehicle raised, inspect the petrol tank and filler neck for punctures, cracks and other damage. The connection between the filler neck and tank is especially critical. Sometimes a rubber filler neck or connecting hose will leak due to loose retaining clamps or deteriorated rubber.

22   Carefully check all rubber hoses and metal fuel lines leading away from the petrol tank. Check for loose connections, deteriorated hoses, crimped lines and other damage. Pay particular attention to the vent pipes and hoses which often loop up around the filler neck and can become blocked or crimped. Follow the lines to the front of the vehicle carefully inspecting them all the way. Renew damaged sections as necessary.

23   From within the engine compartment, check the security of all fuel hose attachments and inspect the fuel hoses and vacuum hoses for kinks, chafing and deterioration.

24   Check the operation of the throttle linkage and lubricate the linkage components with a few drops of light oil.

Exhaust system checks

25   With the engine cold (at least an hour after the vehicle has been driven), check the complete exhaust system from the engine to the end of the tailpipe. Ideally the inspection should be carried out with the vehicle on a hoist to permit unrestricted access. If a hoist is not available, raise and support the vehicle on axle stands.

26 Check the exhaust pipes and connections for evidence of leaks, severe corrosion and damage. Make sure that all brackets and mountings are in good condition and tight. Leakage at any of the joints or in other parts of the system will usually show up as a black sooty stain in the vicinity of the leak. Holts Flexiwrap and Holts Gun Gum exhaust repair systems can be used for effective repairs to exhaust pipes and silencer boxes, including ends and bends. Holts Flexiwrap is an MOT-approved permanent exhaust repair. Holts Firegum is suitable for the assembly of all exhaust system joints.

27 Rattles and other noises can often be traced to the exhaust system, especially the brackets and mountings. Try to move the pipes and silencers. If the components can come into contact with the body or suspension parts, secure the system with new mountings or if possible, separate the joints and twist the pipes as necessary to provide additional clearance.

4 Ignition system

Warning: *Voltages produced by an electronic ignition system are considerably higher than those produced by conventional systems. Extreme care must be taken when working on the system with the ignition switched on. Persons with surgically-implanted cardiac pacemaker devices should keep well clear of the ignition circuits, components and test equipment.*

Ignition timing check and adjustment

1 Before the ignition timing can be checked, the timing marks must be identified and, if necessary, clarified. When looking at the crankshaft pulley, the timing mark will be seen as a V-notch cut into the inner rim. When looking at the timing chain cover, the timing marks will be seen as raised lines with their value beside them (photo). Mark the pulley V-notch and the appropriate line on the timing chain cover (see Specifications for correct timing value) with white paint.

2 Start the engine and allow it to reach the normal operating temperature, ensuring that the idle speed is correct, then stop the engine and connect a stroboscopic timing light, according to the equipment manufacturer's instructions. Disconnect the vacuum pipe from the distributor, and plug it temporarily.

3 Restart the engine, and aim the timing light at the timing marks; the highlighted marks should stand out clearly and appear stationary. Check that the pulley mark aligns with the correct timing chain cover line, or falls within the specified tolerance.

4 If adjustment is required, slacken the distributor adjustment bolt, until the distributor body is just able to rotate, then turn the body until the timing marks align. Retighten the bolt and recheck the ignition timing to ensure that it has not altered.

5 If the engine speed is now increased, the pulley mark should appear to drift away from the timing chain cover mark as the distributor

4.1 Crankshaft pulley V-notch (A) and timing marks (B) on timing chain cover

automatic advance mechanism comes into operation; if this is not the case, then the advance mechanism should be examined.

6 Unplug and reconnect the vacuum pipe; the ignition timing should be seen to advance slightly. If the ignition timing does not alter then, the distributor vacuum capsule may be faulty and should be examined.

7 On completion of the adjustments, stop the engine and disconnect the timing light.

Spark plug check and renewal

8 The correct functioning of the spark plugs is vital for the correct running and efficiency of the engine. It is essential that the plugs fitted are appropriate for the engine, and the suitable type is specified at the beginning of this Chapter. If this type is used and the engine is in good condition, the spark plugs should not need attention between scheduled replacement intervals. Spark plug cleaning is rarely necessary, and should not be attempted unless specialised equipment is available as damage can easily be caused to the firing ends.

9 To remove the plugs, first open the bonnet and mark the HT leads one to four to correspond to the cylinder the lead serves (No 1 cylinder is at the crankshaft pulley end of the engine). Pull the HT leads from the plugs by gripping the end fitting, not the lead, otherwise the lead connection may be fractured (photo).

10 It is advisable to remove the dirt from the spark plug recesses using a clean brush, vacuum cleaner or compressed air before removing the plugs, to prevent the dirt dropping into the cylinders.

11 Unscrew the plugs using a spark plug spanner, suitable box spanner or a deep socket and extension bar (photo). Keep the socket squarely on the spark plug – if it is forcibly moved to either side, the porcelain top of the spark plug may be broken off. As each plug is removed, examine it as follows.

12 Examination of the spark plugs will give a good indication of the condition of the engine. If the insulator nose of the spark plug is clean and white, with no deposits, this is indicative of a weak fuel mixture or too hot a plug (a hot plug transfers heat away from the electrode slowly, a cold plug transfers heat away quickly).

13 If the tip and insulator nose are covered with hard black-looking deposits, then this is indicative that the fuel mixture is too rich. Should the plug be black and oily, then it is likely that the engine is fairly worn, as well as the mixture being too rich.

14 If the insulator nose is covered with light-tan to greyish-brown deposits, then the mixture is correct and it is likely that the engine is in good condition.

15 The spark plug gap is of considerable importance as, if it is too large or too small, the size of the spark and its efficiency will be seriously impaired. For best results, the spark plug gap should be set in accordance with the Specifications at the beginning of this Chapter.

16 To set it, measure the gap with a feeler gauge, and then bend the outer plug electrode until the correct gap is achieved (photo). The centre electrode should never be bent, as this may crack the insulation and cause plug failure, if nothing worse.

17 Special spark plug electrode gap adjusting tools are available from most motor accessory shops (photos).

18 Before fitting the spark plugs, check that the threaded connector sleeves are tight, and that the plug exterior surfaces and threads are clean. Apply a light coating of copper-based brake grease (such as Holts Copaslip) to the spark plug threads, to aid removal next time.

19 Screw in the spark plugs by hand where possible, then tighten them to the specified torque. Take extra care to enter the plug threads correctly as the cylinder head is of aluminium alloy.

20 Reconnect the HT leads in their correct order, as marked on removal.

Spark plug HT leads, distributor cap and rotor arm check and renewal

21 The spark plug HT leads should be checked whenever new spark plugs are installed in the engine.

22 Ensure that the leads are numbered before removing them to avoid confusion when refitting. Pull the HT leads from the plugs by gripping the end fitting, not the lead, otherwise the lead connection may be fractured.

23 Check inside the end fitting for signs of corrosion, which will look like a white crusty powder. Push the end fitting back onto the spark plug, ensuring that it is a tight fit on the plug. If it isn't, remove the lead again and use pliers to carefully crimp the metal connector inside the end fitting until it fits securely on the end of the spark plug.

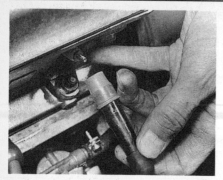

4.9 Pull the HT lead from the spark plug by gripping the end fitting

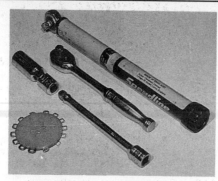

4.11 Tools required for removing, refitting and adjusting the spark plugs

4.16 Measuring the spark plug electrode gap using a feeler gauge

4.17A Measuring the spark plug electrode gap using a wire gauge

4.17B Adjusting the spark plug electrode gap using a special tool

4.25 Disconnecting an HT lead from the distributor cap

24   Using a clean rag, wipe the entire length of the lead to remove any built-up dirt and grease. Once the lead is clean, check for burns, cracks and other damage. Do not bend the lead excessively or pull the lead lengthwise – the conductor inside might break.

25   Disconnect the other end of the lead from the distributor (photo) – again, pull only on the end fitting. Check for corrosion and a tight fit in the same manner as the spark plug end. If an ohmmeter is available, check the resistance of the HT lead by connecting the meter between the spark plug end of the lead and the segment inside the distributor cap. Refit the lead securely on completion.

26   Check the remaining HT leads one at a time, in the same way.

27   If new HT leads are required, purchase a set for your specific vehicle and engine.

28   Remove the distributor cap, wipe it clean and carefully inspect it inside and out for signs of cracks, carbon tracks (tracking) and worn, burned or loose contacts; check that the cap's carbon brush is unworn, free to move against spring pressure and making good contact with the rotor arm. Similarly inspect the rotor arm. Renew these components if any defects are found. It is common practice to renew the cap and rotor arm whenever new HT leads are fitted. When fitting a new cap, remove the HT leads from the old cap one at a time and fit them to the new cap in the exact same location – do not simultaneously remove all the leads from the old cap, or firing order confusion may occur.

29   Even with the ignition system in first class condition, some engines may still occasionally experience poor starting attributable to damp ignition components. To disperse moisture, a water-repelling aerosol spray such as Holts Wet Start can be very effective. Holts Damp Start should be used for providing a sealing coat to exclude moisture from the ignition system, and in extreme difficulty, Holts Cold Start will help to start a vehicle when only a very poor spark occurs.

Distributor – lubrication

30   Remove the distributor cap and rotor arm, and lubricate the components of the distributor with light oil as follows.

   (a)   The felt underneath the rotor arm with 3 drops of oil.
   (b)   The vacuum control unit lever with 1 drop of oil.
   (c)   The rotating base friction points with 3 drops of oil.
   (d)   Remove the cover screw and lubricate the centrifugal weights with 5 drops of oil.

31   Refit the rotor arm and distributor cap.

5   Clutch

Clutch cable adjustment

1   The clutch cable should be adjusted such that there is no free play in the pedal; the pedal should be level with, or up to 10 mm below, the height of the brake pedal.

2   To adjust the cable, follow the cable through to the clutch operating lever, which is situated on the side of the bellhousing adjacent to the gearbox. Turn the nut on the threaded portion of the cable until the specified pedal height is achieved; turning the nut in a clockwise direction will raise the height of the pedal (photo).

5.2 Adjusting the clutch cable – note anti-rattle clip (arrowed)

6.3A Remove the retaining clip ...

6.3B ... withdraw the speedometer drive ...

6.3C ... and measure the oil level (see text)

6.4 Use only good quality oil when topping-up the transmission

6.7 Draining the transmission oil

General check

3   Check that the clutch pedal moves smoothly and freely through its full travel, and that the clutch itself functions correctly, with no trace of slip or drag. If excessive effort is required to operate the clutch, check that the cable is correctly routed and undamaged, then remove the pedal to ensure its pivot is properly greased before suspecting a fault in the clutch itself; if the cable is worn or damaged it must be renewed (Chapter 6).

6   Transmission

Oil level check

1   The oil level must be checked with the vehicle standing on its wheels on level ground. Also, the level must be checked before the vehicle is driven, or at least five minutes after the engine has been switched off. If the oil is checked immediately after driving the vehicle, some of the oil will remain distributed around the transmission components, resulting in an inaccurate level reading.
2   The level is checked by measuring its height on the speedometer drivegear. The speedometer drive is located on the gearbox casing, and can be positively identified by tracing the cable from the speedometer head.
3   Wipe clean the area around the speedometer drive, then remove the bolt and clip which retain it. Lift the drive from the gearbox housing and note the oil level on the drive; this should be between 4 and 11 mm when measured from the bottom of the drivegear (photos).
4   If topping-up is necessary, pour the oil into the hole vacated by the speedometer drive (photo).
5   Recheck the oil level, and refit the speedometer drive, ensuring that the drivegear meshes correctly.

Oil renewal

6   Before starting this procedure, make sure that you have plenty of clean rags and newspapers handy to mop up any spills. Ideally, the gearbox oil should be warm, as it will drain better and more

contaminants will be removed with it. To avoid any possibility of scalding and to protect yourself from possible skin irritants and other harmful contaminants in used oils, it is advisable to wear non-permeable gloves when carrying out this work. Access to the underside of the vehicle will be greatly improved if it can be raised on a lift, driven onto ramps or jacked up and supported on axle stands. Whichever method is chosen, make sure that the vehicle remains level, or if it is at an angle, that the drain plug (located at the bottom of the gearbox casing, below the nearside driveshaft) is at the lowest point.
7   Using a spanner (or preferably a suitable socket and bar) slacken the drain plug about half a turn. Position the draining container under the drain plug, then remove the plug completely. If possible, try to keep the plug pressed into the casing while unscrewing it by hand the last couple of turns. As the plug releases from the threads, move it away sharply so the stream of oil issuing from the gearbox runs into the container, not up your sleeve! (photo).
8   Allow some time for the old oil to drain, noting that it may be necessary to reposition the container as the oil flow slows to a trickle.
9   After all the oil has drained, wipe off the drain plug with a clean rag and renew the sealing washer if necessary. Clean the area around the drain plug opening, refit the plug and tighten securely.
10   To refill the gearbox, follow the instructions for topping-up as detailed above.

7   Driveshafts

Driveshaft rubber gaiter and CV joint check

1   With the vehicle raised and securely supported on stands, turn the steering onto full-lock then slowly rotate the roadwheel. Inspect the condition of the outer constant velocity (CV) joint rubber gaiters while squeezing the gaiters to open out the folds. Check for signs of cracking, splits or deterioration of the rubber which may allow the grease to escape and lead to water and grit entry into the joint. Also check the security and condition of the retaining clips. Repeat these checks on the inner CV joints (photo). If any damage or deterioration is found, the gaiters should be renewed as described in Chapter 8.

7.1 Checking a driveshaft rubber gaiter

2   At the same time check the general condition of the CV joints themselves by first holding the driveshaft and attempting to rotate the wheel. Repeat this check by holding the inner joint and attempting to rotate the driveshaft. Any appreciable movement indicates wear in the joints, wear in the driveshaft splines or loose driveshaft retaining nut.

8   Braking system

Hydraulic fluid level check

1   The brake master cylinder and fluid reservoir is mounted on the front of the vacuum servo unit in the engine compartment. The maximum and minimum marks are indicated on the side of the reservoir, and the fluid level should be maintained between these marks at all times.
2   If topping-up is necessary, first wipe the area around the filler cap with a clean rag before removing the cap. When adding fluid, pour it carefully into the reservoir to avoid spilling it on surrounding painted surfaces. Be sure to use only the specified brake hydraulic fluid, since mixing different types of fluid can cause damage to the system (photo). See 'Lubricants fluids and capacities' at the beginning of this Chapter.
Warning: Brake hydraulic fluid can harm your eyes and damage painted surfaces, so use extreme caution when handling and pouring it. Do not use fluid that has been standing open for some time as it absorbs moisture from the air. Excess moisture can cause a dangerous loss of braking effectiveness.
3   When adding fluid it is a good idea to inspect the reservoir for contamination. The system should be drained and refilled if deposits, dirt particles or contamination are seen in the fluid.
4   After filling the reservoir to the proper level, make sure that the cap is refitted securely, to avoid leaks and the entry of foreign matter.
5   The fluid level in the master cylinder reservoir will drop slightly as the brake pads and shoes wear down during normal operation. If the reservoir requires repeated replenishing to maintain the proper level, this is an indication of a hydraulic leak somewhere in the system which should be investigated immediately.

Hydraulic fluid renewal

6   The procedure is similar to that for the bleeding of the hydraulic system as described in Chapter 9, except that the brake fluid reservoir should be emptied by syphoning, using a clean poultry baster or similar before starting, and allowance should be made for the old fluid to be removed from the circuit when bleeding a section of the circuit.

Vacuum servo unit check

7   To test the operation of the servo unit, depress the footbrake four or five times to exhaust the vacuum then start the engine. As the engine starts there should be a noticeable 'give' in the brake pedal as vacuum builds up. Allow the engine to run for at least two minutes and then switch it off. If the brake pedal is now depressed again, it should be possible to detect a hiss from the servo when the pedal is depressed. After about four or five applications no further hissing will be heard and the pedal will feel considerably firmer.

Hydraulic pipes and hoses check

8   The brake hydraulic system consists of a number of metal hydraulic pipes which run from the master cylinder around the engine compartment to the front brakes and pressure-regulating valves and along the underbody to the rear brakes. Flexible hoses are fitted at front and rear to cater for steering and suspension movement.
9   When checking the system, first look for signs of leakage at the pipe or hose unions, then examine the flexible hoses for signs of cracking, chafing or deterioration of the rubber. Bend them sharply between the fingers (but do not actually bend them double, or the casing may be damaged) and check that this does not reveal previously-hidden cracks, cuts or splits (photo). Check that all pipes and hoses are securely fastened in their clips.
10   Carefully work along the length of the metal hydraulic pipes looking for dents, kinks, damage of any sort or corrosion. Corrosion should be polished off; if the depth of pitting is significant the pipe must be renewed.

Front brake pad, caliper and disc check

11   Jack up the front of the vehicle and support it securely on axle stands, then remove the roadwheel.
12   For a quick check, the thickness of friction material remaining on each brake pad can be measured through the slot in the caliper body (photo). If any pad's friction material is worn to the specified thickness or less, all four pads must be renewed.
13   For a comprehensive check, the brake pads should be removed and cleaned. This will permit the operation of the caliper to be checked and the condition of the brake disc itself to be fully examined on both sides (Chapter 9).

Rear brake shoe, wheel cylinder and drum check

14   The rear brakes are equipped with a self-adjusting mechanism, to automatically compensate for friction material wear, and therefore should not require periodic adjustment. If, however, reduced braking efficiency is experienced, then the self-adjusting mechanism could be at fault and should be checked (Chapter 9).
15   To inspect the condition of the friction material, the brake drums should be removed and cleaned. This will also allow the wheel cylinders to be checked, and the condition of the brake drum itself to be fully examined (Chapter 9).

Handbrake check and adjustment

16   The handbrake should be capable of holding the parked vehicle stationary, even on steep slopes, when applied with moderate force. The mechanism should be firm and positive in feel with no trace of stiffness or sponginess from the cables, and should release immediately the handbrake lever is released. If the mechanism is faulty in any of these respects, it must be checked immediately.
17   To check the setting, apply the handbrake firmly several times to establish correct shoe-to-drum clearance, then release fully the lever. Applying normal, moderate pressure, pull the handbrake lever to the fully-applied position and count the number of notches required to do so; if the number of notches is not as specified, adjustment is required.
18   To adjust the handbrake, chock the front wheels, then jack up the rear of the car and support it on axle stands. From inside the vehicle, unclip the handbrake lever trim (photo).
19   The handbrake adjusting mechanism is situated at the point just forward of where the handbrake lever protrudes through the floorpan into the car. It should be noted that the right-hand cable adjusts the right-hand brake and the left-hand cable adjusts the left-hand brake. The procedure for adjusting either brake is identical; care must be taken, however, that both brakes are adjusted by the same amount, ie when the handbrake is operated both brakes operate simultaneously and with the same amount of force.
20   Set the handbrake lever on the fourth notch of the ratchet mechanism and slacken the locknut which secures the cable adjustment nut. Adjust the cable by turning the adjustment nut until the

8.2 Use only good quality hydraulic fluid of the specified type when topping-up brake master cylinder fluid reservoir

8.9 Checking a braking system flexible hose

8.12 Front brake pad friction material can be checked through the slot in the caliper body

8.18 Removing the handbrake lever trim

8.20 Adjusting the handbrake

brake is felt to bind as the roadwheel is turned (photo). Now check that the brake is locked when the lever is applied between five and eight notches, but is free to turn when the lever is released.

21   Retighten the locknut, and then adjust the opposite brake in the same manner.

22   When adjustment is complete, refit the plastic trim and lower the car.

9   Suspension and steering

Front suspension and steering check

1   Raise the front of the vehicle and securely support it on axle stands.

2   Visually inspect the balljoint dust covers and the steering gear gaiters for splits, chafing or deterioration (photo). Any wear of these components will cause loss of lubricant, as well as allowing dirt and water entry, resulting in rapid deterioration of the balljoints or steering gear.

3   Grasp the roadwheel at the 12 o'clock and 6 o'clock positions, and try to rock it (photo). Very slight free play may be felt, but if the movement is appreciable further investigation is necessary to determine the source. Continue rocking the wheel while an assistant depresses the footbrake. If the movement is now eliminated or significantly reduced, it is likely that the hub bearings are at fault. If the free play is still evident with the footbrake depressed, then there is wear in the suspension joints or mountings.

4   Now grasp the wheel at the 9 o'clock and 3 o'clock positions, and try to rock it as before. Any movement felt now may again be caused by wear in the hub bearings or the steering track-rod balljoints. If the outer balljoint is worn the visual movement will be obvious. If the inner joint is suspect, it can be felt by placing a hand over the steering gear rubber gaiter and gripping the track-rod. If the wheel is now rocked, movement will be felt at the inner joint if wear has taken place.

5   Using a large screwdriver or flat bar, check for wear in the suspension mounting bushes by levering between the relevant suspension component and its attachment point. Some movement is to be expected as the mountings are made of rubber, but excessive wear should be obvious. Also check the condition of any visible rubber bushes, looking for splits, cracks or contamination of the rubber.

9.2 Check the steering gear rubber gaiters for signs of chafing or deterioration

9.3 Rocking the roadwheel to check suspension/steering wear

9.9 Remove the dust cap from the hub

Condition	Probable cause	Corrective action	Condition	Probable cause	Corrective action
Shoulder wear	• Underinflation (wear on both sides) • Incorrect wheel camber (wear on one side) • Hard cornering	• Check and adjust pressure • Repair or renew suspension parts • Reduce speed	**Feathered edge** **Toe wear**	• Incorrect toe setting	• Adjust front wheel alignment
Centre wear	• Overinflation	• Measure and adjust pressure	**Uneven wear**	• Incorrect camber or castor • Malfunctioning suspension • Unbalanced wheel • Out-of-round brake disc/drum	• Repair or renew suspension parts • Repair or renew suspension parts • Balance tyres • Machine or renew disc/drum

Fig. 1.2 Tyre tread wear patterns and causes (Sec 9)

6   With the vehicle standing on its wheels, have an assistant turn the steering wheel back and forth about an eighth of a turn each way. There should be very little, if any lost movement between the steering wheel and roadwheels. If this is not the case, closely observe the joints and mountings previously described, but in addition check the steering column universal joints for wear, and also check the steering gear itself.

Rear hub bearing check and adjustment

7   Jack up the rear of the vehicle, and support it securely on axle stands.
8   Check the hub bearings by gripping the roadwheel at the 3 o'clock and 9 o'clock positions, and rocking it from side to side. Some movement is necessary, but if the movement is excessive, the bearings will have to be adjusted.
9   If adjustment is necessary, remove the roadwheel. Then, using a hammer and cold chisel, tap off the dust cap from the end of the hub (photo).
10   Extract the split pin and take off the nut retainer.
11   Tighten the hub nut to a torque of 15 Nm (11 lbf ft) (photo), at the same time rotating the brake drum in an anti-clockwise direction.
12   Tap the brake drum around its circumference with a mallet, to relieve the bearing tapers.
13   Unscrew the nut half a turn (180°) and then retighten it to a torque of 5 Nm (4 lbf ft).
14   Fit the nut retainer so that two of its slots line up with the split pin hole. Insert a new split pin (photo), bending the ends around the nut retainer slots.
15   Tap the dust cap back into position.
16   Recheck the play as described above, remembering that a small amount of movement is essential.
17   Repeat the operations on the opposite hub, refit the roadwheels and lower the vehicle to the ground.

Suspension strut/shock absorber check

18   Check for any signs of fluid leakage around the suspension strut/shock absorber body, or from the rubber gaiter around the piston rod. Should any fluid be noticed, the unit is defective internally and should be renewed. **Note:** *Suspension struts/shock absorbers should always be renewed in pairs on the same axle.*

19   The efficiency of the suspension strut/shock absorber may be checked by bouncing the vehicle at each corner. Generally speaking, the body will return to its normal position and stop after being depressed. If it rises and returns on a rebound, the suspension unit is probably suspect. Examine also the upper and lower mountings for any signs of wear.

Rear suspension check

20   Chock the front wheels, then jack up the front of the vehicle and support it on axle stands.
21   Working as described previously for the front suspension, check the rear suspension torsion beam axle for any signs of wear or damage and the pivot bracket bushes for deterioration.

Wheel and tyre maintenance and tyre pressure checks

22   Periodically remove the wheels and clean any dirt or mud from their inside and outside surfaces. Examine the wheel rims for signs of rusting, corrosion or other damage. Light alloy wheels are easily damaged by 'kerbing' whilst parking, and similarly steel wheels may become dented or buckled. Renewal of the wheel is very often the only course of remedial action possible.
23   To check that the roadwheels are securely fastened, remove the roadwheel trim (if necessary), then slacken each wheel nut or bolt in turn through one-quarter of a turn and tighten it to the specified torque wrench setting. Refit the trim, where applicable.
24   The tyres originally fitted are equipped with tread wear indicators which will appear flush with the surface of the tread, thus producing the effect of a continuous band of rubber across the width of the tyre when the tread depth is reduced to approximately 1.6 mm (0.063 in); **at this point, the tyre must be renewed immediately.** Tread wear can be monitored with a simple inexpensive device, known as a tread depth indicator gauge (photo).
25   Note any abnormal tread wear with reference to Fig. 1.2. Tread pattern irregularities such as feathering, flat spots and more wear on one side than the other are indications of front wheel alignment and/or balance problems. If any of these conditions are noted, they should be rectified as soon as possible.
26   General tyre wear is influenced to a large degree by driving style – harsh braking and acceleration, or fast cornering, will all produce more rapid tyre wear. Interchanging of tyres may result in more even wear,

9.11 Initially tighten the hub nut to the correct torque

9.14 Secure the hub nut using a new split pin

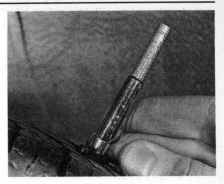

9.24 Checking tyre tread depth with a depth gauge

but it is worth bearing in mind that if this is completely effective, the added expense is incurred of replacing simultaneously a complete set of tyres, which may prove financially restrictive for many owners.

27   Front tyres may wear unevenly as a result of wheel misalignment. The front wheels should always be correctly aligned according to the settings specified (Chapter 10).

28   Regularly check the tyres for damage in the form of cuts or bulges, especially in the sidewalls. Remove any nails or stones embedded in the tread before they penetrate the tyre to cause deflation. If removal of a nail does reveal that the tyre has been punctured, refit the nail so that its point of penetration is marked, then immediately change the wheel and have the tyre repaired by a tyre dealer. Do not drive on a tyre in such a condition. If in any doubt as to the possible consequences of any damage found, consult your local tyre dealer for advice.

29   Ensure that tyre pressures are checked regularly and maintained correctly. Checking should be carried out with the tyres cold, and not immediately after the car has been in use (photo). If the pressures are checked with the tyres hot, a fictitiously-high reading will be obtained owing to heat expansion. Under no circumstances should an attempt be made to reduce the pressures to the quoted cold reading in this instance, or effective underinflation will result.

30   Underinflation will cause overheating of the tyre owing to excessive flexing of the casing, and the tread will not sit correctly on the road surface. This will cause a consequent loss of adhesion and excessive wear, not to mention the danger of sudden tyre failure due to heat build-up.

31   Overinflation will cause rapid wear of the centre part of the tyre tread coupled with reduced adhesion, harsher ride, and the danger of shock damage occurring in the tyre casing.

32   The balance of each wheel and tyre assembly should be maintained to avoid excessive wear, not only to the tyres but also to the steering and suspension components. Wheel imbalance is normally signified by vibration through the car's bodyshell, although in many

cases it is particularly noticeable through the steering wheel. Conversely, it should be noted that wear or damage in suspension or steering components may cause excessive tyre wear. Out-of-round or out-of-true tyres, damaged wheels and wheel bearing wear also fall into this category. Balancing will not usually cure vibration caused by such wear.

33   Wheel balancing may be carried out with the wheel either on or off the car. If balanced on the car, ensure that the wheel-to-hub relationship is marked in some way prior to subsequent wheel removal so that it may be refitted in its original position.

34   Legal restrictions apply to many aspects of tyre fitting and usage and in the UK this information is contained in the Motor Vehicle Construction and Use Regulations. It is suggested that a copy of these regulations is obtained from your local police if in doubt as to current legal requirements with regard to tyre type and condition, minimum tread depth, etc.

10   Bodywork

Hinges and locks – check and lubrication

1   Lubricate the hinges of the bonnet, doors and tailgate with a light oil.

2   Lightly lubricate the bonnet release mechanism with a lithium-based grease.

3   The door and tailgate latches, strikers and locks must also be lubricated with a lithium-based grease, applied sparingly. **Do not** lubricate the steering lock mechanism with oil or any other lubricant which might foul the ignition switch contacts; if the lock is stiff, try to introduce a graphite-based powder into the mechanism.

4   Check carefully the security and operation of all hinges, latches and locks, adjusting them where required.

5   Check the condition and operation of the tailgate struts, renewing them if either is leaking or no longer able to support the tailgate securely when raised.

Seat belt check

6   Carefully examine the seat belt webbing for cuts or any signs of serious fraying or deterioration. If the seat belt is of the retractable type, pull the belt all the way out and examine the full extent of the webbing.

7   The seat belts are designed to lock up during a sudden stop or impact, yet allow free movement during normal driving. Fasten and unfasten the belt, ensuring that the locking mechanism holds securely and releases properly when intended. Check also that the retracting mechanism operates correctly when the belt is released.

11   Electrical system

Battery check and maintenance

Caution: *Before carrying out any work on the vehicle battery, read through the precautions given in 'Safety first!' at the beginning of this manual.*

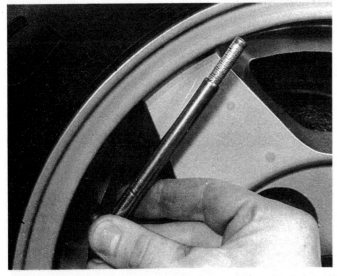

9.29 Checking the tyre pressures with a tyre pressure gauge

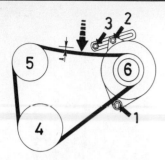

Fig. 1.3 Alternator drivebelt adjustment (Sec 11)

1 Alternator pivot bolt	5 Water pump pulley
2 Alternator clamp bolt	6 Alternator pulley
3 Alternator bracket bolt	A Drivebelt deflection –
4 Crankshaft pulley	10 to 15 mm

1   The battery is located at the rear of the engine bay on the left-hand side.

2   The electrolyte level should be maintained just above the tops of the cells. If topping-up is necessary, add **distilled** water to each cell as necessary after unscrewing the cell caps or lifting up the top cover (photo).

3   The exterior of the battery should be inspected periodically for damage such as a cracked case or cover.

4   Check the tightness of the battery cable clamps to ensure good electrical connections, and check the entire length of each cable for cracks and frayed conductors.

5   If corrosion (visible as white, fluffy deposits) is evident, remove the cables from the battery terminals, clean them with a small wire brush, then refit them. Corrosion can be kept to a minimum by applying a layer of petroleum jelly to the clamps and terminals after they are reconnected.

6   Make sure that the battery tray is in good condition and the retaining clamp is tight.

7   Corrosion on the tray, retaining clamp and the battery itself can be removed with a solution of water and baking soda. Thoroughly rinse all cleaned areas with plain water.

8   Any metal parts of the vehicle damaged by corrosion should be covered with a zinc-based primer then painted.

9   Further information on the battery, charging and jump starting can be found in Chapter 12 and in the preliminary sections of this manual.

Alternator drivebelt check, adjustment and renewal

Drivebelt check and adjustment

10   The drivebelt should be visually inspected for signs of chafing, fraying, splitting and cracking. If any of these signs are apparent, renew the drivebelt at the earliest opportunity.

11   The drivebelt tension is correct when, with an applied load of approximately 2 kg, there is 10 to 15 mm of lateral movement at the midpoint position of the drivebelt between the alternator pulley and the water pump pulley (photo).

12   To adjust the drivebelt, slacken the alternator bracket bolt and the alternator pivot and clamp bolts, and rock the alternator backwards or forwards until the correct drivebelt tension is obtained (photo). It is easier if the alternator pivot and clamp bolts are only slackened slightly, so that some force is required to move it. In this way, the correct tension of the drivebelt can be arrived at more quickly than making frequent adjustments.

13   Once the correct drivebelt tension has been obtained, retighten the alternator bracket bolt and the alternator pivot and clamp bolts, and recheck the tension.

Drivebelt renewal

14   To renew the drivebelt, if it has become worn or stretched, slacken the alternator bracket bolt and the alternator pivot and clamp bolts and move the alternator in towards the water pump as far as it will go.

15   Remove the old drivebelt by slipping it over the crankshaft, alternator and water pump pulleys, and discard it.

16   Carefully slip the new belt over the three pulleys, taking care not to contaminate it with any oil or grease, and adjust the tension as described above.

Note: *Following renewal it is advisable to recheck the tension after approximately 250 miles (400 km), due to the initial stretch of the new drivebelt.*

11.2 Checking the battery electrolyte level

11.11 Checking the alternator drivebelt tension

11.12 Rock the alternator backwards or forwards until the correct drivebelt tension is achieved

11.21 Topping-up the washer system reservoir

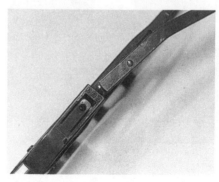

11.26 Disconnecting a wiper blade from the arm

Lights, horn and direction indicators operational check

17   Check the operation of all the electrical equipment, ie lights, direction indicators, horn, etc. Refer to the appropriate Sections of Chapter 12 for details if any of the circuits are found to be inoperative.

18   Note that stop-light switch adjustment is described in Chapter 9.

19   Visually check all accessible wiring connectors, harnesses and retaining clips for security, and for signs of chafing or damage. Rectify any faults found.

Windscreen and rear window washer/wiper system check

Washer system reservoir top-up

20   The reservoir for the windscreen and the rear window washer (where fitted) systems is located on the left-hand side of the engine compartment.

21   Check, and if necessary top-up, the washer fluid level in the reservoir. When topping-up the reservoir, a screenwash such as Turtle Wax High Tech Screen Wash should be added in the quantities recommended on the bottle (photo). It is permissible to use only clean water in Summer, though this is best mixed with a screenwash additive of the type recommended. In Winter, mix the water either with methylated spirit or with a combined screenwash additive which has antifreeze properties. Follow the manufacturer's instructions for the mixing ratio.

22   **Never** use strong detergents (washing-up liquids, etc.) or engine antifreeze in the washer fluid. Not only can they cause smearing of the glass, but they can also damage the vehicle's paintwork.

23   Check the security of the pump wires and the washer tubing; if any of the jets is blocked, clear the obstruction using a thin wire probe.

Washer jet adjustment

24   Check the operation of the windscreen and rear window washers. Adjust the nozzles using a pin if necessary, aiming the spray to a point slightly above the centre of the swept area.

Wiper blade check and renewal

25   Check the condition of the wiper blades; if they are cracked or show any signs of deterioration, or if the glass swept area is smeared, renew them. For maximum clarity of vision, wiper blades should be renewed annually, as a matter of course.

26   To remove a wiper blade, pull the arm fully away from the glass until it locks. Swivel the blade through 90°, press the locking tab with a fingernail, and slide the blade out of the arm's hooked end (photo). On refitting, ensure that the blade locks securely into the arm.

Chapter 2 Engine

Contents

Part A: In-vehicle engine repair procedures
Compression test – description and interpretation.............................. 2
Crankshaft oil seals – renewal 11
Cylinder head – removal and refitting 6
Engine oil and filter renewal...See Chapter 1
Engine oil level check..See Chapter 1
Engine/transmission mounting rubbers – inspection and renewal.. 13
Flywheel – removal, inspection and refitting................................... 12
General engine checks...See Chapter 1
General information 1
Oil cooler – general information, removal and refitting.................... 8
Oil pump – removal, inspection and refitting................................... 9
Rocker cover – removal and refitting... 4
Rocker gear – removal, inspection and refitting.............................. 5
Sump – removal and refitting... 10
Timing cover, chain and sprockets – removal, inspection and refitting 7
Top Dead Centre (TDC) for No 1 piston – locating........................... 3
Valve clearances – adjustment....................................See Chapter 1

Part B: Engine removal and general overhaul procedures
Camshaft and followers – removal, inspection and refitting............. 22
Crankshaft – inspection... 27
Crankshaft – refitting and main bearing running clearance check.... 31
Crankshaft – removal... 24
Cylinder block/crankcase – cleaning and inspection....................... 25
Cylinder head – dismantling.. 19
Cylinder head – reassembly.. 21
Cylinder head and valves – cleaning and inspection....................... 20
Engine – initial start-up after overhaul... 33
Engine overhaul – dismantling sequence.. 18
Engine overhaul – general information 15
Engine overhaul – reassembly sequence... 29
Engine/transmission – removal and refitting................................... 17
Engine/transmission removal – methods and precautions............... 16
General information 14
Main and big-end bearings – inspection... 28
Piston/connecting rod assembly – dismantling, inspection and reassembly 26
Piston/connecting rod assembly – refitting and big-end bearing running clearance check... 32
Piston/connecting rod assembly – removal...................................... 23
Piston rings – refitting.. 30

Specifications

Engine (general)
Type... Four-cylinder in-line, four stroke, liquid-cooled
Designation:
    1.3 low-compression .... Skoda 781.135
    1.3 high-compression .... Skoda 781.136
Bore .... 75.50 mm
Stroke.. 72.00 mm
Capacity .... 1289 cc
Firing order .... 1–3–4–2 (No 1 cylinder at crankshaft pulley end)
Direction of crankshaft rotation.. Clockwise (when viewed from right-hand side of vehicle)
Compression ratio:
    135 engine.. 8.8 : 1
    136 engine.. 9.7 : 1
Power output:
    135 engine.. 59 ps (43 kW) @ 5000 rpm
    136 engine.. 63 ps (46 kW) @ 5000 rpm

Cylinder block
Material.. Aluminium alloy
Cylinder liner diameter:
    Standard – class A .... 75.500 mm nominal
    Standard – class B... 75.510 mm nominal
    Standard – class C... 75.520 mm nominal
    Tolerance on nominal diameter....................... + 0.009 mm/– 0 mm
Cylinder liner protrusion above cylinder block surface:
    Standard .... 0.07 to 0.13 mm
    Maximum difference between any two liners.... 0.04 mm

Crankshaft
Number of main bearings	3
Main bearing journal diameter:	
Standard	60.00 mm
1st regrind	59.75 mm
2nd regrind	59.50 mm
3rd regrind	59.25 mm
Diametrical tolerance (all journals)	–0.010 to –0.029 mm
Main bearing shell thickness:	
Standard	2.495 mm
1st regrind	2.620 mm
2nd regrind	2.745 mm
3rd regrind	2.870 mm
Thickness tolerance (all bearings)	+0.000 to –0.010 mm
Main bearing running clearance	0.016 to 0.065 mm
Crankpin journal diameter:	
Standard	45.00 mm
1st regrind	44.75 mm
2nd regrind	44.50 mm
3rd regrind	44.25 mm
Diametrical tolerance (all journals)	–0.009 to –0.025 mm
Crankpin bearing shell thickness:	
Standard	1.490 mm
1st regrind	1.615 mm
2nd regrind	1.740 mm
3rd regrind	1.865 mm
Thickness tolerance (all bearings)	+0.000 to –0.007 mm
Big-end bearing running clearance	0.019 to 0.060 mm
Main bearing No 1 journal width:	
Standard	31.500 mm
1st regrind	31.625 mm
2nd regrind	31.750 mm
3rd regrind	31.875 mm
Width tolerance	–0.000 to +0.025 mm
Thrustwasher thickness:	
Standard	1.490 mm
1st regrind	1.615 mm
2nd regrind	1.740 mm
3rd regrind	1.865 mm
Thickness tolerance (all washers)	+0.000 to –0.010 mm
Crankshaft endfloat	0.020 to 0.106 mm

Pistons and piston rings
Piston diameter:		
Standard – class A	75.475 mm	
Standard – class B	75.485 mm	
Standard – class C	75.495 mm	
Diametrical tolerance (all pistons)	±0.009 mm	
Piston-to-bore clearance	0.025 mm	
Piston ring-to-groove clearance:		
Top compression ring	0.040 to 0.072 mm	
Second compression ring	0.030 to 0.062 mm	
	New	**Service limit**
Piston ring end gap:		
Compression rings	0.25 to 0.40 mm	1.00 mm
Oil scraper ring	0.20 to 0.35 mm	1.00 mm

Gudgeon pins
Diameter	19.997 to 20.000 mm
Small-end bush diameter	19.999 to 20.005 mm
Pin bore diameter in piston	19.998 to 20.006 mm
Gudgeon pin clearances:	
Pin-to-piston	0.002 to 0.007 mm
Pin-to-small-end bush	0.001 to 0.008 mm

Connecting rods
Length between centres	133 ± 0.1 mm
Big-end cap endfloat	0.065 to 0.182 mm

Cylinder head
Material	Aluminium alloy
Valve seat angle	45°
Valve seat width:	
Inlet valve	1.5 mm
Exhaust valve	1.7 mm

Camshaft and followers

Drive	Chain, from crankshaft at pulley end
Number of bearings	3
Camshaft journal diameter:	
Pulley end	38.950 to 38.975 mm
Middle	38.450 to 38.475 mm
Flywheel end	29.959 to 29.980 mm
Camshaft bearing internal diameter:	
Pulley end	39.000 to 39.025 mm
Middle	38.500 to 38.525 mm
Flywheel end	30.000 to 30.021 mm
Camshaft bearing running clearance	0.025 to 0.075 mm
Camshaft endfloat	0.020 to 0.066 mm
Cam follower outer diameter:	
Standard	20.980 to 21.000 mm
Oversize	21.193 to 21.200 mm
Cam follower bore internal diameter:	
Standard	21.000 to 21.021 mm
Oversize	21.200 to 21.221 mm

Valves

Seat angle	45°
Head diameter:	
Inlet	34.00 ± 0.12 mm
Exhaust	30.00 ± 0.12 mm
Stem diameter (standard):	
Inlet	7.982 ± 0.015 mm
Exhaust	7.975 ± 0.015 mm
Stem-to-guide clearance:	
Inlet	0.018 to 0.037 mm
Exhaust	0.025 to 0.037 mm
Valve timing (at nominal clearance of 0.43 mm):	
Inlet opens	12° BTDC
Inlet closes	48° ABDC
Exhaust opens	42° BBDC
Exhaust closes	8° ATDC
Valve spring free length:	
Inner spring	43.60 mm
Outer spring	45.85 mm

Lubrication system

System pressure:	
Minimum @ 1500 rpm	3.5 bars
Maximum	5.8 bars
Oil pump type	Gear-driven, force-feed
Oil pump clearances:	
Drivegear shaft-to-cover:	
Standard	0.02 to 0.06 mm
Wear limit	0.15 mm
Pin-to-driven gear:	
Standard	0.014 to 0.050 mm
Wear limit	0.1 mm
Gear-to-pump cover (endfloat) – maximum	0.1 mm

Torque wrench settings

	Nm	lbf ft
Cylinder head bolts:		
Stage 1	17 to 20	13 to 15
Stage 2	Angle-tighten through 90°	Angle-tighten through 90°
Stage 3	Angle-tighten a further 90°	Angle-tighten a further 90°
Cylinder head nuts	20 to 23	15 to 17
Rocker cover nuts	2 to 3	2
Rocker gear retaining bolts	25 to 30	18 to 22
Timing chain cover bolts	5 to 8	4 to 6
Cam follower cover nuts	2 to 3	2
Sump bolts	7 to 9	5 to 7
Oil pump pick-up/strainer	5 to 8	4 to 6
Flywheel bolts	55 to 65	41 to 48
Flywheel cover plate bolts	8 to 10	6 to 8
Camshaft sprocket bolt	30 to 35	22 to 26
Crankshaft pulley bolt	100 to 120	74 to 89
Main bearing cap bolt	67 to 75	49 to 55
Connecting rod bearing cap nut	36 to 40	27 to 30
Oil pressure switch	20 to 25	15 to 18
Cylinder block oil gallery plugs:		
12 mm thread	20 to 30	15 to 22
16 mm thread	50 to 55	37 to 41
Engine/transmission left-hand and right-hand mountings:		
Through-bolts	42 to 50	31 to 37
Mounting bracket-to-body bolts	39 to 45	29 to 33

Part A: In-vehicle engine repair procedures

1 General information

How to use this Chapter

This Part of Chapter 2 describes those repair procedures that can reasonably be carried out on the engine while it remains in the vehicle. If the engine has been removed from the vehicle and is being dismantled as described in Part B, any preliminary dismantling procedures can be ignored.

Note that while it may be possible physically to overhaul items such as the piston/connecting rod assemblies while the engine is in the vehicle, such tasks are not usually carried out as separate operations and usually require the execution of several additional procedures (not to mention the cleaning of components and of oilways); for this reason, all such tasks are classed as major overhaul procedures, and are described in Part B of this Chapter.

Part B describes the removal of the engine/transmission unit from the vehicle and the full overhaul procedures that can then be carried out.

For ease of reference, all specifications are given in the one Specifications Section at the beginning of the Chapter.

Engine description

The engine is an overhead valve (OHV), in-line four-cylinder unit, which is mounted transversely at the front of the vehicle; the clutch and transmission are situated on the left-hand end of the engine.

The engine is available in two different forms: a low-compression version and a high-compression version. The low-compression engine, designated the '135', is fitted to all Estate, Pick-up models, and to all later Hatchback and Van models from approximately August 1991 on. Pre-August 1991 Hatchback and Van models are fitted with the high-compression engine, which is designated the '136'. Apart from the different compression ratios, achieved by the use of different pistons (136 has flat-topped pistons whereas 135 has a recess in the piston crown), both engines are of identical construction.

The cylinder block, cylinder head and rocker cover are all cast in aluminium alloy. The cylinder bores are formed by replaceable cast-iron cylinder liners that are located at their lower ends; sealing gaskets are fitted at the base of each liner to prevent the escape of coolant into the sump.

The crankshaft has three main bearings. The clutch and flywheel are located on a flange at the left-hand end. A double sprocket fitted onto the right-hand end serves to drive the camshaft via a double-row timing chain. The main bearings and the big-end bearings are of the shell type, whilst the connecting rod small-end bearings are of the bronze bush type, being pressed into the connecting rod and reamed to suit.

The camshaft has a helical gear on its right-hand end which drives the distributor. The camshaft also drives the oil pump via the distributor shaft.

The force-feed lubrication system consists of a gear-driven pump, which draws oil from the sump through a strainer and circulates the lubricant to the various engine components, via a filter mounted externally on the cylinder block. An oil cooler is offered as an optional extra, to help keep the oil temperature stable under arduous operating conditions.

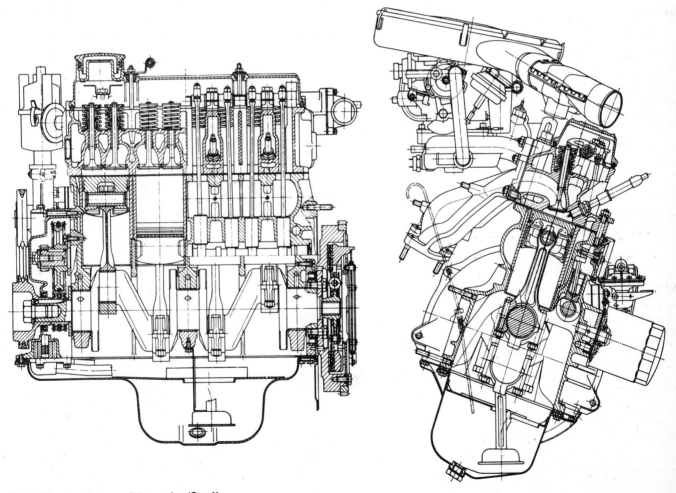

Fig. 2.1 Sectional views of the engine (Sec 1)

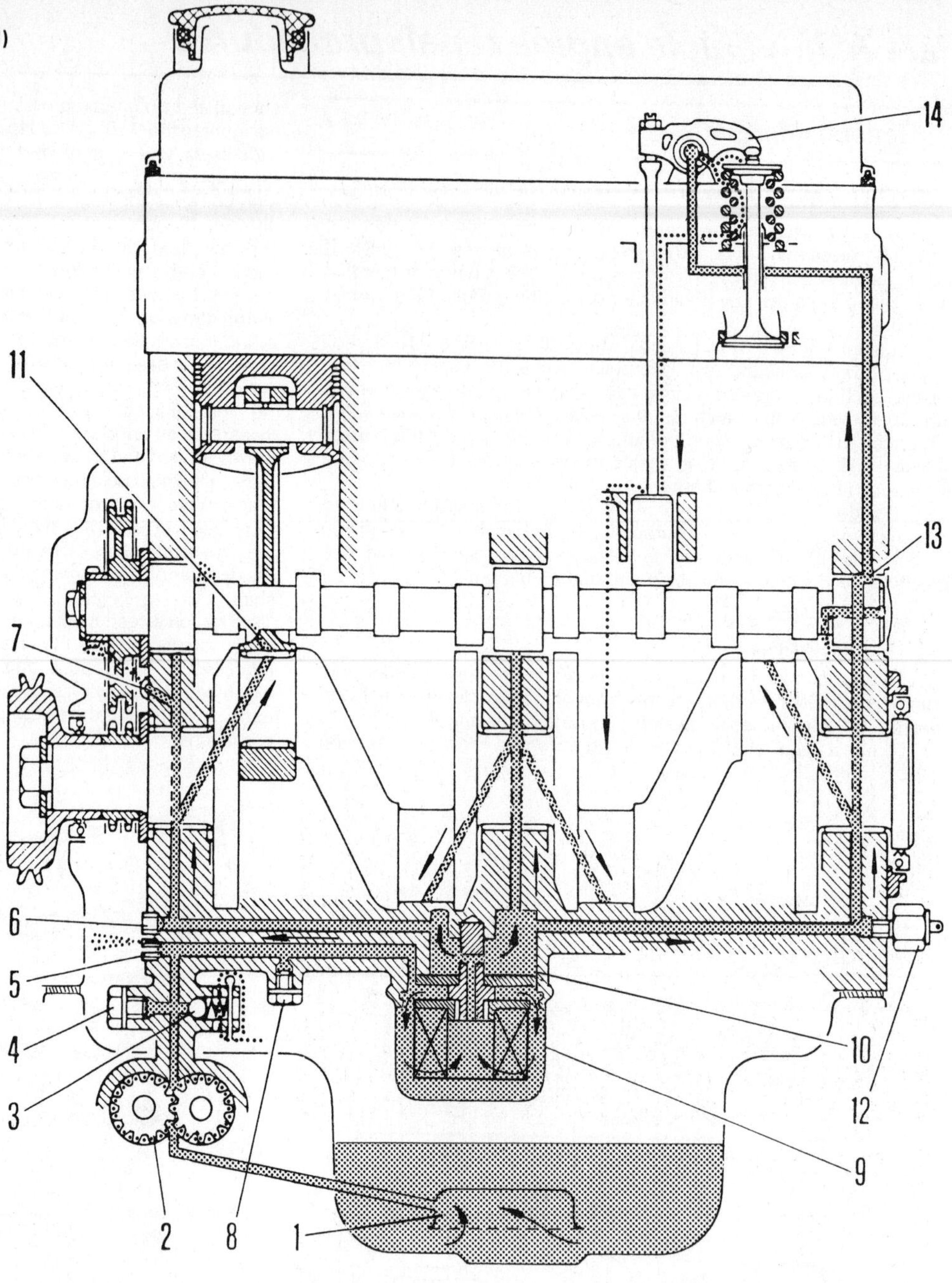

Fig. 2.2 Engine lubrication system (Sec 1)

1   Pick-up strainer
2   Oil pump
3   Pressure relief valve
4   Plug
5   Jet (timing chain lubrication)
6   Plug
7   Jet (distributor drivegear lubrication)
8   Plug
9   Oil filter
10   Bypass
11   Connecting rod oil jet
12   Oil pressure switch
13   Intermittent feed to rocker gear
14   Rocker gear

Repair operations possible with the engine in the vehicle

The following work can be carried out with the engine in the vehicle.

(a)   Compression pressure – testing.
(b)   Rocker cover – removal and refitting.
(c)   Rocker gear – removal and refitting.
(d)   Cylinder head – removal and refitting.
(e)   Timing cover – removal and refitting.
(f)   Timing chain and sprockets – removal and refitting.
(g)   Oil cooler – removal and refitting.
(h)   Oil pump – removal, inspection and refitting.
(i)   Sump – removal and refitting.
(j)   Cylinder head and pistons – decarbonising.
(k)   Crankshaft oil seals – renewal.
(l)   Flywheel – removal, inspection and refitting.
(m)   Engine/transmission mountings – inspection and renewal.

2   Compression test – description and interpretation

1   When engine performance is down, or if misfiring occurs which cannot be attributed to the ignition or fuel systems, a compression test can provide diagnostic clues as to the engine's condition. If the test is performed regularly, it can give warning of trouble before any other symptoms become apparent.

2   The engine must be fully warmed up to normal operating temperature, the battery must be fully charged, and the spark plugs must be removed (Chapter 1). The aid of an assistant will also be required.

3   Disable the ignition system by disconnecting the ignition HT coil lead from the distributor cap and earthing it on the cylinder block. Use a jumper lead or similar wire to make a good connection.

4   Fit a compression tester to the No 1 cylinder spark plug hole – the type of tester which screws into the plug thread is to be preferred.

5 Have the assistant hold the throttle wide open and crank the engine on the starter motor; after one or two revolutions, the compression pressure should build up to a maximum figure and then stabilise. Record the highest reading obtained.

6 Repeat the test on the remaining cylinders, recording the pressure in each.

7 All cylinders should produce very similar pressures, of the order of 11 to 15 bars. Any one cylinder reading below 10 bars, or a difference of more than 1.5 bars between cylinders, suggests a fault. Note that the compression should build up quickly in a healthy engine; low compression on the first stroke, followed by gradually increasing pressure on successive strokes, indicates worn piston rings. A low compression reading on the first stroke, which does not build up during successive strokes, indicates leaking valves or a blown head gasket (a cracked head could also be the cause). Deposits on the undersides of the valve heads can also cause low compression.

8 If the pressure in any cylinder is reduced to 10 bars or less, carry out the following test to isolate the cause. Introduce a teaspoonful of clean oil into that cylinder through its spark plug hole and repeat the test.

9 If the addition of oil temporarily improves the compression pressure, this indicates that bore or piston wear is responsible for the pressure loss. No improvement suggests that leaking or burnt valves, or a blown head gasket, may be to blame.

10 A low reading from two adjacent cylinders is almost certainly due to the head gasket having blown between them; the presence of coolant in the engine oil will confirm this.

11 If one cylinder is about 20 percent lower than the others and the engine has a slightly rough idle, a worn camshaft lobe could be the cause.

12 If the compression reading is unusually high, the combustion chambers are probably coated with carbon deposits. If this is the case, the cylinder head should be removed and decarbonised.

13 On completion of the test, refit the spark plugs and reconnect the ignition system.

3 Top Dead Centre (TDC) for No 1 piston – locating

1 Top dead centre (TDC) is the highest point in its travel up-and-down its cylinder bore that each piston reaches as the crankshaft rotates. While each piston reaches TDC both at the top of the compression stroke and again at the top of the exhaust stroke, for the purpose of timing the engine, TDC refers to the piston position (usually No 1) at the top of its compression stroke.

2 No 1 piston and cylinder are at the right-hand end of the engine. Note that the crankshaft rotates clockwise when viewed from the right-hand side of the vehicle.

3 Disconnect the battery negative terminal, and remove all the spark plugs as described in Chapter 1.

4 Unclip the distributor cap and remove the cap and HT leads.

5 Turn the steering onto full-right lock. Slacken and remove the three engine undershield right-hand side cover retaining screws, and remove the cover to gain access to the crankshaft pulley retaining bolt.

6 Using a socket and extension bar, applied to the crankshaft pulley bolt, rotate the crankshaft clockwise until the notch on the crankshaft pulley inner rim is aligned with the '0' on the timing chain cover (photo).

7 With the crankshaft in this position Nos 1 and 4 cylinders are now at TDC, one of them on the compression stroke. If the distributor rotor arm is pointing at the notch in the distributor rim, then No 1 cylinder is correctly positioned (photo). If the rotor arm is pointing in the opposite direction, No 4 cylinder is on compression. Rotate the crankshaft one full turn (360°) clockwise until the rotor arm points at the notch. No 1 cylinder will then be at TDC on the compression stroke.

8 Once No 1 cylinder has been positioned at TDC on the compression stroke, TDC for any of the other cylinders can then be located by rotating the crankshaft clockwise 180° at a time and following the firing order (see Specifications).

3.6 Crankshaft pulley timing mark at TDC

3.7 Distributor rotor arm aligned with notch (arrowed) showing No 1 cylinder firing position

4.2 Disconnecting the breather hose from the rocker cover filler neck

4.3 Free the fuel hose retaining clip ...

4.4 ... and manoeuvre the rocker cover away from the engine

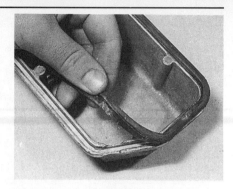

4.5 Ensure that the rocker cover seal is correctly seated in its groove

4   Rocker cover – removal and refitting

Removal

1   Disconnect the battery negative terminal.
2   Disconnect the breather hose from the rocker cover oil filler neck (photo).
3   Slacken and remove the two rocker cover retaining nuts and free the fuel feed hose retaining clip from the stud (photo). Remove the two washers and stud seals.
4   Lift off the rocker cover (photo) and carefully remove the rubber seal from its groove. Check the seal for signs of damage or distortion, and renew it if necessary.

Refitting

5   Carefully clean the cylinder head mating surfaces and the cover groove, removing all traces of oil. Fit the rubber seal to the rocker cover, ensuring it is correctly located in the groove (photo).
6   Refit the cover to the cylinder head, ensuring that the seal remains seated in its groove, then refit the seals, washers and nuts to the cover studs, not forgetting to refit the fuel hose retaining clip. Tighten both nuts to the specified torque setting.
7   Connect the breather hose to the cover oil filler neck, and reconnect the battery.

5   Rocker gear – removal, inspection and refitting

Removal

1   Remove the rocker cover as described in Section 4.
2   Using a 10 mm Allen key, slacken and remove the two cylinder head bolts which secure the left- and right-hand rocker pedestals to the cylinder head.

3   Evenly and progressively slacken the four rocker gear retaining bolts by half a turn at a time until all valve spring pressure has been relieved from the rocker arms. Remove the bolts, noting the correct fitted position of the oil splash plate which is fitted to the top of the right-hand pedestal, and lift the rocker gear assembly off the cylinder head (photo).
4   If necessary, the rocker gear assembly can be dismantled by removing the circlip from one end of the rocker shaft and sliding the various components off the end of the shaft. Keeping all components in their correct fitted order, make a note of each component's correct fitted position as it is removed, to ensure it is positioned correctly on reassembly (photos).

Inspection

5   With the rocker gear dismantled, examine the rocker arm and shaft bearing surfaces for wear ridges and scoring. If there are obvious signs of wear the affected rocker arm(s) and/or shaft must be renewed.

Refitting

6   If the rocker gear was dismantled, reassemble it by reversing the dismantling sequence, and secure all components in position with the circlip. Ensure the circlip is correctly located in its groove, and check that all rocker arms are free to rotate smoothly around the shaft.
7   Lower the rocker gear into position on the cylinder head, ensuring that all the rocker arm adjusting screws correctly engage with their respective pushrod ends (photo).
8   Refit the four rocker gear retaining bolts and, ensuring that the oil splash plate is correctly positioned on the right-hand pedestal, tighten them evenly and progressively to the specified torque setting (photos).
9   Refit the two cylinder head bolts securing the left- and right-hand pedestals in position and tighten them first to the specified stage 1 torque setting, and then through the angles specified for their stage 2 and 3 tightening. Refer to Section 6, paragraph 26 for further information.
10 Adjust the valve clearances as described in Chapter 1.
11 Refit the rocker cover as described in Section 4.

5.3 Slacken the retaining bolts and lift the rocker gear away from the cylinder head

5.4A To dismantle the rocker gear, remove the circlip ...

5.4B ... and slide off the various components keeping them in their correct fitted order

5.7 On refitting ensure all rocker arm adjusting screws are correctly located in the pushrod ends

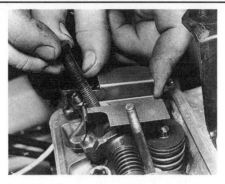

5.8A Do not forget to refit the oil splash plate to the right-hand pedestal when installing the rocker gear bolts

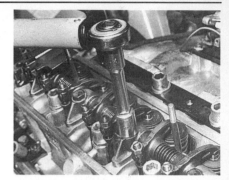

5.8B Tighten the rocker gear retaining bolts to the specified torque setting as described in text

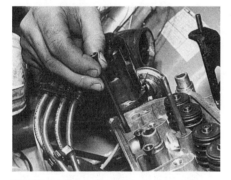

6.5 Lift out the pushrods from the engine and store them in a cardboard template

6.9 Disconnect all the relevant cooling system hoses from the thermostat housing and manifold

6.11A Working as described in text, slacken and remove the four cylinder head nuts ...

6.11B ... and the remaining cylinder head bolts

6.14 Removing the cylinder head assembly complete with manifolds

6.15 If the crankshaft is to be rotated with the head removed, the liners must be clamped in position as shown

6 Cylinder head – removal and refitting

Removal

1 Disconnect the battery negative lead.
2 Drain the cooling system as described in Chapter 1.
3 Remove the air cleaner assembly as described in Chapter 4.
4 Remove the rocker gear as described in Section 5.
5 Lift out each pushrod in turn (photo) and store it in its correct fitted order by pushing it through a clearly-marked cardboard template. This will help ensure that the pushrods are refitted in their original positions on reassembly.
6 Note that the following text assumes that the cylinder head will be removed with both inlet and exhaust manifolds attached; this is easier, but makes it a bulky and heavy assembly to handle. If it is wished first to remove the manifolds, proceed as described in Sections 13 and 14 of Chapter 4.
7 Working as described in Chapter 4, disconnect the exhaust system downpipe from the manifold.

8 Disconnect the following from the carburettor and inlet manifold, as described in the relevant Sections of Chapter 4.
    (a) Carburettor wiring connector.
    (b) Throttle cable.
    (c) Braking system vacuum servo unit hose.
    (d) Coolant hose(s).
9 Disconnect the wiring connector from the coolant gauge temperature sender unit. Disconnect the radiator top hose and expansion tank hose from the thermostat housing, referring to Chapter 3 for further information (photo).
10 Slacken and remove the alternator upper mounting bolt, and free the alternator from its upper mounting bracket.
11 Working in the **reverse** of the sequence shown in photo 6.26A, progressively slacken the four cylinder head nuts, situated along the front edge of the head, and remove them. Still following the sequence, slacken the eight remaining cylinder head bolts by one turn at a time. Remove each bolt along with its washer (photos), and store it in its correct fitted order by pushing it through a clearly-marked cardboard template. Note the correct fitted position of the engine lifting bracket fitted beneath the three rear bolts.

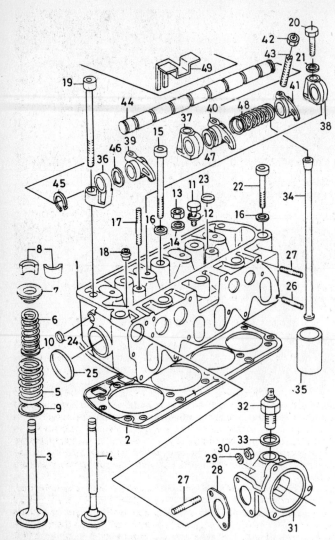

Fig. 2.3 Exploded view of the cylinder head and associated components (Secs 5 and 6)

1 Cylinder head	27 Stud
2 Cylinder head gasket	28 Gasket
3 Inlet valve	29 Spring washer
4 Exhaust valve	30 Nut – thermostat housing
5 Outer valve spring	to cylinder head
6 Inner valve spring	31 Thermostat housing
7 Spring retainer	32 Coolant temperature
8 Collets	gauge sender unit
9 Outer spring seat	33 Sealing washer
10 Inner spring seat	34 Pushrod
11 Bolt – alternator bracket to	35 Cam follower
cylinder head	36 Rocker gear pedestal
12 Spring washer	37 Rocker gear pedestal
13 Cylinder head nut	38 Rocker gear pedestal
14 Flat washer	39 Rocker arm
15 Cylinder head bolt	40 Rocker arm
16 Flat washer	41 Rocker arm
17 Rocker cover stud	42 Rocker arm adjusting
18 Valve guide oil seal	screw locknut
19 Cylinder head bolt	43 Rocker arm adjusting
20 Bolt – rocker gear to	screw
cylinder head	44 Rocker shaft
21 Flat washer	45 Circlip
22 Cylinder head bolt	46 Wave washer
23 Plug	47 Flat washer
24 Plug	48 Spring
25 Plug	49 Oil splash plate
26 Stud	

12 The joint between the cylinder head and gasket and the cylinder block/crankcase must now be broken without disturbing the wet liners; although these liners are better located and sealed than some wet-liner engines, there is still a risk of coolant and foreign matter leaking into the sump if the cylinder head is lifted carelessly. If care is not taken and the liners are moved, there is also a possibility of the bottom seals being disturbed, causing leakage after refitting the head. **Caution:** *If the liner bottom seals are disturbed, it will be necessary to remove the pistons and liners in order to fit new seals.*

13 To break the joint, use the exhaust manifold as a leverage point, and gently 'rock' the cylinder head free towards the front of the vehicle.

14 When the joint is broken, lift the cylinder head away; use assistance if possible as it is a heavy assembly, especially if it is complete with the manifolds (photo). Remove the gasket and discard it.

15 **Do not** attempt to rotate the crankshaft with the cylinder head removed, otherwise the cylinder liners may be displaced. Operations that would normally require the rotation of the crankshaft (eg cleaning the piston crowns), must be carried out with great care to ensure that no particles of dirt or foreign matter are left behind. If the crankshaft is to be turned, the liners must first be clamped in position using a couple of suitable bolts and large flat washers (photo).

16 If the cylinder head is to be dismantled, then refer to the relevant Sections in Part B of this Chapter.

Preparation for refitting

17 Check the condition of the cylinder head bolts, paying particular attention to their threads, whenever they are removed. Keeping all the bolts in their correct fitted order, wash them and wipe dry, then check each for any sign of visible wear or damage, renewing any bolt if necessary. Considering the strain which the cylinder head bolts are under, it is recommended that they are renewed as a complete set whenever they are removed, regardless of their apparent condition.

18 The mating faces of the cylinder head, liners and cylinder block/crankcase must be perfectly clean before refitting the head. Use a hard plastic or wood scraper to remove all traces of gasket and carbon; also clean the piston crowns. Take particular care, as the soft aluminium alloy is easily damaged. Also, make sure that the carbon is not allowed to enter the oil and water passages – this is particularly important for the lubrication system, as carbon could block the oil supply to any of the engine's components. Using adhesive tape and paper, seal the water, oil and bolt holes in the cylinder block/crankcase. To prevent carbon entering the gap between the pistons and bores, smear a little grease in the gap. After cleaning each piston, use a small brush to remove all traces of grease and carbon from the gap, then wipe away the remainder with a clean rag. Clean all the pistons in the same way.

19 Check the mating surfaces of the cylinder block/crankcase and the cylinder head for nicks, deep scratches and other damage. If slight, they may be removed carefully with a file, but if excessive, machining may be the only alternative to renewal.

6.21 Ensure the gasket is fitted the correct way up so that its holes are correctly aligned with block oilways and coolant passages (arrowed)

6.26A Cylinder head fastener tightening sequence

6.26B Tighten all the cylinder head bolts to their specified torque setting as described in text ...

20   If warpage is suspected of the cylinder head gasket surface, use a straight-edge to check it for distortion. Refer to Part B of this Chapter if necessary.

Refitting

21   Wipe clean the mating surfaces of the cylinder head and cylinder block/crankcase and position a new gasket on the cylinder block/crankcase surface. Ensure the gasket is installed the correct way up, so that the holes in the gasket align with the oilways on the left- and right-hand ends of the cylinder block (photo).
22   Locate the cylinder head on the studs, and carefully lower it into position.
23   Keeping all the cylinder head bolts and washers in their correct fitted order, wash them and wipe dry (if not already done), then lightly oil under the head and on the threads of each bolt. Carefully enter each bolt, (except the two which are also used to retain the rocker gear pedestals) into its original hole. Do not forget to refit the engine lifting bracket. Screw each bolt in by hand only until finger-tight.
24   Remove the pushrods from the cardboard template, and insert them into their original positions in the cylinder head, ensuring that each pushrod is correctly located in its cam follower.
25   Refit the rocker gear as described in Section 5. Tighten its four

small inner retaining bolts to the specified torque, but tighten the two cylinder head bolts finger-tight only.
26   Working progressively and in the sequence shown in photo 6.26A (numbers 1 to 10), use first a torque wrench, then an ordinary socket extension bar, to tighten the cylinder head bolts in the stages given in the Specifications Section of this Chapter. To tighten the bolts through the angles specified, simply use a felt-tip pen or a dab of white paint to make alignment marks between the cylinder head and outer edge of each bolt head; the second stage then tightens each bolt through 90° (a quarter of a turn) so that the marks are at right angles to each other. The third stage tightens them through a further 90° so that all the marks are then opposite each other (half a turn apart). If any bolt is overtightened past its mark, slacken it through 90°, then re-tighten until the marks are opposite (photos).
27   Once the ten cylinder head bolts have been correctly tightened, apply a drop of engine oil to the threads and underside of the heads of the cylinder head nuts. Refit the nuts and washers onto the studs situated along the front edge of the cylinder head. Tighten the four nuts to their specified torque setting in the order shown in photo 6.26A (numbers 11 to 14) (photo).
28   Adjust the valve clearances as described in Chapter 1, then refit the rocker cover as described in Section 4 of this Chapter.
29   Connect all disturbed coolant hoses and reconnect the coolant temperature sensor wiring. It is recommended that the old Skoda hose clips (where fitted) are replaced with standard worm-drive type hose clips.
30   Working as described in the relevant Sections of Chapter 4, connect or refit all disturbed wiring and hoses to the inlet manifold and fuel system components, bearing in mind the point made above concerning the old hose clips. Reconnect and adjust the throttle cable.
31   Working as described in Chapter 4, reconnect the exhaust system downpipe to the manifold.
32   Refit the alternator upper mounting bolt and adjust the drivebelt tension as described in Chapter 1.
33   Refit the air cleaner assembly as described in Chapter 4, and reconnect the battery negative lead.
34   Refill the cooling system as described in Chapter 1.

6.27 ... then tighten the four cylinder head nuts to their specified torque setting

7 Timing cover, chain and sprockets – removal, inspection and refitting

Removal

1   Position No 1 cylinder at TDC as described in Section 3, then remove the distributor, complete with extension tube, as described in Chapter 5.
2   Remove the alternator as described in Chapter 12.

7.5 Slacken and remove the retaining bolt and washer and slide off the crankshaft pulley

7.6 Undo the timing cover retaining bolts and remove the cover

7.8A Remove the camshaft bolt, along with its tab washer and dished washer ...

3   Remove the oil pick-up/strainer and withdraw the oil pump gears as described in Section 9.

4   To prevent crankshaft rotation while the pulley bolt is unscrewed, select top gear and have an assistant apply the brakes hard. If the engine has been removed from the vehicle, lock the flywheel using the arrangement shown in photo 12.10A.

5   Slacken and remove the pulley retaining bolt and washer (photo), then slide the pulley off the crankshaft.

6   Slacken and remove all the timing chain cover retaining bolts and screws (photo). Manoeuvre the cover downwards and away from the engine. Remove the gasket and discard it.

7   Using a flat-bladed screwdriver, bend back the tab of the camshaft bolt tab washer. To prevent camshaft rotation while the bolt is slackened, select top gear and have an assistant apply the brakes hard. Alternatively, the sprocket can be retained with a holding tool fabricated from two lengths of steel strip (one long, the other short) and three nuts and bolts. One nut and bolt form the pivot of the forked tool, with the remaining two nuts and bolts at the tips of the 'forks' to engage with the sprocket spokes, as shown in photo 7.20B.

8   Unscrew the camshaft bolt and remove it along with the tab washer and dished washer. Discard the tab washer; a new one must be used on refitting. Withdraw the distributor drivegear from the camshaft end, noting which way around it is fitted (photos).

9   Prior to removing the timing chain and sprockets, note the position of the sprocket timing marks and crankshaft and camshaft keyways as shown in Fig. 2.4.

10   Simultaneously withdraw the timing chain and sprockets from the crankshaft and camshaft, and manoeuvre the assembly away from the engine.

11   Remove the Woodruff key from the crankshaft keyway, noting which way around it is fitted. If the camshaft Woodruff key is a loose fit in the camshaft, remove it and store it with the sprocket for safe keeping.

12   With the Woodruff key removed, withdraw the shim, guide spacer

and outer thrustwasher from the crankshaft end, noting which way around the guide spacer and thrustwasher are fitted.

Inspection

13   Examine the teeth on both the crankshaft and camshaft sprockets for signs of wear or damage such as chipped, hooked or missing teeth. If there is any sign of wear or damage on either sprocket, both sprockets and the chain should be renewed as a set.

14   Inspect the links of the timing chain for signs of wear on the rollers. The extent of wear on the chain can be judged by checking the amount by which the chain can be bent sideways: a new chain will have very little sideways movement. If there is an excessive amount of side play in the timing chain, the chain must be renewed. Note that it is a sensible precaution to renew the chain, regardless of its apparent condition, at about 30 000 miles or at a lesser mileage if the engine is undergoing a major overhaul. Although not strictly necessary, it is always worth renewing the chain and sprockets as a matched set, since it is false economy to run a new chain on worn sprockets and *vice-versa*.

15   Inspect all other components for signs of wear or damage, and renew as necessary.

Refitting

16   Slide the outer thrustwasher over the end of the crankshaft, ensuring that its oil grooves are facing away from the bearing cap, then align the washer locating tab with its cutout at the bottom of the cap, and press the thrustwasher into position in its recess. With the thrustwasher in position, slide on the guide spacer, noting that its chamfered inner edge must face inwards, and refit the shim (photos).

17   Refit the Woodruff key to the crankshaft keyway so that its tapered end is innermost (photo). Also refit the Woodruff key to the camshaft keyway if it was removed.

18   Referring to Fig. 2.4, engage the camshaft and crankshaft sprockets with the timing chain. The dot on the camshaft sprocket must be aligned with the twelfth timing chain roller along from the roller which aligns with the dot on the crankshaft sprocket, counting the roller above the crankshaft sprocket dot as number 1.

19   Check that the crankshaft and camshaft Woodruff keys are positioned as shown in Fig. 2.4. Offer up the chain and sprocket assembly, and simultaneously slide on the sprockets, ensuring that the timing dot on each sprocket is facing outwards. With the sprockets in position, recheck the position of the timing dots (photos).

20   Locate the distributor drivegear on the camshaft end, noting that its flange must face inwards, then refit the dished washer so that its concave face is outermost. Fit a new tab washer, engaging its locating peg with the slot in the drivegear, and refit the camshaft bolt. Tighten the bolt to the specified torque whilst using the method employed on removal to prevent rotation. Secure the bolt by bending up the tab washer against one of the flats of the bolt head (photos).

21   Remove all traces of oil and gasket from the mating surfaces of the timing chain cover and block. Inspect the crankshaft oil seal in the cover for signs of damage or deterioration, and renew it if necessary as described in Section 11.

22   Fit a new gasket over the locating pegs in the cylinder block, using a smear of grease to hold it in place. Carefully manoeuvre the timing chain cover into position, and locate the cover on the pegs. Refit the cover retaining bolts and screws, and (where possible) tighten them to

Fig. 2.4 Crankshaft and camshaft Woodruff key and sprocket timing mark positions with No 1 cylinder at TDC (Sec 7)

7.8B ... and withdraw the distributor drivegear

7.16A Refit the outer thrustwasher, ensuring its oil grooves are facing outwards, and locate its tab with the bearing cap cut-out (arrows)

7.16B Slide on the guide spacer with its chamfered inner edge facing inwards ...

7.16C ... and refit the shim

7.17 Refit the Woodruff key so that its tapered end is innermost

7.19A Locate the timing chain and sprocket assembly on the crankshaft and camshaft ends ...

7.19B ... then recheck that the timing dots (arrows) are still positioned as described in text

7.20A Ensure the tab washer locating peg is correctly engaged with the drivegear ...

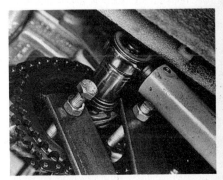

7.20B ... then tighten the camshaft bolt to the specified torque. Note use of home-made holding tool to prevent camshaft rotation

7.20C Bend tab washer up against one of camshaft bolt flats to secure it in position

7.22A Locate a new gasket over pegs (arrow) on block mating surface

7.22B Refit the timing cover and trim off the ends of the gasket which protrude beyond sump mating face

7.24A Ensure thrustwasher locating tabs are aligned with bearing cap cut-outs ...

7.24B ... then tighten the crankshaft pulley retaining bolt to the specified torque

the specified torque. Using a sharp knife, carefully trim off the ends of the gasket which protrude beyond the cylinder block sump mating face (photos).

23   Align the crankshaft pulley slot with the Woodruff key and carefully slide the pulley onto the crankshaft, taking great care not to damage the oil seal lip. Refit the retaining bolt and washer, and tighten it by hand only.

24   Check that the inner and outer thrustwasher locating tabs are aligned with the cut-outs on the right-hand main bearing cap, and that the thrustwashers are correctly seated in their recesses. Tighten the crankshaft pulley bolt to the specified torque whilst preventing rotation using the method employed on removal. Note that if the thrustwashers are not properly seated, the crankshaft will lock up as the bolt is tightened, and the thrustwashers will be damaged. Check that the crankshaft rotates freely before proceeding further (photos).

25   Refit the oil pump gears and the oil pick-up/strainer as described in Section 9, then refit the sump as described in Section 10.

26   Refit the alternator as described in Chapter 12.

27   Refit the distributor as described in Chapter 5.

8   Oil cooler – general information, removal and refitting

General information

1   An oil cooler is offered as an optional extra, to help keep the oil temperature stable under arduous operating conditions. The oil cooler is mounted on the right-hand side of the radiator, and is joined to the engine by two rubber hoses. The feed hose to the cooler is bolted onto the timing chain cover, just above the oil pump outlet, and the return hose is bolted onto the front of the cylinder block just to the right of the oil filter.

Removal

2   Position a suitable container beneath the oil cooler unions on the cylinder block. Slacken and remove the union bolts, noting the fitted positions of the sealing washers fitted on either side of each hose union. Discard the washers; they must be renewed whenever they are disturbed.

3   Allow the oil to drain from the oil cooler hoses into the container, then plug the hose ends and the holes in the cylinder block to prevent the entry of dirt into the lubrication system.

4   Slacken and remove the mounting bolt, and manoeuvre the oil cooler out from the engine compartment.

Refitting

5   Refitting is a reversal of the removal procedure, positioning new sealing washers on each side of both hose unions and tightening all bolts securely. On completion, top-up the oil level as described in Chapter 1, then run the engine for a short while to circulate the oil around the cooler before stopping the engine and checking the oil level for a second time.

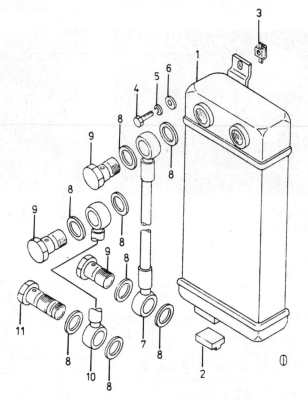

Fig. 2.5 Exploded view of the oil cooler and hoses (Sec 8)

1 Oil cooler	7 Hose
2 Mounting rubber	8 Sealing washer
3 Caged nut	9 Union bolt
4 Bolt – oil cooler to body	10 Hose
5 Spring washer	11 Union bolt
6 Flat washer	

9   Oil pump – removal, inspection and refitting

Removal

1   Remove the sump as described in Section 10.

2   Undo the four bolts securing the oil pump pick-up/strainer to the underside of the timing cover, and the single bolt securing it to the centre main bearing cap. Carefully lower the pick-up/strainer away from the timing cover, noting that the oil pump gears will drop out as soon as the cover is removed (photos). Remove the gasket (where fitted) and discard it.

Inspection

3   Inspect the oil pump gears and the pump body for signs of wear ridges or obvious damage such as chipped teeth. If the necessary

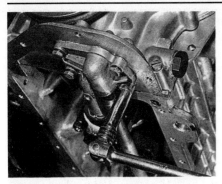

9.2A Undo the oil pump pick-up/strainer retaining bolts ...

9.2B ... then carefully lower it away from the engine ...

9.2C ... and withdraw the oil pump gears

9.4 Checking oil pump gear-to-cover clearance (endfloat)

9.5A Extract the split pin (arrowed) ...

9.5B ... and withdraw the pressure relief valve ball and spring from the pick-up/strainer

Fig. 2.6 Exploded view of the oil pump components (Sec 9)

1   Oil pump pick-up/strainer
2   Spring washer
3   Bolt – pick-up/strainer to timing cover
4   Bolt – pick-up/strainer to bearing cap
5   Gasket (where fitted)
6   Oil pump drivegear
7   Oil pump driven gear
8   Oil pump driven gear shaft
9   Oil pressure relief valve ball
10 Oil pressure relief valve spring
11 Split pin

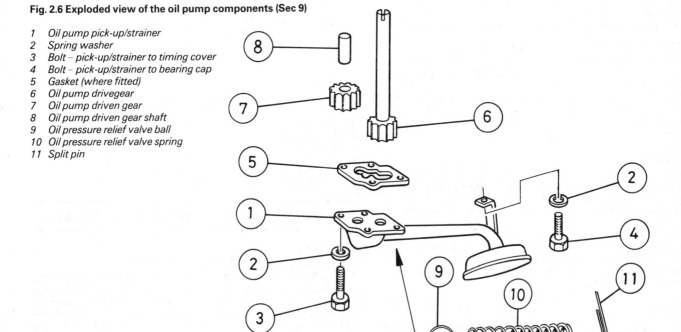

H23932

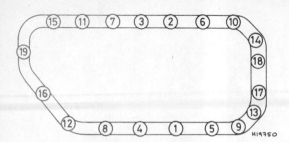

Fig. 2.7 Sump bolt tightening sequence (Sec 10)

measuring equipment is available, the extent of wear on the pump shafts and body can be determined by direct measurement. If there is any obvious sign of wear, or if the tolerances given in the Specifications are exceeded, both the pump gears and the timing chain cover (which incorporates the oil pump body) must be renewed as a complete set. Refer to Section 7 for information on timing chain cover removal and refitting.

4   Temporarily insert the gears into the pump body, and use a straight-edge and feeler blades to measure the gear-to-cover clearance (endfloat) (photo). Skoda state that there must be a maximum of 0.1 mm clearance between the gears and cover. If there is approximately 0.1 mm clearance present, then the pick-up/strainer should be refitted without a gasket. If there is very little or no measurable clearance, then a gasket must be positioned behind the cover on refitting to provide the necessary clearance. If the clearance exceeds 0.1 mm, then the pump body and/or gears are worn, and the oil pump assembly must be renewed.

5   Extract the split pin from the pick-up/strainer assembly, and withdraw the oil pressure relief valve spring and ball (photos). Inspect the ball and spring for signs of wear or damage, and renew as necessary. If a new ball is to be fitted, insert the ball into position in the pick-up/strainer then, using a hammer and suitable soft-metal drift, tap the ball firmly into its seat; this will help the ball to seat properly and ensure correct operation of the valve. On refitting, secure the ball and spring in position with a new split pin.

Refitting

6   Where necessary, stick a new gasket onto the pick-up/strainer pipe mating surface, using a dab of grease to hold it in position.

7   Generously lubricate the oil pump gears and shafts, then insert the gears into the pump body. Holding them in position, offer up the pick-up/strainer and insert its five retaining bolts. Tighten the pick-up/strainer pipe retaining bolts to the specified torque.

8   Refit the sump as described in Section 10.

10   Sump – removal and refitting

Removal

1   Disconnect the battery negative lead.

10.4 Undo the bolt securing the coolant pipe to the right-hand end of the sump

2   Apply the handbrake, then jack up the front of the vehicle and support it on axle stands.

3   Drain the engine oil, then clean and refit the engine oil drain plug, tightening it to the specified torque wrench setting. If the engine is nearing its service interval when the oil and filter are due for renewal, it is recommended that the filter is also removed and a new one fitted. After reassembly, the engine can then be replenished with fresh engine oil. Refer to Chapter 1 for further information.

4   From underneath the front of the vehicle, slacken and remove the bolt securing the coolant pipe to the bracket on the right-hand end of the sump (photo).

5   Working in the **reverse** of the sequence shown in Fig. 2.7, evenly and progressively slacken and remove the sump retaining bolts, noting the correct fitted position of the coolant pipe bracket which is fitted under the right-hand sump bolt.

6   Break the joint by striking the sump with the palm of the hand, then lower the sump away from the engine and withdraw it.

7   While the sump is removed, take the opportunity to clean the oil pump pick-up/strainer pipe mesh using a suitable solvent. Inspect the strainer mesh for signs of clogging or splitting and renew if necessary, referring to Section 9 for further information.

Refitting

8   Clean all traces of oil from the mating surfaces of the cylinder block/crankcase and sump, then use a clean rag to wipe out the sump and the engine's interior.

9   Fit a new sump gasket to the sump mating surface and offer up the sump to the cylinder block/crankcase (photos). Refit the sump retaining bolts, not forgetting the coolant pipe bracket, and tighten them finger-tight only.

10.9A Fit a new gasket to the sump ...

10.9B ... and refit the sump to the engine

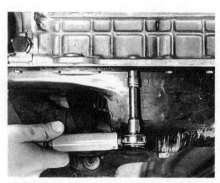

10.10 Tighten the sump retaining bolts to the specified torque setting as described in text

11.2 Use a large flat-bladed screwdriver to prise out the crankshaft right-hand oil seal

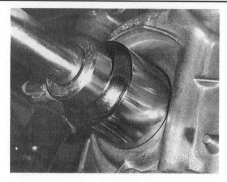

11.4 Tap the new seal into position using a suitable tubular drift which bears only on the seal's hard outer edge

11.7 Using a self-tapping screw to remove the crankshaft left-hand oil seal

10   Working in the sequence shown in Fig. 2.7, tighten the sump bolts to the specified torque (photo).
11   Refit the coolant pipe retaining bolt and tighten it securely, then lower the vehicle to the ground and reconnect the battery negative lead.
12   Refill the engine with oil as described in Chapter 1.

11   Crankshaft oil seals – renewal

Right-hand (pulley end) oil seal

1   Remove the crankshaft pulley as described in Section 7, paragraphs 4 and 5.
2   Carefully lever the old seal out of the timing chain cover using a suitable flat-bladed screwdriver, taking great care not to damage the cover or crankshaft (photo). Alternatively, punch or drill two small holes opposite each other in the seal then screw a self-tapping screw into each and pull on the screws with pliers to extract the seal.
3   Clean the seal housing and polish off any burrs or raised edges on the crankshaft which may have caused the seal to fail in the first place.
4   Lubricate the lips of the new seal with clean engine oil, and press it into position until its outer edge is flush with the timing chain cover surface. If necessary, the seal can be tapped into position using a suitable tubular drift, such as a socket, which bears only on the hard outer edge of the seal (photo). Note that the sealing lips must face inwards.
5   Clean off any traces of oil, then refit the crankshaft pulley as described in Section 7, paragraphs 23 and 24. Note that should the

crankshaft lock up as described, the sump will have to be removed to check the thrustwasher location.

Left-hand (flywheel end) oil seal

6   Remove the flywheel as described in Section 12.
7   Carefully punch or drill two small holes opposite each other in the seal. Screw a self-tapping screw into each hole and pull on the screws with pliers to extract the seal (photo).
8   Clean the seal housing and polish off any burrs or raised edges on the crankshaft which may have caused the seal to fail in the first place.
9   Lubricate the lips of the new seal and the crankshaft shoulder with clean engine oil, then offer the seal to the cylinder block/crankcase, ensuring its sealing lip is facing inwards.
10   Ease the sealing lip of the seal over the crankshaft shoulder by hand only, and press the seal evenly into its housing until its outer flange seats evenly on the housing shoulder. If necessary, a soft-faced mallet can be used to tap the seal gently into place.
11   Clean off any traces of oil, then refit the flywheel as described in Section 12.

12   Flywheel – removal, inspection and refitting

Removal

1   Remove the transmission as described in Chapter 7, then remove the clutch assembly as described in Chapter 6.
2   Prevent the flywheel from turning by locking the ring gear teeth as shown in photo 12.10A, or by bolting a strap between the flywheel and the cylinder block/crankcase.
3   Using a flat-bladed screwdriver, bend back the tabs of the flywheel retaining bolt locking plate. Slacken and remove the flywheel retaining bolts along with the locking plate; discard the locking plate, which must be renewed whenever it is disturbed.
4   Mark the relative positions of the flywheel centre and the crankshaft (photo). The marks are used when refitting to ensure the flywheel is installed in its original fitted position; this is essential as the flywheel is balanced on the engine during manufacture.
5   Remove the flywheel. Do not drop it, as it is very heavy.

Inspection

6   If the clutch mating surface of the flywheel is deeply scored, cracked or otherwise damaged, the flywheel must be renewed, unless it is possible to have it surface-ground. Seek the advice of a Skoda dealer or engine reconditioning specialist.
7   If the ring gear is badly worn or has missing teeth, it must be renewed, but this job is best left to a Skoda dealer or engine reconditioning specialist. The temperature to which the new ring gear must be heated for installation (180° to 200°C) is critical and, if not done accurately, the hardness of the teeth will be destroyed.

Refitting

8   Clean the mating surfaces of the flywheel and crankshaft, then fit the flywheel to the crankshaft. If the original flywheel is being refitted,

12.4 Prior to removing the flywheel, mark its correct fitted relationship with the crankshaft

12.9 A new locking plate must be used on refitting

12.10A Tighten the retaining bolts to the specified torque setting, noting the locking tool used to prevent flywheel rotation ...

12.10B ... and secure them in position with the locking plate tabs

13.8A Slacken and remove the connecting rod rear mounting nut ...

13.8B ... and withdraw the washer and rubber bush

13.8C Undo the front mounting bolt and remove the rod from the vehicle

aligning the marks made when dismantling. Note that if a new flywheel is being fitted, it can be installed in any position.

9   Offer up the new locking plate (photo), then refit the flywheel bolts and tighten them by hand only.

10   Lock the flywheel using the method employed on dismantling, and tighten the retaining bolts to the specified torque wrench setting. Secure the bolts in position by bending up the locking plate tabs against the flats of each bolt head (photos).

11   Refit the clutch as described in Chapter 6, then remove the locking tool and refit the transmission as described in Chapter 7.

13   Engine/transmission mounting rubbers – inspection and renewal

Inspection

1   If improved access is required, raise the front of the vehicle and support it securely on axle stands.

2   Check each mounting rubber to see if it is cracked, hardened or separated from the metal at any point; renew the mounting if any such damage or deterioration is evident.

3   Check that all the mounting's fasteners are securely tightened; use a torque wrench to check if possible.

4   Using a large screwdriver or a pry bar, check for wear in the mounting by carefully levering against it to check for free play; where this is not possible, enlist the aid of an assistant to move the engine/transmission unit back and forth or from side to side while you watch the mounting. While some free play is to be expected even from new components, excessive wear should be obvious. If excessive free play is found, check first that the fasteners are correctly tightened before deciding that renewal of the mounting rubber is required.

Renewal – general information

Right-hand mounting

5   The right-hand engine mounting rubber is an integral part of the water pump casing. Removal and refitting of the mounting rubber from the pump requires the use of a hydraulic press and several special mandrels and spacers. Therefore if the mounting requires renewal, remove the water pump as described in Chapter 3 and take it to your Skoda dealer. The dealer will have access to the equipment required to remove the old mounting rubber and install the new one.

Left-hand mounting

6   The left-hand engine mounting rubber is an integral part of the transmission end cover. Removal and refitting of the mounting rubber from the cover requires the use of a special Skoda service tool. Therefore if the mounting requires renewal, remove the transmission as described in Chapter 7 and take it to your Skoda dealer. The dealer will have access to the necessary puller and will be able to remove the old mounting rubber and install the new one.

Rear mounting

7   The rear mounting rubber is an integral part of the rear mounting connecting rod. If the mounting rubber requires renewal it will be necessary to remove the connecting rod and take it to a Skoda dealer. The dealer will have access to the equipment required to press out the old mounting rubber and install the new one.

8   To remove the connecting rod, firmly apply the handbrake, then jack up the front of the vehicle and support it on axle stands. Undo the nut securing the rear of the rod to the mounting bracket on the front subframe, and slide the washer and rubber bush off the threaded end of the rod. Undo the bolt securing the rod to the engine mounting bracket, and remove the rod from underneath the vehicle, noting the second rubber bush and washer which are fitted to the threaded end of the rod (photos). Inspect the bushes for signs of wear and renew as necessary.

9   Refitting is a reversal of the removal procedure. Ensure that the connecting rod mounting nut and bolt are securely tightened.

Part B: Engine removal and general overhaul procedures

14 General information

Included in this part of Chapter 2 are details of removing the engine/transmission unit from the vehicle and general overhaul procedures for the cylinder head, cylinder block/crankcase and all other engine internal components.

The information given ranges from advice concerning preparation for an overhaul and the purchase of replacement parts, to detailed step-by-step procedures covering removal, inspection, renovation and refitting of engine internal components.

After Section 18, all instructions are based on the assumption that the engine has been removed from the vehicle. For information concerning in-vehicle engine repair, as well as the removal and refitting of those external components necessary for full overhaul, refer to Part A of this Chapter and to Section 18. Ignore any preliminary dismantling operations described in Part A that are no longer relevant once the engine has been removed from the vehicle.

All Specifications relating to engine overhaul are at the beginning of this Chapter.

15 Engine overhaul – general information

It is not always easy to determine when, or if, an engine should be completely overhauled, as a number of factors must be considered.

High mileage is not necessarily an indication that an overhaul is needed, while low mileage does not preclude the need for an overhaul.

Frequency of servicing is probably the most important consideration; an engine which has had regular and frequent oil and filter changes, as well as other required maintenance, should give many thousands of miles of reliable service. Conversely, a neglected engine may require an overhaul very early in its life.

Excessive oil consumption is an indication that piston rings, valve seals and/or valve guides are in need of attention. Make sure that oil leaks are not responsible before deciding that the rings and/or guides are worn. Perform a compression test, as described in Section 2, to determine the likely cause of the problem.

Check the oil pressure with a gauge fitted in place of the oil pressure switch and compare it with that specified. If it is extremely low, the main and big-end bearings and/or the oil pump are probably worn out.

Loss of power, rough running, knocking or metallic engine noises, excessive valve gear noise and high fuel consumption may also point to the need for an overhaul, especially if they are all present at the same time. If a complete service does not remedy the situation, major mechanical work is the only solution.

An engine overhaul involves restoring all internal parts to the specification of a new engine. During an overhaul, the cylinder liners, the pistons and the piston rings are renewed. New main and big-end bearings are generally fitted and if necessary, the crankshaft may be reground to restore the journals. The valves are also serviced as well, since they are usually in less-than-perfect condition at this point. While the engine is being overhauled, other components, such as the distributor, starter and alternator, can be overhauled as well. The end result should be an as-new engine that will give many trouble-free miles.

Note: *Critical cooling system components such as the hoses, thermostat and water pump should be renewed when an engine is overhauled. The radiator should be checked carefully to ensure that it is not clogged or*

Fig. 2.8 Exploded view of the cylinder block and associated components (Sec 15)

1   Cylinder block
2   Cylinder liner
3   Cylinder liner sealing washer
4   Stud
5   Plug
6   Oil gallery plug (12 mm thread)
7   Sealing washer
8   Stud
9   Rear crankshaft oil seal
10 Bolt – rear oil seal housing to block
11 Spring washer
12 Gasket (where fitted)
13 Main bearing cap bolt
14 Main bearing cap
15 Stud
16 Stud
17 Stud
18 Upper main bearing shell
19 Lower main bearing shell
20 Stud
21 Stud
22 Timing chain oil jet
23 Oilway plug
24 Oilway plug
25 Locating pin
26 Oil gallery plug (16 mm thread)
27 Sealing washer
28 Oil pressure switch
29 Adaptor
30 Stud
31 Plug
32 Coolant drain plug
33 Sealing washer
34 Stud
35 Locating dowel

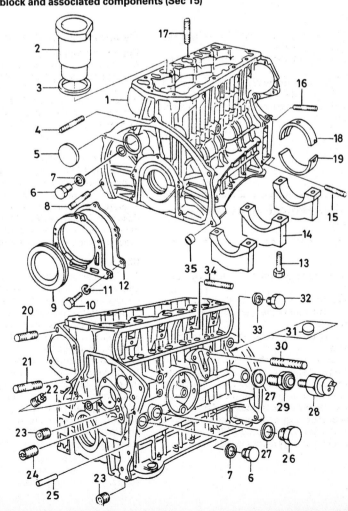

leaking. It is also a good idea to renew the oil pump whenever the engine is overhauled.

Before beginning the engine overhaul, read through the entire procedure to familiarize yourself with the scope and requirements of the job. Overhauling an engine is not difficult if you follow carefully all of the instructions, have the necessary tools and equipment and pay close attention to all specifications; however, it can be time-consuming. Plan on the vehicle being off the road for a minimum of two weeks, especially if parts must be taken to an engineering works for repair or reconditioning. Check on the availability of parts and make sure that any necessary special tools and equipment are obtained in advance. Most work can be done with typical hand tools, although a number of precision measuring tools are required for inspecting parts to determine if they must be renewed. Often the engineering works will handle the inspection of parts and offer advice concerning reconditioning and renewal.

Note: *Always wait until the engine has been completely dismantled and all components, especially the cylinder block/crankcase, the cylinder liners and the crankshaft have been inspected before deciding what service and repair operations must be performed by an engineering works. Since the condition of these components will be the major factor to consider when determining whether to overhaul the original engine or buy a reconditioned unit, do not purchase parts or have overhaul work done on other components until they have been thoroughly inspected. As a general rule, time is the primary cost of an overhaul, so it does not pay to fit worn or substandard parts.*

As a final note, to ensure maximum life and minimum trouble from a reconditioned engine, everything must be assembled with care in a spotlessly-clean environment.

16   Engine/transmission removal – methods and precautions

If you have decided that the engine must be removed for overhaul or major repair work, several preliminary steps should be taken.

Locating a suitable place to work is extremely important. Adequate work space, along with storage space for the vehicle, will be needed. If a workshop or garage is not available, at the very least a flat, level, clean work surface is required.

Cleaning the engine compartment and engine/transmission before beginning the removal procedure will help keep tools clean and organized.

An engine hoist or A-frame will also be necessary. Make sure the equipment is rated in excess of the combined weight of the engine and transmission. Safety is of primary importance, considering the potential hazards involved in lowering the engine/transmission out of the vehicle.

If the engine/transmission is being removed by a novice, a helper should be available. Advice and aid from someone more experienced would also be helpful. There are many instances when one person cannot simultaneously perform all of the operations required when lifting the engine out of the vehicle.

Plan the operation ahead of time. Before starting work, arrange to obtain or hire all of the tools and equipment you will need. Some of the equipment necessary to perform engine/transmission removal and installation safely and with relative ease are (in addition to an engine hoist) a heavy- duty trolley jack, a complete sets of spanners and sockets as described in the front of this Manual, wooden blocks and plenty of rags and cleaning solvent for mopping up spilled oil, coolant and fuel. If the hoist must be hired, make sure that you arrange for it in advance, and perform all of the operations possible without it beforehand. This will save you money and time.

Plan for the vehicle to be out of use for quite a while. An engineering works will be required to perform some of the work which the do-it-yourselfer cannot accomplish without special equipment. These places often have a busy schedule, so it would be a good idea to consult them before removing the engine in order to estimate the amount of time required to rebuild or repair components that may need work.

Always be extremely careful when removing and refitting the engine/transmission. Serious injury can result from careless actions. Plan ahead, take your time and a job of this nature, although major, can be accomplished successfully.

17   Engine/transmission – removal and refitting

Removal

Note: *The engine can be removed from the vehicle only as a complete unit with the transmission; the two are then separated for overhaul. The engine/transmission unit is lowered out of the vehicle. The vehicle must therefore be securely supported at a height which leaves sufficient clearance for the combined engine/transmission unit to be withdrawn from underneath.*

1   Park the vehicle on firm, level ground, then remove the bonnet as described in Chapter 11.
2   If the engine is to be dismantled, drain the oil and remove the oil filter (see Chapter 1). Clean and refit the drain plug, tightening it securely.
3   Firmly apply the handbrake and slacken the front wheel bolts. Jack up the front of the vehicle and support it securely on axle stands, bearing in mind the note made at the start of this Section. Remove both front roadwheels.
4   Drain the transmission oil as described in Chapter 1, then clean and refit the drain plug and tighten it securely.
5   Drain the cooling system as described in Chapter 1.
6   Remove the air cleaner assembly as described in Chapter 4.
7   Disconnect the battery and remove the alternator as described in Chapter 12.
8   Rotate the clutch adjusting nut in an anti-clockwise direction to obtain maximum clutch cable free play. Release the inner cable from the clutch release lever and free the outer cable from its mounting bracket.
9   Unscrew the knurled retaining ring and disconnect the speedometer cable from its drive, located at the rear of the transmission.
10   Displace the rubber insulating boot from the starter motor solenoid main terminal, then remove the nut and disconnect the battery lead. Carefully disconnect the spade connector from the solenoid.
11   Disconnect the wiring connectors from the oil pressure switch, situated on the front of the cylinder block, and the reversing light switch, located on the underside of the transmission (photo).
12   Release the retaining clip, then disconnect the feed hose from the fuel pump/filter union. Plug the hose end to minimise the loss of fuel. **Warning:** *Take appropriate fire precautions when dealing with fuel.*
13   Disconnect the following from the carburettor and inlet manifold as described in the relevant Sections of Chapter 4 (photos).

(a)   Carburettor wiring connector.
(b)   Throttle cable.
(c)   Braking system vacuum servo unit hose.
(d)   Coolant hose(s).

14   Working as described in Chapter 3, disconnect the wiring connector from the coolant gauge temperature sender unit and disconnect the radiator top hose and expansion tank hose from the thermostat housing. Slacken the retaining clips and disconnect the radiator bottom hose from the front of the coolant metal pipe, and the heater hose from the rear of the pipe (photos).
15   Trace the LT wiring back from the distributor to the ignition unit, and disconnect the wiring connectors; the connectors are different sizes, to prevent them being reconnected incorrectly. Disconnect the ignition coil HT lead from the centre of the distributor, and position it clear of the engine.
16   Working from underneath the vehicle, slacken and remove the retaining bolt and disconnect the transmission earth strap from the vehicle underbody.
17   Working as described in Chapter 7, Section 2, disconnect the gearchange linkage selector rod and steady rod from the transmission. Release the driveshaft inner constant velocity joints from the transmission as described in Chapter 7, Section 4, paragraphs 3 to 6. Ensure the driveshafts and gearchange linkage rods are positioned clear of the engine/transmission so that they will not hinder the removal procedure.
18   On models equipped with an oil cooler, disconnect the oil cooler hoses from the block, referring to Section 8 for further information.
19   Attach lifting chains to the bracket on the rear of the cylinder head and take the weight of the engine/transmission unit on an engine hoist. Ensure that the chains do not contact any other component.
20   Undo the nut securing the engine/transmission rear connecting rod to the subframe bracket. Remove the bolt securing the rod to the

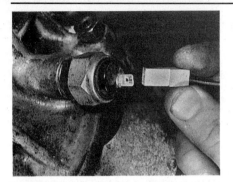

17.11 Disconnecting the oil pressure switch wiring connector

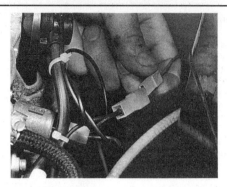

17.13A Disconnect the wiring connector ...

17.13B ... and all the relevant cooling system hoses form the carburettor and inlet manifold (arrows)

17.14A Disconnect the radiator bottom hose ...

17.14B ... and the heater hose from the metal coolant pipe on the right-hand side of the engine

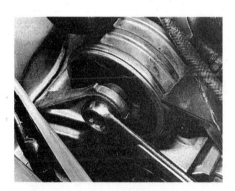

17.21A Slacken the engine/transmission right-hand mounting through-bolt ...

17.21B ... then tap out the plug from the valance ...

17.21C ... and withdraw the through-bolt via the hole

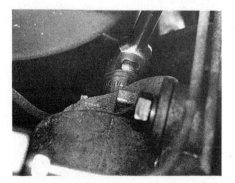

17.22 Slackening the engine/transmission left-hand mounting through-bolt

17.26 Rock the engine to settle it on its mountings, then tighten the mounting through-bolts

engine bracket and remove the connecting rod from underneath the vehicle.

21   Slacken the engine/transmission right-hand mounting through-bolt and remove the nut. To gain the required clearance to remove the through-bolt, tap out the plug from the right-hand valance, using a hammer and a suitable punch. The through-bolt can then be withdrawn through the hole and out from under the wing (photos).

22   Slacken and remove the left-hand mounting through-bolt and remove its square nut from the front of the mounting bracket (photo). Note that there is no need to disturb either the left- or right-hand mounting brackets; they should be left in their original positions since they provide excellent alignment points when the engine is being lifted into position on refitting.

23   Make a final check that all components that will prevent the removal of the engine/transmission from the vehicle have been removed, disconnected or positioned clear of the unit so that they will not hinder removal. Note that removal of the engine/transmission unit from underneath the vehicle will be considerably easier if the assembly is lowered onto a wheeled trolley or, alternatively, a trolley jack with an interposed block of wood; the unit can then be wheeled out from under the vehicle rather than dragged.

24   Carefully lower the engine/transmission out of the vehicle, ensuring that nothing is trapped or damaged. Once the engine is lowered onto its platform, detach the chains and manoeuvre the unit out from under the vehicle.

25   If the engine and transmission are to be separated for overhaul, first remove the starter motor. Undo the flywheel cover plate retaining bolts, and remove the plate from the transmission. Slacken and remove the remaining bolts securing the transmission housing to the engine, noting the correct fitted position of the clutch cable bracket. Move the gearbox squarely away from the engine to release it from its locating dowels, and separate the two. If necessary, also remove the clutch as described in Chapter 6.

Refitting

26   Refitting is the reverse of removal, following where necessary the instructions given in the other Chapters of this manual. Note the following additional points.

(a)   Prior to assembling the engine and transmission, overhaul and lubricate the clutch components as described in Chapter 6.

(b)   Carefully raise the engine/transmission unit into position, then refit the left- and right-hand mounting through-bolts and tighten them by hand only. Refit the rear mounting connecting rod, tightening its retaining nut and bolt securely, then rock the engine/transmission unit to settle its mounting rubbers in position before tightening both through-bolts to the specified torque (photo).

(c)   Tighten all nuts and bolts to their specified torque wrench settings, where given.

(d)   Ensure that all hoses and pipes are securely reconnected to their original positions and, where necessary, are securely held in position with their retaining clips. Note that it is recommended that all old Skoda type hose clips be replaced with worm drive type hose clips.

(e)   On completion, refill the engine and transmission with the specified type and amount of oil, and refill the cooling system as described in Chapter 1.

18   Engine overhaul – dismantling sequence

1   It is much easier to dismantle and work on the engine if it is mounted on a portable engine stand. These stands can often be hired from a tool hire shop. Before the engine is mounted on a stand, the flywheel should be removed, as described in Section 12, so that the stand bolts can be tightened into the end of the cylinder block/crankcase.

2   If a stand is not available, it is possible to dismantle the engine with it blocked up on a sturdy workbench or on the floor. Be extra careful not to tip or drop the engine when working without a stand.

3   If you are going to obtain a reconditioned engine, all external components must be removed first to be transferred to the replacement

engine (just as they will if you are doing a complete engine overhaul yourself). These components include the following:

(a)   Alternator mounting brackets (Chapter 12).
(b)   Distributor, HT leads and spark plugs (Chapter 5).
(c)   Thermostat and housing (Chapter 3).
(d)   Carburettor (Chapter 4).
(e)   All electrical switches and sensors.
(f)   Inlet and exhaust manifolds (Chapter 4).
(g)   Oil filter (Chapter 1).
(h)   Fuel pump and filter (Chapter 4).
(i)   Flywheel (Section 12).

Note: *When removing the external components from the engine, pay close attention to details that may be helpful or important during refitting. Note the fitted position of gaskets, seals, spacers, pins, washers, bolts and other small items.*

4   If you are obtaining a short engine (which consists of the engine cylinder block/crankcase, crankshaft, pistons and connecting rods all assembled), then the cylinder head, sump, oil pump, and timing chain and sprockets will have to be removed also.

5   If you are planning a complete overhaul, the engine can be dismantled and the components removed in the following order:

(a)   Inlet and exhaust manifolds (Chapter 4).
(b)   Cylinder head (Section 6).
(c)   Sump (Section 10).
(d)   Oil pump (Section 9).
(e)   Timing cover, chain and sprockets (Section 7).
(f)   Camshaft and followers (Section 22).
(g)   Piston/connecting rod assemblies (Section 23).
(h)   Crankshaft (Section 24).

6   Before beginning the dismantling and overhaul procedures, make sure that you have all the necessary tools. Refer to the introductory pages at the beginning of this Manual for further information.

19   Cylinder head – dismantling

Note: *New or reconditioned cylinder heads are available from the manufacturer and from engine overhaul specialists. Due to the fact that some specialist tools are required for the dismantling and inspection procedures, and new components may not be readily available, it may be more practical and economical for the home mechanic to purchase a reconditioned head rather than dismantle, inspect and recondition the original head.*

1   Remove the cylinder head as described in Section 6.

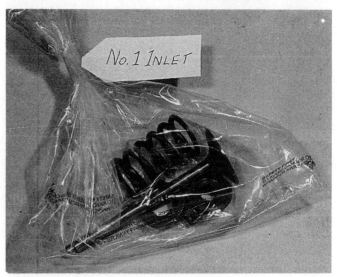

19.6 Store all valve components in a labelled plastic bag to ensure that they are refitted in their original positions

2   Using a valve spring compressor, compress each valve spring in turn until the split collets can be removed. Release the compressor and lift off the spring retainer and both the outer and inner springs.

3   If, when the valve spring compressor is screwed down, the spring retainer refuses to free and expose the split collets, gently tap the top of the tool, directly over the retainer with a light hammer. This will free the retainer.

4   Lift both the inner and outer spring seats off the valve guide, then use a pair of pliers to carefully extract the valve stem seal from the guide.

5   Withdraw the valve through the combustion chamber.

6   It is essential that each valve is stored together with its collets, retainer, springs and spring seats, and that all valves are kept in their correct sequence unless they are so badly worn that they are to be renewed. If they are going to be kept and used again, place each valve assembly in a labelled polythene bag or similar small container (photo).

20   Cylinder head and valves – cleaning and inspection

1   Thorough cleaning of the cylinder head and valve components, followed by a detailed inspection, will enable you to decide how much valve service work must be carried out during the engine overhaul.

Note: *If the engine has been severely overheated, it is best to assume that the cylinder head is warped and to check carefully for signs of this.*

Cleaning

2   Scrape away all traces of old gasket material and sealing compound from the cylinder head; see Section 6 for details.

3   Scrape away the carbon from the combustion chambers and ports, then wash the cylinder head thoroughly with paraffin or a suitable solvent.

4   Scrape off any heavy carbon deposits that may have formed on the valves, then use a power-operated wire brush to remove deposits from the valve heads and stems.

Inspection

Note: *Be sure to perform all the following inspection procedures before concluding that the services of a Skoda dealer or engine overhaul specialist are required. Make a list of all items that require attention.*

Cylinder head

5   Inspect the head very carefully for cracks, evidence of coolant leakage and other damage. If cracks are found, a new cylinder head should be obtained.

6   Use a straight-edge and feeler gauge blade to check that the cylinder head gasket surface is not distorted. Since Skoda quote no specified figures for the maximum distortion allowed, if distortion of the gasket face is found it will be necessary to consult a Skoda dealer as to what is acceptable and what is not. The dealer will also be able to inform you if it is possible to resurface the cylinder head or whether it will be necessary to purchase a new one.

7   Examine the valve seats in each of the combustion chambers. If they are severely pitted, cracked or burned then they will need to be renewed or re-cut by an engine overhaul specialist. If there is only slight pitting, this can be removed by grinding-in the valve heads and seats with fine valve-grinding compound as described below. If the valve seats are to be re-cut, this must be done only after the valve guides have been checked and, if necessary, reamed.

8   Inspect the valve guides for visible signs of wear and damage. If the necessary measuring equipment is available, measure the diameter of the existing valve stems (see below) and the bore of the guides, then calculate the clearance and compare the result with the specified value. If no measuring equipment is available a rough idea of valve guide wear can be gained by inserting each valve into its respective guide and with the valve head held approximately 10 mm above the cylinder head surface, checking the side-to-side movement of the valve in its guide. Very little side play should be present. Note that the valve guides are an integral part of the cylinder head, and are not available separately. Therefore if the specified stem-to-guide clearance is exceeded or the side play seems excessive, it will be necessary to have the valve guides reamed and install a new set of valves which have oversize stems

20.10 Measuring a valve stem diameter

(8.25 mm nominal diameter). This work should be entrusted to a Skoda dealer who will have access to the necessary tools and can obtain a set of oversize valves.

Valves

9   Examine the head of each valve for pitting, burning, cracks and general wear and check the valve stem for scoring and wear ridges. Rotate the valve and check for any obvious indication that it is bent. Look for pits and excessive wear on the tip of each valve stem. Renew any valve that shows any such signs of wear or damage.

10   If the valve appears satisfactory at this stage, measure the valve stem diameter at several points using a micrometer (photo). Any significant difference in the readings obtained indicates wear of the valve stem. Should any of these conditions be apparent, the valve(s) must be renewed.

11   If the valves are in satisfactory condition, they should be ground (lapped) into their respective seats to ensure a smooth gas-tight seal. If the seat is only lightly pitted, or if it has been re-cut, fine grinding compound **only** should be used to produce the required finish. Coarse valve-grinding compound should **not** be used unless a seat is badly burned or deeply pitted; if this is the case the cylinder head and valves should be inspected by an expert to decide whether seat re-cutting or even the renewal of the valve or seat insert is required.

12   Valve grinding is carried out as follows. Place the cylinder head upside-down on a bench.

13   Smear a trace of (the appropriate grade of) valve-grinding compound on the seat face, and press a suction grinding tool onto the valve head. With a semi-rotary action, grind the valve head to its seat, lifting the valve occasionally to redistribute the grinding compound. A light spring placed under the valve head will greatly ease this operation.

14   If coarse grinding compound is being used, work only until a dull, matt even surface is produced on both the valve seat and the valve, then wipe off the used compound and repeat the process with fine compound. When a smooth unbroken ring of light grey matt finish is produced on both the valve and seat, the grinding operation is complete. **Do not** grind in the valves any further than absolutely necessary, or the seat will be sunk excessively into the cylinder head.

15   When all the valves have been ground-in, carefully wash off **all** traces of grinding compound using paraffin or a suitable solvent before reassembly of the cylinder head. It will be appreciated that even a small quantity of grinding compound left in the cylinder head could cause rapid wear.

Valve components

16   Examine the valve springs for signs of damage and discoloration, and stand each spring on a flat surface and check it for squareness. Using a pair of vernier calipers, measure the free length of each spring, and compare it to the specified free length given in the Specifications at the start of this Chapter (photo). If any of the springs are damaged, distorted or are significantly shorter than their specified free length, obtain a complete new set of both inner and outer springs.

20.16 Measuring valve spring free length

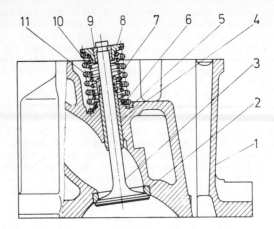

Fig. 2.9 Sectional view of the cylinder head and valve components (Sec 21)

1	Cylinder head	7	Valve guide oil seal
2	Valve seat	8	Spring retainer
3	Valve	9	Collets
4	Valve guide	10	Inner spring
5	Outer spring seat	11	Outer spring
6	Inner spring seat		

21   Cylinder head – reassembly

1   Lubricate the stems of the valves and insert them into their original locations. If new valves are being fitted, insert them into the locations to which they have been ground (photo).
2   Working on the first valve, first refit the inner and outer spring seats over the valve guide. If genuine Skoda valve guide seals are being fitted, fit one of the plastic seal protectors supplied with the seal kit to the end of the valve stem; the plastic protector protects the seal lip from being damaged as it passes over the valve end. Dip the new valve guide seal in fresh engine oil then carefully locate it over the valve and onto the guide. Take care not to damage the seal as it is passed over the valve stem. Use

a suitable socket or metal tube to press the seal firmly onto the guide then, where fitted, remove the seal protector (photos).
3   Locate the inner and outer springs on their seats, and refit the spring retainer (photos).
4   Compress the valve spring and locate the split collets in the recess in the valve stem (photo). Use a little grease to hold the collets in place. Release the compressor, then repeat the procedure on the remaining valves.

21.1 Lubricate the valve stem then insert into its guide ...

21.2A ... and refit the inner ...

21.2B ... and outer spring seats

21.2C Carefully slide the valve guide oil seal onto the valve stem. Note the seal protector (arrowed) which is supplied with genuine oil seals

21.2D Use a socket to press the seal onto the valve guide

21.3A Refit the inner and outer valve springs ...

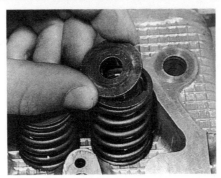

21.3B ... and install the spring retainer

21.4 Compress the valve spring and install the collets, using a dab of grease to hold them in position

5   With all the valves installed, place the cylinder head flat on the bench and, using a hammer and interposed block of wood, tap the end of each valve stem to settle the components.

22 Camshaft and followers – removal, inspection and refitting

Removal

1   Remove the rocker gear as described in Section 5.
2   Lift out each pushrod in turn, and store it in its correct fitted order by pushing it through a clearly-marked cardboard template. This will help ensure that the pushrods are refitted in their original positions on reassembly.
3   Undo the four retaining nuts securing the cam follower cover to the front of the cylinder block, then remove the washers and seals from the cover studs. Carefully prise the cover away from the cylinder block, and remove it along with its rubber seal.
4   Withdraw each cam follower in turn, and either label the individual followers or place them in a small partitioned container. This will help ensure that if the followers are to be re-used they are refitted in their original positions; this is essential to minimise the amount of wear between the followers and cam lobes (photos).
5   Remove the timing chain and sprockets as described in Section 7.
6   Prior to removing the camshaft, check the endfloat as follows. Temporarily refit the distributor drivegear, dished washer, tab washer and sprocket bolt to the end of the camshaft, and tighten the bolt to the specified torque. Set up a dial gauge on the end of the camshaft, and measure the endfloat whilst moving the camshaft to and fro (photo). If the endfloat exceeds the specified limit, renew the camshaft thrustplate on refitting.
7   Remove the temporarily-installed components, then slacken and remove the three screws securing the camshaft thrustplate to the cylinder block. Remove the plate and withdraw the camshaft from the block (photos).

Inspection

8   Inspect the cam followers for wear ridges and pitting of their camshaft lobe contact surfaces. Insert each follower into its respective bore in the cylinder block, and check that it is free to move smoothly up and down, but that there is no excessive side-to-side movement of the follower. If the necessary measuring equipment is available, the amount of wear on the followers and their bores in the cylinder block can be checked by direct measurement (photo).
9   If any of the cam followers are badly marked or excessively-worn (compare with the figures quoted in the Specifications), it will be necessary to renew the affected follower(s). If the amount of side-to-side movement of any follower in its bore seems excessive, or if any of the bores in the cylinder block have worn beyond their specified limits, it will be necessary to have the bores in the cylinder block reamed and to install oversize cam followers. This task should be entrusted to a Skoda dealer, who will be able to obtain a set of oversize followers and will have the necessary tools to ream out the bores.
10   Examine the camshaft lobes and bearing journals for signs of wear such as pitting or scoring, along with the camshaft bearings which are in the cylinder block. If the necessary measuring equipment is available, measure the diameter of the camshaft journals (photo) and the internal diameter of each bearing in the cylinder block, and compare the results to the figures given in the Specifications. The bearing running clearance can be calculated by subtracting the camshaft journal outer diameter from the bearing internal diameter.
11   If the camshaft lobes or the bearing journals are badly worn, the camshaft must be renewed. If the camshaft bearings are excessively-worn (compare with the figures quoted in the Specifications), then the advice of a Skoda dealer or engine repair specialist must be sought. It may be possible to have the cylinder block bored out and camshaft bearing shells installed. If this is not possible, the block will have to be renewed.
12   Inspect the camshaft thrustplate for signs of scuffing, and renew if worn.

Refitting

13   Liberally oil the camshaft lobes and bearing journals, then slide the camshaft into position in the cylinder block.

22.4A Withdraw the cam followers from the block ...

22.4B ... and store them in a partitioned container

22.6 Checking camshaft endfloat

22.7A Undo the thrustplate retaining screws ...

22.7B ... remove the thrustplate ...

22.7C ... and withdraw the camshaft

22.8 Measuring a cam follower diameter

22.10 Measuring a camshaft bearing journal

22.17A Ensure seal is correctly located in cam follower cover groove

22.17B Cam follower cover cut-out (arrowed) aligns with fuel pump aperture in cylinder block

22.17C Fit the seals and washers onto the cover studs ...

22.17D ... then tighten the retaining nuts

14   Fit the camshaft thrustplate over the camshaft end, and securely tighten its three retaining screws. Check the camshaft endfloat as described in paragraph 6.
15   Refit the timing chain and sprockets as described in Section 7.
16   Liberally oil the outer surfaces of the cam followers, and insert them into their respective bores in the cylinder block. If the original followers are being re-used, ensure they are refitted in their original locations to minimise wear.
17   Examine the cam follower cover seal for signs of damage or deterioration, and renew if necessary; if the seal is undamaged it can be re-used. Ensure the cover and block mating surfaces are clean, and the seal is correctly located in its groove in the cover. Refit the cover to the cylinder block, noting that the cut-out on the outer rim of the cover must face downwards so that it aligns with the cylinder block fuel pump aperture. Slide the seals and flat washers onto the cover studs, then refit the cover retaining nuts and tighten them to the specified torque setting (photos).
18   Remove the pushrods from the cardboard template, and insert

them into their original positions in the cylinder head, ensuring that each pushrod is correctly located in its cam follower.
19   Refit the rocker gear as described in Section 5, adjusting the valve clearances as described in Chapter 1 before installing the rocker cover.

23   Piston/connecting rod assembly – removal

1   Remove the cylinder head, sump and oil pump gears as described in Sections 6, 9 and 10. Ensure the cylinder liners are securely clamped in position.
2   Prior to removing the connecting rods, note the two numbers which are stamped on one side of each assembly, next to the connecting rod/big-end cap mating surface; one on the big-end cap and one on the connecting rod (photo). These numbers indicate the cylinder number of

Fig. 2.10 Exploded view of the crankshaft, camshaft and associated components (Secs 22 to 24)

1 Crankshaft
2 Woodruff key
3 Flywheel
4 Flywheel ring gear
5 Dowel pin
6 Flywheel retaining bolt
7 Locking plate
8 Crankshaft thrustwashers
9 Guide spacer
10 Shim
11 Crankshaft sprocket
12 Camshaft sprocket
13 Timing chain
14 Distributor drivegear
15 Dished washer
16 Tab washer
17 Camshaft bolt
18 Crankshaft pulley
19 Washer
20 Crankshaft pulley retaining bolt
21 Camshaft thrustplate retaining screw
22 Spring washer
23 Camshaft thrustplate
24 Woodruff key
25 Camshaft
26 Piston top compression ring
27 Piston second compression ring
28 Piston oil control ring
29 Piston
30 Gudgeon pin
31 Circlip
32 Connecting rod
33 Small-end bush
34 Connecting rod big-end bearing cap bolt
35 Connecting rod big-end bearing cap nut
36 Big-end bearing shells

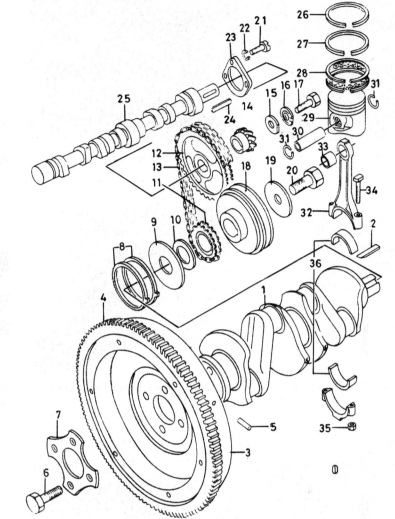

23.2 Connecting rod assemblies are numbered with their cylinder number

each respective connecting rod assembly, No 1 cylinder being at the right-hand end (nearest the timing chain). If any of these numbers are no longer visible or the number stamped on the assembly does not correspond to the cylinder to which it is fitted, use a hammer and centre-punch or paint to mark each connecting rod and big-end bearing cap with its respective cylinder number on the flat, machined surface provided.

3 With the connecting rods still installed on the crankshaft, use a feeler blade to check the amount of endfloat between the caps and crankshaft webs. If the measured endfloat greatly exceeds the specified tolerance, then the affected connecting rods will require renewal.

4 Rotate the crankshaft until Nos 2 and 3 cylinder pistons are at the bottom of their stroke.

5 Unscrew and remove the big-end bearing cap nuts, and withdraw the cap, complete with bearing shell, from the connecting rod. If only the bearing shells are being attended to, push the connecting rod up and off the crankpin, ensuring that the connecting rod big-ends do not mark the cylinder bore walls, then remove the upper bearing shell. Keep the cap, nuts and (if they are to be refitted) the bearing shells together in their correct sequence.

6 With Nos 2 and 3 cylinder big-ends disconnected, repeat the procedure (exercising great care to prevent damage to any of the components) to remove Nos 1 and 4 cylinder bearing caps.

7 Remove the ridge of carbon from the top of each bore. Push each piston/connecting rod assembly up, and remove it from the top of the bore, taking great care to ensure the connecting rod big-ends do not mark the cylinder bore walls. Immediately refit the bearing cap, shells and nuts to each piston/connecting rod assembly so that they are all kept together as a matched set.

24.4 Using a dial gauge to measure crankshaft endfloat

24   Crankshaft – removal

1   Remove the cylinder head and the timing chain and sprockets as described in Sections 6 and 7. Ensure the cylinder liners are securely clamped in position.

2   Free the connecting rod big-end caps from the crankshaft and, if necessary, remove the connecting rods as described in Section 23.

3   Prior to removing the crankshaft, temporarily refit the following components to the right-hand end of the crankshaft and check the endfloat as follows. Slide the outer thrustwasher onto the crankshaft, ensuring that its oil grooves are facing away from the bearing cap, then locate the thrustwasher tab with its cut-out in the bearing cap, and press the thrustwasher into its recess; check that the inner thrustwasher tab is also correctly located in its cap cut-out. With the thrustwasher in position, slide on the large spacer (chamfered inner edge facing towards block), the shim, the Woodruff key (tapered end innermost) and the timing chain sprocket. Fit the crankshaft pulley, pulley bolt and washer; tighten the bolt to the specified torque, preventing flywheel rotation using the arrangement shown in photo 12.10A. Note that if the thrustwashers are not properly located, the crankshaft will lock up as the bolt is tightened, and both thrustwashers will be damaged.

4   Position a dial gauge with its probe in contact with the end of the crankshaft. Push the crankshaft fully one way, and zero the gauge. Push the crankshaft fully the other way and check the endfloat (photo). The result can be compared with the value given in the Specifications, and will give an indication as to whether new thrustwashers are required.

5   If a dial gauge is not available, feeler gauges can be used. First push the crankshaft fully towards the flywheel end of the engine, then use feeler gauges to measure the gap between the web of No 1 crankpin and the thrustwasher (photo).

6   Once crankshaft endfloat has been checked, remove all the components which were temporarily installed on the crankshaft

right-hand end. Remove the flywheel as described in Section 12.

7   Slacken and remove its retaining screws, and slide the flywheel-end oil seal housing off the end of the crankshaft, noting whether a gasket is fitted behind the housing or not (photo). If there is a gasket, remove and discard it; a new one must be fitted on reassembly.

8   Identification numbers should be visible on each main bearing cap. The caps are numbered 1 to 3, with No 1 being the right-hand (pulley-end) cap (photo). If no marks are visible, stamp the bearing caps with a centre punch as was done for the connecting rods, and mark them in such a way as to indicate their fitted direction.

9   Slacken and remove the main bearing cap bolts, and withdraw the caps complete with bearing shells.

10   Remove the crankshaft, and slide the thrustwasher off its right-hand end, noting which way around it is fitted. Remove the upper main bearing shells from the cylinder block, and store them with their respective partners from the main bearing caps so that all shells can be identified and (if necessary) refitted in their original locations.

25   Cylinder block/crankcase – cleaning and inspection

Cleaning

1   For complete cleaning, remove the liners (see paragraph 19 below), oil gallery plugs, and all external components and electrical switches/sensors.

2   Scrape all traces of gasket from the cylinder block and crankcase, taking care not to damage the gasket/sealing surfaces.

3   If any of the castings are extremely dirty, all should be steam-cleaned.

4   After the castings are returned, clean all oil holes and oil galleries one more time. Flush all internal passages with warm water until the water runs clear, then dry thoroughly and apply a light film of oil to all liner surfaces to prevent rusting. If you have access to compressed air, use it to speed up the drying process, and to blow out all the oil holes and galleries (photo). **Warning:** *Wear eye protection when using compressed air!*

5   If the castings are not very dirty, you can do an adequate cleaning job with hot soapy water (as hot as you can stand!), and a stiff brush. Take plenty of time, and do a thorough job. Regardless of the cleaning method used, be sure to clean all oil holes and galleries very thoroughly, and to dry all components well; protect the liners as described above to prevent rusting.

6   All threaded holes must be clean, to ensure accurate torque readings during reassembly. To clean all threads, run the proper-size tap into each of the holes to remove rust, corrosion, thread sealant or sludge, and to restore damaged threads. If possible, use compressed air to clear the holes of debris produced by this operation; a good alternative is to inject aerosol-applied water-dispersant lubricant into each hole, using the long spout usually supplied. **Warning:** *Wear eye protection when cleaning out these holes in this way!*

7   Fit new sealing washers to the oil gallery plugs, then refit them to the cylinder block and tighten them to the specified torque setting.

8   If the engine is not going to be reassembled right away, cover it with a large plastic bag to keep it clean; protect the liners as described above to prevent rusting.

24.5 Checking crankshaft endfloat using feeler blades

24.7 Undo the retaining screws and remove the flywheel-end oil seal housing

24.8 Main bearing caps are numbered for identification purposes

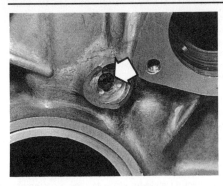

25.4 Compressed air should be used to clean all cylinder block oilways (tlming chain oil jet shown – arrowed)

25.20 Fit a sealing washer of the required thickness to the base of the liner ...

25.21 ... and install the liner in the block

25.22A Using a straight-edge and feeler blade to check liner protrusion

25.22B Once liner protrusions are within specified limits, clamp all the liners in position

Inspection

9   Visually check the castings for cracks and corrosion. Look for stripped threads in the threaded holes. If there has been any history of internal water leakage, it may be worthwhile having an engine overhaul specialist check the cylinder block/crankcase with special equipment. If defects are found have them repaired, if possible, or renew the assembly.

10   Remove the liners as described in paragraph 19, and check the bore of each liner for scuffing and scoring. The liners are grouped into three size classes to allow for manufacturing tolerances; the size group is stamped on the side of the each liner.

11   Measure the diameter of each cylinder liner just below the wear ridge at the top of the bore, halfway down the bore, and just up from the base of the bore. Take measurements both parallel to the crankshaft axis and at right-angles to it.

12   Compare the results with the Specifications for the relevant class of liner given at the beginning of this Chapter; if any measurement exceeds the tolerances specified, the liner must be renewed.

13   To measure the piston-to-bore clearance, either measure the bore and piston skirt as described in Section 26 and subtract the skirt diameter from the bore measurement, or insert each piston into the original bore, select a feeler gauge blade, and slip it into the bore along with the piston. The piston must be aligned exactly in its normal attitude, and the feeler gauge blade must be between the piston and bore on one of the thrust faces, just up from the bottom of the bore.

14   If the clearance is excessive a new piston will be required. If the piston binds at the lower end of the bore and is loose towards the top, the bore is tapered. If tight spots are encountered as the piston/feeler gauge blade is rotated in the bore, the bore is out-of-round.

15   Repeat this procedure for the remaining pistons and cylinder liners.

16   If the cylinder liner walls are badly scuffed or scored, or if they are excessively-worn, out-of-round or tapered, obtain new cylinder liners; new pistons will also be required. Skoda state that all the pistons and liners installed in the engine must be of the same size class. The liner size class is stamped on the outer surface of the liner, and the piston size class is stamped on the piston crown (see Section 26).

17   If the bores are in reasonably good condition and not worn to the specified limits, and if the piston-to-bore clearances can be maintained properly, then it may only be necessary to renew the piston rings.

18   If this is the case, the bores should be honed to allow the new rings to bed in correctly and provide the best possible seal. The conventional type of hone has spring-loaded stones, and is used with a power drill. You will also need some paraffin or honing oil, and rags. The hone should be moved up and down the bore to produce a crosshatch pattern, and plenty of honing oil should be used. Ideally, the crosshatch lines should intersect at approximately a 60° angle. Do not take off more material than is necessary to produce the required finish. If new pistons are being fitted, the piston manufacturers may specify a finish with a different angle, so their instructions should be followed. Do not withdraw the hone from the bore while it is still being turned – stop it first. After honing a bore, wipe out all traces of the honing oil. If equipment of this type is not available, or if you are not sure whether you are competent to undertake the task yourself, an engine overhaul specialist will carry out the work at moderate cost.

19   To remove the liners, invert the cylinder block/crankcase and support it on blocks of wood, then use a hard wood drift to tap out each liner from the crankshaft side. When all the liners are released, tip the cylinder block/crankcase on its side, and remove each liner from the cylinder head side. Remove the sealing washer from the base of the liner, and measure its thickness. The washer is available in various sizes, and is used to adjust the cylinder liner protrusion (see paragraph 22); obtain a new washer of the relevant thickness for each liner to use on refitting. If the liners are to be re-used, mark each one by sticking masking tape on its right-hand (timing chain) face and writing the cylinder number on the tape.

20   To install the liners, thoroughly clean the liner mating surfaces in the cylinder block/crankcase, and use fine abrasive paper to polish away any burrs or sharp edges which might damage the liner sealing washer. Clean the liners and wipe dry, then fit a new sealing washer of the required thickness to the base of each liner (photo). Apply a thin coat of engine oil to the bore.

21   If the original liners are being refitted, use the marks made on

removal to ensure that each is refitted the same way round into its original bore. Insert each liner into the cylinder block/crankcase, taking great care not to displace the washer, and press it home as far as possible by hand (photo). Using a hammer and a block of wood, tap each liner lightly but fully onto its locating shoulder.

22   With all four liners installed, using a dial gauge or a straight-edge and feeler blade, check that the protrusion of each liner above the upper surface of the cylinder block is within the limits given in the Specifications, and that the maximum difference between any two liners is not exceeded. If this is not the case, it will be necessary to remove the appropriate liner and to obtain another sealing washer of the required thickness. Washers are available in three thicknesses; 0.10 mm, 0.12 mm and 0.14 mm. Fit the necessary washer to the liner, then install the liner and recheck the protrusion. Repeat as necessary until all liner protrusions are within the specified limits and the maximum difference between any two is not exceeded, then securely clamp the liners in position (photos).

26 Piston/connecting rod assembly – dismantling, inspection and reassembly

Dismantling

1   Using a small flat-bladed screwdriver, carefully prise both the circlips from the gudgeon pin bore and discard them; new circlips must be used on reassembly (photo). Prior to removing the piston, note the position of the piston arrow and connecting rod oilway (see paragraph 11).

2   Push the gudgeon pin out of the piston, then separate the piston from the connecting rod. If the gudgeon pin is a tight fit in the piston, removal can be eased by gently warming the piston; the heat will expand the piston sufficiently to release its grip on the pin. The pin can then be tapped out of position, using a hammer and suitable drift, ensuring that the piston is securely supported.

Inspection

3   Examine the pistons for ovality, scoring and scratches, and for wear of the piston ring grooves. Use a micrometer to measure the piston diameter at a point 8 mm up from the base of the skirt and at right-angles to the gudgeon pin axis. Check the piston-to-bore clearance as described in Section 25 (photo).

4   If the piston shows visible signs of wear, or has worn beyond the specified tolerance for its size class, it must be renewed. As mentioned in Section 25, all the cylinder liners and pistons fitted to one engine must be of the same size class. The piston size class is stamped on the piston crown (see Fig. 2.11) and must be stated when ordering new pistons.

5   If new rings are to be fitted to the original pistons, expand the old rings over the top of the pistons. The use of two or three old feeler gauge blades will be helpful in preventing the rings dropping into empty grooves (photo).

6   When the original piston rings have been removed, ensure that the ring grooves in the piston are free of carbon by cleaning them using an old ring. Break the ring in half to do this. Protect your fingers: the edges of the ring may be sharp.

7   Check the ring-to-groove clearance by inserting each ring from the outside together with a feeler gauge blade between the ring's top surface and the piston land. Check the ring end gaps by inserting each ring into the cylinder bore and pushing it in with the piston crown to ensure that it is square in the bore, approximately 15 mm from the top; use feeler gauges to measure the gap (photos). Desired values are given in the Specifications.

8   Inspect the connecting rods for signs of damage, and check that they are not visibly bent. If any connecting rod shows any sign of damage or is not perfectly straight, it must be renewed. The connecting rods are grouped into two weight groups to allow for manufacturing tolerances. The weight group of each assembly is indicated by a dot of paint on the big-end bearing cap; lighter rods are marked with a dot of yellow paint and the heavier rods are marked with a dot of blue paint. Skoda state that all four connecting rods must be of the same weight group, therefore it will be necessary to state the required weight group when ordering new connecting rods. If the weight group markings are no longer visible, take the original connecting rod along to your Skoda dealer, who will be able to identify its weight group by weighing it.

9   Inspect the gudgeon pin and connecting rod small-end bush for signs of wear and scuffing. Insert the pin into the small-end bush, and check that there is no detectable clearance between them. If the necessary measuring equipment is available, the condition of the connecting rod small-end bush and gudgeon pin can be obtained by direct measurement; subtract the pin outer diameter from the bush internal diameter to calculate the pin-to-bore clearance (photo). If either component is visibly worn or any of the measurements exceeds the tolerances given in the Specifications, then both the gudgeon pin and small-end bush should be renewed as a pair. Small-end bush renewal should be entrusted to a Skoda dealer who will have the necessary tooling required for the task.

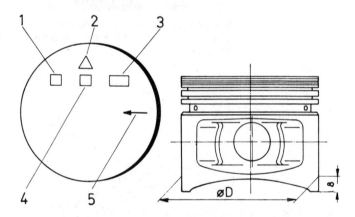

Fig. 2.11 Piston crown markings and diameter measuring point (Sec 26)

1   Manufacturer's number
2   Manufacturer's mark
3   Piston size class (diameter)

4   Production date
5   Arrow (points towards the front of cylinder block)

26.1 Use a small flat-bladed screwdriver to prise out piston circlips

26.3 Measuring piston diameter

26.5 Removing piston rings using feeler gauge blades

26.7A Measuring piston ring-to-groove clearance

26.7B Measuring piston ring end gap

26.9 Measuring gudgeon pin diameter

26.12 Align the gudgeon pin with the connecting rod small-end bore, then press the pin in ...

26.13 ... and secure it in position with second circlip. Note arrow (arrowed) cast near gudgeon pin bore

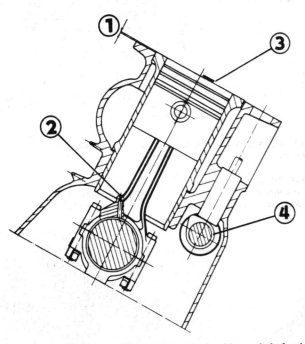

Fig. 2.12 Sectional view of the cylinder block with crankshaft, piston and connecting rod and camshaft installed (Sec 26)

1 Liner projection above cylinder block gasket face
2 Connecting rod oilway
3 Arrow on piston crown (pointing towards front of cylinder block)
4 Camshaft

Reassembly

10   Fit a new circlip to one of the grooves in the piston gudgeon pin bore. Lubricate the gudgeon pin bore and the connecting rod small end with clean engine oil, and press the gudgeon pin into opposite end of the piston.

11   Offer up the connecting rod to the piston, ensuring that the arrow on the piston (either on the piston crown or next to the gudgeon pin bore) is pointing away from the oilway on the connecting rod, ie so that when the assembly is installed in the engine, the arrow is pointing towards the front (oil filter side) of the cylinder block and the connecting rod oilway is facing the rear (Fig. 2.12).

12   With the piston and connecting rod positioned as described above, align the small-end bore with the gudgeon pin and press the pin fully into the piston until it abuts the circlip (photo). If the pin is a tight fit, gently warm the piston to aid installation. The gudgeon pin can then be gently tapped into position, using a hammer and suitable drift, ensuring that the piston is securely supported.

13   Check that the connecting rod is free to pivot smoothly on the gudgeon pin then secure the pin in position with the second new circlip, ensuring the circlip is correctly located in its groove (photo).

14   Fit the piston rings as described in Section 30.

27 Crankshaft – inspection

1   Clean the crankshaft and dry it with compressed air, if available. **Warning:** *Wear eye protection when using compressed air!* Be sure to clean the oil holes with a pipe cleaner or similar probe.

2   Check the main and crankpin (big-end) bearing journals for uneven wear, scoring, pitting and cracking.

3   Rub a penny across each journal several times. If a journal picks up

27.3 Using a penny to check condition of a crankshaft journal

27.5 Measuring the diameter of a crankshaft journal

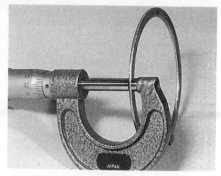

27.9 Measuring crankshaft thrustwasher thickness

copper from the penny, it is too rough (photo). (Note that from 1992, UK 'copper' coins are in fact made of ferrous metal.)

4   Remove any burrs from the crankshaft oil holes with a stone, file or scraper.

5   Using a micrometer, measure the diameter of the main bearing and crankpin (big-end) journals and compare the results with the Specifications at the beginning of this Chapter; the journal measurements can then be used to determine whether the crankshaft is standard or has been reground. Check carefully that each journal's diameter is within the tolerances of the relevant size group. If any diameter measured is incorrect for the group indicated, re-check the measurement carefully (photo).

6   By measuring the diameter at a number of points around each journal's circumference, you will be able to determine whether or not the journal is out-of-round. Take the measurement at each end of the journal (near the webs) to determine if the journal is tapered.

7   If the crankshaft journals are damaged, tapered, out-of-round or worn beyond the tolerances specified at the start of this Chapter, the crankshaft must be ground down to the next specified size and the appropriate set of oversize bearing shells fitted. Skoda manufacture three different oversizes of main bearing shells, big-end bearing shells and thrustwashers. This task must be entrusted to a Skoda dealer or a suitably-equipped engine overhaul specialist.

8   Check the oil seal journals at each end of the crankshaft for wear and damage. If either seal has worn a deep groove in its journal, consult an engine overhaul specialist who will be able to advise whether a repair is possible or whether a new crankshaft is necessary.

9   Using a micrometer, measure the crankshaft thrustwasher thickness, and compare the readings obtained with the measurements given in the Specifications (photo). If either of the thrustwashers are worn beyond the specified tolerances for their relevant size group, renew both washers as a pair. Note that if the crankshaft has been reground then one of the thrustwashers will be thicker than the other. Ensure that the thicker of the thrustwashers is always installed as the inner thrustwasher (ie next to the crankshaft web).

28   Main and big-end bearings – inspection

1   Even though the main and big-end bearings should be renewed during the engine overhaul, the old bearings should be retained for close examination, as they may reveal valuable information about the condition of the engine. The bearing shells are available in four different thicknesses (see Sections 31 and 32).

2   Bearing failure occurs because of lack of lubrication, the presence of dirt or other foreign particles, overloading the engine, and corrosion. Regardless of the cause of bearing failure, it must be corrected before the engine is reassembled to prevent it from happening again.

3   When examining the bearing shells, remove them from the cylinder block/crankcase, the main bearing caps, the connecting rods and the connecting rod big-end bearing caps and lay them out on a clean surface in the same general position as their location in the engine. This will enable you to match any bearing problems with the corresponding crankshaft journal. **Do not** touch any shell's bearing surface with your fingers while checking it, or the delicate surface may be scratched.

4   Dirt and other foreign particles get into the engine in a variety of ways. It may be left in the engine during assembly, or it may pass

through filters or the crankcase ventilation system. It may get into the oil and from there into the bearings. Metal chips (from machining operations and from normal engine wear) are often present. Abrasives are sometimes left in engine components after reconditioning, especially when parts are not thoroughly cleaned using the proper cleaning methods. Whatever the source, these foreign objects often end up embedded in the soft bearing material and are easily recognized. Large particles will not embed in the bearing, and will score or gouge the bearing and journal. The best prevention for this cause of bearing failure is to clean all parts thoroughly and keep everything spotlessly-clean during engine assembly. Frequent and regular engine oil and filter changes are also recommended.

5   Lack of lubrication (or lubrication breakdown) has a number of interrelated causes. Excessive heat (which thins the oil), overloading (which squeezes the oil from the bearing face) and oil leakage (from excessive bearing clearances, worn oil pump or high engine speeds) all contribute to lubrication breakdown. Blocked oil passages, which usually are the result of misaligned oil holes in a bearing shell, will also oil starve a bearing and destroy it. When lack of lubrication is the cause of bearing failure, the bearing material is wiped or extruded from the steel backing of the bearing. Temperatures may increase to the point where the steel backing turns blue from overheating.

6   Driving habits can have a definite effect on bearing life. Full-throttle, low-speed operation (labouring the engine) puts very high loads on bearings, squeezing out the oil film. These loads cause the bearings to flex, which produces fine cracks in the bearing face (fatigue failure). Eventually the bearing material will loosen in pieces and tear away from the steel backing.

7   Short-distance driving leads to corrosion of bearings because insufficient engine heat is produced to drive off the condensed water and corrosive gases. These products collect in the engine oil, forming acid and sludge. As the oil is carried to the engine bearings, the acid attacks and corrodes the bearing material.

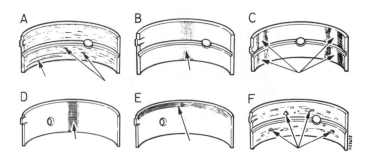

Fig. 2.13 Typical bearing shell failures (Sec 28)

A   Scratched by dirt; dirt embedded into bearing material
B   Lack of oil; overlay wiped out
C   Improper seating; bright (polished) sections
D   Tapered journal; overlay gone from entire surface
E   Radius ride
F   Fatigue failure; craters or pockets

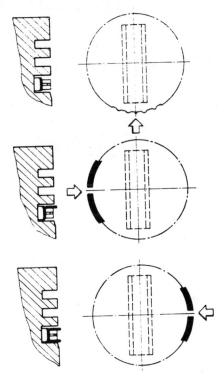

Fig. 2.14 Piston oil control ring fitting sequence and end gap positions (Sec 30)

8   Incorrect bearing installation during engine assembly will lead to bearing failure as well. Tight fitting bearings leave insufficient bearing running clearance and will result in oil starvation. Dirt or foreign particles trapped behind a bearing shell result in high spots on the bearing which lead to failure.

9   **Do not** touch any shell's bearing surface with your fingers during reassembly; there is a risk of scratching the delicate surface or of depositing particles of dirt on it.

29 Engine overhaul – reassembly sequence

1   Before reassembly begins ensure that all new parts have been obtained and that all necessary tools are available. Read through the entire procedure to familiarise yourself with the work involved, and to ensure that all items necessary for reassembly of the engine are at hand. In addition to all normal tools and materials, a thread-locking compound will be needed. A tube of liquid sealant will also be required for the joint faces that are fitted without gaskets.

2   In order to save time and avoid problems, engine reassembly can be carried out in the following order.

   (a) Crankshaft (Section 31).
   (b) Piston/connecting rod assemblies (Section 32).
   (c) Cylinder head (Section 6).
   (d) Camshaft and followers (Section 22).
   (e) Timing chain and sprockets (Section 7).
   (f) Flywheel (Section 12).
   (g) Sump (Section 10).
   (h) Engine external components.

3   At this stage, all engine components should be absolutely clean and dry, with all faults repaired and should be laid out (or in individual containers) on a completely clean work surface.

30 Piston rings – refitting

1   Before installing new piston rings, check the ring end gaps and the ring-to-groove clearance as described in Section 26.

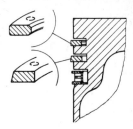

Fig. 2.15 Piston compression ring orientation (Sec 30)

2   When measuring new rings, lay out each piston set with a piston/connecting rod assembly and keep them together as a matched set from now on.

3   If the end gap of a new ring is found to be too large or too small, double-check to ensure that you have rings of the correct size class before proceeding. If the end gap is still too small, it must be opened up by careful filing of the ring ends using a fine file; if it is too large, this is not as serious unless the specified service limit is exceeded, in which case very careful checking is required of the dimensions of all components as well as of the new parts.

4   Once all rings have been checked, they can be installed; ensure that each ring is fitted only to its matched piston and bore.

5   Install the new rings by fitting them over the top of the piston, starting with the oil control ring spring. Position the control ring spring and side rail end gaps as shown in Fig. 2.14.

6   Once the oil control ring is correctly fitted, install the top and second compression rings. The second ring is easily distinguished from the top ring due to its tapered outer face. Note that both compression rings must be installed with the manufacturer's marking uppermost (see Fig. 2.15).

31 Crankshaft – refitting and main bearing running clearance check

Selection of bearing shells

1   To select the required main bearing shells it will first be necessary to determine the size group of the crankshaft main bearing journals; ie, are they standard or have they been reground? To do this, measure the main bearing journal diameter and compare the measurements obtained with the figures given in the Specifications at the start of this Chapter to find which size group the main bearing journals belong (see Section 27 for further information).

2   Alternatively, the size group of the crankshaft journals can be determined by measuring the thickness of the original bearing shells, using a suitable micrometer, then comparing then readings obtained with those given in the table below (photo). Note that great care must be taken not to mark the surface of the bearing shells. It is preferable to use the crankshaft journal measurements since the bearing shells are far more difficult to measure accurately and more likely to wear, therefore giving a false reading.

3   Once the main bearing journal size group is known, the correct thickness bearing shells can be selected from the table below.

Main bearing journal size group	Thickness of required bearing shell
Standard	2.495 mm
1st regrind	2.620 mm
2nd regrind	2.745 mm
3rd regrind	2.870 mm

Note that all new bearing shells have a manufacturing tolerance of + 0.000 to –0.010 mm.

Main bearing running clearance check

4   Clean the backs of the bearing shells and the bearing locations in both the cylinder block/crankcase and the main bearing caps.

5   Press the bearing shells into their locations, ensuring that the tab on each shell engages in the notch in the cylinder block/crankcase or main bearing cap location, and taking care not to touch any shell's bearing surface with your fingers. Note that it is not possible to interchange

31.2 Measuring bearing shell thickness

31.5A Lower main bearing shells are plain and have a central locating tab (arrowed) ...

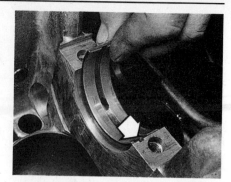

31.5B ... whilst upper main bearing shells are grooved and have an offset locating tab (arrowed)

31.11 Place the length of Plastigage on the journal to be measured, parallel to the crankshaft axis

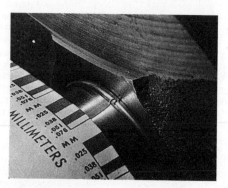

31.14 Using the scale on the envelope provided to check (at its widest point) the width of the crushed Plastigage and measure the bearing running clearance

31.20A Fit the inner thrustwasher to the crankshaft, so that its oil grooves face the crankshaft web ...

31.20B ... then carefully lower the crankshaft into the cylinder block

31.21 Align the thrustwasher tab with the cut-out in the bearing cap when installing No 1 cap (arrows)

upper and lower main bearing shells, since their locating tabs are offset (photos).

6   If the original main bearing shells are being re-used, these must be refitted to their original locations in the cylinder block/crankcase and main bearing caps.

7   The main bearing running clearance should be checked if there is any doubt about the amount of crankshaft wear that has taken place, if the crankshaft has been reground and is to be refitted with non-genuine undersized bearing shells, or if non-genuine bearing shells are to be fitted. If the original or a newly-reground crankshaft and genuine Skoda bearings are to be installed, the shell selection procedure given above will produce the correct clearances and a further check will not be necessary. If the clearance is to be checked, it can be done in either of two ways.

8   One method (which will be difficult to achieve without a range of internal micrometers or internal/external expanding calipers) is to refit the main bearing caps to the cylinder block/crankcase, with bearing shells in place. With the bearing cap retaining bolts tightened to the specified torque, measure the internal diameter of each assembled pair

of bearing shells. If the diameter of each corresponding crankshaft journal is measured and then subtracted from the bearing internal diameter, the result will be the main bearing running clearance.

9   The second (and more accurate) method is to use an American product known as Plastigage. This consists of a fine thread of perfectly-round plastic which is compressed between the bearing shell and the journal. When the shell is removed, the plastic is deformed and can be measured with a special card gauge supplied with the kit. The running clearance is determined from this gauge. Plastigage is sometimes difficult to obtain, but enquiries at one of the larger specialist quality motor factors should produce the name of a stockist in your area. The procedure for using Plastigage is as follows.

10   With the main bearing upper shells in place, carefully lay the crankshaft in position. Do not use any lubricant; the crankshaft journals and bearing shells must be perfectly clean and dry.

11   Cut three lengths of the appropriate size Plastigage (they should be slightly shorter than the width of the main bearings) and place one length on each crankshaft journal axis (photo).

12   With the main bearing lower shells in position, refit the main

31.22 Tighten the main bearing cap bolts evenly and progressively to the specified torque setting

31.24 Fit a new seal to the flywheel end oil seal housing ...

31.25 ... then slide the housing over the crankshaft and onto its locating dowels (arrows)

bearing caps and tighten their retaining bolts to the specified torque setting. Take great care not to disturb the Plastigage or rotate the crankshaft at any time during this operation.

13   Once all bearing cap bolts have been tightened to the specified torque, carefully undo the bolts and remove the bearing caps, again taking great care not to disturb the Plastigage or rotate the crankshaft.

14   Compare the width of the crushed Plastigage on each journal with the scale printed on the Plastigage envelope to obtain the main bearing running clearance (photo).

15   If the clearance is not as specified, the bearing shells may be the wrong size (or excessively-worn if the original shells are being re-used). Before deciding that different size shells are needed, make sure that no dirt or oil was trapped between the bearing shells and the caps or cylinder block/crankcase when the clearance was measured. If the Plastigage was wider at one end than at the other, the journal may be tapered.

16   If the main bearing running clearance is excessive even with new bearing shells of the correct size fitted, it will be necessary to have the crankshaft ground down to the next specified size and to fit oversize main bearing shells (see Section 27).

17   If all is well, carefully scrape away all traces of the Plastigage material from the crankshaft and bearing shells, using a fingernail or other object which is unlikely to score the shells.

Final refitting

18   Carefully lift the crankshaft out of the cylinder block once more.

19   Place the bearing shells in their locations as described in paragraphs 4 to 6 above. If new shells are being fitted, ensure that all traces of the protective grease are cleaned off using paraffin. Wipe dry the shells and bearing journals with a lint-free cloth. Liberally lubricate each bearing shell in the cylinder block/crankcase.

20   Slide the inner thrustwasher onto the right-hand end of the crankshaft, ensuring its lubrication grooves are facing towards the crankshaft web. Carefully lower the crankshaft into position in the block, then lubricate the bearing shells and crankshaft journals with clean engine oil. Position the thrustwasher locating tab so that it is pointing directly upwards; this will ensure that it aligns with the cut-out in the bearing cap when the cap is installed (photos).

21   Refit the main bearing caps using the marks made or noted on removal to ensure that they are refitted in their original positions. Align the thrustwasher tab with the cut-out in the right-hand bearing cap, and press the thrustwasher into its recess (photo).

22   Install the main bearing cap bolts, and tighten them evenly and progressively to the specified torque setting (photo).

23   Check that the crankshaft is free to turn, then check the endfloat as described in Section 24. Note that great care must be taken to ensure that the inner and outer thrustwasher locating tabs are properly seated in their grooves on the main bearing cap before the crankshaft pulley bolt is tightened. If the thrustwashers are not properly seated, the crankshaft will lock up as the bolt is tightened, and the thrustwashers will be damaged.

24   Remove all traces of gasket or sealant from the flywheel end oil seal housing and cylinder block mating surfaces. Carefully lever the old seal out of the housing, and press a new seal into position so that it seats evenly on the housing shoulder. If necessary, a soft-faced mallet can be used to tap the seal gently into place (photo). Note that the oil seal sealing lip should face inwards.

25   If an oil seal housing gasket was noted on removal, fit a new gasket over the locating dowels on the cylinder block. If no gasket was noted on removal, apply a thin film of gasket sealant to the oil seal housing mating surface. Ease the oil seal onto the crankshaft end, taking care not to damage its sealing lip. Slide the housing into position on the cylinder block, so that it engages with its locating dowels (photo). Refit the housing retaining screws, and tighten them securely. If a gasket has been fitted, use a sharp knife to trim off the ends of the gasket which protrude beyond the cylinder block sump mating face.

26   Install the connecting rod assemblies as described in Section 32.

32 Piston/connecting rod assembly – refitting and big-end bearing running clearance check

Selection of bearing shells

1   To select the required big-end bearing shells, it will first be necessary to determine the size group of the crankpin (big-end) journals; ie, are they standard or have they been reground? To do this, measure the crankpin journal diameter and compare the measurements obtained with the figures given in the Specifications at the start of this Chapter to find to which size group the journals belong (see Section 27 for further information).

2   Alternatively, the size group of the crankpins can be determined by measuring the thickness of the original bearing shells, using a suitable micrometer, then comparing the readings obtained with those given in the table below. Note that great care must be taken not to mark the surface of the bearing shells. It is preferable to use the crankpin journal measurements since the bearing shells are far more difficult to measure accurately and more likely to wear, therefore giving a false reading.

3   Once the crankpin journal size group is known, the correct thickness bearing shells can be selected from the table below.

Crankpin journal size group	Thickness of required bearing shell
Standard	1.490 mm
1st regrind	1.615 mm
2nd regrind	1.740 mm
3rd regrind	1.865 mm

Note that all new bearing shells have a manufacturing tolerance of + 0.000 to –0.007 mm.

Big-end bearing running clearance check

4   Refer to Section 31, paragraph 7. If the clearance is to be checked, it can be done in either of two ways.

5   One method is to refit the big-end bearing cap to the connecting rod, with bearing shells in place. With the cap retaining nuts tightened to the specified torque, use an internal micrometer or vernier caliper to measure the internal diameter of each assembled pair of bearing shells. If the diameter of each corresponding crankpin journal is measured and then subtracted from the bearing internal diameter, the result will be the big-end bearing running clearance.

6   The second method is to use Plastigage as described in Section 31,

paragraphs 9 to 17. Place a strand of Plastigage on each (cleaned) crankpin journal and refit the (clean) piston/connecting rod assemblies, shells and big-end bearing caps, tightening the nuts to the specified torque wrench settings. Take care not to disturb the Plastigage or rotate the connecting rod at any time during this operation. Dismantle the assemblies without rotating the crankshaft, and use the scale printed on the Plastigage envelope to obtain the big-end bearing running clearance. On completion of the measurement, carefully scrape off all traces of Plastigage from the journal and shells, using a fingernail or other object which will not score the components.

Final refitting

7   Note that the following procedure assumes that the cylinder liners have been refitted to the cylinder block/crankcase and clamped in position as described in Section 25, and that the crankshaft and main bearing caps are in place. It is of course possible to refit the piston/connecting rod assemblies before installing the crankshaft (see Section 31).

8   Clean the backs of the bearing shells and the bearing recesses in both the connecting rod and the big-end bearing cap. If new shells are being fitted, ensure that all traces of the protective grease are cleaned off using paraffin. Wipe dry the shells and connecting rods with a lint-free cloth.

9   Press the bearing shells into their locations, ensuring that the tab on each shell engages in the notch in the connecting rod or big-end bearing cap, and taking care not to touch any shell's bearing surface with your fingers. Note that if the original bearing shells are to be re-used they must be installed in their original fitted positions.

10   Lubricate the cylinder bores, the pistons and piston rings, then lay out each piston/connecting rod assembly in its respective position.

11   Starting with assembly No 1, make sure that the piston rings are still spaced as described in Section 30, then clamp them in position with a piston ring compressor.

12   Insert the piston/connecting rod assembly into the top of liner No 1, ensuring that the arrow on the piston crown or near the gudgeon pin bore (as applicable) points towards the front (fuel pump side) of the engine; note that the oilway on the connecting rod should face towards the rear of the engine. Using a block of wood or a hammer handle against the piston crown, tap the assembly into the liner until the piston crown is flush with the top of the liner (photo).

13   Check that the bearing shell is still correctly installed, then liberally lubricate the crankpin and both bearing shells. Taking great care not to mark the liner bores, pull the piston/connecting rod assembly down the bore and onto the crankpin. Refit the big-end bearing cap and shell, noting that the cap and connecting rod faces with the stamped marks must match. Refit the bearing cap nuts, noting that the collar of the nut must face the bearing cap, and tighten them evenly and progressively to the specified torque setting (photos). After the nuts are tightened, check that the crankshaft is free to rotate before moving onto the next assembly.

14   Repeat the procedure for the remaining three piston/connecting rod assemblies.

15   With all piston/connecting rod assemblies installed, check that the crankshaft is free to rotate before proceeding further. Some stiffness is to be expected with new components, but there must be no tight spots or binding.

32.12 Using a piston ring compressor to clamp piston rings while piston/connecting rod assembly is fitted to cylinder liner

33   Engine – initial start-up after overhaul

1   With the engine refitted in the vehicle, double-check the engine oil and coolant levels. Make a final check that everything has been reconnected, and that there are no tools or rags left in the engine compartment.

2   With the spark plugs removed and the ignition system disabled by earthing the ignition coil HT lead with a jumper lead, turn the engine on the starter until the oil pressure warning light goes out.

3   Refit the spark plugs and connect all the spark plug (HT) leads, referring to Chapter 1 for further information.

4   Start the engine, noting that this may take a little longer than usual due to the fuel system components being empty. This can be avoided by manually filling the carburettor float chamber using the fuel pump priming lever.

5   While the engine is idling, check for fuel, water and oil leaks. Don't be alarmed if there are some odd smells and smoke from parts getting hot and burning off oil deposits.

6   Keep the engine idling until hot water is felt circulating through the top hose, check the ignition timing and idle speed and mixture, then switch it off.

7   After a few minutes, recheck the oil and coolant levels as described in Chapter 1, and top-up as necessary.

8   If they were tightened as described, there is no need to re-tighten the cylinder head bolts once the engine has first run after reassembly.

9   If new pistons, rings or crankshaft bearings have been fitted, the engine must be run-in for the first 500 miles (800 km). Do not operate the engine at full-throttle or allow it to labour in any gear during this period. It is recommended that the oil and filter be changed at the end of this period.

32.13A Refit the bearing cap, aligning the stamped marks (arrow) ...

32.13B ... then refit the bearing cap nuts, noting that the collar of the nut must abut the cap

32.13C Tighten the bearing cap nuts evenly and progressively to the specified torque setting

Chapter 3
Cooling, heating and ventilation systems

Contents

Antifreeze mixture ....See Chapter 1
Coolant draining ....See Chapter 1
Coolant filling ....See Chapter 1
Coolant level check ....See Chapter 1
Cooling system electrical switches – testing, removal and refitting   6
Cooling system hoses – renewal 2
General cooling system checks ....See Chapter 1
General information 1
Heater control valve – removal and refitting 9
Heater controls – removal and refitting................................ 13
Heater/fresh air blower motor – removal and refitting....................... 11

Heater/fresh air blower control switch – removal and refitting......... 12
Heater matrix – removal and refitting................................. 8
Heater unit – removal and refitting.................................. 10
Radiator, expansion tank and filler cap – removal, inspection and
refitting 3
Radiator cooling fan – testing, removal and refitting................. 5
System flushing...See Chapter 1
Thermostat – removal, testing and refitting 4
Water pump – removal and refitting.................................. 7
Water pump drivebelt check, adjustment and renewal.....See Chapter 1

Specifications

System type	Pressurised, with front-mounted radiator and electric cooling fan

Thermostat
Type	Wax
Starts to open at	86° to 90°C
Fully-open at	103°C
Lift height	8 mm

Expansion tank cap
Release pressure	0.9 to 1.1 bars

Radiator cooling fan
Cut-in temperature	95° to 99°C
Cut-out temperature	88°C

Torque wrench settings
	Nm	lbf ft
Thermostat housing cover bolts	7 to 9	5 to 7
Water pump-to-cylinder block nuts	16 to 24	12 to 18
Cylinder block drain plug	15 to 25	11 to 18

1 General information

Cooling system

1 The cooling system is of the pressurised, pump-assisted thermo-syphon type. It consists of the front-mounted radiator (which is of aluminium alloy, with moulded plastic side tanks), a translucent expansion tank mounted on the left-hand inner wing, a thermostatically-controlled electric cooling fan mounted on the rear of the radiator, a thermostat and a centrifugal water pump, as well as the connecting pipes and hoses. A coolant drain plug is located in the bottom pipe (photos). There is another drain plug in the cylinder block, just forward of the clutch housing on the fuel pump side of the crankcase.

2 The location of the system's components and the direction of coolant flow are shown in Fig. 3.1.

Warning: *Do not attempt to remove the expansion tank filler cap or disturb any part of the cooling system while it is hot, as there is a very great risk of scalding. If the expansion tank filler cap must be removed before the engine and radiator have fully cooled down (though not recommended) the pressure in the cooling system must first be released. Cover the cap with a thick layer of cloth, to avoid scalding, and slowly unscrew the filler cap until a hissing sound can be heard. When the pressure is fully released, the hissing will stop. The filler cap can then be further unscrewed until it is fully released and can be removed; if more hissing sounds are heard, wait until they have stopped before unscrewing the cap completely. At all times, keep well away from the filler opening.*

Warning: *Do not allow antifreeze to come in contact with your skin or*

Fig. 3.1 Cooling system layout, direction of flow (arrows) and main component locations (Sec 1)

1   Radiator
2   Cooling fan thermo-switch
3   Hose
4   Water pump
5   Drain plug
6 to 10 Hoses
11 Heater control valve
12 Engine
13 Cooling fan
14 Hose
15 Expansion tank
16 Expansion tank/coolant filler cap
17 Choke
18 Carburettor
19 Engine idle air vent line
20 Brake vacuum servo hose
21 Hose
22 Temperature switch
23 Drain plug
24 Thermostat
25 Expansion tank hose
26 Heater fan
27 Heater

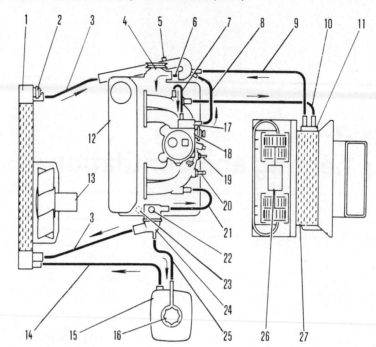

painted surfaces of the vehicle. Rinse off spills immediately with plenty of water. Never leave antifreeze lying around in an open container or in a puddle in the driveway or on the garage floor. Children and pets are attracted by its sweet smell, but antifreeze is fatal if ingested.
Warning: If the engine is hot, the radiator cooling fan may start rotating, so be careful to keep hands, hair and loose clothing well clear when working in the engine compartment.

Heating and ventilation systems

3   The heater has a three-speed blower located on the engine side of the bulkhead. Face level vents are fitted in the centre and at each end of the facia, and air ducts are located in the front footwells. Illuminated sliding controls for air temperature and distribution are housed (with the heater blower switch) in the centre of the facia, and operate flap valves to deflect the air flowing through the heater. Cold air enters through the grille at the rear of the bonnet, is boosted when required by the blower's radial fan and flows through the ducts, according to the control setting;

stale air is exhausted through rear-mounted ducts. If warm air is required, the cold air is passed over the heater matrix which is heated by the engine's coolant.

2   Cooling system hoses – renewal

Note: Refer to the warnings given in Section 1 of this Chapter before starting work.

1   If the checks described in Chapter 1 reveal a faulty hose, it must be renewed as follows. First drain the cooling system (Chapter 1); if the antifreeze is not due for renewal, the drained coolant may be re-used if collected in a clean container. Although the hoses can be removed with relative ease when new or hot, **do not** attempt to disconnect any part of the system when it is still hot (see Section 1).
2   To disconnect any hose, use a screwdriver to slacken the clips, then

1.1A Cooling system expansion tank

1.1B Cooling system drain plug in the bottom pipe to the water pump

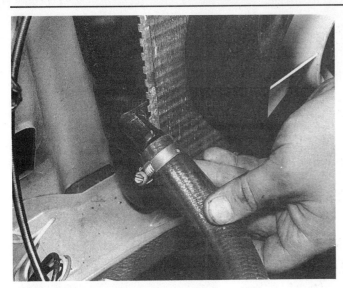

2.4 Coolant hose connection

move them along the hose clear of the outlet. Carefully work the hose off its outlets. If the hose clips are of the wire or 'sardine can' type, it is recommended that they be replaced with worm drive type hose clips on reassembly.

3   Note that the radiator hose outlets are fragile; do not use excessive force when attempting to remove the hoses. If a hose proves stubborn, try to release it by rotating it on its outlets before attempting to work it off. If all else fails, cut the hose with a sharp knife then slit it so that it can be peeled off in two pieces.

4   When refitting a hose, first slide the clips onto the hose, then work the hose onto its outlets (photo). If the hose is stiff, use soap as a lubricant or soften it by first soaking it in boiling water, but take care to avoid scalding.

5   Work each hose end fully onto its outlet, check that the hose is settled correctly and is properly routed, then slide each clip along the hose until it is behind the outlet flared end before tightening it securely.

6   Refill the system with coolant (Chapter 1).

7   Check carefully for leaks as soon as possible after disturbing any part of the cooling system.

3   Radiator, expansion tank and filler cap – removal, inspection and refitting

Note: *Refer to the warnings given in Section 1 of this Chapter before starting work.*

Removal

Note: *Minor leaks from the radiator can be cured without removing the radiator, using a product such as Holts Radweld.*

Radiator

1   Drain the cooling system (Chapter 1).
2   Undo the retaining nut, detach the cooling fan earth lead from the horn mounting stud (photo) and remove the horn.
3   Disconnect the coolant hoses from the radiator.
4   Disconnect the electric cooling fan thermostatic switch wires.
5   Undo the two radiator retaining bolts at the top (photo).
6   Pivot the radiator back at the top, lift it clear of its bottom mountings and withdraw the radiator complete with the cooling fan, taking care not to damage its matrix (photos).

Expansion tank and filler cap

7   Drain or syphon the coolant from the expansion tank, plug or clamp the connecting hose to the radiator, then undo the retaining nuts and remove the tank from the vehicle.

Inspection

Radiator

8   To allow full visual inspection of the radiator, detach the cooling fan from it as described in Section 5. If the radiator was removed because of clogging (causing overheating) then try reverse-flushing (Chapter 1) or, in severe cases, use a radiator cleanser strictly in accordance with its manufacturer's instructions; ensure that the cleanser is suitable for use in an aluminium alloy radiator.

9   Use a soft brush, an air line or garden hose to clear the radiator matrix of leaves, insects, etc.

3.2 Detaching the cooling fan earth lead

3.5 Undo the radiator retaining bolts

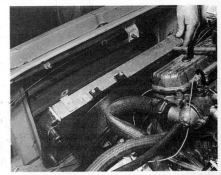

3.6A Pivot the top of the radiator to the rear ...

3.6B ... then lift it clear

3.12 Radiator mounting rubber

4.3 Thermostat housing showing the hose connections (1), one of the retaining bolts (2) and the coolant temperature sensor (3)

4.4A Unscrew the retaining bolts ...

4.4B ... and remove the cover and the thermostat

4.10A Thermostat directional arrow points up

4.10B Fit the thermostat into its housing ...

4.10C ... locate the new gasket and refit the cover

10   Minor leaks from the radiator can be cured using Holts Radweld. Major leaks or extensive damage should be repaired by a specialist, or the radiator should be renewed or exchanged for a reconditioned unit.

11   If the radiator is to be repaired or exchanged, detach first the thermostatic switch (Sec 6) and any remaining coolant hoses.

12   Check the condition of the mountings and renew them if necessary (photo).

Expansion tank and filler cap

13   Empty any remaining coolant from the tank, and flush it with fresh water to clean it. If the tank is leaking it must be renewed, but it is worth first attempting a repair using a proprietary sealant or suitable adhesive.

14   The expansion tank filler cap should be cleaned and checked whenever it is removed. Check that its sealing surfaces and threads are clean and undamaged, and that they mate correctly with those of the expansion tank.

15   The expansion tank filler cap's performance can be checked only by using a cap pressure-tester (cooling system tester) with a suitable adaptor. On applying pressure, the cap's pressure relief valve should hold until the specified pressure is reached, at which point the valve should open.

16   If there is any doubt about the cap's efficiency it must be renewed; ensure that the replacement is of exactly the correct type and rating.

Refitting

Radiator

17   Refitting is the reverse of the removal procedure, noting the following points.

(a)   *Ensure that the radiator is seated correctly, without strain on its mountings.*

(b)   *Position the hose clips carefully so that they do not foul any other component.*

(c)   *Refill the cooling system (Chapter 1).*

Expansion tank and filler cap

18   Refitting is the reverse of the removal procedure, noting the following points.

(a)   *Ensure that the hoses, especially that between the tank and the*

radiator, are correctly routed with no kinks or sharp bends, and are secured by the clips provided.

(b)   *Refill the cooling system (Chapter 1).*

4   Thermostat – removal, testing and refitting

Note: *Refer to the warnings given in Section 1 of this Chapter before starting work.*

Removal

1   Drain the cooling system (Chapter 1). If the antifreeze is not due for renewal, the drained coolant may be re-used if it is collected in a clean container.

2   The thermostat is located in a housing on the transmission end of the inlet manifold.

3   The hoses can be left attached to the thermostat housing cover, unless they (or the housing cover) are to be renewed, in which case loosen the retaining clips and detach the coolant hoses from the thermostat housing (photo).

4   Unscrew the housing cover bolts and withdraw the cover. If the cover does not readily separate from the housing, lever them apart, but take care not to damage the sealing faces as these are of aluminium alloy. Note its direction of fitting, and remove the thermostat (photos).

Testing

5   Inspect the thermostat to make sure that no riveted or soldered joints are broken or loose. Check also that the jiggle pin is in position and moves freely.

6   If on inspection the thermostat is in the open position at room temperature, it is faulty and must be renewed as a matter of course.

7   To test it fully, suspend the (closed) thermostat on a length of string in a container of cold water, with a thermometer beside it; ensure that neither touches the side of the container.

8   Heat the water and check the temperature at which the thermostat begins to open; compare this value with that specified. Continue to heat

5.4 Two of the cooling-fan-to radiator attachment bolts

5.5 Removing the cooling fan-to-mounting bracket retaining nuts

the water until the thermostat is fully open; the temperature at which this should happen is stamped into the unit. Remove the thermostat and measure the height of the fully-opened valve, then allow the thermostat to cool down and check that it closes fully. (If the fully-open temperature is above 100°C, it will not be possible to complete the test using water in an open pan.)

9   If the thermostat does not open and close as described, if it sticks in either position, or if it does not open at the specified temperature, it must be renewed.

Refitting

10   Refitting is the reverse of the removal procedure, noting the following points (photos).

(a) Clean the thermostat housing and housing cover mating surfaces thoroughly prior to refitting the thermostat.
(b) Ensure that the thermostat is correctly orientated when located in its housing with the arrow pointing up.
(c) Always fit a new cover gasket, lightly smeared with jointing compound.
(d) Tighten the thermostat cover bolts to the specified torque.
(e) Ensure the coolant hose clips are positioned so that they do not foul any other component, then tighten them securely.
(f) Refill the cooling system (Chapter 1).
(g) Check that there is no leakage from the thermostat housing on completion.

5   Radiator cooling fan – testing, removal and refitting

Testing

1   The cooling fan is supplied with current via the ignition switch and fusebox; the circuit being completed by the radiator-mounted thermostatic switch.
2   If the fan does not appear to work, run the engine until normal operating temperature is reached, then allow it to idle. If the fan does not cut in within a few minutes, switch off the ignition and disconnect the two wires from the thermostatic switch. Bridge these two wires with a length of spare wire, and switch on the ignition. If the fan now operates, the thermostatic switch is probably faulty, and must be tested further (Section 6). If the fan does not operate, the fault is either in the circuit (not forgetting the fuse), or the fan motor is faulty.

Removal

3   The cooling fan is removed together with the radiator as described in Section 3.

4   With the radiator removed, undo the four retaining bolts (two at the top, two at the bottom) and detach the cooling fan and mounting bracket unit (photo).
5   The fan can be detached from its mounting bracket by unscrewing the three retaining nuts (photo).

Refitting

6   Refit in the reverse order of removal.

6   Cooling system electrical switches – testing, removal and refitting

Note: Refer to the warnings given in Section 1 of this Chapter before starting work.

Testing

Radiator cooling fan thermo-switch

1   Refer to the previous Section for details of a quick test which should eliminate most faulty switches. If the switch is to be renewed, or tested thoroughly, then it must be removed.
2   To carry out a thorough test of the switch, use two spare wires to connect to it either a multimeter (set to the resistance function) or a battery and bulb test circuit. Suspend the switch in a pan of water which is being heated. Measure the temperature of the water with a thermometer. Do not let either the switch or the thermometer touch the pan itself.
3   The switch contacts should close (ie, the bulb should light or the meter should show continuity) when the water reaches the cut-in temperature specified. Stop heating the water and allow it to cool down; the switch contacts should open at the cut-out temperature specified.
4   If the switch's performance is significantly different from that specified, or if it does not work at all, it must be renewed.

Coolant temperature gauge sender unit

5   The coolant temperature gauge mounted in the instrument panel is fed with a stabilised voltage supply from the instrument panel feed, its earth being controlled by the sender unit.
6   The sender unit is screwed into the thermostat housing. It contains a thermistor, which is an element whose electrical resistance decreases at a predetermined rate as its temperature rises; thus when the coolant is cold, the sender's resistance is high, current flow through the gauge is reduced and the gauge needle points to the cold end of the scale. If the unit is faulty it must be renewed.
7   If the gauge develops a fault, check first the other instruments; if they do not work at all, check the instrument panel feed. If the fault is in the temperature gauge alone, check it as follows.

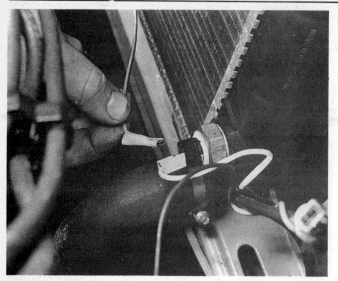

6.12A Disconnect the wires ...

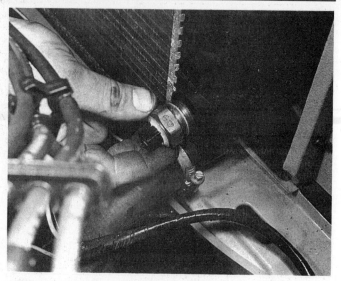

6.12B ... and unscrew the cooling fan thermostatic switch

8   If the gauge needle remains at the cold end of the scale, disconnect the sender unit wire and earth it to the cylinder head; if the needle then deflects when the ignition is switched on the sender unit is proven faulty and must be renewed. If the needle still does not move, remove the instrument panel (Chapter 12) and check the continuity of the wire between the gauge and the sender unit and the feed to the gauge unit. If continuity is shown, and the fault still exists, then the gauge is faulty and the gauge unit must be renewed.

9   If the gauge needle remains at the hot end of the scale, disconnect the sender unit wire; if the needle then returns to the cold end of the scale when the ignition is switched on, the sender unit is proven faulty and must be renewed. If the needle still does not move, check the remainder of the circuit as described above.

Removal

Radiator cooling fan thermostatic switch

10   When the engine and radiator are cold, drain the cooling system down to the level of the switch (Chapter 1). Alternatively, unscrew the expansion tank filler cap to release any remaining pressure and have ready a suitable plug that can be used temporarily to stop the escape of coolant while the switch is removed. If the latter method is used, take care not to damage the radiator, and do not use anything which will leave foreign matter inside the radiator.

11   Disconnect the battery negative lead.

12   Disconnect the wiring connectors from the switch, unscrew the switch and withdraw it from the radiator (photos).

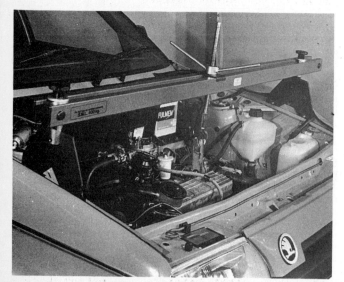

7.6 Engine support bar in position for removal of the water pump

Coolant temperature gauge sender unit

13   Prepare for removal as described in paragraph 10.

14   Disconnect the battery negative lead.

15   Disconnect the unit's wiring, and unscrew the unit from the thermostat housing.

Refitting

Radiator cooling fan thermostatic switch

16   On refitting, renew the sealing ring if it is worn or compressed. Carefully clean the switch seat in the radiator before pressing in the sealing ring and switch. Refit the locking ring and rotate it to tighten it securely. Reconnect the switch and battery, then refill the cooling system or check the coolant level, as necessary (Chapter 1).

Coolant temperature gauge sender unit

17   On refitting, apply a suitable sealant to the unit threads. Reconnect the unit and battery, then refill the cooling system or check the coolant level, as necessary (Chapter 1).

7   Water pump – removal and refitting

Note: *Refer to the warnings given in Section 1 of this Chapter before starting work.*

Removal

1   First drain the cooling system (Chapter 1). If the antifreeze is not due for renewal, the drained coolant may be re-used if it is collected in a clean container.

2   To provide improved access, remove the air cleaner assembly as described in Chapter 4.

3   Loosen the alternator clamping bolts and remove the drivebelt.

4   Loosen the retaining clips and detach the hoses from the water pump.

5   Check that the handbrake is firmly applied, then jack up the front of the vehicle and support it on axle stands.

6   The water pump is an integral part of the engine right-hand mounting, and its removal necessitates supporting the weight of the engine. This can be achieved by positioning a jack with interposed block of wood under the engine and raising it so that it takes the weight (rather than lifts) the engine from underneath. Alternatively, attach lifting eyes to the engine lifting bracket on the cylinder head, and fit a hoist or support bar to take the weight of the engine from above (photo).

7   From underneath the vehicle, undo the nut securing the engine/transmission rear connecting rod to the subframe bracket. Remove the bolt securing the rod to the engine bracket, and remove the connecting rod from underneath.

7.9 Undo the three right-hand mounting bolts

7.10 Water pump/right-hand engine mounting removal

7.12 Locating a new water pump gasket

8.3 Disconnecting the heater hoses

8.6A Prise free the plastic retainer ...

8.6B ... and withdraw the heater matrix

8 Loosen the right-hand mounting through-bolt, and remove the nut. To gain the required clearance for through-bolt removal, use a hammer and suitable punch to tap out the plug from the right-hand valance (see Chapter 2, Section 17); the through-bolt can then be withdrawn through the hole and out from under the wing.
9 Loosen the three bolts securing the right-hand mounting bracket to the body, and manoeuvre the bracket out of position (photo). It may be necessary to lower the engine a little to permit this, in which case, check that the exhaust mountings and other associated engine fittings are not stretched or damaged. Disconnect any items likely to be damaged as the engine is lowered.
10 Unscrew and remove the four water pump securing nuts. Lower the engine just enough to enable the water pump to be withdrawn from the mounting studs and removed from the car (photo).
11 Scrape clean the gasket faces, taking care not to damage the corresponding mating surfaces of the water pump and the engine. Note that the gasket must be renewed. If the connecting hoses are in poor condition they must be renewed, with their retaining clips.

Refitting

12 Refitting is a reversal of the removal procedure. Use a new gasket and smear the mating faces with a suitable sealant (photo).
13 Tighten the fastenings to their specified torque wrench settings. Refill the cooling system with the specified quantity of antifreeze, and check for any sign of leaks from the water pump joints. Detach and remove the engine support hoist.
14 Refit the drivebelt and adjust its tension as described in Chapter 1.
15 Refit the air cleaner as described in Chapter 4.

8 Heater matrix – removal and refitting

Note: *Refer to the warnings given in Section 1 of this Chapter before starting work.*

Removal

Note: *Minor leaks from the heater matrix could be cured without removing the matrix, using a product such as Holts Radweld.*

1 The heater matrix (radiator) can be removed from the heater, leaving the heater unit in position in the vehicle. First drain the cooling system (Chapter 1); if the antifreeze is not due for renewal, the drained coolant may be re-used if it is collected in a clean container.
2 Refer to Chapter 12 for details and remove the windscreen wiper motor.
3 Loosen the retaining clips and detach the coolant supply and return hoses from their connections to the matrix (on the right-hand side of the heater unit). Allow for a small amount of coolant spillage as the hoses are detached (photo).
4 Loosen the clamp screw and disconnect the heater control cable from the control valve lever on the right-hand side.
5 Unscrew the retaining nut and detach the earth lead from the heater-to-bulkhead mounting stud on the right-hand side.
6 Prise free and detach the plastic retainer, then carefully withdraw the matrix from the heater body (photos).

Refitting

7 Refit in the reverse order of removal. When reconnecting the control cable, ensure that it is fitted so that the control lever at the panel and the lever on the side of the heater unit are both set in the 'hot' position. In this position, the lever on the side of the heater will be fully forward.
8 Refill the cooling system on completion, and check for any sign of leaks at the heater hose connections.

9 Heater control valve – removal and refitting

Note: *Refer to the warnings given in Section 1 of this Chapter before starting work.*

Removal

1 Drain the cooling system (Chapter 1); if the antifreeze is not due for renewal, the drained coolant may be re-used if it is collected in a clean container.
2 Loosen the retaining clips and detach the coolant supply and return hoses from their connections to the control valve which is located in the end of the matrix (on the right-hand side of the heater unit). Allow for a small amount of coolant spillage as the hoses are detached.

Fig. 3.2 Heater unit (Sec 9)

1   Rubber seal
2   Blower motor
3   Housing
4   Bypass flap
5   Heater matrix
6   Heater case
7   Control flap
8   Packing
9   Plug
10 Bush
11 Bypass flap
12 Control flap
13 Blower control switch

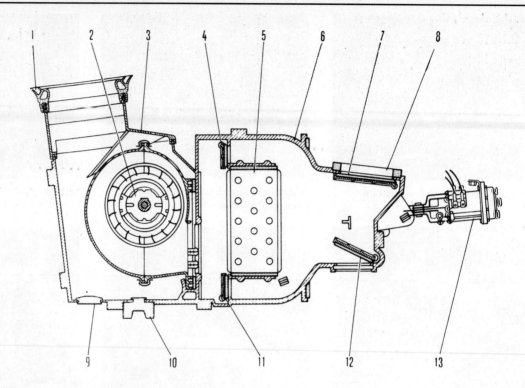

9.4 Control valve lever (1) and valve retaining screws (2)

3   Loosen the clamp screw and detach the control cable from the control valve lever.
4   Undo the four retaining screws and withdraw the control valve (photo).

Refitting

5   Refit in the reverse order of removal. Check the mating faces are clean, and fit a new seal ring. Ensure that the valve assembly is correctly orientated when fitted to the matrix, with the lever position as shown. Check that the lever/cable adjustment allows the valve to open and close fully.
6   Refill the cooling system on completion, and check for any sign of leaks at the heater hose connections.

10   Heater unit – removal and refitting

Note: Refer to the warnings given in Section 1 of this Chapter before starting work.

Removal

1   Disconnect and remove the battery (refer to Chapter 12 for details).
2   Drain the cooling system (Chapter 1); if the antifreeze is not due for renewal, the drained coolant may be re-used if it is collected in a clean container.
3   Disconnect the control cables from the control levers at the heater unit. For access to the cable attachments within the vehicle, it will be necessary to remove the central switch panel, the glovebox and the plate on the left-hand side (photos).
4   Working in the engine compartment, lift the air intake duct clear from the top of the heater unit (photo).
5   The heater/fresh air blower unit is now accessible, and can be lifted from its location in the heater unit housing (photo). As it is lifted clear, note their connections then detach the wires from their terminal connectors to the blower.
6   Fold back the carpet from the bulkhead at the front of the vehicle, to provide access to the lower heater duct connection just above the central tunnel. Carefully prise the duct free from its heater air outlet connection (photo).
7   Unscrew and remove the two heater retaining nuts on the engine side of the bulkhead. Check that all connections are detached from the heater unit, and carefully withdraw it from the bulkhead. As it is withdrawn, arrange for an assistant to disengage the heater unit from the upper air ducts within the vehicle.

Refitting

8   Refit in the reverse order of removal. Ensure that all connections are correctly and securely made.
9   Top up the cooling system on completion, and check for any sign of leaks at the heater hose connections.

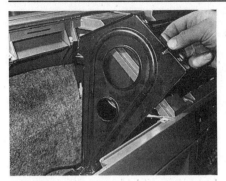

10.3A Remove the plate ...

10.3B ... for access to the heater/ventilation control cable attachment on the left-hand side

10.3C Heater/ventilation control cable attachment on the right-hand side

10.4 Removing the air intake duct from the heater unit

10.5 Heater/fresh air blower motor removal

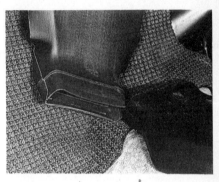

10.6 Detaching the lower air duct at the centre

11.4A Prise free the retaining clips ...

11.4B ... to release the heater blower housings

11.4C Prise free the centre clips to release the housing and heater blower motor

11.5A Dropper resistor attached to the heater unit

11.5B Dropper resistor retaining screws (arrowed)

12.4 Heater control switch retaining nut

11   Heater/fresh air blower motor – removal and refitting

Removal

1   Disconnect and remove the battery (refer to Chapter 12 for details).
2   Lift clear the air intake duct from the top of the heater unit.
3   The heater/fresh air blower is now accessible and can be lifted from its location in the heater unit housing. As it is lifted clear, note their connections and detach the wires from their terminal connectors to the blower.
4   Release the spring retaining clips, separate the housing and lift out the heater motor (photos).
5   A 'dropper' resistor, which is switched in series with the blower motor at low and intermediate speeds, is attached to the heater blower housing. If required, this can be removed by detaching the wire and undoing the two retaining screws (photos).

Refitting

6   Refitting is a reversal of the removal procedure. Check that the retaining clips are securely fitted, and on completion also check for satisfactory operation of the blower.

12   Heater/fresh air blower control switch – removal and refitting

Removal

1   Disconnect the battery earth lead.
2   Remove the heater/fresh air motor from its location in the heater unit, and disconnect the heater control wires. Refer to Section 11 for details.
3   Remove the central switch panel (directly above the heater controls). Refer to Chapter 12 for details.
4   Pull free the blower control knob from the switch, then undo the retaining nut and push the switch through the panel (photo).

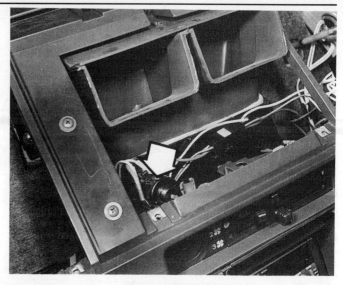

12.5 Heater control switch (arrowed) being removed

5   Detach the switch wires from the connector to the right of its location in the panel, then remove the switch from the vehicle, pulling the heater motor wires through the bulkhead as it is removed (photo).
6   If the reason for removal of the switch is a problem with low and/or intermediate speed operation, check the blower motor dropper resistor (see Section 11).

Refitting

7   Refit in the reverse order of removal. Ensure that the wiring connections are securely made.

13   Heater controls – removal and refitting

Removal

1   Remove the central switch panel (directly above the heater controls). Refer to Chapter 12 for details.
2   Remove the instrument panel to allow access to the right-hand side of the heater unit. Refer to Chapter 12 for details.
3   Remove the glovebox lid and the glovebox. Refer to Chapter 11 for details.
4   Undo the four retaining screws, and remove the plate from the left-hand side for access to the heater on that side (see photo 10.3A).
5   Undo the three control panel retaining screws, two at the top and one lower down to the left of centre (in the top face of the ashtray supporting plate).
6   Note their connections, then release and disconnect the control cables from the control unit. To disconnect the blower switch and/or its wiring connections, refer to Section 11 in this Chapter.
7   Withdraw the control unit.

Refitting

8   Refit in the reverse order of removal. Ensure that the wiring and cable connections are secure. Check that the heater and ventilation control valves have full and free movement before refitting the central facia panel, glovebox and instrument panel assemblies.

Chapter 4 Fuel and exhaust systems

Contents

Air cleaner assembly – removal and refitting 2
Air cleaner filter element renewal ....See Chapter 1
Carburettor – fault diagnosis, overhaul and adjustments.................. 12
Carburettor – general information 10
Carburettor – removal and refitting... 11
Exhaust manifold – removal and refitting.. 14
Exhaust system – general information and component
replacement 15
Exhaust system check ....See Chapter 1
Fuel filter renewal ....See Chapter 1
Fuel gauge sender unit – removal, refitting and testing...................... 4

Fuel pump – testing, removal and refitting 3
Fuel tank – removal and refitting 5
Fuel tank filler components – removal and refitting........................... 6
General fuel system checks......................................See Chapter 1
General information and precautions 1
Idle speed and mixture adjustment..........................See Chapter 1
Inlet manifold – removal and refitting... 13
Throttle cable – removal, refitting and adjustment........................... 7
Throttle pedal – removal and refitting 8
Unleaded petrol – general information and usage 9

Specifications

Fuel pump
Make and type .... Jikov OD diaphragm
Actuation.. Mechanical from camshaft
Delivery pressure .... 0.3 bars

Carburettor (general)
Type and designation .... Pierburg 2E3 or Jikov 28-30 LEKR
Carburettor number:
    Jikov 443 751 220 100
    Pierburg 4301-360.6
Choke type... Automatic

Carburettor adjustment data
Idle speed.. See Chapter 1
Idle mixture CO content .... See Chapter 1
Float height .... 29 ± 1 mm

Carburettor calibration

	Primary	Secondary
Venturi diameter	20 mm	24 mm
Jet sizes:		
Main jet..	92.5	120
Emulsion tube..	100	100
Idle fuel jet..	45	–
Idle air jet..	130	–
Auxiliary fuel jet diameter	–	0.55 mm
Auxiliary air jet diameter..	–	1.2 mm
Part-load enrichment jet diameter	0.5 mm	–
Full-load enrichment jet..	–	85
Accelerator pump jet diameter..	0.15 mm	–
Needle valve diameter	1.5 mm	–

Torque wrench settings

	Nm	lbf ft
Fuel pump..	12 to 16	9 to 12
Carburettor retaining screws	7 to 10	5 to 7
Inlet manifold nuts..	18 to 24	13 to 18
Exhaust manifold nuts..	18 to 24	13 to 18

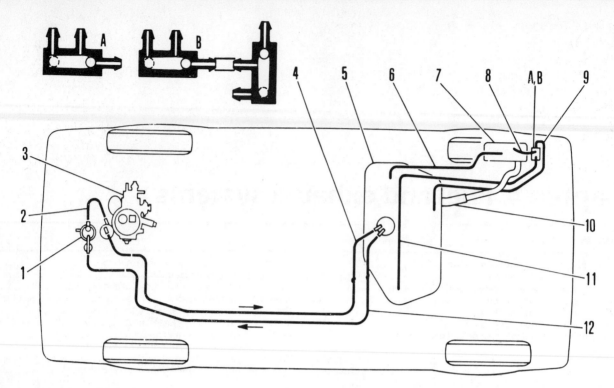

Fig. 4.1 Fuel system layout (Sec 1)

1	Fuel pump	5	Fuel tank	9	Vent hose	A	Piping
2	Hose	6	Breather hose	10	Filler hose	B	Piping (to EEC
3	Carburettor	7	Fuel filler	11	Vent hose		requirements)
4	Fuel return hose	8	Vent hose	12	Fuel supply line		

1   General information and precautions

The fuel system consists of a fuel tank mounted under the floor pan (just forward of the rear axle), a mechanical fuel pump and a carburettor. The system layout is shown in Fig. 4.1. The fuel pump is operated by an eccentric on the camshaft, and is mounted on the side of the cylinder block. The air cleaner assembly contains a disposable paper filter element. Air intake temperature is thermostatically controlled.

The carburettor is a Pierburg 2E3 type, although in some instances it is manufactured under licence by Jikov and is designated Jikov 28-30 LEKR; in either instance, the carburettors are identical. To reduce emissions and to improve driveability when the engine is cold, the inlet manifold is heated by the engine coolant. Mixture enrichment for cold starting is by a thermostatically-controlled automatic choke.

A conventional type three-section exhaust system is fitted, suspended by rubber mountings.

Warning: *Many of the procedures in this Chapter require the removal of*

fuel lines and connections which may result in some fuel spillage. Before carrying out any operation on the fuel system, refer to the precautions given in 'Safety first!' at the beginning of this manual, and follow them implicitly. Petrol is a highly-dangerous and volatile liquid, and the precautions necessary when handling it cannot be overstressed.

2   Air cleaner assembly – removal and refitting

Removal

1   Remove the air cleaner element (Chapter 1). Loosen the retaining clip which secures the air intake duct connecting hose to the air cleaner intake duct (photo).
2   Undo the three retaining nuts within the filter body, then remove the retaining ring and the rubber seal. Undo the retaining nut, remove the washer from the filter attachment to the mounting bracket, then

2.1 Air cleaner duct-to-hose connection

2.2A Remove the air cleaner retaining ring ...

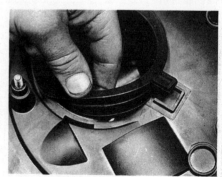

2.2B ... and the rubber seal

2.2C Remove the filter retaining nut and washer from the mounting bracket attachment

2.3A Detaching the intake duct from the air cleaner

2.3B Air temperature sensor removal

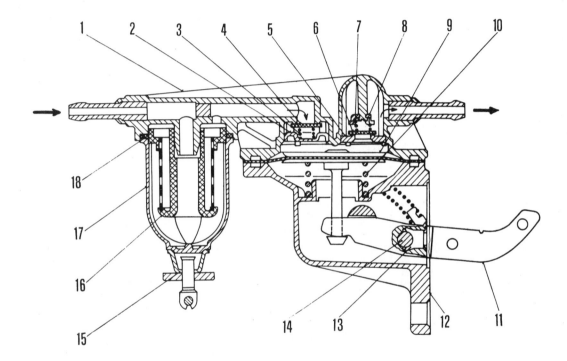

Fig. 4.2 Sectional view of the early type fuel pump and filter (Sec 3)

1	Upper body	6	Outlet valve plate	11	Pump hand primer	16	Filter element
2	Inlet valve cap	7	Outlet valve spring	12	Lower body	17	Filter bowl
3	Inlet valve spring	8	Outlet valve rest	13	Shim	18	Filter bowl seal
4	Inlet valve plate	9	Diaphragm	14	Lever pivot		
5	Outlet valve seat	10	Diaphragm spring	15	Filter clip		

carefully lift the air cleaner from the carburettor (photos). As it is lifted clear, disconnect the filter from the intake duct connecting hose. Also, note their connections then detach the vacuum and breather hoses from the base of the air cleaner.

3 If required, the air intake duct can be detached from the air cleaner by carefully prising the retainers from the lugs. The air intake temperature sensor can be unscrewed and removed from the intake duct as shown (photos).

Refitting

4 Refitting is a reversal of the removal procedure. Ensure that all hoses are correctly and securely reconnected.

3 Fuel pump – testing, removal and refitting

Note: *Refer to the warning note in Section 1 before proceeding.*

Testing

1 To test the fuel pump on the engine, temporarily disconnect the outlet hose from the pump (to the carburettor).

2 On early models, the fuel pump is equipped with a hand primer. To test the operation of this type of pump, hold a wad of rag over the pump outlet, and simultaneously actuate the hand primer lever on the side of the pump (photo).

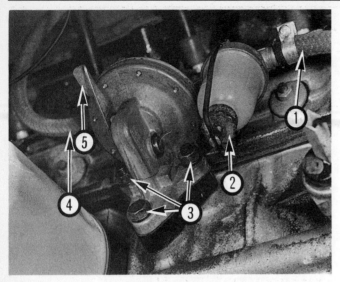

3.2 Early type fuel pump and filter viewed from underneath

1   *Fuel inlet hose*
2   *Fuel filter and securing nut*
3   *Fuel pump retaining nuts*
4   *Fuel outlet hose*
5   *Hand priming lever*

3   The fuel pump on later models does not have a hand primer. The engine will need to be turned using the starter motor in order to make the check. Prevent the engine starting by detaching the HT lead from the centre of the distributor cap and earthing it.

4   Regular spurts of fuel should be ejected from the outlet as the pump is actuated. If pump operation proves to be satisfactory, reconnect the fuel line and the ignition HT lead to the coil. If the pump is defective, remove it as follows for inspection and if necessary renewal.

Removal

5   Identify the pump inlet and outlet hoses, then loosen the retaining clips, disconnect the hoses from the pump (photo) and plug them. Place wads of rag to catch any spilled fuel, and cover the hose unions to prevent the entry of dirt and the escape of fuel.

6   Unscrew the nuts securing the pump to the engine, and remove the washers.

7   Withdraw the fuel pump together with the attached fuel filter (earlier pump type only) from the engine, and remove the insulating block (photo).

8   On the earlier type fuel pump fitted with a hand primer and a fuel filter, remove the filter from the pump by unscrewing the securing nut, then withdraw the filter bowl and filter (photos).

9   The later type pump cannot be dismantled, and if defective it must therefore be renewed as a unit. With the earlier type pump, the upper body can be removed to inspect the diaphragm and the inlet and outlet valves. Make an alignment mark across the fitted position of the upper to lower pump body, undo the retaining screws and separate the two bodies.

10   Check the valves on the underside of the upper cover. If their condition is suspect, the top cover will need to be renewed as they are not individually renewable. Check the diaphragm and its spring for signs of deterioration, and renew as necessary (photos).

11   On the earlier type pump, renew the fuel filter if it is dirty or if it is due for renewal (see Chapter 1). Also renew the fuel filter bowl seal if its condition is suspect prior to refitting the filter bowl (photo).

Refitting

12   Refitting is the reverse of the removal procedure; ensure that all of the mating surfaces are clean, and renew the insulating block if its sealing surfaces are marked or damaged. Tighten the pump mounting nuts to the specified torque.

3.5 Disconnecting the feed pipe hose from the fuel pump

3.7 Removing the fuel pump and filter

3.8A Removing the pump filter bowl ...

3.8B ... and filter

3.10A Underside view of the fuel pump upper cover showing location of the inlet and outlet valves (arrowed)

3.10B Removing the diaphragm and spring

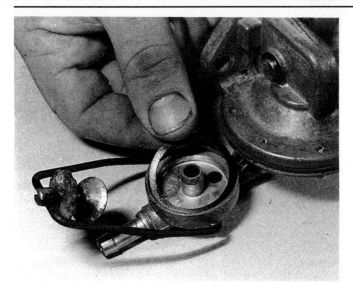

3.11 Fuel filter bowl seal renewal

4 Fuel gauge sender unit – removal, refitting and testing

Note: *Refer to the warning note in Section 1 before proceeding.*

Removal

1   Disconnect the battery negative lead.
2   If applicable, remove the rear seat. Refer to Chapter 11 for details.
3   The sender unit access cover is located in the floorpan, forward of the rear axle, and is removed from within the vehicle. On some models, the access cover is secured by two screws; where this is the case, undo and remove the screws. Prise free and remove the fuel sender access cover (photo).
4   Note the connections, then disconnect the sender unit wiring and hoses (photo).
5   Release the sender unit locking ring by turning it anti-clockwise using a tool similar to the Skoda tool (number MP8-502) shown in Fig. 4.3. Where necessary, a pair of slip-jointed pliers will probably suffice, but take care not to damage the wiring terminals and hose connections on the top face of the sender unit.
6   Withdraw the sender unit, noting the sealing ring; this must be renewed if worn or damaged.

Refitting

7   Refitting is the reverse of the removal procedure. Position the float arm in line with the vehicle centre-line and pointing to the rear.

Testing

8   The fuel gauge mounted in the instrument panel receives a voltage supply from the instrument panel feed (via the ignition switch). It incorporates a 'fuel level low' warning light.
9   If the gauge develops a fault, check first the other instruments; if

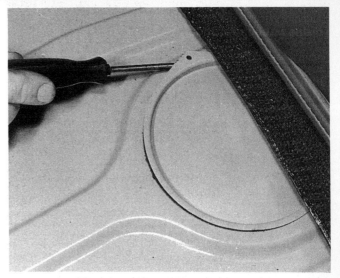

4.3 Prising free the fuel gauge sender cover

they do not work at all, check the instrument panel feed. If the readings are erratic, there may be a fault necessitating the renewal of the printed circuit (Chapter 12). If the fault is in the fuel gauge alone, check it as follows.
10   Gain access to the sender unit wires as described earlier. With the ignition on, disconnect the yellow wire: the gauge reading should fall to zero. Reconnect the yellow wire, and disconnect the blue wire: the gauge reading should rise to maximum.
11   If the gauge behaves as just described but the readings are known to be incorrect in use, the sender unit is probably faulty and the instrument is OK. If the gauge does not move, the instrument or the wiring is at fault and the sender unit is probably OK.
12   Still with the ignition on, disconnect the black wire. If the low fuel warning light was on, it should now go out. Earth the black wire and the light should come on.
13   If the warning light behaves as just described but does not come on in use, the warning light switch in the sender unit is faulty. If the warning light does not come on when tested, the bulb or the wiring is at fault.

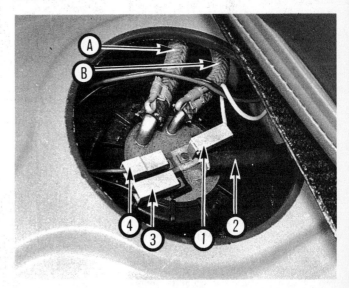

4.4 Fuel gauge sender unit and connections

A   *Fuel feed*
B   *Fuel return*
1   *Yellow wire (gauge positive)*
2   *Green wire (earth)*
3   *Blue wire (gauge negative)*
4   *Black wire (fuel level warning light)*

Fig. 4.3 Fuel gauge sender unit removal/refitting tool (Sec 4)

Fig. 4.4 Fuel tank and associated components (Sec 5)

10 Clip
11 Strip
12 Fuel line
13 Hose
14 Hose
15 Bypass tube
17 Nut
18 Fuel gauge sender
19 Gasket
20 Fuel tank
21 Seal strip
22 Tank retaining strap (LH)
23 Seal strip
24 Bolt
25 Washer
26 Washer
27 Tank retaining strap (RH)
30 Clip
31 Strip
32 Air hose
33 Ventilation hose
34 Connector
35 Air hose
36 Air hose
40 Filler neck
41 Seal ring
42 Washer
43 Nut
44 Filler cap
45 Bolt
46 Washer
47 Washer
48 Clip
49 Strip
50 Hose
51 Filler neck insert and clip (later models)
52 In-line fuel filter (later models)

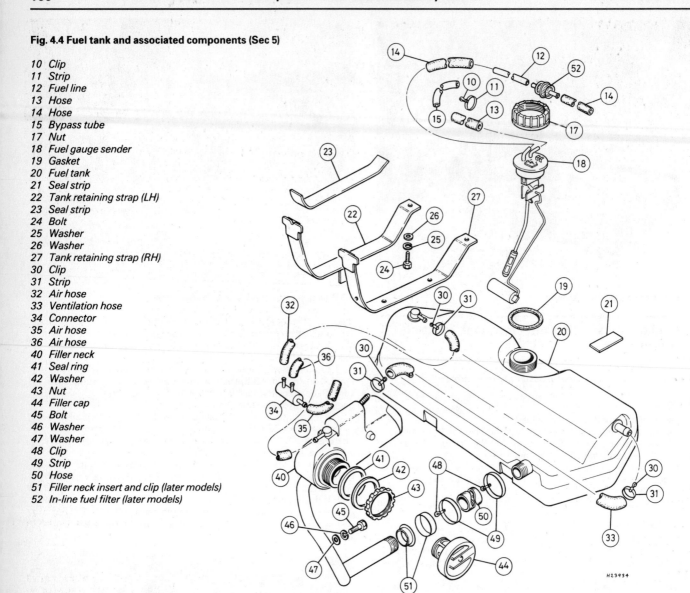

5   Fuel tank – removal and refitting

Note: *Refer to the warning note in Section 1 before proceeding.*

Removal

1   A fuel tank drain plug is not provided; it is therefore preferable to carry out the removal operation when the tank is nearly empty. Before proceeding, disconnect the battery negative lead, and syphon or hand-pump the remaining fuel from the tank.

2   Chock the front wheels, jack up the rear of the vehicle and support it on axle stands, allowing sufficient room under the vehicle to lower and withdraw the tank. Remove the right-hand rear wheel to improve access on that side.

3   Remove the access cover and disconnect the wiring, fuel supply and return hoses from the top of the sender unit as described in the previous Section.

4   Working underneath the vehicle, unscrew the retaining clip and detach the fuel filler pipe from the tank.

5   Prise open the retaining clips, and release the handbrake cables from their locating clips on the underside of the tank retaining strap and the rear axle beam each side. Move each cable out of the way, and tie them back so that they are clear of the fuel tank.

6   Support the weight of the fuel tank, then undo the retaining strap

5.6 Fuel tank strap and retaining bolt

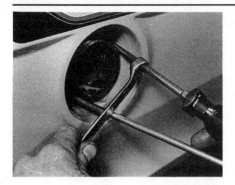

6.3A Method of loosening the fuel filler pipe nut

6.3B Fuel filler pipe nut and washer removal

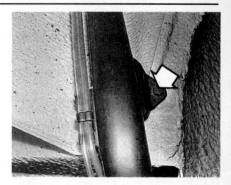

6.4 Bolt (arrowed) attaching fuel filler pipe and vent hoses to the rear wheel arch

6.5 Fuel filler pipe hose attachment to fuel tank

6.6 Fuel filler pipe unit viewed from underneath

bolts (photo), pivot the straps downwards and lower the fuel tank. As the tank is lowered, guide it clear of the surrounding components and withdraw it from under the vehicle. Allow for the spillage of any remaining fuel in the tank. Plug all hoses and cover their unions to prevent the entry of dirt and the escape of fuel.

7   If the tank is contaminated with sediment or water, wash it out with clean fuel. If the tank is damaged or leaks, it should be inspected by a fuel tank repair specialist for possible repair, or else renewed. **Do not** attempt to repair a fuel tank yourself by welding or brazing.

Refitting

8   Refitting is the reverse of the removal procedure. Ensure that all hoses are correctly routed and securely fastened so that there can be no risk of fuel leakage.

6 Fuel tank filler components – removal and refitting

Note: *Refer to the warning note in Section 1 before proceeding.*

Removal

1   A fuel tank drain plug is not provided; it is therefore preferable to carry out the removal operation when the tank is nearly empty. Before proceeding, disconnect the battery negative lead, and syphon or hand-pump the remaining fuel from the tank.
2   Chock the front wheels, then jack up the rear of the vehicle and support it on axle stands. Remove the right-hand rear wheel to provide increased access under the wheel arch.
3   Remove the fuel filler cap, then unscrew the recessed castle nut and its seal washer securing the filler pipe to the rear wing. Loosen the nut using a pair of screwdrivers located at opposite points and a ring spanner engaged as shown (photos).
4   Unscrew the filler pipe-to-wheel arch retaining bolt (photo).

5   Loosen the filler pipe hose-to-fuel tank retaining clip, and detach the hose (photo).
6   Lower the filler pipe unit (photo). Disconnect the breather hoses by releasing their clips. Plug all hoses, and cover open unions to prevent the entry of dirt and the escape of fuel.

Refitting

7   Refitting is the reverse of the removal procedure. Ensure that all hoses are correctly routed and securely fastened so that there can be no risk of fuel leakage.

7 Throttle cable – removal, refitting and adjustment

Removal

1   Working inside the engine compartment, open the throttle and release the inner cable nipple from the throttle quadrant, then detach the outer cable from the support/adjustment bracket (photos).
2   Working inside the vehicle, release the cable nipple from the clevis at the top of the pedal.
3   Release the throttle cable to bulkhead retaining clip, withdraw the cable into the engine compartment, and remove it.

Refitting

4   Refitting is the reverse of the removal procedure; adjust the cable as follows.

Adjustment

5   The position of the cable must be set so that when the throttle pedal is fully released, there is a small measure of slack in the cable, so

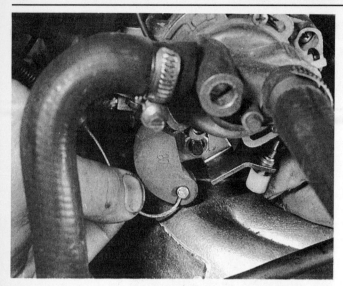

7.1A Disconnecting the throttle inner cable from the quadrant at the carburettor

7.1B Detaching the throttle cable from the support/adjustment bracket

ensuring that the throttle is fully closed. Have an assistant fully depress the pedal and check that the throttle opens fully, then check that it returns to the at-rest position when released.

6   Adjustment is made by repositioning the clip on the cable outer at the support/adjustment bracket. Check for satisfactory operation after adjustment.

8   Throttle pedal – removal and refitting

Removal

1   Disconnect the throttle cable inner wire from the pedal (Section 7).
2   Unhook the return spring, and remove the clip securing the pedal to the pivot shaft; withdraw the pedal (photo).

Refitting

3   Refitting is the reverse of the removal procedure. Adjust the cable if necessary on completion (Section 7).

8.2 Throttle pedal removal

9   Unleaded petrol – general information and usage

Note: *The information given in this Chapter is correct at the time of writing, and applies only to petrol currently available in the UK. If updated information is thought to be required, check with a Skoda dealer. If travelling abroad, consult one of the motoring organisations (or a similar authority) for advice on the petrols available and their suitability for your vehicle.*

1   The fuel recommended by Skoda for their Favorit models is given in the Specifications Section of Chapter 1, followed by the equivalent petrol currently on sale in the UK.
2   RON and MON are different testing standards; RON stands for Research Octane Number (also written as RM), while MON stands for Motor Octane Number (also written as MM).
3   All models are designed to run on 95 (RON) octane petrol. Super/Super Plus (unleaded) petrol can be used without modification, if nothing else is available.

10   Carburettor – general information

1   The carburettor is a Pierburg 2E3 type, although in some instances it is manufactured under licence by Jikov, and is designated Jikov 28-30 LEKR. In either instance, the carburettor is identical, being of downdraught progressive twin choke type, with a vacuum-controlled secondary throttle (photo).
2   The function of the carburettor is to supply the correct air/fuel mixture to the engine in accordance with the varying operating conditions. The 2E3 carburettor achieves this in the following manner.
3   Fuel enters the carburettor through a filter, and is collected in the float chamber. The level of fuel in the float chamber is controlled by the float and a needle valve located in the fuel inlet. As the level of fuel in the chamber lowers, the float drops and the needle valve opens. As the fuel reaches its correct level, the float closes the needle valve and the fuel supply is correspondingly cut. An air channel between the float chamber and the air filter prevents the possibility of a pressure build-up within the float chamber, and also reduces the effect of a clogged air filter on the fuel/air mixture.
4   A semi-automatic cold start (choke) system is used. When the engine is cold, the choke is actuated by depressing the throttle pedal once (or twice in frosty weather). This actuates the fast idle cam; the bi-metal spring in the automatic choke housing closes off the choke valve, and the fast idle cam is simultaneously moved to the fast idle position. As the throttle pedal is released, the throttle valve is moved to

10.1 General view of the Pierburg 2E3 carburettor

1   Gas bubble separator
2   Secondary throttle diaphragm
3   Automatic choke housing
4   Choke pull-down unit
5   Accelerator pump
6   Timing thermo-valve
7   Float chamber vent
8   Full-load (Stage II) enrichment nozzle

the cold start position, with the fast idle adjustment screw in contact with the highest step of the fast idle stepped cam.

5   When the ignition is switched on, the idle cut-off valve is opened, allowing fuel supply to the carburettor and the bi-metal spring in the choke cover is actuated. Cranking the engine on the starter motor causes a vacuum downside of the choke valve, and fuel is drawn from the primary choke system. The mixture is prevented from becoming too rich by the choke valve being eccentrically mounted so that as the air is allowed past the slightly-opened valve.

6   When the engine starts, the vacuum in the venturi causes a pull-down diaphragm to open the choke valve via connecting linkages, and additional air enters the system to prevent the mixture becoming too rich. A stop screw limits the movement of the diaphragm rod. An air bleed into the pull-down unit via the timing thermo-valve reduces the effect of the vacuum pull-down diaphragm in cold conditions. When the thermo-valve closes, pull-down effect is increased and the choke valve opens further.

7   As the engine warms up, any movement of the throttle pedal causes the throttle acting lever to turn and release the fast idle cam. The fast idle adjuster screw resets onto the warm-up section of the fast idle cam, and the throttle valve opening is reduced accordingly.

8   As the engine approaches its normal operating temperature, the bi-metal spring and lever progressively open the choke valve to weaken the mixture. The fast idle screw moves into contact with the final stage warm-up step on the fast idle cam. At normal operating temperature, the fast idle adjustment screw is no longer in contact with the fast idle cam, and the idle speed is determined by the position of the throttle valve and the amount of mixture passing through the idle bypass circuit.

9   To prevent the mixture becoming too rich when accelerating during the warm-up stage, the primary throttle valve and choke valve are mechanically connected, and this moves the choke valve to a mid-range setting.

10   To prevent flooding in the event of the throttle being fully opened when the engine is still cold, a wide-open kick mechanism operates, whereby a cam on the throttle lever returns the choke lever anti-clockwise to partially open the flap.

11   An accelerator pump is fitted and is designed to operate only when the throttle valve is less than half-open. The pump is actuated mechanically by a lever and cam attached to the primary throttle linkage. It discharges fuel into the primary venturi, any excess fuel being returned to the float chamber through a calibrated channel.

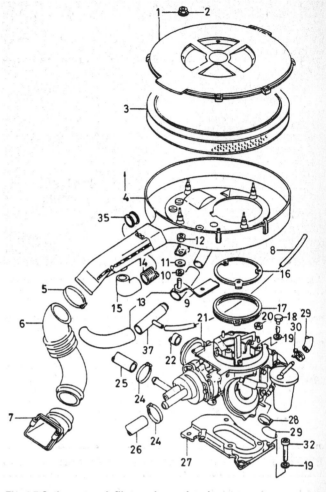

Fig. 4.5 Carburettor, air filter and associated components (Secs 2 and 10)

1	Air cleaner cover	17	Gasket
2	Nut	18	Screw
3	Filter element	19	Washer
4	Air cleaner body	20	Nut
5	Clip	21	Carburettor
6	Intake hose	22	Hose
7	Adaptor	24	Clip
8	Vent hose	25	Coolant outlet pipe
9	Bracket	26	Coolant inlet hose
10	Rubber insert	27	Mounting flange and
11	Washer		gasket
12	Nut	28	Clip
13	Vent hose	29	Fuel hose
14	Hot air hose	30	Clip
15	Elbow	32	Screw
16	Retaining plate	35	End piece
		37	T-piece

12   A calibrated main jet regulates the amount of fuel supplied from the float chamber to the main airstream. A combined emulsion tube/air correction jet, located in the base of the float chamber well, mixes the fuel and air prior to discharge through an auxiliary venturi into the main airstream.

13   At idle speed and light throttle operating conditions, the fuel outlet channel and the enrichment channel are closed off under vacuum pressure acting on the diaphragm. When the throttle is opened, the manifold vacuum drops, the diaphragm returns under spring pressure, the fuel channel valve is opened and the additional fuel required is supplied.

14   During operation at low speeds, only the primary venturi is in operation. When the air velocity through the primary venturi reaches a

Fig. 4.6 General view of the 2E3 carburettor (Sec 11)

1   Thermo-valve
2   Fuel inlet and filter
3   Choke valve
4   Float chamber vent
5   Gas bubble separator (vapour trap)
6   Secondary full-load enrichment tube
7   Secondary throttle diaphragm vacuum chamber
8   Automatic choke housing
9   Choke housing cover
10 Throttle quadrant
11 Throttle lever
12 Idle mixture screw
13 Throttle stop screw
14 Choke pull-down unit
15 Idle cut-off valve

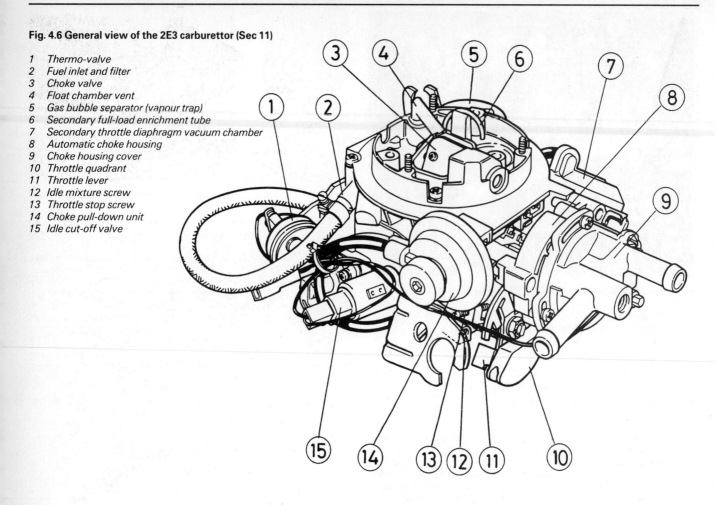

certain level, depression acting on the secondary diaphragm brings the secondary throttle into operation. A progression jet prevents any hesitation as the secondary throttle valve starts to open. Once the secondary throttle valve is opened, the operation of the secondary circuit is much the same as that of the primary circuit.

15   At full-load and high engine speed, the air velocity creates a depression sufficient to draw fuel from the float chamber into the vertical tube, then through the calibrated bushing and into the upper part of the secondary air intake. From here it is discharged into the airstream from the full-load enrichment tube.

16   The inlet manifold is coolant-heated to improve atomization of the air/fuel mixture. The throttle body is heated electrically for the same purpose.

17   A gas bubble separator (vapour trap) is fixed to a bracket on the side of the carburettor. Its function is to ensure a continuous fuel flow to the float chamber at higher temperatures, when excess vapours could otherwise cause uneven running and poor starting.

18   The gas bubble separator is part of a calibrated fuel return system. Fuel drawn by the pump and not immediately required by the carburettor is returned to the tank. This ensures that only relatively cool fuel is supplied to the carburettor.

11   Carburettor – removal and refitting

Note: *Refer to the warning note in Section 1 before proceeding.*

Removal

1   Remove the air cleaner assembly (Section 2).
2   Disconnect the throttle cable from the carburettor and the support/adjustment bracket (Section 7).
3   With the engine cold, slacken the expansion tank filler cap. Clamp

the coolant hoses near to their carburettor connections in order to minimise coolant spillage, then loosen their retaining clips and disconnect the hoses from the carburettor (photo). If the hoses are not clamped, the cooling system will need to be partially drained as described in Chapter 1.

4   Detach the green wire (from the main loom) at the carburettor.
5   Detach the brown earth lead from its connection to the carburettor mounting bolt (photo).
6   Disconnect the three hoses from the gas bubble separator (photo).

11.3 Detach the coolant hoses from the automatic choke unit

11.5 Disconnect the earth lead

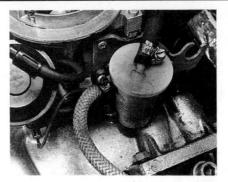

11.6 Gas bubble separator

11.7 Carburettor retaining screws (arrowed)

7   Undo the three retaining screws, and carefully lift the carburettor clear from the insulation spacer and manifold (photo).

Refitting

8   Refitting is a reversal of the removal procedure. Fit a new carburettor-to-manifold gasket, and take care not to overtighten the fastenings. Adjust the throttle cable as described in Section 7.
9   Refit the air cleaner assembly as described in Section 2.
10   Check the coolant level and top-up if necessary as described in Chapter 1.

12   Carburettor – fault diagnosis, overhaul and adjustments

Fault diagnosis

1   Faults with the carburettor are usually associated with dirt entering the float chamber and blocking the jets, causing a weak mixture or power failure within a certain engine speed range. If this is the case, then a thorough clean will normally cure the problem. If the carburettor is well-worn, uneven running may be caused by air entering through the throttle valve spindle bearings.

Overhaul

2   Although it is possible to undertake some operations with the carburettor in position, the following paragraphs describe cleaning and adjustment procedures which can be carried out by the home mechanic after the carburettor has been removed from the inlet manifold. If the carburettor is worn or damaged, it should either be renewed or overhauled by a specialist who will be able to restore the carburettor to its original calibration.
3   Note the location and routing of the choke vacuum hoses and disconnect them.
4   Undo the four retaining screws and lift the carburettor upper body

from the lower body, taking care not to break the gasket as the two bodies are separated (a replacement gasket may not be readily available).
5   Empty any remaining fuel from the float chamber. Inspect the float chamber for signs of corrosion or a build-up of sediment or deposits.
6   Tap out the pivot pin and remove the float, then withdraw the needle valve. Shake the float to check that no fuel has leaked into it, and also check the pivot pin for any signs of excessive wear. Inspect the needle valve to ensure that the anti-vibration ball is free in the valve end, and check that the needle valve tip is free of excessive wear marks.
7   Extract the fuel filter from the fuel inlet port. A small screw can be tightened into the filter to enable it to be gripped and withdrawn from its orifice in the carburettor. This filter must be renewed once it has been removed from the carburettor.

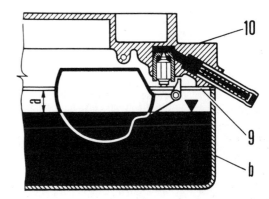

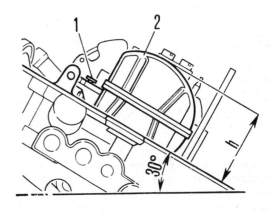

Fig. 4.8 Float level setting (Sec 12)

a   8.5 to 10.5 mm   2   Float
b   Float chamber   9   Gasket
h   28 to 30 mm   10   Carburettor upper body
1   Valve pin

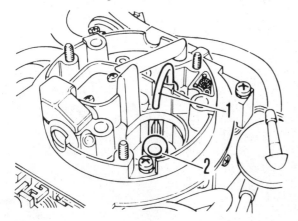

Fig. 4.7 Injector nozzle (1) to be vertically aligned with the centre of the atomizer (2) (Sec 12)

12.9 Accelerator pump unit (1) – also shown is the throttle body heater (2)

8   Unscrew the mixture screw and inspect the tip for signs of ridges or damage.

9   Undo the four retaining screws and withdraw the accelerator pump unit. Check the diaphragm for fatigue and damage (photo).

10   Carefully prise free the accelerator pump injector from its location in the body. Once removed, the injector can be tested by shaking it to ensure that the outlet ball can be heard moving. If the ball cannot be heard, it is seized and the injector will need to be renewed.

11   Note their respective locations, then remove the primary idle jet unit and both main jets. **Note:** *It is not possible to remove any of the remaining jets or the emulsion tubes.* Check that the channels from the float chamber to the emulsion tube wells are clear.

12   Undo the two retaining screws and withdraw the power valve unit. Check the operation of the diaphragm and inspect it for any sign of damage.

13   Check the condition of the secondary throttle vacuum hose. If a vacuum pump is available, connect it to the vacuum connector and operate the pump until the diaphragm is activated. If the diaphragm fails to operate, or if it will not hold the vacuum for at least 10 seconds, it must be renewed.

14   To remove the choke diaphragm unit, drive out the retaining pin securing the unit to the upper body (photo), undo the three retaining screws and withdraw the choke housing. The pull-down diaphragm can be removed by extracting the star fixing clip.

15   Clean the carburettor housings, the internal channels, the float chamber, jets and all associated items in clean petrol, and blow dry with an air line. For more stubborn blockages, spraying a carburettor cleaner into all channels and passages in the carburettor housings will usually clear them of gum and dirt. Although the choke housing cover can be removed for inspection purposes, the setting of the choke and fast idle

screw are best left to a Skoda dealer or a carburettor specialist, as specialised equipment is required. **Note:** *Do not apply high-pressure compressed air into the channels if the diaphragm is still in position or it will almost certainly be damaged.*

16   New gaskets must be obtained for reassembly. Where the choke diaphragm unit and housing have been removed, a new roll pin and star clip must be used to secure them when refitting. Renew any components which are not in good condition, including the vacuum hoses, all linkages and their associated connections.

17   Prior to reassembly, ensure that all mating surfaces, jets and passages are perfectly clean.

18   Reassemble in the reverse order of dismantling, noting the following special points and adjustment checks possible during assembly (photos).

   (a)   Ensure that the main jets are correctly repositioned.

   (b)   The seal on the pump injector must be renewed prior to inserting it. When fitted, the nozzle of the injector should be centrally located over the atomizer as indicated (Fig. 4.7). Check that the height of the nozzle above the edge of the upper face of the venturi is between 22 to 24 mm.

   (c)   When refitting the mixture screw, renew the small seal, then insert the screw and tighten it gently by hand to the point where it is just felt to seat, then from this point, unscrew the screw three full turns. This will give an approximate setting in order to start the engine.

   (d)   The float needle valve must be fitted to its seat so that the ball faces outwards. When fitted, the top of the needle valve should engage in the float slot.

   (e)   The float height should be checked before refitting the upper housing to the lower housing. To check the setting, hold the upper housing at an angle of 30°, and with the float tag gently touching the ball of the fully-closed needle valve, check that the distance between the upper body (less gasket) and the top of the float is as given in the Specifications and in Fig. 4.8.

   (f)   Where it is found to be incorrect, check that the needle valve is correctly seated. No adjustment to the plastic float is possible. If the float height is incorrect, the float and/or the needle valve must be renewed.

   (g)   If the choke housing cover was removed, ensure that the index mark of the housing cover aligns with the corresponding mark on the upper housing as they are assembled. Tighten the three retaining screws to secure.

19   Refit the carburettor with reference to the previous Section, then check the idle speed and mixture settings as described in Chapter 1.

13   Inlet manifold – removal and refitting

Note: *Refer to the warning note in Section 1 before proceeding.*

Removal

1   Although it is possible to remove the inlet manifold with the carburettor attached, it is preferable to remove the carburettor first, in order to improve the access to the manifold fastenings (Section 11).

12.14 Choke diaphragm unit retaining pin removal

12.18A Choke housing and cover alignment index marks

12.18B Choke housing cover screws (arrowed)

13.2 Disconnect the brake servo hose from the inlet manifold

2   Disconnect the vacuum hose to the brake servo at the inlet manifold (photo).
3   With the engine cold, slacken the expansion tank filler cap. Clamp the coolant hoses to the manifold to minimise coolant loss, then loosen the retaining clips and detach the hoses from the manifold (photos).
4   Unscrew the six retaining nuts, remove the flat washers and withdraw the manifold from the locating studs. Take care not to damage the gasket, unless it is to be renewed in any case (photo).
5   If the gasket is damaged or in poor condition, it must be renewed. As a combined inlet/exhaust manifold is used, the exhaust manifold will need to be removed to enable it to be replaced (Section 14).

Refitting

6   Refit in the reverse order of removal. Ensure that the mating surfaces of the manifold and cylinder head are clean and in good condition prior to reassembly. Check that all hose connections are secure, and check for any sign of leakage on completion. Check and if necessary top-up the coolant level, referring to Chapter 1 for details.

14   Exhaust manifold – removal and refitting

Removal

1   Remove the inlet manifold as described in the previous Section.
2   Undo the four downpipe-to-manifold flange nuts, and separate the downpipe from the manifold.
3   Undo the three retaining nuts securing the warm air cowl over the top of the exhaust manifold. Detach the air duct from the cowl, then remove the cowl and the duct (photo).
4   Undo the six retaining nuts, and withdraw the manifold from the cylinder head (photo). Remove the gasket.

Refitting

5   Refitting is a reversal of the removal procedure. Ensure that the gasket mating surfaces of the manifold and the downpipe are clean, and be sure to fit a new gasket (photo). Tighten the retaining nuts to the specified torque. Note that the warm air cowl can be relocated before refitting the inlet manifold.

15   Exhaust system – general information and component replacement

1   The exhaust system components are shown in Fig. 4.9. The system is suspended under the vehicle by means of rubber mountings, and consists of three sections. The downpipe and the tailpipe can be removed leaving the centre section of the exhaust system in position, but to remove the complete system or the centre section, it is first necessary to disconnect the tailpipe from the centre section.

13.3A Coolant hose removal from the inlet manifold on the right-hand side

13.3B Coolant hose removal from the inlet manifold on the left-hand side

13.4 Inlet manifold removal

14.3 Removing the warm air cowl from the exhaust manifold

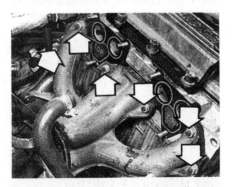

14.4 Exhaust manifold and retaining nuts (arrowed). Note the orientation of the combined inlet/exhaust manifold gasket

14.5 Fit a new exhaust/inlet manifold gasket

Fig. 4.9 Inlet manifold, exhaust manifold and exhaust system components (Secs 13, 14 and 15)

1 Inlet manifold
2 Coolant hose
3 Vacuum hose connection
4 Seal ring
5 Nut
6 Washer
7 Gasket (inlet/exhaust)
8 Washer
9 Hose connector
10 Exhaust manifold
11 Bolt
12 Warm air shroud
13 Bolt
14 Gasket
15 Locknut
16 Exhaust downpipe
17 Seal ring
18 Flexible mounting rubber
19 Circlip
20 Exhaust centre section
21 Bolt
22 Retainer plate
23 Coupling spring
24 Flexible mounting rubber
25 Exhaust rear section
26 Washer
27 Clip
28 Bolt
30 Plug
31 Insulating tube
32 Clip
33 Hose
34 Clip
35 Strip
36 Heater feed hose
37 Clip
39 Vacuum hose connector
40 Seal ring

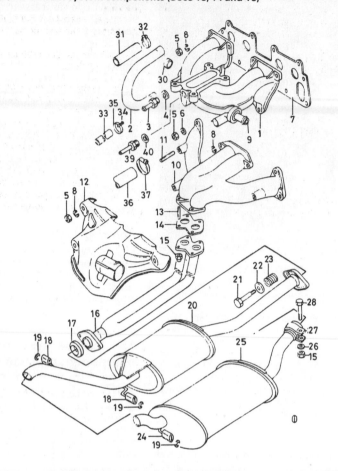

15.3A Detaching the downpipe at the centre section flange joint

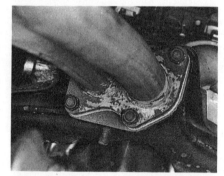

15.3B Downpipe-to-exhaust manifold flange joint

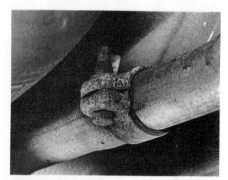

15.4A Exhaust tailpipe-to-centre section joint and clamp

15.4B Exhaust system hanger

15.7 New gasket fitted to the manifold-to-downpipe flange

2   To remove the system or part of the system, first jack up the front or rear of the vehicle (as applicable) and support on axle stands. Alternatively, position the vehicle over an inspection pit or on ramps.

3   To remove the downpipe, unscrew and remove the two downpipe-to-centre section flange nuts, and release the coil springs. Reach up to the downpipe-to-manifold flange nuts using a socket and extension, and unscrew the retaining nuts. Detach the downpipe from the joints at each end, then lower and remove it from the vehicle (photos).

4   To remove the tailpipe, loosen the tailpipe-to-centre section joint clamp, release the tailpipe from the hangers, and withdraw the pipe to the rear (photos). The tailpipe-to-centre section connection will probably require leverage or careful tapping to separate. Where the joint is seriously corroded and the section(s) are to be replaced, the joint can be cut through using a hacksaw.

5   The centre section of the exhaust can be removed together with, or separate from, the front downpipe as required. First separate the centre section from the rear section (as described in the previous paragraph), then detach the centre section at the downpipe or manifold as required,

release the pipe from the suspended hangers and remove it from the vehicle.

6   Renew all gaskets and seals as a matter of course; check, and renew if necessary, all fasteners, the clamp (if appropriate) and the rubber mountings.

7   Refitting is the reverse of the removal procedure, noting the following points.

(a)   Ensure that the mating faces of the joints and flanges are clean prior to assembly. Always fit a new manifold-to-downpipe gasket (photo).

(b)   Assemble the system loosely on its mountings, and check that it cannot touch any part of the body or suspension, even when deflected within the full extent of the rubber mountings.

(c)   Apply a smear of anti-seize compound (such as Holts Copaslip) to the threads of all nuts (except self-locking nuts) and bolts, as well as to the sleeve joint.

(d)   When the engine is restarted, check that the system is free of leaks before lowering the vehicle to the ground.

Chapter 5 Ignition system

Contents

Distributor – lubrication ....See Chapter 1
Distributor – removal, overhaul and refitting........................ 2
General information and precautions 1
Ignition control unit – checking, removal and refitting.................... 3
Ignition HT coil – removal, testing and refitting.................................. 4
Ignition system – testing.. 5
Ignition timing check and adjustment ....See Chapter 1
Spark plug check and renewal...................................See Chapter 1
Spark plug HT leads, distributor cap and rotor arm check
and renewal ....See Chapter 1

Specifications

General

System type..	Electronic breakerless
Firing order...	1–3–4–2
Location of No 1 cylinder	Crankshaft pulley end

Spark plugs

Make and type..	See Chapter 1

Distributor

Type	PAL Kromeriz 443 213 204 860
Direction of rotor arm rotation..	Clockwise
Pick-up coil resistance	7000 ± 500 ohms

Ignition coil

Type	PAL Kromeriz 443 212 215 820
Output (open-circuit, maximum)	40 kV

Torque wrench settings

	Nm	lbf ft
Distributor extension tube bolts	5 to 8	4 to 6

---

1 General information and precautions

The ignition system is fully electronic in operation and of the inductive type, incorporating a breakerless distributor (driven from the camshaft) and an ignition control unit module, as well as the spark plugs, HT leads, ignition HT coil and associated wiring.

The system is divided into two circuits: primary (low tension/LT) and secondary (high tension/HT). The primary circuit consists of the battery, ignition switch, ignition HT coil primary windings, ignition control unit, distributor pick-up coil and wiring. The secondary circuit consists of the ignition HT coil secondary windings, the distributor cap and rotor arm, the spark plugs, and the HT leads connecting these.

The distributor incorporates features which vary the ignition timing in response to changes of speed and load. This is achieved centrifugally (by spring-loaded weights, advance increasing with engine speed) and by inlet manifold vacuum (through a diaphragm attached to the distributor body, advance increasing with high vacuum).

A pick-up coil in the distributor generates a weak magnetic field when the ignition is switched on. As the engine rotates, the reluctor poles pass the pick-up coil, disturbing the magnetic field and sending a signal current to the control unit. This signal is fed to the ignition control unit, where it is used to trigger the higher voltage and current needed to drive the ignition coil.

The high voltage needed at the spark plugs is produced in the coil when the LT current is suddenly interrupted by the control unit. The high voltage is fed through the coil HT lead to the rotor arm, from where it jumps to the appropriate contact in the distributor cap and travels along the spark plug lead to the spark plug. Finally, the high voltage jumps the spark plug electrode gap and produces the spark necessary to ignite the fuel/air mixture in the cylinder.

Refer to Chapter 10 for details of the ignition switch.

Warning: *The voltages produced by the electronic ignition system are considerably higher than those produced by conventional (contact breaker) systems. Extreme care must be taken when working on the system with the ignition switched on. Persons with surgically-implanted cardiac pacemaker devices should keep well clear of the ignition circuits, components and test equipment.*

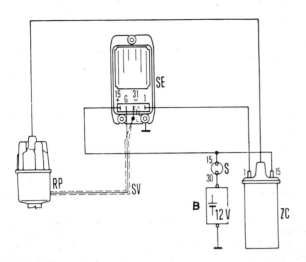

Fig. 5.1 Ignition system circuit diagram (Sec 1)

B   Battery
RP Distributor
S   Ignition switch

SE Ignition control unit
SV Screened cable
ZC Ignition coil

2   Distributor – removal, overhaul and refitting

Removal

1   Disconnect the battery negative terminal.
2   Mark the HT leads for position, then detach them from the spark plugs. If possible, do not detach the HT leads from the distributor cap, but if you do, mark the location of each lead on the cap first, to aid refitting.
3   Disconnect the vacuum pipe from the advance unit (photo).
4   Release the retaining clips, detach the distributor cap and position it out of the way.
5   Pull back the rubber cover from the ignition control unit (attached to the right-hand inner wing). Note their connections, then detach the two LT leads from the spade terminals in the control unit.
6   Set the engine at TDC, No 1 cylinder on compression. See Chapter 2, Section 3.
7   The distributor can be removed and refitted in one of two ways, according to preference. It can either be removed complete with the extension tube, or separately. The latter method is preferable when the distributor is to be overhauled.
8   To remove the distributor complete with the extension tube, undo the two extension tube flange-to-timing cover retaining bolts, then withdraw the distributor and tube from the timing cover (photos).
9   As the distributor and tube are withdrawn, it will be noted that the rotor will turn as the shaft pinion disengages from the helical drive gear on the camshaft. Note the final position of the rotor once the distributor is withdrawn to provide a guide to the required preset position when refitting.
10   To detach the distributor from the extension tube, first mark their relative positions to ensure correct timing when refitting, then slacken the clamp nut and bolt, and withdraw the distributor (photos).
11   Do not disturb the crankshaft setting while the distributor is removed, nor rotate the distributor shaft (unless the unit is to be overhauled).
12   Remove the O-ring seal from the groove in the distributor; this must be renewed whenever it is disturbed.

Overhaul

13   Withdraw the rotor arm.
14   Release the circlip and withdraw the wavy spring washer and the reluctor (photos).
15   Undo the retaining screws from the distributor body. Note the positions of the retaining clips and the special nuts. Withdraw the screws, extract the nuts and lift out the pick-up coil (photos).

2.3 Disconnecting the hose from the distributor vacuum advance unit

2.8A Distributor extension tube retaining bolts (arrowed)

2.8B Withdrawing the distributor (with extension tube)

2.10A Distributor/extension tube clamp nut and alignment index marks

2.10B Withdrawing distributor (leaving extension tube in position)

Fig. 5.2 Exploded view of the distributor (Sec 2)

1   Distributor cap
2   Carbon contact
3   Rotor arm
5   Circlip
6   Spring washer
7   Reluctor
9   Special nut
10 Pick-up coil
11 Special nut
12 Rotating plate
13 Terminal
14 Support plate
15 Shim (0.5, 0.10 or 0.16 mm)
17 Circlip
18 Retainer spring
19 Rotor bush
20 Spring
21 Circlip
22 Washer
24 Weight
25 Screw
26 Spring washers
27 Flat washer
28 Screw
31 Washers
32 Coupling
33 Retainer spring
34 Screw
35 Shaft
37 Vacuum unit
38 Spring clip
39 Bushes
40 Pin

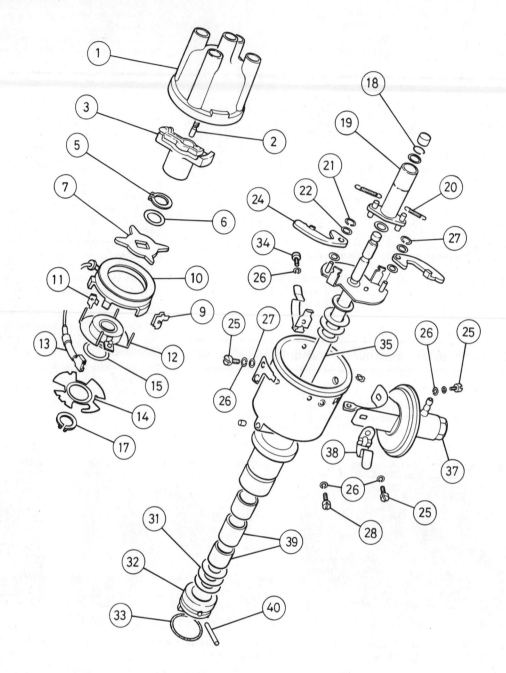

2.14A Remove the circlip ...

2.14B ... the wavy washer ...

2.14C ... and the reluctor

2.15A Undo the retaining screws ...

2.15B ....and release the special nuts....

2.15C ....noting their differences and locations as they are withdrawn

2.15D Remove the pick-up coil

2.16 Disengaging the vacuum control unit

2.17A Extract the rotating plate assembly

2.17B Underside view of the rotating plate assembly

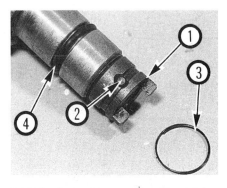

2.19 Distributor drive coupling (1), retaining pin (2), spring (3) and oil seal (4)

2.25A Showing correct location for rotating plate

2.25B General view of the distributor mechanical advance assembly

2.25C New gasket location on extension tube

2.26 Extension shaft position – No 1 cylinder at TDC

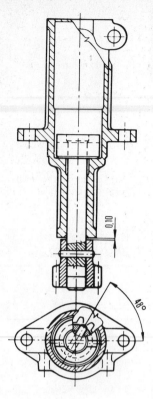

Fig. 5.3 Sectional view of the extension shaft bracket showing the required endfloat (0.10 mm) and the pinion-to-shaft fitting position (Sec 2)

16   Disconnect and remove the vacuum control unit (photo).

17   Remove the rotating plate assembly (photos).

18   Check the distributor shaft endfloat and axial play for excessive wear. If required, the distributor can be further dismantled as follows.

19   Remove the spring from the distributor drive coupling, then use a scriber or similar implement to mark the relationship of the coupling to the shaft. It is essential that the coupling is refitted correctly in relationship to the rotor arm on refitting. Release the distributor shaft by driving out the retaining pin and removing the coupling (photo); note the thrustwasher behind it.

20   Withdraw the shaft, noting the thrustwashers underneath the centrifugal advance assembly.

21   Clean and lubricate the advance weights and springs. Renew the springs (if available) if they have stretched.

22   Clean and examine all components, and renew as necessary. If wear is extensive, it may be more satisfactory to renew the distributor complete.

23   Clean and inspect the distributor cap. If there are any signs of hairline cracks or other damage, the cap must be renewed. Use an

ohmmeter or continuity tester to check that there is no continuity between any of the cap's terminal segments. Similarly, check that there is no continuity between the rotor arm body and its brass segment; note that the arm has a built-in resistance for the suppression of radio interference.

24   If the distributor extension tube has been removed, inspect the tube, shaft and pinion gear for excessive wear. Insert feeler gauges between the base of the bracket and the top of the drive pinion. Ideally, the endfloat of the shaft in the bracket should be 0.10 mm (Fig. 5.3). Although it is possible to renew the shaft and gear, it is a task best entrusted to a Skoda dealer, to ensure that the gear is correctly located on the shaft and that the endfloat of the shaft in the bracket is correct.

25   Reassembly is the reverse of the dismantling procedure, noting the following points (photos).

(a)   When fitting the rotating plate, locate it so that its slot aligns with the lug in the distributor body inner wall.

(b)   Apply a few drops of oil to the advance assembly pivots and springs, shaft and bearing surfaces.

(c)   Using the marks made on dismantling, ensure that the coupling is located correctly on the shaft end (in relationship to the rotor arm) before driving in the pin to secure it, then ensure that the spring is fitted over the pin ends.

(d)   Lightly grease the vacuum capsule arm before reconnecting it.

(e)   Ensure that the retainer plates are correctly relocated as noted during removal.

(f)   Renew the O-ring seal in the groove in the distributor body, and smear it with engine oil to ease fitting.

(g)   Fit a new gasket to the underside of the extension tube flange (if it was removed).

Refitting – old distributor

26   First check that No 1 cylinder is still at TDC. Turn the distributor shaft to align the rotor arm tip with the notch in the distributor body. If the extension tube is still on the engine, check that the distributor drive dog aligns with the engagement slot of the extension shaft (photo). If refitting the distributor and extension tube as an assembly, align the rotor arm to the pre-setting position noted during removal (paragraph 9).

27   With the index marks in alignment, refit the distributor. If necessary, turn the rotor arm very slightly to allow the drive dog or the gear teeth to mesh. Refit the mounting bolts and tighten them to the specified torque.

28   Refit the distributor cap, ensuring that it is correctly located, then reconnect the HT leads (Chapter 1).

29   Reconnect the vacuum pipe and the distributor-to-ignition control unit LT wiring.

30   Check the ignition timing and adjust if necessary (Chapter 1).

Refitting – new distributor

31   If a new distributor is to be fitted (or if no marks were made on removal), the procedure is basically the same, except that there will be no alignment marks between the distributor and the extension tube. Assuming that the distributor is fitted so that the rotor arm tip aligns with the notch on the distributor body when the engine is at TDC, the initial timing will be sufficiently accurate to enable the engine to run. The ignition timing can then be checked and adjusted if necessary as described in Chapter 1.

3   Ignition control unit – checking, removal and refitting

Caution: *Do not attempt to open or repair the control unit; if it is faulty, it must be renewed.*

Checking

1   The ignition control unit is located on the right-hand inner front wing, just to the rear of the headlamp unit on that side.

2   Before assuming that it is at fault, pull back the rubber gaiter from the control unit and check that the wiring connections are clean and secure (photo). It is essential that there is good electrical contact

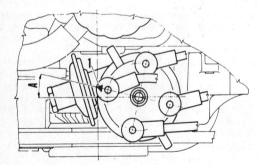

Fig. 5.4 Distributor position with No 1 cylinder at TDC, showing No 1 cylinder HT lead location and rotor arm angle (A) of 13° (approx) (Sec 2)

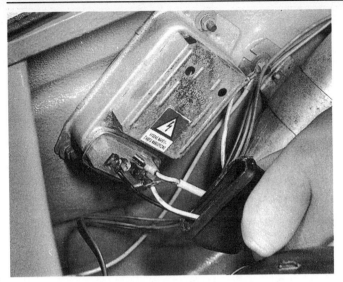

3.2 Ignition system control unit showing wiring connections

4.1 Ignition coil location

between the control unit and the distributor, and at all LT wiring connections.
3   Further checks of the ignition system, including the control unit, are described in Section 5.

Removal

4   Before removing the ignition control unit, first disconnect the battery negative terminal.
5   Pull free the rubber grommet from the control unit, then noting the respective connections, detach the wires from their control unit connectors.
6   Remove the securing nuts and withdraw the control unit, taking care not to damage it.

Refitting

7   Refit by reversing the removal operations, making sure that the LT and earth connections are well made.
8   Reconnect the battery and check for correct operation on completion.

4   Ignition HT coil – removal, testing and refitting

Removal

1   The coil is mounted on the right-hand inner wing, to the rear of the ignition control unit (photo).
2   Disconnect the battery negative terminal.
3   Disconnect the HT lead from the coil.
4   Note the locations of the LT connections on the coil, then disconnect them from the coil.
5   Slacken the mounting nuts and withdraw the coil. Note the location of the earth lead under one of the nuts.

Testing

6   Testing of the coil can be carried out without removing it, but first disconnect the leads from it as just described.
7   Use a multi-meter, set to its resistance function, to check the resistance of the primary winding (LT '+' to '–' terminals) and the secondary winding (LT '+' to HT lead terminals). No values are specified, but typically results of around 0.5 ohm for the primary and 5000 ohms for the secondary can be expected. If either winding is open-circuit (infinite resistance) the coil is definitely faulty.
8   If the coil is faulty, it must be renewed.

Refitting

9   Refitting is the reverse of the removal procedure.

5   Ignition system – testing

Note: *Refer to the warning given in Section 1 of this Chapter before starting work. Always switch off the ignition before disconnecting or connecting any component and when using a multi-meter to check resistances.*

General

1   The components of electronic ignition systems are normally very reliable. Faults are more likely to be due to loose or dirty connections or to 'tracking' of HT voltage due to dirt, dampness or damaged insulation than to the failure of any of the system's components. **Always** check all wiring thoroughly before condemning an electrical component, and work methodically to eliminate all other possibilities before deciding that a particular component is faulty.
2   When checking for a spark, hold the end of the HT lead being tested 10 mm from the engine block. For preference, secure the lead with crocodile clips, or use a proprietary air gap spark tester, rather than holding it by hand with an insulated tool.
3   Do not allow the coil to produce HT which cannot go anywhere, as the insulation and/or the control unit can be damaged. Either set up a spark gap as just described, or earth the coil HT lead.
4   Do not try to diagnose misfires by pulling off one HT lead at a time. This combines the risks of personal electric shock and insulation damage.

Engine will not start

Preliminary checks

5   If the engine will not turn at all, or only turns very slowly, check the battery and starter motor. Connect a voltmeter across the battery terminals (meter positive probe to battery positive terminal). Disconnect the ignition coil HT lead from the distributor cap and earth it, then note the voltage reading obtained while turning over the engine on the starter for a maximum of ten seconds. If the reading obtained is less than approximately 9.5 volts, check the battery, starter motor and charging system (Chapter 12).
6   If the engine turns at normal speed but will not start, check the HT circuit by connecting a timing light (following the manufacturer's instructions) and turning the engine on the starter motor. If the light flashes, voltage is reaching the spark plugs, so these should be checked first. If the light does not flash, check the HT leads themselves followed by the distributor cap, carbon brush and rotor arm (Chapter 1, and Section 2 of this Chapter).
7   If there is a spark, check the fuel system for faults (Chapter 4).
8   If there is still no spark, check the voltage at the ignition HT coil '+' terminal (black and orange wires); it should be the same as the battery voltage (ie, at least 11.7 volts). If the voltage drop between the battery and the coil is more than 1 volt, check the feed back through the ignition switch to the battery and its earth until the fault is found.

9　If the feed to the HT coil is sound, check the coil's primary winding (and also the secondary winding, while the opportunity exists) as described in Section 4. Renew the coil if it is faulty, but be careful to check carefully the condition of the LT connections themselves before doing so, to ensure that the fault is not due to dirty or poorly-fastened connectors.

10　If the HT coil is in good condition, the fault is probably within the ignition control unit or distributor pick-up coil. By way of a quick check, connect a low-wattage 12-volt bulb across the coil LT terminals. If the bulb flashes or flickers when the engine is turned on the starter, the control unit and distributor are probably OK.

11　If the control unit and distributor are sound, and the entire LT circuit is in good condition, the fault, if it lies in the ignition system, must be in the HT circuit components. These should be checked carefully, as outlined above.

12　If the test bulb did not flash or flicker, the fault is in either the distributor pick-up coil or the ignition control unit. Further checking can be carried out as follows.

Specific checks

13　Construct an ignition system test box as shown in Fig. 5.5.

14　Disconnect the coil HT lead from the distributor cap. Position the end of the lead approximately 10 mm from the engine block, or connect it to an air gap spark checking device.

15　Disconnect the distributor-to-control unit wiring. Connect the test box to the control unit as shown, and switch on the ignition.

16　Checking is now carried out with switch S2 first in one position, then in the other. In each position the effect is tried of pushing switch S1 a few times – this simulates the normal triggering input from the distributor. Observe what happens to the indicator light in the test box and to the spark gap. Possible results, and the sequence to follow, are given in the following table.

Switch S2 in position 1

Indicator light	Spark	Conclusion
On, flickering when S1 is pushed	Yes	Control unit and ignition coil OK. Possible distributor fault
On, flickering when S1 is pushed	No	Ignition coil defective
On steadily, not flickering when S1 is pushed	No	Control unit defective
Off	No	Proceed to next check

Switch S2 in position 2

Indicator light	Spark	Conclusion
On steadily, not flickering when S1 is pushed	No	Internal short-circuit in control unit. *Switch off immediately to avoid further damage.*
On, flickering when S1 is pushed	No	Ignition coil defective

17　If the above checks indicate that the control unit and coil are working correctly, measure the resistance of the distributor pick-up coil. If the resistance is not as specified, renew the distributor.

Engine misfires

18　An irregular misfire suggests either a loose connection or intermittent fault on the primary circuit, or an HT fault on the coil side of the rotor arm.

19　With the ignition switched off, check carefully through the system ensuring that all connections are clean and securely fastened. If the equipment is available, check the LT circuit as described above.

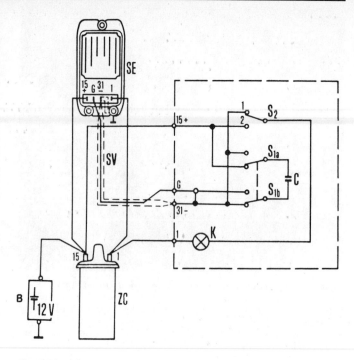

Fig. 5.5 Ignition system test box and wiring (Sec 5)

B	Vehicle battery	S2	Toggle switch (1-pole, 2-way)
C	Capacitor (2 microfarads)	SE	Control unit
K	Indicator light (12 volts, 2 watts maximum)	SV	Screened cable
		ZC	Ignition coil
S1	Pushbutton switch (2-pole, 2-way)		

20　Check that the HT coil, the distributor cap and the HT leads are clean and dry. Check the leads themselves and the spark plugs (by substitution, if necessary), then check the distributor cap, carbon brush and rotor arm (Chapter 1).

21　Regular misfiring is almost certainly due to a fault in the distributor cap, HT leads or spark plugs. Use a timing light as described above to check whether HT voltage is present at all leads.

22　If HT voltage is not present on one particular lead, the fault will be in that lead or in the distributor cap. If HT is present on all leads, the fault will be in the spark plugs; check and renew them if there is any doubt about their condition. (Bear in mind that it is possible for even a new spark plug to be defective. It is rare, but it does happen.)

23　If no HT is present, check the HT coil; its secondary windings may be breaking down under load.

Pinking

24　Pinking (pre-ignition) at light throttle and light loads on models up to August 1990 may be cured by fitting an extra washer under the vacuum advance unit cap bolt. This will increase the spring tension and delay the application of vacuum advance. Total washer thickness should be 2.5 to 3.0 mm. Later models have this modification already carried out.

Chapter 6 Clutch

Contents

Clutch assembly – removal, inspection and refitting.......................... 4
Clutch cable – removal, inspection and refitting................................. 2
Clutch cable adjustment ....See Chapter 1
Clutch pedal – removal, inspection and refitting 3
Clutch release mechanism – removal, inspection and refitting 5
General check...See Chapter 1
General information.. 1

Specifications

General
Type .... Single dry plate with a diaphragm spring, cable-operated
Adjustment... See Chapter 1

Friction plate
Diameter.. 190 mm
Lining thickness (new) .... 7.5 to 7.7 mm (under compression of 3000 N)
Lining thickness (minimum) .... 6.1 mm (under compression of 3000 N)

Torque wrench settings

	Nm	lbf ft
Pressure plate retaining bolts	23 to 28	17 to 21
Release fork bolt	18 to 25	13 to 18

1 General information

The clutch consists of a friction plate, a pressure plate assembly, a release bearing and the release mechanism; all of these components are contained in the large cast aluminium alloy bellhousing, sandwiched between the engine and the transmission. The release mechanism is mechanical, being operated by a cable.

The friction plate is fitted between the engine flywheel and the clutch pressure plate, and is allowed to slide on the transmission input shaft splines. It consists of two circular facings of friction material riveted in position to provide the clutch bearing surface, and a spring-cushioned hub to damp out transmission shocks.

The pressure plate assembly is bolted to the engine flywheel; it comprises the clutch cover, the diaphragm spring and the pressure plate. When the engine is running, drive is transmitted from the crankshaft via the flywheel and clutch cover to the friction plate (these last three components being clamped securely together by the pressure plate and diaphragm spring) and from the friction plate to the transmission input shaft.

To interrupt the drive, the spring pressure must be relaxed. This is achieved by a sealed release bearing fitted concentrically around the transmission input shaft; when the driver depresses the clutch pedal, the release bearing is pressed against the fingers at the centre of the diaphragm spring. Since the spring is held between two annular fulcrum rings, the pressure at its centre causes it to deform so that it flattens and thus releases the clamping force it exerts, at its periphery, on the pressure plate.

Depressing the clutch pedal pulls the control cable inner wire, and this in turn rotates the release fork by acting on the lever at the fork's upper end, above the bellhousing. The fork itself is clipped to the release bearing.

Fig. 6.1 Exploded view of the clutch components and release mechanism (Sec 1)

1   *Friction plate*
2   *Pressure plate*
3   *Pressure plate retaining bolt*
4   *Washer*
5   *Release bearing*
6   *Release fork pin*
7   *Release fork*
8   *Release fork bolt*
9   *Release fork lever bush*
10   *Release fork lever*
11   *Cable adjusting nut*
12   *Cap*
13   *Rubber spacer*
14   *Cap*
15   *Spring clip*
16   *Rubber gaiter*
17   *Seat*
18   *Rubber*
19   *Washer*
20   *Sealing washer*
21   *C-clip*
22   *Clutch cable*

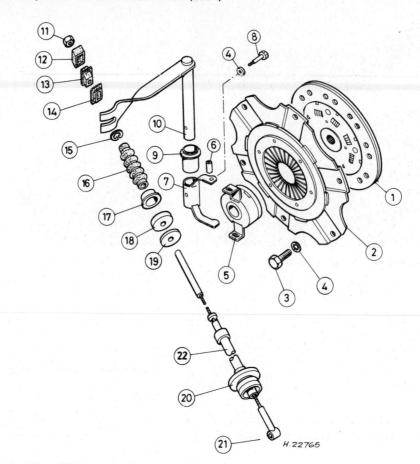

As the friction plate facings wear, the pressure plate moves towards the flywheel; this causes the diaphragm spring fingers to push against the release bearing, thus reducing the clearance which must be present in the mechanism. To ensure correct operation, the clutch cable must be regularly adjusted as described in Chapter 1.

2   Clutch cable – removal, inspection and refitting

Removal

1   Working in the engine compartment, rotate the clutch adjusting nut in an anti-clockwise direction to obtain maximum clutch cable free play. Remove the anti-rattle clip. Release the inner cable from the clutch release lever, and free the outer cable from its mounting bracket (photo).
2   Work back along the length of the cable, and free it from any ties or clamps.
3   Working from inside the vehicle, push back the carpet from around the clutch pedal upper end to gain access to the cable end fitting.
4   Prise off the C-clip and free the cable from the pedal upper end.
5   Return to the engine compartment and withdraw the cable forwards through the bulkhead, noting the rubber sealing ring fitted to the bulkhead end of the cable.

Inspection

6   Examine the cable, looking for worn end fittings or a damaged outer casing and for signs of fraying of the inner cable. Check the cable's operation; the inner cable wire should move smoothly and easily through the outer casing, but remember that a cable that appears serviceable when tested off the vehicle may well be much heavier in operation when compressed into its working position. Renew the cable

if it shows any signs of excessive wear or of damage, transferring the adjusting nut, washers and rubber spacers from the original.

Refitting

7   Apply a thin smear of multi-purpose grease to the cable end fittings. Fit the rubber sealing ring to the bulkhead end of the cable, and pass the cable through the engine compartment bulkhead.

2.1 Slacken the adjusting nut and free the clutch cable from the release lever and mounting bracket

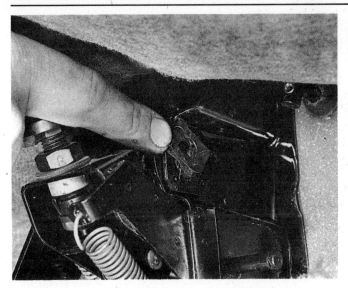

3.6A Remove the retaining clip from the clutch pedal pivot pin ...

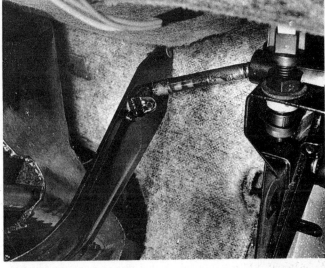

3.6B ... then slide the pedal out the left-hand side of the mounting bracket

8   Working from inside the vehicle, locate the cable with the clutch pedal pin, and secure it in position with the C-clip.
9   Working in the engine compartment, ensure that the cable is correctly routed, then pass the lower end through the mounting bracket and engage the inner cable with the clutch release lever. Secure any cable ties or clamps.
10   Adjust the cable as described in Chapter 1.

3 Clutch pedal – removal, inspection and refitting

Removal

1   Working in the engine compartment, rotate the clutch adjusting nut in an anti-clockwise direction to obtain maximum clutch cable free play.
2   Working from inside the vehicle, push back the carpet from around the clutch pedal upper end to gain access to the cable end fitting.
3   Prise off the C-clip and free the cable from the pedal upper end.
4   Using a pair of pliers, unhook the clutch pedal spring from the pedal.
5   To gain the required clearance to remove the clutch pedal, it is first necessary to drop the steering column as described in Section 14 of Chapter 10.
6   Slide the retaining clip off the right-hand end of the pedal pivot pin. Slide the clutch pedal to the left to disengage it from its mounting, and manoeuvre it out from the under the facia (photos). Note that the clutch pedal pivot bush also acts as the brake pedal pivot. Therefore if the bush is to be withdrawn, insert a suitable screwdriver into the right-hand end of the mounting bracket to retain the brake pedal in position whilst the bush is removed.

Refitting

7   Refitting is the reverse of the removal procedure, applying a thin smear of multi-purpose grease to the pedal pivot pin and bush. On completion, adjust the clutch cable as described in Chapter 1.

4 Clutch assembly – removal, inspection and refitting

Warning: *Dust created by clutch wear and deposited on the clutch components may contain asbestos, which is a health hazard. DO NOT blow it out with compressed air or inhale any of it. DO NOT use petrol or petroleum-based solvents to clean off the dust. Brake system cleaner or*

methylated spirit should be used to flush the dust into a suitable receptacle. After the clutch components are wiped clean with rags, dispose of the contaminated rags and cleaner in a sealed, marked container.
Note: *Although some friction materials may no longer contain asbestos, it is safest to assume that they do, and to take precautions accordingly.*

Removal

1   Unless the complete engine/transmission unit is to be removed from the vehicle and separated for major overhaul (see Chapter 2), the clutch can be reached by removing the transmission as described in Chapter 7.
2   Before disturbing the clutch, use a suitable marker pen or a dab of quick-drying paint to mark the relationship of the pressure plate assembly to the flywheel (photo).
3   Working in a diagonal sequence, slacken the pressure plate retaining bolts by half a turn at a time until spring pressure is released and the bolts can be unscrewed by hand. Remove the bolts along with their washers.
4   Remove the pressure plate assembly from the flywheel, and collect the friction plate, noting which way round the friction plate is fitted (photos).

4.2 Prior to removal, make alignment marks between the pressure plate and flywheel

4.4A Remove the pressure plate from the flywheel ...

4.4B ... and withdraw the friction plate, noting which way around it is fitted

4.18 Use a clutch-aligning tool to centralise the friction plate while tightening the pressure plate bolts to the specified torque

Inspection

Note: *Due to the amount of work necessary to remove and refit clutch components, it is usually considered good practice to renew the clutch friction plate, pressure plate assembly and release bearing as a matched set, even if only one of these is actually worn enough to require renewal.*

5   Remove the clutch assembly.

6   When cleaning clutch components, read first the warning at the beginning of this Section. Remove dust as described, and work in a well-ventilated atmosphere.

7   Check the friction plate facings for signs of wear, damage or oil contamination. If the friction material is cracked, burnt, scored or damaged, or if it is contaminated with oil or grease (shown by shiny black patches), the friction plate must be renewed.

8   If the friction material is still serviceable, check that the centre boss splines are unworn, that the torsion springs are in good condition and securely fastened, and that all the rivets are tightly fastened. If any wear or damage is found, the friction plate must be renewed.

9   If the friction material is fouled with oil, this must be due to an oil leak from the crankshaft left-hand (flywheel end) oil seal, from the sump-to-cylinder block joint or from the transmission input shaft. Renew the seal or repair the joint, as described in Chapter 2 or 7, before installing the new friction plate.

10   Check the pressure plate assembly for obvious signs of wear or damage. Shake it to check for loose rivets or worn or damaged fulcrum rings. Check that the drive straps securing the pressure plate to the cover do not show signs of overheating (such as a deep yellow or blue discoloration). If the diaphragm spring is worn or damaged, or if its pressure is in any way suspect, the pressure plate assembly should be renewed.

11   Examine the machined bearing surfaces of the pressure plate and of the flywheel; they should be clean, completely flat and free from scratches or scoring. If either is discoloured from excessive heat, or shows signs of cracks, it should be renewed, although minor damage of this nature can sometimes be polished away using emery paper. It may also be possible to reclaim a scored flywheel by machining, but this is a job for a specialist. See Chapter 2, Section 12.

12   Check the release bearing as described in Section 5 of this Chapter.

Refitting

13   On reassembly, ensure that the bearing surfaces of the flywheel and pressure plate are completely clean, smooth and free from oil or grease. Use solvent to remove any protective grease from new components.

14   Fit the friction plate so that the longer part of its central, splined, boss is towards the flywheel, and so that the spring hub assembly faces away from the flywheel. Install the pressure plate assembly, aligning the marks made on dismantling (if the original pressure plate is re-used). Note that if a new pressure plate assembly is being fitted, the plate can be installed in any position.

15   Fit the pressure plate retaining bolts and washers, but tighten them only finger-tight so that the friction plate can still be moved.

16   The friction plate must now be centralised so that when the transmission is refitted, its input shaft will pass through the splines at the centre of the friction plate.

17   Centralisation can be achieved by passing a screwdriver or other long bar through the friction plate and into the hole in the crankshaft; the

friction plate can then be moved around until it is centred on the crankshaft hole. Alternatively, a clutch-aligning tool can be used to eliminate the guesswork; these can be obtained from most accessory shops. A clutch-aligning tool can be made up from a length of metal rod or wooden dowel which fits closely inside the crankshaft hole, and has insulating tape wound around it to match the diameter of the friction plate splined hole.

18   When the friction plate is centralised, tighten the pressure plate bolts evenly and in a diagonal sequence to the specified torque (photo).

19   Apply a thin smear of molybdenum disulphide grease to the splines of the friction plate and the transmission input shaft, also to the release bearing bore.

20   Refit the transmission as described in Chapter 7.

5   Clutch release mechanism – removal, inspection and refitting

Note: *Refer to the warning concerning the dangers of asbestos dust at the beginning of Section 4.*

Removal

1   Unless the complete engine/transmission unit is to be removed from the vehicle and separated for major overhaul (see Chapter 2), the clutch release mechanism can be reached only by removing the transmission as described in Chapter 7.

2   Slacken and remove the clutch release fork retaining bolt, then withdraw the release lever from the gearbox whilst retaining the release bearing. The release bearing and fork assembly can then be also removed.

3   Unhook the release bearing from its locating peg on the fork, and separate the two components.

Inspection

4   Check the release mechanism for signs of wear or damage, renewing any component which is worn or damaged. Carefully check all bearing surfaces and points of contact, and renew the release lever pivot bush if worn.

5   When checking the release bearing itself, note that it is often considered worthwhile to renew it as a matter of course. Check that the contact surface rotates smoothly and easily, with no sign of noise or roughness, and that the surface itself is smooth and unworn, with no signs of cracks, pitting or scoring. If there is any doubt about its condition, the bearing must be renewed.

6   When cleaning the clutch components, **do not** use solvents on the release bearing; it is packed with grease which may be washed out if care is not taken.

Refitting

7   Offer up the release bearing to the release fork, engaging the fork

5.7 Engage the release bearing with the release fork pin ...

5.8A ... then slide the bearing and fork assembly onto the guide sleeve and insert the release lever

5.8B Align the release lever hole with that of the release fork, then insert and tighten the retaining bolt

locating pin in the release bearing slot (photo). Apply a smear of molybdenum disulphide grease to the centre of the release bearing and to the shaft of the release lever.

8   Slide the release bearing and fork assembly onto the guide sleeve, and insert the release lever. Align the release fork hole with that of the release lever shaft, then refit the fork retaining bolt and tighten it to the specified torque (photos).

9   Move the release lever to and fro, to check the operation of the release mechanism before refitting the transmission as described in Chapter 7.

Chapter 7 Transmission

Contents

Gearchange linkage – removal, overhaul and refitting...................... 2
General information 1
Oil level check ....See Chapter 1
Oil renewal...See Chapter 1
Oil seals – renewal 4

Reversing light switch – testing, removal and refitting..................... 5
Speedometer drive – removal and refitting.. 3
Transmission – removal and refitting.. 6
Transmission overhaul – general notes and precautions.................. 7

Specifications

Type.. Manual, five forward speeds and one reverse. Synchromesh on forward speeds

Ratios (typical)
1st... 3.308 : 1
2nd.. 1.913 : 1
3rd... 1.267 : 1
4th... 0.927 : 1
5th... 0.717 : 1
Reverse... 2.923 : 1
Final drive:
    Estate and Pick-up models .... 4.167 : 1
    All other models .... 3.895 : 1

Torque wrench settings

	Nm	lbf ft
Transmission-to-engine bolts	40 to 50	30 to 37
Speedometer drivegear lockplate bolt	7 to 10	5 to 8
Reversing light switch	25 to 35	18 to 26
Clutch release bearing guide sleeve screws	5 to 8	4 to 6
Earth cable retaining bolt	15 to 20	11 to 15
Engine/transmission left-hand and right-hand mountings:		
Through-bolts	42 to 50	31 to 37
Mounting bracket-to-body bolts	39 to 45	29 to 33
Flywheel cover plate bolts	8 to 10	6 to 8

1 General information

The transmission is contained in a cast aluminium alloy casing bolted to the engine's left-hand end, and consists of the gearbox and final drive/differential. The whole assembly is often called a 'transaxle'.

Drive is transmitted from the crankshaft via the clutch to the input shaft, which has a splined extension to accept the clutch friction plate, and rotates in sealed ball-bearings. From the input shaft, drive is transmitted to the output shaft, which rotates in a roller bearing at its right-hand end and a sealed ball-bearing at its left-hand end.

From the output shaft, the drive is transmitted to the differential crownwheel, which rotates with the differential case and planetary gears, thus driving the sun gears and driveshafts. The rotation of the planetary gears on their shaft allows the inner roadwheel to rotate at a slower speed than the outer when the vehicle is cornering.

The input and output shafts are arranged side by side, parallel to the crankshaft and driveshafts, so that their gear pinion teeth are in constant mesh. In the neutral position, the output shaft gear pinions rotate freely so that drive cannot be transmitted to the crownwheel.

Gear selection is by a floor-mounted lever acting through a remote control linkage on the selector mechanism. The selector mechanism causes the appropriate selector fork to move its respective synchro-sleeve along the shaft to lock the gear pinion to the synchro-hub. Since the synchro-hubs are splined to the output shaft, this locks the pinion to the shaft so that drive can be transmitted. To ensure that gear changing can be made quickly and quietly, a synchromesh system is fitted to all forward gears, consisting of baulk rings and spring-loaded fingers as well as the gear pinions and synchro-hubs; the synchromesh cones are formed on the mating faces of the baulk rings and gear pinions.

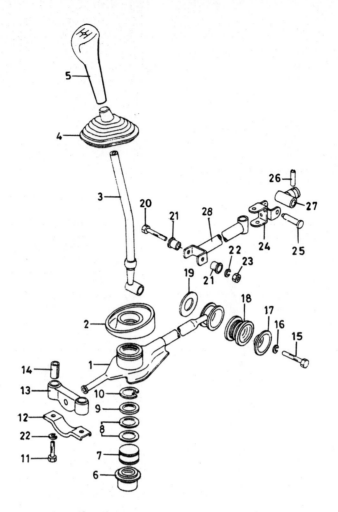

Fig. 7.1 Gearchange linkage/mechanism components (Sec 2)

1	Gearchange steady rod
2	Steady rod upper gaiter
3	Gearchange lever
4	Gearchange lever gaiter
5	Gearchange lever knob
6	Lower gaiter
7	Gearchange lever seat
8	Washers
9	Washer
10	Circlip
11	Bolt – steady rod to body
12	Mounting plate
13	Mounting rubber
14	Spacer
15	Bolt – steady rod to transmission
16	Washer
17	Washer
18	Mounting rubber
19	Washer
20	Bolt – selector rod to gearchange lever
21	Pivot bush
22	Washer
23	Nut
24	Selector rod joint
25	Selector rod joint pivot pin
26	Roll pin
27	Selector rod front section
28	Selector rod rear section

2 Gearchange linkage – removal, overhaul and refitting

Removal

1   Park the vehicle on level ground, switch off the ignition, check that the transmission is in neutral, and apply the handbrake firmly. Jack up the front of the vehicle, and support it securely on axle stands.
2   From inside the car, pull the knob off the gearchange lever.
3   Working underneath the car, using a hammer and suitable punch, tap the roll pin out of the selector rod and disconnect the rod from the transmission. Discard the pin, which must be renewed whenever it is disturbed. Slacken the nut and bolt which secure the selector rod to the gearchange lever, then withdraw the bolt and collect the washers fitted between the selector rod and gearchange lever (photos). Manoeuvre the selector rod out from under the car.
4   Slacken and remove the bolt securing the front end of the gearchange linkage steady rod to the transmission housing, then free the rod and remove the two large mounting washers. Undo the two

bolts securing the rear of the steady rod to the vehicle underbody, and remove the bolts along with the mounting plate, noting the two spacers which are fitted to the mounting rubber. Free the steady rod upper rubber gaiter from the vehicle underbody, then carefully lower the rod and lever assembly downwards and out from under the car (photos).
5   If necessary, remove the gearchange lever gaiter from the vehicle.

Overhaul

6   Remove the upper steady rod upper gaiter to gain access to the gearchange lever circlip. Extract the circlip and withdraw the washers. The gearchange lever can then be tapped upwards out of the steady rod, and the gearchange lever seat and lower gaiter removed.
7   Thoroughly clean all components, and examine them for signs of wear or damage, paying particular attention to the rubber mountings and gaiters. Renew damaged components as necessary.
8   On reassembly, apply a smear of multi-purpose grease to the gearchange lever ball and seat, and refit the assembly to the steady rod. Refit the washers, securing them in position with the circlip, ensuring it is correctly located in its groove. Fit the steady rod upper gaiter.

2.3A Tap out the roll pin from the front of the selector rod ...

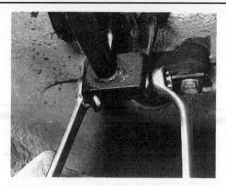

2.3B ... then undo the nut and bolt

2.4A Remove the bolt securing the steady rod to the transmission ...

2.4B ... and the two rear steady rod mounting bolts

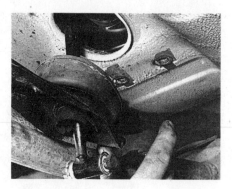

2.4C Free the gaiter from the underbody

Refitting

9   Refitting is the reverse of the removal procedure, noting the following points (photos).

  (a) Apply a smear of multi-purpose grease to all linkage pivot points.
  (b) Securely tighten all nuts and bolts, noting that a thread-locking compound should be applied to the threads of the bolt securing the steady rod to the transmission housing.
  (c) On completion, check that the linkage operates smoothly and that all rubber gaiters are correctly located in their grooves.

3   Speedometer drive – removal and refitting

Removal

1   Working in the engine compartment, unscrew the knurled retaining ring securing the speedometer cable to its drive, situated at the rear of the transmission, and disconnect the cable (photo).
2   Hold the speedometer drive assembly (to prevent it from falling down into the transmission) then slacken and remove the retaining bolt and lockplate, and lift the assembly out of the transmission (photos).

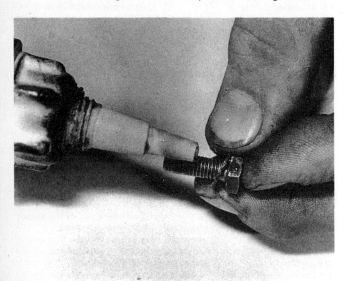

2.9A On refitting apply thread-locking compound to the steady rod front mounting bolt ...

2.9B ... and secure the selector rod with a new roll pin

3.1 Unscrew the knurled retaining ring, and disconnect the speedometer cable from the transmission

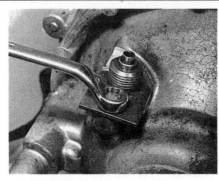

3.2A Undo the retaining bolt, remove the lockplate ...

3.2B ... and withdraw the speedometer drive assembly

4.5 Carefully lever the inner constant velocity joint out of the transmission

4.6 Insert a suitable rod to support the sun gear if both driveshafts are to be withdrawn

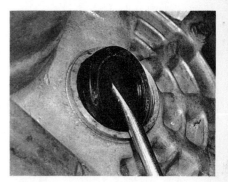

4.7 Lever out the oil seal using a large flat-bladed screwdriver ...

3   Examine the speedometer drivegear for signs of chipped or missing teeth; renew if damaged. Inspect the speedometer drive O-ring for signs of damage or deterioration, and renew if necessary.

Refitting

4   Apply a smear of oil to the O-ring, then ease the speedometer gear assembly back into position in the transmission. Hold it in position, and locate the lockplate with the slots in the housing. Refit the lockplate retaining bolt, and tighten it to the specified torque.

5   Reconnect the speedometer cable to the drivegear, and securely tighten its knurled retaining ring.

4   Oil seals – renewal

Driveshaft oil seal

1   Chock the rear wheels of the vehicle, firmly apply the handbrake, then jack up the front of the vehicle and support it on axle stands. Remove the appropriate front roadwheel.

2   Drain the transmission oil as described in Chapter 1.

3   Disconnect the track rod balljoint from the hub carrier steering arm as described in Chapter 10.

4   Remove the pinch-bolt, and disconnect the suspension lower arm balljoint from the hub carrier as described in Chapter 10.

5   Insert a suitable flat bar in between the inner constant velocity joint and transmission housing. Carefully lever the joint out of position, taking care not to damage the transmission housing or the constant velocity joint metal shield (photo).

6   Withdraw the inner constant velocity joint from the transmission, and support the driveshaft to avoid damaging the constant velocity joints or gaiters. If both driveshafts are to be withdrawn, prevent the sun gear falling down inside the transmission by inserting a clean metal rod or wooden dowel of approximately 24 mm diameter until the gear is securely supported (photo).

7   Carefully prise the oil seal out of the transmission with a large flat-bladed screwdriver (photo).

8   Remove all traces of dirt from the area around the oil seal aperture, then apply a smear of grease to the outer lip of the new oil seal. Fit the new seal into its aperture, and drive it squarely into position using a suitable tubular drift (such as a socket) which bears only on the hard outer edge of the seal, until it abuts its locating shoulder (photo).

9   Prior to refitting the driveshaft, check that the inner constant velocity joint shoulder is smooth and free of burrs and scratches. Small burrs or scratches can be removed using emery cloth; larger imperfections may require the renewal of the joint. Examine the circlip which is fitted to the groove in the inner constant velocity joint splines for signs of damage, and renew it if there is any doubt about its condition.

10   Thoroughly clean the driveshaft splines, then apply a thin film of grease to the oil seal lips and to the inner constant velocity joint splines and shoulder. Remove the sun gear support, if applicable.

11   Ensure that the circlip is located securely in its groove. Engage the joint splines with those of the differential sun gear, taking care not to damage the oil seal (photo). Push the joint fully into the transmission, and check that it is securely retained by the circlip by firmly grasping the inner joint body and trying to pull the driveshaft out of the sun gear.

12   Refit the suspension lower arm balljoint to the hub carrier, and connect the track rod balljoint to the hub carrier steering arm. Refer to Chapter 10 for further information.

13   Refit the roadwheel, lower the vehicle to the ground and tighten the wheel bolts to the specified torque (Chapter 1 Specifications).

14   Refill the transmission with the correct type and quantity of oil as described in Chapter 1.

Selector shaft oil seal

15   Park the vehicle on level ground, switch off the ignition, check that the transmission is in neutral and apply the handbrake firmly. Jack up the front of the vehicle, and support it securely on axle stands.

16   Using a hammer and punch, tap the roll pin out of the selector rod and disconnect the rod from the transmission. Discard the roll pin, which must be renewed whenever it is disturbed.

4.8 ... and tap the new seal into position with a tubular drift

4.11 Take care not to damage the oil seal lip when refitting the constant velocity joint

4.17A Remove the selector shaft gaiter ...

4.17B ... then extract the old oil seal

4.19 Tap the selector shaft seal into position using a tubular drift such as a socket

4.22 Clutch release bearing guide sleeve is retained by two screws

17   Remove the selector shaft gaiter. Using a screwdriver or long-nosed pliers, carefully lever the seal out of the housing and slide it off the end of the shaft (photos).

18   Before fitting a new seal, check the selector shaft seal rubbing surface for signs of burrs, scratches or other damage which may have caused the seal to fail in the first place. It may be possible to polish away minor faults of this sort using fine abrasive paper; more serious defects will require the renewal of the selector shaft.

19   Apply a smear of grease to the outer edge and sealing lip of the new seal, then carefully slide the seal along the selector rod. Press the seal fully into position in the gearbox housing and refit the gaiter, ensuring that it is correctly located with the seal shoulder (photo).

20   Reconnect the selector rod to the shaft, and align the roll pin holes. Tap a new roll pin into position using a hammer and punch, then lower the car to the ground.

Input shaft oil seal

21   Remove the transmission as described in Section 6, then remove the clutch release fork as described in Chapter 6.

22   Undo the two screws securing the clutch release bearing guide sleeve in position (photo), and slide the guide off the input shaft. Carefully lever the oil seal out of the guide using a suitable flat-bladed screwdriver.

23   Before fitting a new seal, check the seal rubbing surface on the input shaft for signs of burrs, scratches or other damage which may have caused the seal to fail in the first place. It may be possible to polish away minor faults of this sort using fine abrasive paper; more serious defects will require the renewal of the input shaft. Ensure that the input shaft is clean and greased to protect the seal lips on refitting.

24   Dip the new seal in clean oil and fit it to the guide sleeve, noting that the seal sealing lip must face inwards when the sleeve is installed. Carefully slide the guide sleeve into position, then refit the retaining screws and tighten them to the specified torque.

25   Reassemble and lubricate the clutch release mechanism as described in Chapter 6, then wipe off any surplus oil or grease and refit the transmission to the vehicle.

5 Reversing light switch – testing, removal and refitting

Testing

1   The reversing light circuit is controlled by a plunger-type switch, screwed into the underside of the transmission casing. If a fault develops in the circuit, first ensure that the bulb or the circuit fuse has not blown.

2   To test the switch, disconnect its wires and use a multimeter (set to the resistance function), or a battery and bulb test circuit, to check that there is continuity between the switch terminals only when reverse gear is selected. If this is not the case, the switch is faulty and must be renewed.

Removal

3   Chock the rear wheels of the vehicle, firmly apply the handbrake, then jack up the front of the vehicle and support it on axle stands. Either drain the transmission oil as described in Chapter 1, or be prepared for some loss of oil as the switch is unscrewed.

4   Disconnect the battery negative terminal, and disconnect the reversing light switch wiring connectors (photo).

5   Unscrew the switch from the transmission and withdraw it, then plug the opening to prevent the entry of dirt; if the transmission has not been drained, work quickly to minimise oil loss.

Refitting

6   Wipe the threads of the switch and those of the transmission clean. If a sealing washer is fitted, renew it whenever it is disturbed to prevent leaks; if no sealing washer is fitted, apply a smear of sealant to the switch threads.

7   Refit the switch, working quickly if the transmission oil was not drained, and tighten it the specified torque. Reconnect the wiring connectors and test the operation of the circuit.

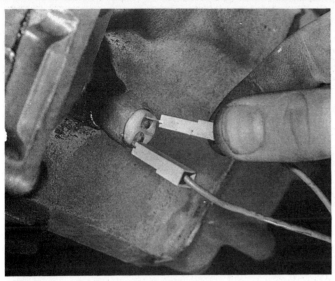

5.4 Disconnecting the reversing light switch wiring connectors

8   Lower the vehicle to the ground, then refill or top-up the transmission oil as described in Chapter 1.

6   Transmission – removal and refitting

Removal

1   Disconnect the battery negative terminal.
2   Remove the starter motor as described in Chapter 12.

3   Working in the engine compartment, rotate the clutch adjusting nut in an anti-clockwise direction to obtain maximum clutch cable free play. Release the inner cable from the clutch release lever, and free the outer cable from its mounting bracket.
4   Unscrew the knurled retaining ring, and disconnect the speedometer cable from its drive located at the rear of the transmission.
5   Firmly apply the handbrake and chock the rear wheels, then jack up the front of the vehicle and support it on axle stands. Remove both front roadwheels.
6   Drain the transmission oil as described in Chapter 1.
7   Remove the exhaust system downpipe as described in Chapter 4.
8   Slacken and remove the retaining screws, and remove the engine undershield and the left-hand undershield side cover.
9   Disconnect the wiring connectors from the reversing light switch.
10   Working from underneath the vehicle, slacken and remove its retaining bolt, then disconnect the transmission earth strap from the vehicle underbody (photo).
11   Disconnect the gearchange linkage selector rod and steady rod from the transmission as described in Section 2.
12   Release the driveshaft inner constant velocity joints from the transmission as described in Section 4, paragraphs 3 to 6.
13   Undo the flywheel lower cover plate retaining nuts and bolt, and remove the plate from the transmission (photos).
14   Undo the nut securing the rear engine/transmission connecting rod to the subframe bracket, then remove the bolt securing the rod to the engine bracket, and remove the connecting rod from underneath the vehicle.
15   Place a jack with interposed block of wood beneath the engine to take the weight of the engine. Alternatively, attach lifting eyes to the engine lifting bracket on the cylinder head and fit a hoist or support bar to take the weight of the engine (photo).
16   Place a jack and block of wood beneath the transmission.
17   Slacken and remove the through-bolt from the left-hand engine/transmission mounting, and remove its square nut from the front of the mounting bracket. Loosen the right-hand mounting through-bolt.
18   Remove all the remaining transmission housing-to-engine bolts, noting the correct location of the clutch cable mounting bracket, then

6.10 Remove the bolt securing the earth strap to the vehicle body

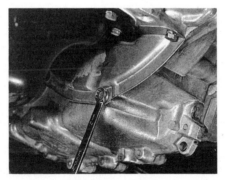

6.13A Remove the retaining bolts ...

6.13B ... and remove the flywheel lower cover plate

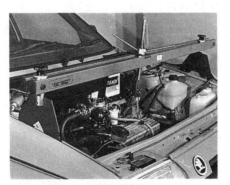

6.15 An engine support bar can be used to take the weight of the engine while the gearbox is removed

6.18 Note the correct fitted position of the clutch cable bracket when removing the transmission housing bolts

6.19A Lower the engine/transmission unit until the left-hand mounting is clear of its bracket ...

6.19B ... then release the transmission from the engine ...

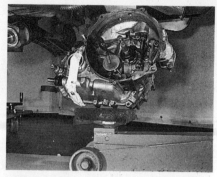

6.19C ... and manoeuvre it out from under the vehicle

Fig. 7.2 Exploded view of transmission shafts (Sec 7)

1   Nut
2   Spring
3   Thrust ring
4   Synchro clutch sleeve
5   Synchro clutch spring
6   Synchro clutch body
7   Synchro clutch pawl
8   Synchro ring
9   5th gear pinion
10 Bearing
11 Spacer
12 Shim (available in various thicknesses)
13 Bearing
14 Complete input shaft assembly
15 Bearing
16 Input shaft oil seal
17 Clutch release bearing guide sleeve
18 Screw
19 Gate
20 Bearing
21 Shim
22 Bolt
23 Output shaft
24 1st gear pinion
25 Synchro ring
26 Synchro clutch spring
27 Circlip
28 Synchro clutch pawl
29 Synchro clutch body
30 Synchro clutch sleeve
31 2nd gear pinion
32 Holder
33 Friction ring
34 3rd gear pinion
35 Synchro clutch body
36 Synchro clutch sleeve
37 4th gear pinion
38 Bearing
39 Circlip
40 5th gear pinion
41 Reverse gear shaft
42 Reverse gear pinion assembly
43 Pin

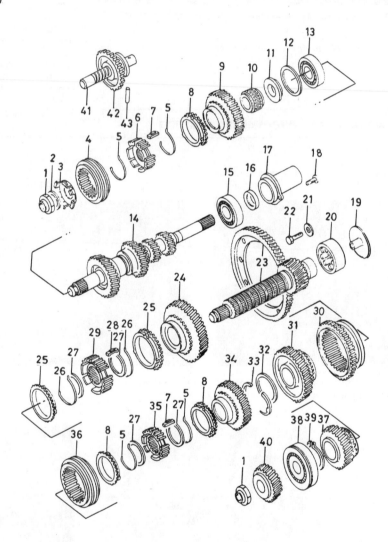

make a final check that all necessary components have been disconnected (photo). Ensure the driveshafts and gearchange linkage are positioned clear of the transmission unit so that they do not hinder the removal procedure.

19   Carefully lower the engine and transmission until the left-hand mounting is clear of its bracket, then release the transmission from the engine. It may initially be tight owing to the locating dowels. Do not allow the weight of the transmission to hang on the input shaft. Once the transmission is free, lower the jack and remove the unit out from under the vehicle (photos).

Refitting

20   The transmission is refitted by reversing the removal procedure, bearing in mind the following points.

(a)   Make sure the dowels are correctly positioned prior to installation.

(b)   Apply a little high-melting-point grease to the splines of the transmission input shaft. Do not apply too much, otherwise there is a possibility of the grease contaminating the clutch friction plate.

(c)   Tighten all nuts and bolts to the specified torque.

(d)   Reconnect the gearchange linkage selector and steady rods as described in Section 2.

(e)   Install the driveshafts as described in Section 4, paragraphs 9 to 12.

(f)   Adjust the clutch cable as described in Chapter 1.

(g)   On completion, refill the transmission with the specified type and quantity of oil as described in Chapter 1.

7   Transmission overhaul – general information

Overhauling a manual transmission unit is a difficult and involved job for the DIY home mechanic. In addition to dismantling and reassembling many small parts, clearances must be precisely measured and, if necessary, changed by selecting shims and spacers. Transmission internal components are also often difficult to obtain, and in many instances, extremely expensive. Because of this, if the transmission develops a fault or becomes noisy, the best course of action is to have the unit overhauled by a specialist repairer, or to obtain an exchange reconditioned unit.

Nevertheless, it is not impossible for the more experienced mechanic to overhaul the transmission, provided the special tools are available and the job is done in a deliberate step-by-step manner so that nothing is overlooked.

The tools necessary for an overhaul include internal and external circlip pliers, bearing pullers, a slide hammer, a set of pin punches, a dial test indicator, and possibly a hydraulic press. In addition, a large, sturdy workbench and a vice will be required.

During dismantling of the transmission, make careful notes of how each component is fitted, to make reassembly easier and accurate.

Before dismantling the transmission, it will help if you have some idea what area is malfunctioning. Certain problems can be closely related to specific areas in the transmission which can make component examination and replacement easier. Refer to the Fault Diagnosis Section at the beginning of this Manual for more information.

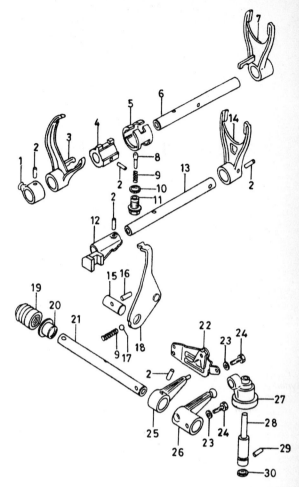

Fig. 7.3 Exploded view of the transmission selector mechanism (Sec 7)

1	Holder	15	Reverse gear shift lever pin
2	Pin	16	Pin
3	1st and 2nd gear selector fork	17	Ball
4	Shift pin	18	Reverse gear shift lever
5	Lock element	19	Selector shaft gaiter
6	Selector fork shaft	20	Selector shaft oil seal
7	3rd and 4th gear selector fork	21	Selector shaft
8	Detent pin	22	Gate
9	Spring	23	Washer
10	Sealing washer	24	Bolt
11	Bolt	25	Gate pin
12	Shift pin	26	Gear lever
13	Selector fork shaft	27	Angular lever
14	5th gear selector fork	28	Angular lever pin
		29	Pin
		30	O-ring

Chapter 8 Driveshafts

Contents

Driveshafts – removal and refitting.. 2
Driveshaft overhaul – general information................................. 4
Driveshaft rubber gaiters – renewal... 3

Driveshaft rubber gaiter and CV joint check .... See Chapter 1
General information 1

Specifications

Type.. Unequal-length solid steel shafts, splined to inner and outer constant velocity joints, dynamic damper on right-hand shaft of some models

Lubrication (overhaul only – see text)
Lubricant type/specification:
    Inner joint .... Shell GLEP 240
    Outer joint .... Shell GL 245 MO
Quantity:
    Inner joint .... 100 g
    Outer joint .... 80 g

Torque wrench settings

	Nm	lbf ft
Driveshaft nuts	240 to 270	177 to 199
Roadwheel bolts	60 to 90	44 to 66
Dynamic damper clamp screws	11 to 15	8 to 11

1 General information

The drive is transmitted from the differential sun gears to the front roadwheels by two unequal-length steel driveshaft assemblies; on some models, the (longer) right-hand driveshaft is fitted with a dynamic damper to reduce harmonic vibrations and resonance.

Both driveshafts are splined at their outer ends to accept the wheel hubs, and are threaded so that each hub can be fastened by a large nut. The inner end of each driveshaft is splined to accept the differential sun gear, and has a groove to accept the circlip which secures the driveshaft to the sun gear.

Two constant velocity joints are fitted to each driveshaft, to ensure the smooth and efficient transmission of drive at all the angles possible as the roadwheels move up and down with the suspension, and as they turn from side to side under steering. Each outer joint is of the Birfield-Rzeppa ball-and-cage type, but the inner joint is of the tripod type and is plunge-accepting, to allow for the differences in driveshaft effective length at the extremes of suspension travel.

Note: *The only replacement parts listed are the constant velocity joint assemblies, the rubber gaiters and their clips, the shaft itself and the various circlips. If any joint is worn or damaged, it cannot be reconditioned but must be renewed. Always renew all circlips, and note that it is not recommended to re-use gaiter clips.*

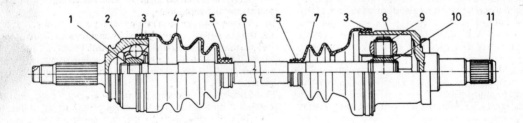

Fig. 8.1 Cutaway view of driveshaft assembly (Sec 1)

1	Circlip	4	Rubber gaiter
2	Outer joint	5	Small gaiter clip
3	Large gaiter clip	6	Shaft

7	Rubber gaiter	10	Circlip
8	Inner joint body	11	Circlip
9	Inner joint inner race assembly		

2.2 Using a punch to release driveshaft nut staking – roadwheel removed for clarity

2.8 Tapping driveshaft out of hub carrier assembly

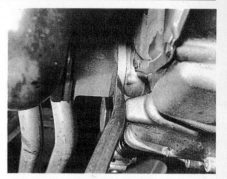

2.10 Levering driveshaft out of transmission – note care taken to avoid damaging joint metal shield

2.11 Insert sun gear support if both driveshafts are to be removed

2.13 Driveshaft inboard end, showing circlip groove

2.14 Take care not to damage transmission oil seal or rubber gaiter when refitting driveshaft

2 Driveshafts – removal and refitting

Note: *If either or both driveshafts have been removed, the vehicle should not be moved, or the front hub bearings may be damaged. If it is absolutely necessary to move the vehicle, either refit temporarily the driveshaft(s) and tighten the driveshaft nut(s), or preload the bearings using a bolt, nut and washers to clamp the bearing inboard inner race against the hub itself. As well as any other parts which may be required, ensure that new inboard circlips and driveshaft nuts are available* **before** *the driveshafts are removed.*

Removal

1   With the vehicle standing on its wheels, apply the handbrake firmly and select first or reverse gear.
2   Remove the roadwheel centre cap. Relieve the staking of the driveshaft nut using a hammer and punch (photo) or (if necessary) an electric drill, then use a suitable socket, a strong T-bar and a long extension tube to slacken the nut; do not unscrew it yet. If the nut is particularly tight, have an assistant apply the brakes hard.
3   Slacken the remaining roadwheel bolts, then jack up the front of the vehicle and support it securely on axle stands (see *'Jacking, towing and wheel changing'*). Remove the roadwheel, then unscrew the driveshaft nut. The nut must be renewed as a matter of course whenever it is disturbed.
4   Drain the transmission oil (Chapter 1).
5   Open the bonnet and slacken, by one or two turns only, each of the two suspension strut top mounting nuts.
6   Disconnect the track rod balljoint from the hub carrier steering arm (Chapter 10).
7   Removing its pinch-bolt, disconnect the suspension lower arm balljoint from the hub carrier (Chapter 10).
8   Sharply tug the hub carrier outwards off the driveshaft splines; it may be necessary to use a soft-faced mallet (having refitted first the used driveshaft nut to protect the shaft's threaded end) to tap the driveshaft out of the hub (photo). Take care not to stretch or kink the brake flexible hose.

9   Tie or wedge the strut assembly, complete with the hub carrier and brake caliper, clear of the driveshaft end.
10   Use a suitable lever to prise out the driveshaft until the circlip compresses into its groove and is released from the differential sun gear (photo). Take care not to damage the metal shield on the inner joint's inboard end.
11   Withdraw the driveshaft assembly. If both driveshafts are to be removed, prevent the sun gear falling down inside the transmission by inserting into the transmission aperture a clean metal rod or wooden dowel of 24 mm diameter until the gear is securely supported (photo). Discard the circlip at the driveshaft's inboard end; it must be renewed as a matter of course whenever it is disturbed.

Refitting

12   Thoroughly clean the driveshaft itself and the apertures in the transmission and hub carrier to prevent the entry of dirt during reassembly. Apply a thin film of grease to the oil seal lips and to the driveshaft splines and shoulders. Check that all gaiter clips are securely fastened.
13   Ensure that a new circlip is fitted to the inboard end of each driveshaft and is located securely in its groove (photo). Remove the sun gear support, if applicable.
14   Taking care not to damage the oil seal lips, insert the driveshaft into the transmission, and engage its splines with those of the sun gear. Press firmly the driveshaft into place until the circlip engages correctly behind (inboard of) the sun gear. If it is necessary to use tools to tap the driveshaft into place, be very careful not to damage the rubber gaiter (photo).
15   Check that the circlip is properly engaged by grasping the inner joint body firmly and trying to pull the driveshaft out of the sun gear.
16   Refit the driveshaft to the hub carrier (photo), and fit a new driveshaft nut.
17   Refit the suspension lower arm balljoint to the hub carrier, refit the pinch-bolt and tighten the pinch-bolt nut to the specified torque.
18   Connect the track rod balljoint to the hub carrier steering arm, tighten the balljoint nut to the specified torque, and fit a new split pin (Chapter 10).
19   Refit the roadwheel.

2.16 Refitting the driveshaft to the hub carrier

2.20A Tighten the new driveshaft nut to the specified torque wrench setting ...

2.20B ... and stake it into the driveshaft groove to secure it – roadwheel removed for clarity

20   Lower the vehicle to the ground and tighten the driveshaft nut and roadwheel bolts to their specified torque settings. Using a hammer and punch, secure the driveshaft nut by staking its collar into the driveshaft groove (photos).

21   Refit the roadwheel centre cap; where applicable, do not forget to tighten the remaining roadwheel bolts to the specified torque setting.

22   Refill the transmission with oil (Chapter 1).

---

3   Driveshaft rubber gaiters – renewal

Outer joint

Note: *This operation is a great deal easier if the driveshaft is removed from the vehicle, as described below. However, it is possible to dismantle an outer joint without removing the driveshaft from the transmission, provided that care is taken to hold the driveshaft into the transmission while the hub carrier and outer joint are removed. If this approach is to be used, refer to Section 2, paragraphs 1 to 3, then 5 to 9.*

1   Remove the driveshaft (Sec 2).

2   Clamp the driveshaft in a soft-jawed vice. If it is necessary to remove the dynamic damper (where fitted), unscrew the two Allen-headed clamp screws and withdraw it.

3   Cut the gaiter clips and peel back the gaiter from the joint (photo).

4   Using a sharply-pointed punch or scribing tool, mark the relationship of the joint body to the shaft itself, then use a hammer and a drift (applied to the joint inner race only) to tap the joint off the shaft splines until the circlip compresses into its groove and is released from the inner race (photo).

5   Withdraw the joint from the shaft and slide off the gaiter; if it is to be

re-used, wrap insulating tape around the shaft to protect the gaiter from any sharp edges. Check the gaiter for splits, cracking or other signs of damage, and renew it if necessary. Renew both clips.

6   Remove and discard the circlip from the shaft end. Using a clean rag, wipe as much of the old grease as possible out of the joint.

7   On refitting, wind a thin layer of insulating tape around the shaft to protect the gaiter from the shaft splines and other sharp edges. Fit the small gaiter clip, then slide on the gaiter and check that it is seated correctly in its shaft groove before removing the tape.

8   Fit a new circlip to the groove nearest the shaft's end, apply a smear of grease and press the outer joint into place so that the shaft end, the circlip and the joint inner race are all aligned, also the marks made on removal. Using a soft-faced mallet and protecting the joint's threaded end by refitting temporarily the used driveshaft nut, tap the outer joint on to the shaft until the circlip compresses into its groove and passes through the inner race (photo).

9   Check that the circlip is correctly engaged by trying to pull the joint off the shaft.

10   Fill the joint with the specified type of grease; pack any surplus into the gaiter.

11   Position the gaiter on the joint body groove, and equalise air pressure on both sides of the gaiter by carefully lifting one of its lips using a small screwdriver, then fasten the gaiter clips.

12   If the dynamic damper (where fitted) was disturbed, refit it as described in paragraph 27 or 28, as appropriate, below.

13   Refit the driveshaft (Section 2).

Inner joint

Note: *The following text assumes that the driveshaft will be removed and the inner joint dismantled. It is, however, possible to remove the*

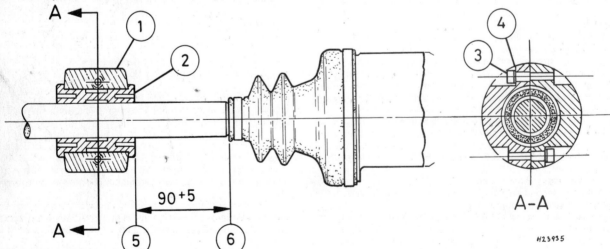

Fig. 8.2 Showing location (dimension in mm) of dynamic damper for early models, without locating groove in shaft – cross-section A – A applicable to all models (Sec 3)

1 Metal clamp	3 Clamp screw	5 Damper inboard end
2 Plastic insert	4 Spring washer	6 Inner joint gaiter groove outboard end

3.3 It may be necessary to cut gaiter clips to release gaiters

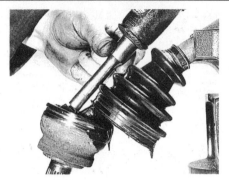

3.4 Driving outer constant velocity joint off driveshaft end

3.8 Refitting outer constant velocity joint to driveshaft

3.15 Releasing inner joint gaiter clip

3.16A Unscrew dynamic damper clamp screws ...

3.16B ... to withdraw damper from driveshaft – note broad groove in shaft for 1992-on models

outer joint only (see note above) and to remove and refit the inner joint gaiter along the driveshaft; if this approach is to be adopted, remove the dynamic damper (where fitted), clean off any rust deposits or similar using emery cloth, and wrap insulating tape around any sharp edges on the shaft to protect the gaiter's sealing lip.

14   Remove the driveshaft (Section 2).

15   Release or cut the gaiter clips, and peel back the gaiter from the joint (photo).

16   Clamp the driveshaft in a soft-jawed vice. If it is necessary to remove the dynamic damper (where fitted), unscrew the two Allen-headed clamp screws and withdraw it (photos).

17   Using a sharply-pointed punch or scribing tool, mark the relationship of the joint body to the shaft itself, then pull off the joint body, being careful not to lose any of the needle rollers from the joint's three bearings.

18   Mark the relationship of the joint inner race to the shaft itself, then remove the circlip from the shaft inboard end. Pull the inner race off the shaft splines; again, take care not to lose any of the needle rollers from the joint's bearings.

19   Slide off the gaiter; if it is to be re-used, wrap insulating tape around the shaft to protect the gaiter from the remaining circlip and any other sharp edges. Check the gaiter for splits, cracking or other signs of damage and renew it if necessary. Renew both clips.

20   Using a clean rag, wipe as much of the old grease as possible out of the joint components.

21   On reassembly, wind a thin layer of insulating tape around the shaft to protect the gaiter from the shaft splines, the remaining circlip and any other sharp edges. Fit the small gaiter clip, then slide on the gaiter, and check that it is seated correctly in its shaft groove before removing the tape.

22   Aligning the marks made on removal, slide the joint inner race on to the shaft splines, then secure it by fitting a new circlip to the groove nearest the shaft's end. If the inner race has to be tapped into place, take care not to lose any of the needle rollers from the joint's three bearings.

23   Aligning the marks made on removal, slide the joint body into place.

24   Fill the joint with the specified type of grease; pack any surplus into the gaiter.

25   Position the gaiter on the joint body groove, and move the body in and out several times to distribute the grease around the joint components, and to settle the gaiter in place. Equalise air pressure on both sides of the gaiter by carefully lifting one of its lips using a small screwdriver, then fasten the gaiter clips.

26   If the dynamic damper (where fitted) was disturbed, refit it as follows.

27   On models built before 1992 (without a broad groove in the right-hand driveshaft), clean thoroughly and degrease the surface of the shaft from 80 to 170 mm outboard of the inner joint gaiter groove. Using any proprietary steel-to-rubber/plastics adhesive, glue the two halves of the damper's plastic insert on to the shaft at the point shown in Fig. 8.2. Arranging them so that their joint is at right-angles to that of the plastic insert, fit the metal clamps with their screws and washers, tightening the screws to their specified torque wrench setting. When the adhesive is dry, check that the damper is securely fixed to the shaft; when the driveshaft is refitted to the vehicle (and allowing for extremes of suspension movement), check that the damper is at least 5 mm clear of any other part of the vehicle, in particular the body or suspension.

28   On 1992 models, clean the shaft and damper components carefully, and fit the two halves of the damper's plastic insert into the shaft's broad groove. Arranging them so that their joint is at right-angles to that of the plastic insert, fit the metal clamps with their screws and washers, tightening the screws to their specified torque wrench setting. There is no need to use adhesive; provided that the damper is located correctly in the groove so that it cannot slide along the shaft, it can be free to rotate on the shaft.

29   Refit the driveshaft (Sec 2).

4   Driveshaft overhaul – general information

1   If any of the checks described in Chapter 1 reveal wear in any driveshaft joint, first remove the roadwheel centre cap. If the staking is still effective, the driveshaft nut should be correctly tightened; if in doubt, use a torque wrench to check that the nut is securely fastened, re- stake it (Section 2), then refit the centre cap. Repeat this check on the other driveshaft nut.

2 Road-test the vehicle, and listen for a metallic clicking from the front as the vehicle is driven slowly in a circle on full-lock. If a clicking noise is heard, this indicates wear in the outer constant velocity joint which means that the joint must be renewed; reconditioning is not possible.

3 If the outer joint is worn, it can be renewed separately (see note, Section 1); the procedure is as described in Section 3, paragraphs 1 to 12.

4 If vibration, consistent with road speed, is felt through the vehicle when accelerating, there is a possibility of wear in the inner constant velocity joints.

5 Remove the driveshafts (Section 2), then dismantle them (Section 3) and check the joints; if any wear or free play is found, the worn components must be renewed. Check with particular care the shaft splines as well as the joint components.

Chapter 9 Braking system

Contents

Brake pedal – removal, inspection and refitting.................................... 2
Brake pedal crossover linkage – removal and refitting...................... 4
Brake pedal height – adjustment 3
Braking system warning lights and switches – general 27
Front brake caliper – overhaul 15
Front brake caliper – removal and refitting 14
Front brake disc – inspection, removal and refitting.......................... 16
Front brake disc shield – removal and refitting 17
Front brake pad, caliper and disc check .... See Chapter 1
Front brake pads – renewal 13
General information 1
Handbrake cables – removal, inspection and refitting 25
Handbrake check and adjustment.................... See Chapter 1
Handbrake lever – removal and refitting.. 24
Hydraulic fluid level check .... See Chapter 1
Hydraulic fluid renewal.................................... See Chapter 1
Hydraulic pipes and hoses – renewal 10
Hydraulic pipes and hoses check.................... See Chapter 1

Hydraulic system – bleeding.. 9
Master cylinder – removal, overhaul and refitting............................. 11
Pressure-regulating valve (Pick-up) – checking............................... 18
Pressure-regulating valve (Pick-up) – removal, overhaul and
refitting 19
Pressure-regulating valves (except Pick-up) – removal, overhaul
and refitting 12
Rear brake backplate – removal and refitting 23
Rear brake drum – removal, inspection and refitting......................... 20
Rear brake shoe wheel cylinder and drum check .... See Chapter 1
Rear brake shoes – inspection and renewal.................................... 21
Rear wheel cylinder – removal, overhaul and refitting....................... 22
Stop-light switch – adjustment... 26
Vacuum servo unit – removal and refitting 5
Vacuum servo unit check................................ See Chapter 1
Vacuum servo unit hose – renewal 8
Vacuum servo unit non-return check valve – removal and refitting   7
Vacuum servo unit non-return check valve – testing 6

Specifications

System type	Hydraulically-operated, diagonally-split dual circuit with pressure-regulating valve(s) to rear brakes. Vacuum servo-assisted disc front brakes and drums rear. Cable-operated handbrake on rear drums.

Front brakes

Type	Disc, with single-piston sliding caliper
Make	Lucas-Girling
Disc diameter	236 mm
Disc thickness:	
New	12.9 mm
Minimum	11.4 mm
Disc maximum run-out	0.15 mm
Brake pad thickness – total, including metal backing:	
New	17.5 mm
Minimum	8 mm
Brake pad friction material minimum thickness	2 mm

Rear brakes

Type	Single leading shoe drum
Drum diameter:	
New	200 mm
Maximum	201 mm
Drum maximum ovality	0.10 mm
Brake shoe friction material thickness:	
New	4 mm
Minimum	1 mm

Torque wrench settings

	Nm	lbf ft
Pedal bracket/crossover linkage mounting bracket retaining nuts	13 to 16	10 to 12
Vacuum servo unit mounting nuts..	25 to 30	18 to 22
Master cylinder-to-vacuum servo unit mounting nuts	25 to 30	18 to 22
Pressure-regulating valves – except Pick-up:		
Valve-to-master cylinder...	22 to 24	16 to 18
End plug-to-valve body	12	9
Front brake caliper:		
Guide pin bolts...	20 to 30	15 to 22
Caliper mounting bracket-to-hub carrier bolts........................	50 to 60	37 to 44
Front brake disc securing screw	7 to 9	5 to 7
Front brake disc shield securing screws	4 to 6	3 to 4
Pressure-regulating valve mounting bolts – Pick-up........................	20 to 25	15 to 18
Handbrake cable guide-to-rear suspension torsion beam axle nuts	10 to 15	7 to 11
Rear brake drum securing screws	10 to 15	7 to 11
Rear brake wheel cylinder mounting bolts...............................	10 to 15	7 to 11

1 General information

The braking system is hydraulically operated, and incorporates a vacuum servo unit and master cylinder mounted on the left-hand side of the engine compartment bulkhead, with a disc brake caliper at each front wheel and a drum brake wheel cylinder at each rear wheel.

The master cylinder is of the tandem type and, with the connecting metal pipes and flexible hoses, provides a diagonally-split dual circuit system. The primary circuit operates the right-hand front and left-hand rear brakes, while the secondary operates the left-hand front and right-hand rear. Under normal conditions, both circuits operate in unison. In the event of hydraulic failure of one of the circuits, full brake pressure will still be available at two of the brakes, thus allowing the vehicle to be stopped in a stable manner, albeit at the expense of increased pedal movement.

Hydraulic pressure to the rear brakes is controlled by pressure-regulating valve(s) to prevent the rear wheels locking under heavy braking. On Pick-up models, a load-sensitive valve, linked by a spring to the rear suspension torsion beam axle, regulates pressure according to vehicle load, while on all other models a pressure-sensitive valve is fitted into each circuit at the master cylinder to limit the pressure transmitted to the rear wheel cylinders. Note that the pressure-sensitive valves fitted to Estate and Van models start to operate at higher pressures than those fitted to Hatchback models; the valves fitted to any particular vehicle must always be of the correct type, and matched to each other.

The handbrake operates the rear brakes through a lever assembly, with a cable to each of the brake backplates.

In addition to the stop-lights, there are in the instrument panel a brake (low fluid level) warning light, activated by a float-type sender unit in the master cylinder reservoir filler cap (so that the light comes on whenever the fluid level falls to a dangerously low level), and a handbrake warning light activated by a plunger switch mounted at the base of the handbrake lever, so that the light comes on whenever the handbrake is applied.

The vacuum servo unit uses inlet manifold depression (generated only while the engine is running) to boost the effort applied by the driver at the brake pedal and transmits this increased effort to the master cylinder pistons. It is direct-acting, with its input rod connected via a linkage to the brake pedal, and is of the suspended-vacuum type. Basically it consists of a sealed metal chamber divided into two by a diaphragm, passages between the two being controlled by the input rod. Under normal running conditions, both chambers are at less than atmospheric pressure, but when the brake pedal is applied, a valve opens the rear chamber to atmospheric pressure; the pressure difference forces forwards the diaphragm, carrying with it the output rod to apply increased effort to the master cylinder.

The front brake calipers are of the single-piston sliding type, in which the main caliper body slides on a mounting bracket that is rigidly attached to the hub carrier. Full braking efficiency relies on the ability of the body to slide easily on its mounting bracket, as well as on the condition of the pads and the caliper bore, piston and seals.

The rear brakes each consist of the drum, which is of cast-iron and is fastened to the hub and roadwheel, as well as the backplate which is mounted on the rear suspension trailing arm to carry the shoes and wheel cylinder. The shoes are adjusted automatically to compensate for friction material wear.

Fig. 9.1 Layout of braking system components (Hatchback, Estate and Van models) – left-hand-drive shown, right-hand-drive similar (Sec 1)

1 Vacuum servo unit/master cylinder assembly (LHD version shown)
2 Brake pipe
3 Flexible hose
4 Brake pipe
5 Brake pipe
6 Brake pipe
7 Clip
8 Clip
9 Flexible hose
10 Brake pipe
11 Brake pipe
12 Plastic tie
13 Spring clip

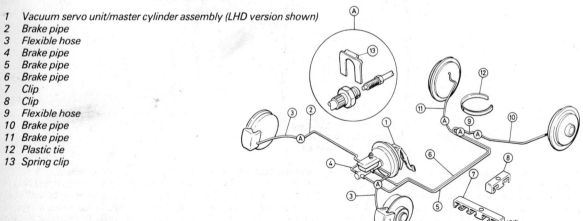

Fig. 9.2 Cross-section through (early type) master cylinder and fluid reservoir (Sec 1)

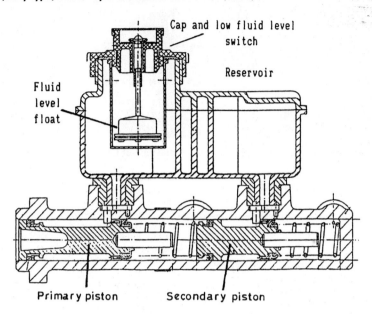

Fig. 9.3 Cross-section through vacuum servo unit (Sec 1)

1 Non-return check valve
2 Hose
3 Hose union
4 Sealing O-ring
5 Washer
6 Seal
7 Rubber bellows

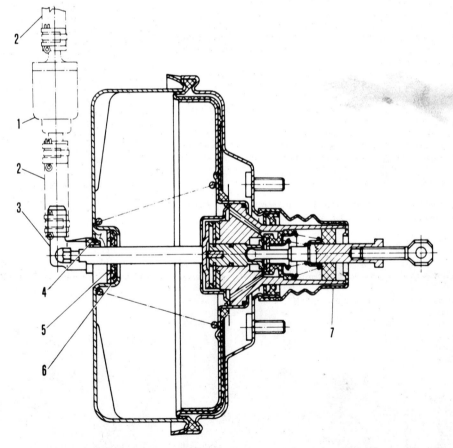

Note: *When servicing any part of the system, work carefully and methodically; also observe scrupulous cleanliness when overhauling any part of the hydraulic system. Always renew components (in axle sets, where applicable) if in doubt about their condition, and use only genuine Skoda replacement parts (or at least those of known good quality). Note the warnings given in 'Safety first!' and at relevant points in this Chapter concerning the dangers of asbestos dust and hydraulic fluid. Although many friction materials no longer contain asbestos, it is safest to assume that they do, and to take precautions accordingly.*

Vehicles built from April 1992 onwards are fitted with master cylinders of 22.2 mm bore (previously 22.0 mm) and vacuum servo units with non-adjustable output rods; the original and modified components may only be used as matched pairs. If either of these is to be renewed on any vehicle, it must be replaced by the correctly-matching component; any Skoda dealer will have details of the identification numbers required to ensure this.

2.2A Unhooking brake pedal return spring

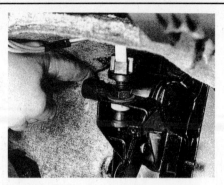
2.2B Withdrawing clutch pedal pivot bush

2.3 Withdrawing brake pedal

2   Brake pedal – removal, inspection and refitting

Removal

1   Remove the clutch pedal (Chapter 6).
2   Unhook the brake pedal return spring from the pedal, then withdraw the clutch pedal's black plastic pivot bush (photos).
3   Remove the C-clip securing the linkage operating rod to the brake pedal pin, then withdraw the pedal, disengaging the linkage operating rod (photo).

Inspection

4   Carefully clean all components, and renew any that are worn or damaged; check with particular care the return spring and the bearing surfaces of the pedal, pedal bracket and the pivot bush. The return spring's specified free length is 60 to 70 mm; if it has stretched to more than this, it must be renewed.

Refitting

5   Refitting is the reverse of the removal procedure, but apply a thin smear of multi-purpose grease to all pivots and bearing surfaces. Check, and adjust if necessary, the pedal height (Section 3).

3   Brake pedal height – adjustment

Note: *While the pedal's height is checked in the passenger compartment, adjustment is made in the engine compartment; the operation is a great deal easier if completed by two people working together.*

1   Working in the passenger compartment, measure the length of the brake pedal-to-crossover linkage operating rod protruding from the bulkhead, ie the distance from the bare metal of the bulkhead (as close as possible to the rubber bellows) to the centre of the pedal's pin (photo). The distance should be between 84.5 and 86.5 mm.
2   If adjustment is required, move to the engine compartment and screw the vacuum servo unit input rod's threaded adjuster sleeve in or out (applying an open-ended spanner to its hexagon) until the pedal height is correct (photo).
3   Returning to the driver's seat, apply the brakes firmly several times, then recheck the pedal height.
4   If significant alteration was required to obtain the correct setting, check (and reset if necessary) the adjustment of the clutch cable (Chapter 1) and the stop-light switch (Section 26).

4   Brake pedal crossover linkage – removal and refitting

Removal

1   Remove the vacuum servo unit if wished (Section 5). If the servo unit is to remain on the linkage mounting bracket, extract the C-clip securing the input rod eye to the crossover rod pin; have an assistant depress the brake pedal until access can be gained through the slot in the side of the mounting bracket.
2   Remove the dust cover and extract the circlip from the crossover rod's left-hand end.
3   Unscrew the nuts securing the linkage left-hand mounting bracket to the bulkhead, then slide the bracket off the crossover rod's end; note the presence of the pivot bush, the washer and (on 1992-on models only) the seal (photos). If the vacuum servo unit is still attached to the bracket, take great care (see Section 5) when disengaging the input rod eye from the crossover rod pin, and do not kink or damage the metal brake pipes.

3.1 Measuring brake pedal height – to centre of pedal pin (arrowed)

3.2 Adjusting brake pedal height – at vacuum servo unit input rod

Fig. 9.4 Brake pedal crossover linkage and vacuum servo unit/master cylinder assembly (Sec 4)

1   Input rod and threaded adjuster
2   Vacuum servo unit assembly
3   Rubber bellows
4   Seal
5   Washer
6   Sealing O-ring
7   Hose union
8   Hose
9   Non-return check valve
10   Washer
11   Spring washer
12   Nut
13   Spring washer
14   Nut
15   Linkage left-hand mounting bracket
16   Linkage right-hand mounting bracket
17   Dust cover
18   Circlip
19   Pivot bush
20   Linkage crossover rod
21   C-clip
22   Pedal-to-linkage operating rod
23   Rubber bellows
24   Washer
25   Clip
26   Seal – 1992-on models only

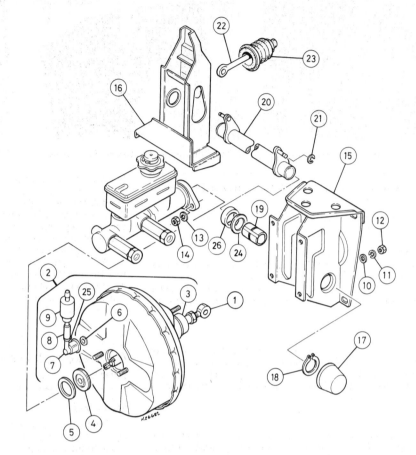

4   With an assistant depressing the brake pedal until access can be gained through the slot in the side of the right-hand mounting bracket, extract the C-clip securing the linkage operating rod eye to the crossover rod pin.

5   Remove the dust cover and extract the circlip from the crossover rod's right-hand end (photo).

6   Slide the crossover rod out of the linkage right-hand mounting bracket; collect the pivot bush and the washer (photo).

7   If the linkage right-hand mounting bracket is to be removed, note that the nuts securing it to the bulkhead also secure the pedal bracket inside the passenger compartment. Either wedge the pedal bracket in place to avoid disturbing the pedals, or disconnect the throttle and clutch cables (Chapters 4 and 6, respectively) and the stop-light switch wires (Section 27) so that the assembly can be removed, as required.

8   Clean all components, and check the bearing surfaces and pivot bushes for signs of wear or damage. Renew any worn or damaged component; the pivot bushes are available separately if required (photo).

Refitting

9   Refitting is the reverse of the removal procedure, noting the following points.

(a)   Apply a thin smear of multi-purpose grease to all pivots and bearing surfaces.

(b)   Tighten all nuts and bolts securely, to the specified torque wrench settings (where given).

(c)   Check, and adjust if necessary, the brake pedal height (Section 3).

4.3A Unscrewing nuts (three of four arrowed) securing crossover linkage left-hand mounting bracket ...

4.3B ... to withdraw mounting bracket

4.5 Remove dust cover from end of crossover rod to expose retaining circlip

4.6 Depress brake pedal until rod can be extracted through mounting bracket slot

4.8 Pivot bushes can be renewed separately if required

5 Vacuum servo unit – removal and refitting

Removal

1   Open the bonnet and disconnect the hose from the vacuum servo unit (photo).

2   Unscrew the two nuts securing the master cylinder to the vacuum servo unit.

3   Very carefully move the master cylinder forwards clear of the servo unit studs and output rod, taking great care not to kink or damage the metal brake pipes. If there is any risk of kinking or damaging any of the pipes, either unclip them from the bulkhead or disconnect them (Section 11) until the master cylinder can be moved clear or removed, as required (photo).

4   Unscrew the four nuts securing the vacuum servo unit to its mounting bracket (photo).

5   With an assistant depressing the brake pedal, ease the vacuum servo unit away from the mounting bracket until the C-clip can be extracted that secures the input rod eye to the crossover rod pin. **Do not** bend the input rod sideways, or the servo piston may be damaged; carefully move the complete vacuum servo unit to disengage the input rod from the pin (photo).

6   If the unit is faulty, it must be renewed (see the note in Section 1). The rubber bellows around the input rod can be renewed separately, as can the washer and seal around the output rod, while the air filter can be cleaned if dirty; if any other component (including the air filter) is faulty, it can be renewed only as part of the complete servo assembly (photo).

Refitting

7   Refitting is the reverse of the removal procedure, noting the following points (photos).

(a)   On early models (vacuum servo unit identification number 443.613.000.003), check that a clearance of between 0.3 and 0.6 mm exists between the tip of the servo output rod and the master cylinder primary piston. To do this, measure the height of the output rod tip above the servo unit's mating surface, and subtract from this the depth of the piston from the master cylinder mating surface (obtained by measuring from the end face of the master cylinder body's boss to the piston, then subtracting the height of the boss above the master cylinder mating surface). If the clearance is incorrect, hold the output rod by means of an open-ended spanner applied to its flats, then screw the tip in or out until it projects the required amount.

(b)   On later models (vacuum servo unit identification number 443.613.000.011), the output rod is non-adjustable. The output rod-to-master cylinder piston clearance (of 0.3 mm) is set on manufacture, and maintained by matching components (see the note in Section 1).

(c)   On all models, if a new servo unit is being fitted (or if this adjustment was disturbed for any reason) check that the centre of the input rod's eye is 116 mm above the unit's mating surface (dimension 'C', photo 5.7C). If adjustment is required, screw the rod's threaded adjuster sleeve in or out. This ensures a brake pedal height basic setting accurate enough to serve as a starting point for correct adjustment once the unit is refitted.

(d)   Apply a thin smear of multi-purpose grease to all pivots and bearing surfaces.

(e)   Refit the servo unit so that the vacuum hose union is towards the vehicle's centre-line, taking care not to bend the input rod sideways. Always renew the vacuum hose union sealing O-ring whenever it is disturbed.

(f)   Tighten all nuts and bolts securely, to the specified torque wrench settings, where given.

(g)   If any brake pipes were disconnected, bleed the air from the system (Section 9) and wash off any spilt hydraulic fluid. Check for any fluid leaks which might subsequently appear.

(h)   Check, and adjust if necessary, the brake pedal height (Section 3).

(i)   Check carefully the operation of the brakes in general, and of the vacuum servo unit in particular.

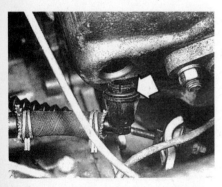

5.1 Always renew sealing O-ring (arrowed) whenever vacuum hose union is unplugged from servo unit

5.3 Take care not to bend or kink brake pipes when withdrawing master cylinder from vacuum servo unit

5.4 Unscrewing vacuum servo unit mounting nuts (three of four arrowed)

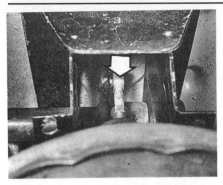

5.5 C-clip secures vacuum servo unit input rod eye (arrowed) to crossover rod pin

5.6 Air filter can be removed from vacuum servo unit for cleaning

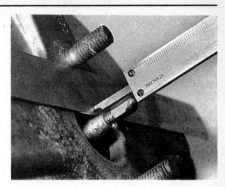

5.7A Measure height of output rod tip above vacuum servo unit mating surface (include thickness of straight-edge, if used) ...

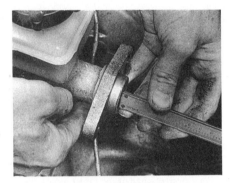

5.7B ... and subtract depth of piston from master cylinder mating surface – subtracting height of boss – to calculate clearance

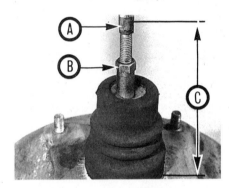

5.7C Hold steady eye (A) and rotate threaded adjuster sleeve (B) until dimension (C) is 116 mm

6 Vacuum servo unit non-return check valve – testing

1 When testing the valve, remember that its function is to allow air to flow in one direction only – out of the vacuum servo unit. If it allows air to flow in both directions, or in neither, it is faulty and must be renewed.
2 To test the valve, disconnect the hose from the vacuum servo unit and blow through the hose; air should pass freely through the valve. Now suck hard; there should be no leakage at all back through the valve.
3 If the valve is faulty it must be renewed (Section 7).

7 Vacuum servo unit non-return check valve – removal and refitting

Removal

1 Cut or release the clips securing the hose to the valve, then disconnect the hose and withdraw the valve, noting which way round it was fitted (photo).

Refitting

2 Refitting is the reverse of the removal procedure, using new clips if required. The valve must be connected so that the arrow (with the word 'Motor') embossed on its body points towards the inlet manifold union.
3 As soon as the engine is restarted, check that there are no signs of air leaks.

8 Vacuum servo unit hose – renewal

1 Cut or release the clips securing the hose, then disconnect the hose from its unions and from the non-return check valve.
2 Refitting is the reverse of the removal procedure, using new clips if required. Ensure the new hose is cut to the correct lengths and is routed correctly; also that the non-return check valve is correctly refitted (Section 7).

7.1 Vacuum servo unit non-return check valve (arrowed) is located in vacuum servo hose

9   Hydraulic system – bleeding

Note: *Hydraulic fluid is poisonous; wash off immediately and thoroughly in case of skin contact, and seek immediate medical advice if any fluid is swallowed or gets into the eyes. Certain types of hydraulic fluid are inflammable, and may ignite when allowed into contact with hot components; when servicing any hydraulic system, it is safest to assume that the fluid is inflammable and to take precautions against the risk of fire as though it is petrol that is being handled. Hydraulic fluid is also an effective paint stripper and will attack plastics; if any is spilt, it should be washed off immediately using copious quantities of fresh water. Finally, it is hygroscopic (it absorbs moisture from the air) – old fluid may be contaminated and unfit for further use. When topping-up or renewing the fluid, always use the recommended type, and ensure that it comes from a freshly-opened sealed container.*

General

1   The correct operation of any hydraulic system is only possible after removing all air from the components and circuit; this is achieved by bleeding the system.
2   During the bleeding procedure, add only clean, unused hydraulic fluid of the recommended type; never re-use fluid that has already been bled from the system. Ensure that sufficient fluid is available before starting work.
3   If there is any possibility of incorrect fluid being already in the system, the brake components and circuit must be flushed completely with uncontaminated, correct fluid, and new seals should be fitted to the various components.
4   If hydraulic fluid has been lost from the system, or air has entered, ensure that the cause is identified and the fault is cured before proceeding further.
5   Park the vehicle on its wheels on level ground; the rear brake wheel cylinders will not bleed properly unless they are in the normal running position (ie, horizontal). Switch off the engine and select first or reverse gear, then chock the wheels and release the handbrake.
6   Check that all pipes and hoses are secure, unions tight and bleed nipples closed. Clean any dirt from around the bleed nipples.
7   Top the master cylinder reservoir up to the 'Max' level line; refit the cap loosely, and remember to maintain the fluid level at least above the 'Min' level line throughout the procedure or there is a risk of further air entering the system.
8   There are a number of one-man, do-it-yourself brake bleeding kits currently available from motor accessory shops. It is recommended that one of these kits is used whenever possible, as they greatly simplify the bleeding operation and also reduce the risk of expelled air and fluid being drawn back into the system. If such a kit is not available, the basic (two-man) method must be used which is described in detail below.
9   If a kit is to be used, prepare the vehicle as described in paragraphs 2 to 7 of this Section, and follow the kit manufacturer's instructions as the procedure may vary slightly according to the type being used; generally they are as outlined below in the relevant sub-Section.
10   Whichever method is used, the same sequence must be followed (paragraphs 11 and 12) to ensure the removal of all air from the system.

Bleeding sequence

11   If the system has been only partially disconnected and suitable precautions were taken to minimise fluid loss, it should be necessary only to bleed that part of the system, or at most the primary or secondary circuit.
12   If the complete system is to be bled, then it should be done working in the following sequence.

   (a)   Right-hand front brake.
   (b)   Left-hand rear brake.
   (c)   Left-hand front brake.
   (d)   Right-hand rear brake.

13   On all models except Pick-ups (ie, those fitted with pressure-sensitive pressure-regulating valves) bleeding the rear brake circuits may take longer due to the restriction of the pressure-regulating valves.

Bleeding – basic (two-person) method

14   Collect a clean glass jar, a suitable length of plastic or rubber tubing

which is a tight fit over the bleed nipples, and a ring spanner to fit the nipples. The help of an assistant will also be required.
15   Remove the dust cap from the first nipple in the sequence. Fit the spanner and tube to the nipple, place the other end of the tube in the jar and pour in sufficient fluid to cover the end of the tube.
16   Ensure that the master cylinder reservoir fluid level is maintained at least above the 'Min' level line throughout the procedure.
17   Have the assistant depress the brake pedal fully several times to build up pressure, then maintain it on the final stroke.
18   While pedal pressure is maintained, unscrew the bleed nipple (approximately one turn) and allow the compressed fluid and air to flow into the jar. The assistant should maintain pedal pressure, following it down to the floor if necessary, and should not release it until instructed to do so. When the flow stops, tighten the bleed nipple again, release the pedal slowly and recheck the reservoir fluid level.
19   Repeat the steps given in the preceding paragraphs until the fluid emerging from the bleed nipple is free from air bubbles. If the master cylinder has been drained and refilled, and air is being bled from the first nipple in the sequence, allow approximately five seconds between cycles for the master cylinder passages to refill (see also Section 11, paragraph 24).
20   When no more air bubbles appear, tighten the bleed nipple securely, remove the tube and spanner and refit the dust cap. Do not overtighten the bleed nipples.
21   Repeat the procedure on all the remaining nipples in the sequence, until all air is removed from the system and the brake pedal feels firm again.

Bleeding – using a one-way valve kit

22   As their name implies, these kits consist of a length of tubing with a one-way valve fitted which prevents expelled air and fluid from being drawn back into the system; some kits include a translucent container which can be positioned so that the air bubbles can be more easily seen flowing from the end of the tube (photo).
23   Such a kit is connected to the bleed nipple, which is then opened. The user returns to the driver's seat and depresses the brake pedal with a smooth, steady stroke and slowly releases it; this is repeated until the expelled fluid is clear of air bubbles.
24   These kits simplify work so much that it is easy to forget the master cylinder reservoir fluid level; ensure that this is maintained at least above the 'Min' level line at all times.

Bleeding – using a pressure bleeding kit

25   These kits are usually operated by the reservoir of pressurised air contained in the spare tyre.
26   By connecting a pressurised, fluid-filled container to the master cylinder reservoir, bleeding can be carried out simply by opening each nipple in turn and allowing the fluid to flow out until no more air bubbles can be seen in the expelled fluid.

9.22 Bleeding the brake hydraulic system using a typical one-way valve kit

10.1 Using a brake hose clamp will minimise fluid loss when brake flexible hoses are disconnected

10.2 Braking system flexible hose/metal brake pipe union clipped to underbody

27   This method has the advantage that the large reservoir of fluid provides an additional safeguard against air being drawn into the system during bleeding. On all models except Pick-ups (ie, those fitted with pressure-sensitive pressure-regulating valves) the reservoir pressure should be as low as possible, while still remaining effective, or the pressure-regulating valves may operate and cause problems in bleeding the rear brake circuits.

28   Pressure bleeding is particularly effective when bleeding 'difficult' systems or when bleeding the complete system at the time of routine fluid renewal.

All methods

29   When bleeding is complete and firm pedal feel is restored, wash off any spilt fluid, tighten securely the bleed nipples and refit their dust caps. Do not overtighten the bleed nipples.

30   Check the hydraulic fluid level, and top-up if necessary (Chapter 1). Check for any fluid leaks which might subsequently appear.

31   Discard any hydraulic fluid that has been bled from the system; it will not be fit for re-use.

32   Check the feel of the brake pedal. If it feels at all spongy, air must still be present in the system, and further bleeding is required. Failure to bleed satisfactorily after a reasonable repetition of the bleeding procedure may be due to worn master cylinder seals.

10   Hydraulic pipes and hoses – renewal

Note: *Before starting work, refer to the note at the beginning of Section 9 concerning the dangers of hydraulic fluid.*

1   If any pipe or hose is to be renewed, minimise fluid loss by removing the master cylinder reservoir cap and then tightening it down on to a piece of polythene (taking care not to damage the sender unit) to obtain an airtight seal. Alternatively, flexible hoses can be sealed (if required) using a proprietary brake hose clamp (photo), while metal brake pipe unions can be plugged (if care is taken not to allow dirt into the system) or capped immediately they are disconnected. Place a wad of rag under any union that is to be disconnected to catch any spilt fluid.

2   If a flexible hose is to be disconnected, unscrew the brake pipe union nut before removing the spring clip which secures the hose to its mounting bracket (photo).

3   To unscrew the union nuts, it is preferable to obtain a brake pipe spanner of the correct size; these are available from motor accessory shops. Failing this, a close-fitting open-ended spanner will be required, though if the nuts are tight or corroded, their flats may be rounded-off if the spanner slips. In such a case, a self-locking wrench is often the only way to unscrew a stubborn union, but it follows that the pipe and the damaged nuts must be renewed on reassembly. Always clean a union

and surrounding area before disconnecting it. If disconnecting a component with more than one union, make a careful note of the connections before disturbing any of them.

4   If a brake pipe is to be renewed it can be obtained, cut to length and with the union nuts and end flares in place, from Skoda dealers. All that is then necessary is to bend it to shape, following the line of the original, before fitting it to the vehicle. Alternatively, most motor accessory shops can make up brake pipes from kits, but this requires very careful measurement of the original to ensure that the replacement is of the correct length. The safest answer is usually to take the original to the shop as a pattern.

5   On refitting, do not overtighten the union nuts; it is not necessary to exercise brute force to obtain a sound joint. When refitting flexible hoses, always renew any sealing washers used.

6   Ensure that the pipes and hoses are correctly routed with no kinks, and that they are secured in the clips or brackets provided. After fitting, remove the polythene from the reservoir, and bleed the hydraulic system (Section 9). Wash off any spilt fluid, and check carefully for fluid leaks.

11   Master cylinder – removal, overhaul and refitting

Note: *Before starting work, refer to the note at the beginning of Section 9 concerning the dangers of hydraulic fluid.*

Removal

1   Remove the master cylinder reservoir cap, disconnecting the sender unit wires, and syphon the hydraulic fluid from the reservoir. **Note:** *Do not syphon the fluid by mouth, as it is poisonous; use a syringe or an old poultry baster.* Alternatively, open any convenient bleed nipple in the system and gently pump the brake pedal to expel the fluid through a plastic tube connected to the nipple (Section 9).

2   Unscrew the union nuts, and disconnect the metal brake pipes (Section 10). Try to keep fluid spillage to a minimum, and wash off any spilt fluid as soon as possible.

3   Unscrew the two nuts securing the master cylinder to the vacuum servo unit and withdraw it (photo).

Overhaul

Note: *Before attempting to overhaul the unit, check the price and availability of individual components, and the price of a new or reconditioned unit, as overhaul may not be viable on economic grounds alone. Also, read through the procedure and check that the special tools and facilities required are available.*

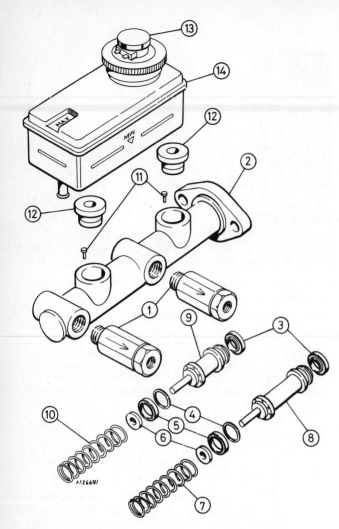

Fig. 9.5 Exploded view of (early type) master cylinder (Sec 11)

1	Pressure-regulating valves – Hatchback, Estate and Van only
2	Master cylinder body
3	Piston seal
4	Washer
5	Piston cup
6	Spring seat
7	Primary piston spring (1.6 mm diameter wire)
8	Primary piston
9	Secondary piston
10	Secondary piston spring (1.8 mm diameter wire)
11	Stop-pin
12	Seal
13	Filler cap and fluid level warning light sender unit
14	Fluid reservoir

All models

4　Remove the master cylinder from the vehicle and clean it thoroughly. Unscrew the pressure-regulating valves, where fitted (Section 12).

5　Prise the reservoir from the master cylinder body, and remove the two seals from the body ports.

6　The modified type of master cylinder introduced on 1992 models requires a slightly different overhaul procedure from this point on. Identify the unit being dismantled by referring to Fig. 9.7, and work according to the relevant sub-Section below.

1987 to 1992 models

7　Press in as far as possible the primary piston, and extract the piston stop-pins from the reservoir inlet ports by holding the assembly upside-down and tapping it on to a clean work surface.

8　Noting the order of removal and the direction of fitting of each component, withdraw the piston assemblies with their springs and seals, tapping the body on to a clean wooden surface to dislodge them.

11.3 Unscrewing master cylinder-to-vacuum servo unit mounting nuts

If necessary, clamp the master cylinder body in a vice (fitted with soft jaw covers) and use low-pressure compressed air (applied through the secondary circuit fluid port) to assist the removal of the secondary piston assembly. **Caution:** *The piston may be ejected with some force.*

9　Thoroughly clean all components using as a cleaning medium only methylated spirit, isopropyl alcohol or clean hydraulic fluid. Never use mineral-based solvents such as petrol or paraffin, which will attack the hydraulic system's rubber components. Dry the components immediately using compressed air or a clean, lint-free cloth.

10　Check all components, and renew any that are worn or damaged. Check particularly the cylinder bores and pistons; the complete assembly should be renewed if these are scratched, worn or corroded. If there is any doubt about the condition of the assembly or of any of its components, renew it (see note, Section 1). Check that the body's inlet and bypass ports are clear.

11　If the assembly is fit for further use, obtain the components required to reassemble it. Renew as a matter of course all seals and rubber cups disturbed on dismantling; these should never be re-used.

12　On reassembly, soak the pistons and the new cups and seals in clean hydraulic fluid. Smear clean fluid into the cylinder bore.

13　Fit the new components to their pistons, using only the fingers to manipulate them into the grooves.

14　Insert the pistons into the bore, using a twisting motion to avoid trapping the seal lips. Ensure that all components are refitted in the correct order and the right way round.

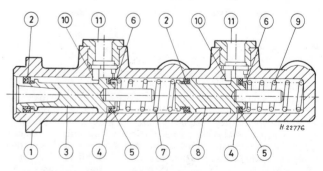

Fig. 9.6 Cross-section through (early type) master cylinder (Sec 11)

1	Master cylinder body
2	Piston seal
3	Primary piston
4	Washer
5	Piston cup
6	Spring seat
7	Primary piston spring (1.6 mm diameter wire)
8	Secondary piston
9	Secondary piston spring (1.8 mm diameter wire)
10	Stop-pin
11	Seal

1987 - 1992

1992 -

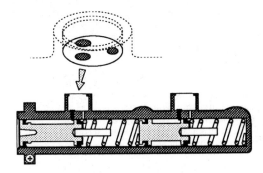
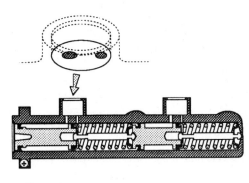

Fig. 9.7 Cross-sections showing differences in early and later types of master cylinder (Sec 11)

15   Press the secondary piston assembly fully up into the bore using a clean metal rod, then refit the stop-pin.

16   Refit the primary piston assembly and its stop-pin.

17   Press new seals into the body ports, then refit the reservoir and, where appropriate, the pressure-regulating valves.

18   Refit the master cylinder to the vehicle.

1992 models

19   Tap the body on to a clean wooden surface to dislodge the piston assemblies with their springs and seals, noting the order of removal and the direction of fitting of each component. The piston assemblies are retained only by the vacuum servo unit on these models; if they are difficult to extract, use low-pressure compressed air (paragraph 8 above).

20   Dismantle, clean, check and prepare the assembly's components as described in paragraphs 9 to 13 above.

21   Assemble the springs on to their respective pushrods, and secure them by clipping the spring seats into place. Ensuring that all components are refitted in the correct order and the right way round, and using a twisting motion to avoid trapping the seal lips, insert the spring assemblies and pistons into the bore.

22   Press new seals into the body ports, then refit the reservoir and, where appropriate, the pressure-regulating valves.

23   Refit the master cylinder to the vehicle.

Refitting

24   Refitting is the reverse of the removal procedure, noting the following points.

(a)   *Refit the master cylinder to the vacuum servo unit, aligning the servo unit output rod with the master cylinder primary piston.*

(b)   *Tighten the master cylinder mounting nuts to their specified torque wrench setting.*

(c)   *Refill the reservoir with new fluid, and bleed the system (Section 9). Check for any fluid leaks which might subsequently appear.*

(d)   *If a new master cylinder has been fitted (or the original was fully drained) start the bleeding procedure by disconnecting each metal brake pipe in turn (front first) and gently pumping the brake pedal until only clear hydraulic fluid emerges. Catch the ejected fluid with a rag wrapped around the master cylinder.*

(e)   *In very difficult cases, disconnect the pipes, plug their ports with the fingers, then uncover each one in turn as the brake pedal is depressed and plug it again as the pedal is released, so that fluid is forcibly drawn in from the reservoir. Refit and tighten securely all pipe unions as soon as the master cylinder is cleared of air and is pumping correctly, then proceed with the normal bleeding procedure.*

12   Pressure-regulating valves (except Pick-up) – removal, overhaul and refitting

Note: *Before starting work, refer to the note at the beginning of Section 9 concerning the dangers of hydraulic fluid.*

If one or both rear roadwheels lock repeatedly under heavy braking, first check that this is not due to adverse road conditions or to incorrectly-inflated or badly-worn tyres, then check the condition of all four brake assemblies before suspecting a pressure-regulating valve fault. Note that the rear valve serves the primary circuit, which includes the left-hand rear brake, while the front valve serves the secondary circuit and the right-hand rear brake; if a fault appears, this may help to isolate the cause.

The valves fitted to Hatchback models are marked with the numbers 003 stamped into the valve body; those fitted to Estate and Van models are marked 004 (or 400, with a dark-coloured end plug). Check that both valves share the same, correct, markings, and if either valve is to be renewed, ensure that the correct type is obtained.

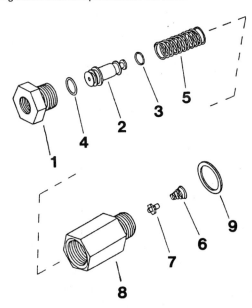

Fig. 9.8 Exploded view of pressure-regulating valve – except Pick-up (Sec 12)

1	End plug	6	Valve spring
2	Piston	7	Plastic valve
3	Small O-ring	8	Body
4	Large O-ring	9	O-ring
5	Piston spring		

Removal

1   Minimise fluid loss either by removing the master cylinder reservoir cap and then tightening it down on to a piece of polythene to obtain an airtight seal (taking care not to damage the sender unit), or by capping or

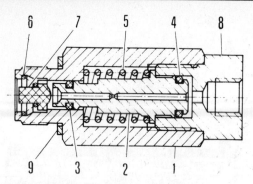

Fig. 9.9 Cross-section through pressure-regulating valve – except Pick-up (Sec 12)

1	Body	6	Valve spring
2	Piston	7	Plastic valve
3	Small O-ring	8	End plug
4	Large O-ring	9	O-ring
5	Piston spring		

plugging the metal brake pipe as it is disconnected from the valve (Section 10). Also plug the valve and master cylinder orifices; take great care not to allow dirt into the system.

2   Unscrew the union nut, and disconnect the metal brake pipe. Try to keep fluid spillage to a minimum, and wash off any spilt fluid as soon as possible.

3   Unscrew the valve, and withdraw it from the master cylinder; remove and discard the sealing O-ring.

Overhaul

Note: *Before attempting to overhaul a valve, check the price and availability of individual components, and the price of a new or reconditioned unit, as overhaul may not be viable on economic grounds alone. Also, read through the procedure, and check that the special tools and facilities required are available.*

4   Remove the valve from the vehicle, and clean it thoroughly.

5   Clamp the valve body carefully in a soft-jawed vice, and unscrew the end plug.

6   Noting the order of removal and the direction of fitting of each component, withdraw the piston assembly with its spring and O-rings, tapping the body on to a clean wooden surface to dislodge them. If necessary, clamp the valve body in a vice (fitted with soft jaw covers) and use low-pressure compressed air to assist removal of the piston assembly. **Caution:** *The piston may be ejected with some force.*

7   Thoroughly clean all components using as a cleaning medium only methylated spirit, isopropyl alcohol or clean hydraulic fluid. Never use mineral-based solvents such as petrol or paraffin, which will attack the hydraulic system's rubber components. Dry the components immediately using compressed air or a clean, lint-free cloth.

8   Check all components, and renew any that are worn or damaged. Check particularly the body bores and the piston; the complete assembly should be renewed if these are scratched, worn or corroded. If

there is any doubt about the condition of the assembly or of any of its components, renew it.

9   If the assembly is fit for further use, obtain the components required to reassemble it. Renew as a matter of course all sealing O-rings disturbed on dismantling; these should never be re-used.

10   On reassembly, soak the piston and the new O-rings in clean hydraulic fluid. Smear clean fluid into the body bore, then insert the valve and its spring.

11   Fit the new O-rings to the piston, using only the fingers to manipulate them into the grooves. Fit the spring to the piston and insert the assembly into the body, ensuring that all components are refitted in the correct order and the right way round.

12   Ensuring that it engages correctly over the piston, refit the end plug, tightening it to its specified torque wrench setting.

13   Refit the valve to the vehicle.

Refitting

14   Refitting is the reverse of the removal procedure, noting the following points.

(a)   Always renew the sealing O-ring.
(b)   Tighten the valve to its specified torque wrench setting into the master cylinder.
(c)   Refill the reservoir with new fluid, and bleed any air from the affected part of the system (Section 9). Check for any fluid leaks which might subsequently appear.

13   Front brake pads – renewal

Warning: *Brake pads must be renewed on both front wheels at the same time – never renew the pads on only one wheel, as uneven braking may result. Also, the dust created by wear of the pads may contain asbestos, which is a health hazard. Never blow it out with compressed air, and don't inhale any of it. An approved filtering mask should be worn when working on the brakes. DO NOT use petroleum-based solvents to clean brake parts. Use brake cleaner or methylated spirit only.*

1   Jack up the front of the vehicle and support it securely on axle stands, then remove the roadwheel (see 'Jacking, towing and wheel changing').

2   If the quick check described in Chapter 1 has shown the condition of the brake pads to be doubtful, they must be removed and checked as follows.

3   Pull the caliper body outwards to compress the piston into the cylinder, then check that the caliper body slides smoothly and easily in the mounting bracket. If not, the guide pins must be cleaned, checked for wear, and lubricated before reassembly.

4   Unscrew the caliper bottom guide pin bolt, if necessary using a slim open-ended spanner to counterhold the head of the guide pin itself (photo). Pivot upwards the caliper body to expose the brake pads. Do not depress the brake pedal until the caliper is reassembled.

5   Noting the exact location of the anti-rattle spring on each, withdraw the brake pads (photo). Mark them so that they will be refitted in their original locations; do not be tempted to interchange pads to compensate for uneven wear.

13.4 Unscrew caliper bottom guide pin bolt, and swing up caliper body ...

13.5 ... note location of anti-rattle springs (arrowed) before removing brake pads

13.6 Measuring thickness of brake pad friction material

Fig. 9.10 Exploded view of front brake caliper (Sec 13)

1 Mounting bracket
2 Guide pin
3 Rubber dust cover
4 Caliper body
5 Piston (fluid) seal
6 Piston
7 Piston (dust) seal
8 Bleed nipple
9 Dust cap
10 Brake pad set
11 Guide pin bolt

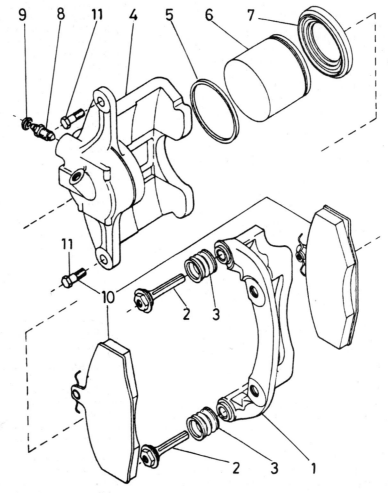

6 First measure the thickness of friction material remaining on each brake pad (photo). Note that, on original Skoda brake pads, the central groove acts as a wear limit indicator; if the friction material is worn so far that the groove is worn away at any point, that pad is worn out and must be renewed.

7 If either pad is worn at any point to the specified minimum thickness or less, all four pads must be renewed (see the warning above). Also, the pads should be renewed if any are fouled with oil or grease; there is no truly satisfactory way of degreasing friction material.

8 If any of the brake pads are worn unevenly, or fouled with oil or grease, trace and rectify the cause before reassembly.

9 If the brake pads are still serviceable, carefully clean them using a clean, fine wire brush or similar, paying particular attention to the sides and back of the metal backing. Clean out the groove in the friction material, and pick out any large embedded particles of dirt or debris. Carefully clean the anti-rattle springs and the pad locations in the caliper body and mounting bracket.

10 If there is any doubt about the ability of the caliper to slide in the mounting bracket, dismantle, clean and lubricate the guide pins as described in Section 15 (photo). Check the brake disc (Section 16).

11 On reassembly, apply a thin smear of high-temperature brake grease (silicone-based or PBC/Poly Butyl Cuprysil-based) or anti-seize compound (eg Holts Copaslip) to the sides and back of each pad's metal backing, and to those surfaces of the caliper body and mounting bracket which bear on the pads. Do not allow the lubricant to foul the friction material.

12 Refit the brake pads, ensuring that the friction material is against the disc.

13 If new brake pads have been fitted, the caliper piston must be pushed back into the cylinder to make room for them. Either use a G-clamp or similar tool, or use suitable pieces of wood as levers. Provided that the master cylinder reservoir has not been overfilled with

hydraulic fluid there should be no spillage, but keep a careful watch on the fluid level while retracting the piston. If the fluid level rises above the 'Max' level line at any time, the surplus should be syphoned off or ejected via a plastic tube connected to the bleed nipple (see Section 11, paragraph 1).

13.10 Remove, clean and lubricate guide pins if caliper body is not free to slide on mounting bracket

14   Pivot down the caliper body over the brake pads, and refit the bottom guide pin bolt. Skoda specify that these bolts must be renewed whenever they are disturbed, as they are coated with locking compound which loses its effectiveness when unscrewed; to this end, new bolts are supplied with genuine Skoda replacement brake pad sets. If new bolts are not available, carefully clean the bolt threads with a clean wire brush, and apply one or two drops of proprietary thread-locking compound to them before refitting. Tighten the bolt to its specified torque wrench setting.

15   Check that the caliper body slides smoothly in the mounting bracket, then depress repeatedly the brake pedal until the pads are pressed into firm contact with the brake disc, and normal pedal travel is restored. Refit the roadwheel.

16   Repeat the full procedure on the opposite brake caliper, then lower the vehicle to the ground and tighten the roadwheel bolts to the specified torque wrench setting (see Chapter 1 Specifications).

17   Check the hydraulic fluid level (Chapter 1).

18   Bear in mind that new pads will take a few hundred miles to bed-in and give maximum efficiency. Avoid hard braking as far as possible during this period, and be prepared for longer stopping distances.

14   Front brake caliper – removal and refitting

Note: *Before starting work, refer to the note at the beginning of Section 9 concerning the dangers of hydraulic fluid, and to the warning at the beginning of Section 13 concerning the dangers of asbestos dust.*

Removal

1   Jack up the front of the vehicle, support it securely on axle stands, then remove the roadwheel (see *'Jacking, towing and wheel changing'*).

2   Minimise fluid loss either by removing the master cylinder reservoir cap and then tightening it down on to a piece of polythene to obtain an airtight seal (taking care not to damage the sender unit), or by using a brake hose clamp, a G-clamp or a similar tool to clamp the flexible hose.

3   Clean the surrounding area, then slacken the flexible hose union.

4   Unscrew the two caliper mounting bracket-to-hub carrier bolts (photo).

5   Withdraw the brake caliper assembly, and slip a clean wooden spacer (of the same thickness as the brake disc) between the brake pads to retain them.

6   Unscrew the caliper from the flexible hose union. If a sealing washer is fitted, discard it; such washers must be renewed whenever they are disturbed. If the caliper is not to be dismantled, plug the fluid orifice to prevent the entry of dirt; similarly, plug the flexible hose union (or wrap it tightly with polythene).

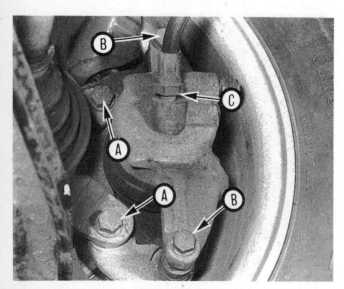

14.4 Caliper mounting bracket-to-hub carrier bolts (A), guide pin bolts (B), and flexible hose union (C)

Refitting

7   Refitting is the reverse of the removal procedure, noting the following points.

(a)   Tighten all nuts and bolts to the specified torque wrench settings.

(b)   If fitted, renew as a matter of course the flexible hose union sealing washer.

(c)   Ensure that the flexible hose is securely tightened into the caliper body, and that it is correctly routed and secured by the clamp provided without being twisted.

(d)   Bleed any air from the system (Section 9). Check for any fluid leaks which might subsequently appear.

15   Front brake caliper – overhaul

Note: *Before starting work, refer to the note at the beginning of Section 9 concerning the dangers of hydraulic fluid and to the warning at the beginning of Section 13 concerning the dangers of asbestos dust.*

1   Prepare to remove the caliper as described in paragraphs 1 to 3 of the previous Section.

2   Unscrew the caliper guide pin bolts, if necessary using a slim open-ended spanner to counterhold the head of each guide pin. Withdraw the caliper body, unscrewing it from the flexible hose union; if a sealing washer is fitted, discard it. Such washers must be renewed whenever they are disturbed. Plug the flexible hose union (or wrap it tightly with polythene).

3   Remove and check the brake pads (Section 13).

4   Extract the guide pins, if necessary by screwing their bolts into them and pulling on the head of each bolt using a self-locking wrench or similar. Peel off the rubber dust cover from each guide pin, and check it for cracks, splits or other damage; these can be renewed separately if required.

5   Unbolt the caliper mounting bracket from the hub carrier.

6   Place a small block of wood in the jaws of the caliper body, and remove the piston by applying a jet of low-pressure compressed air (such as that from a tyre pump) to the fluid entry port. **Caution:** *The piston may be ejected with some force.*

7   Peel off the dust seal, and use a blunt instrument such as a knitting needle to extract the fluid seal from the caliper body's cylinder bore.

8   Thoroughly clean all components using as a cleaning medium only methylated spirit, isopropyl alcohol or clean hydraulic fluid. Never use mineral-based solvents such as petrol or paraffin, which will attack the hydraulic system's rubber components. Dry the components immediately using compressed air or a clean, lint-free cloth. Use compressed air to blow clear the fluid passages.

9   Check all components, and renew any that are worn or damaged. Check particularly the caliper body's cylinder bore and the piston; these should be renewed if they are scratched, worn or corroded in any way.

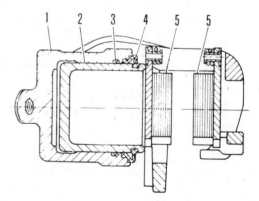

Fig. 9.11 Cross-section through front brake caliper (Sec 15)

1   Caliper body
2   Piston
3   Piston (fluid) seal

4   Piston (dust) seal
5   Brake pads

Similarly check the condition of the guide pins and their bores in the mounting bracket; both guide pins should be undamaged and (when cleaned) a reasonably tight sliding fit in the mounting bracket bores. If there is any doubt about the condition of any of the components, renew it.

10   If the assembly is fit for further use, obtain the components required to reassemble it. Renew as a matter of course all rubber seals, dust covers and caps, and any sealing washers discovered on dismantling; these should never be re-used.

11   On reassembly, ensure that all components are absolutely clean and dry.

12   Soak the piston and the new fluid seal in clean hydraulic fluid for one hour before assembly. Smear clean fluid into the caliper body's cylinder bore, and fit the new fluid seal using only the fingers to manipulate it into the bore's inner groove.

13   Fit the new dust seal over the piston's inner end, then press its outside edge into the bore's outer groove. Press the piston into the caliper body, using a twisting motion and ensuring that the piston enters squarely (through the dust and fluid seals) into the bore. When the piston bottoms in the body, press the dust seal's inner edge into the piston's groove.

14   Unplug the flexible hose, and screw the caliper body on to the hose union, tightening it firmly by hand; if a sealing washer was found on dismantling, do not forget to fit a new replacement.

15   Refit the caliper mounting bracket to the hub carrier, tightening the two mounting bolts to the specified torque wrench setting.

16   Fit a new rubber dust cover to each guide pin, and apply a thin smear of grease to the guide pins before refitting them to their bores; any good-quality silicone-based or PBC/Poly Butyl Cuprysil-based high-temperature brake grease or anti-seize compound (eg Holts Copaslip) can be used.

17   Refit the brake pads (Section 13).

18   Fit the caliper body over the mounting bracket and brake pads, then refit the guide pin bolts. Skoda specify that these bolts must be renewed whenever they are disturbed, as they are coated with locking compound which loses its effectiveness when unscrewed; to this end, new bolts are supplied with genuine Skoda replacement brake pad sets. If new bolts are not available, clean carefully the bolt threads with a clean wire brush, and apply one or two drops of proprietary thread-locking compound to them before refitting. Tighten the bolts to the torque wrench setting specified.

19   Check that the caliper body slides smoothly in the mounting bracket.

20   Ensuring that the flexible hose is correctly routed and secured by the clamp provided without being twisted; tighten the union securely.

21   Bleed any air from the system (Section 9), then depress the brake pedal repeatedly until the pads are pressed into firm contact with the brake disc, and normal pedal travel is restored.

22   Wash off any spilt fluid, and check for any fluid leaks while an assistant applies full pressure to the brake pedal. Refit the roadwheel.

23   Repeat the full procedure on the opposite brake caliper, then lower the vehicle to the ground and tighten the wheel bolts to the specified torque wrench setting.

24   Check the hydraulic fluid level (Chapter 1). Check for any fluid leaks which might subsequently appear.

16 Front brake disc – inspection, removal and refitting

Note: *Before starting work, refer to the warning at the beginning of Section 13 concerning the dangers of asbestos dust.*

Inspection

Note: *To ensure even and consistent braking, both discs should be renewed at the same time, even if only one is faulty.*

1   Jack up the front of the vehicle, and support it securely on axle stands, then remove the roadwheel (see *'Jacking, towing and wheel changing'*).

2   Slowly rotate the brake disc so that the full area of both sides can be checked; remove the brake pads (Section 13) if better access is required to the inboard surface. Light scoring is normal in the area swept by the brake pads, but if heavy scoring is found, the disc must be renewed. The

only alternative to this is to have the disc surface-ground until it is flat again, but this must not reduce the disc to less than the minimum thickness specified.

3   It is normal to find a lip of rust and brake dust around the disc's perimeter; this can be scraped off if required. If, however, a lip has formed due to excessive wear of the brake pad swept area, then the disc's thickness must be measured using a micrometer. Take measurements at four places around the disc at the inside and outside of the pad swept area; if the disc has worn at any point to the specified minimum thickness or less, it must be renewed.

4   If the disc is thought to be warped, it can be checked for run-out (5 mm in from the disc's outer edge) either using a dial gauge mounted on any convenient fixed point, while the disc is slowly rotated, or by using feeler gauges to measure (at several points all around the disc) the clearance between the disc and a fixed point such as the caliper mounting bracket. If the measurements obtained are at the specified maximum or beyond, the disc is excessively warped and must be renewed; however, it is worth checking first that the hub bearing is in good condition (Chapters 1 and/or 10). Also try the effect of removing the disc and turning it through 180° to reposition it on the hub; if run-out is still excessive, the disc must be renewed.

5   Check the disc for cracks, especially around the bolt holes, and any other wear or damage. Renew it if any of these are found.

Removal

6   Jack up the front of the vehicle, support it securely on axle stands, then remove the roadwheel (see *'Jacking, towing and wheel changing'*).

7   With reference to Section 14, unscrew the two brake caliper mounting bracket-to-hub carrier bolts, then withdraw the caliper assembly and secure it out of harm's way, without stretching or kinking the brake hose. Place a clean spacer (of the same thickness as the brake disc) between the pads to prevent them being dislodged.

8   Use chalk or paint to mark the relationship of the disc to the hub, then undo the disc securing screw and withdraw the disc. The screw may be very tight, in which case an impact screwdriver will be needed (photo).

Refitting

9   Refitting is the reverse of the removal procedure, noting the following points.

(a) Ensure that the mating surfaces of the disc and hub are clean and flat (photo).
(b) Align (if applicable) the marks made on removal.
(c) Tighten the disc screw, bolts and roadwheel bolts to their specified torque wrench settings .
(d) If a new disc has been fitted, use a suitable solvent to wipe any preservative coating from the disc before refitting the caliper.

16.8 Unscrewing front brake disc securing screw using an impact driver

16.9 Ensure disc/hub mating surfaces are clean and flat before refitting

17.2 Front brake disc shield securing screws (two of three arrowed)

17   Front brake disc shield – removal and refitting

Note: *Before starting work, refer to the warning at the beginning of Section 13 concerning the dangers of asbestos dust.*

Removal

1   Referring to the relevant Sections of Chapter 10 and of this Chapter, remove the front hub carrier, then detach the brake disc and press out the hub.

2   Unbolt the brake disc shield from the hub carrier and withdraw it (photo).

Refitting

3   Refitting is the reverse of the removal procedure; tighten the shield securing (hexagon-headed) screws to the specified torque wrench setting.

18   Pressure-regulating valve (Pick-up) – checking

1   If one or both rear roadwheels lock repeatedly under heavy braking, first check that this is not due to adverse road conditions or to incorrectly-inflated or badly-worn tyres, then check the condition of all four brake assemblies before suspecting an incorrectly-set pressure-regulating valve or a valve fault.

2   No information is available at the time of writing to help the owner adjust this component; the vehicle must be taken to a Skoda dealer who has the equipment and information required to adjust the system correctly. **Do not** disturb the valve operating lever's adjustment (photo).

19   Pressure-regulating valve (Pick-up) – removal, overhaul and refitting

Note: *Before starting work, refer to the note at the beginning of Section 9 concerning the dangers of hydraulic fluid.*

If a fault is thought to exist, always have the valve's adjustment checked by a Skoda dealer (see previous Section) before deciding that repairs are necessary.

Removal

1   Minimise fluid loss either by removing the master cylinder reservoir cap and then tightening it down on to a piece of polythene to obtain an

18.2 Pick-up model rear brake pressure-regulating valve on underbody, behind rear suspension torsion beam axle – do not disturb adjuster (arrowed)

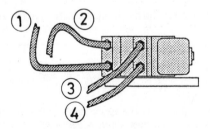

Fig. 9.12 Pick-up model pressure-regulating valve brake pipe connections – seen from above (Sec 19)

1 To right-hand rear brake	3 From master cylinder
2 To left-hand rear brake	(primary circuit)
	4 From master cylinder
	(secondary circuit)

Fig. 9.13 Pick-up model pressure-regulating valve spring setting (Sec 19)

1   *Valve*
2   *Adjuster nut*
3   *Locknut*
4   *Spring*
5   *Rear suspension torsion beam axle*
A   *105.00 ± 0.05 mm*

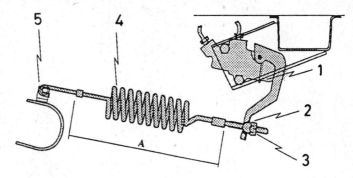

19.5 Adjusting setting of Pick-up pressure-regulating valve spring

airtight seal (taking care not to damage the sender unit), or by capping or plugging each metal brake pipe as it is disconnected from the valve (Section 10). Also plug the valve orifices; take great care not to allow dirt into the system.

2   Slacken the metal brake pipe union nuts; note carefully the connections before disturbing any of the pipes. Unscrew the valve mounting bolts, and unhook the valve spring from the rear suspension torsion beam axle.

3   Unscrew the union nuts and disconnect the metal brake pipes. Try to keep fluid spillage to a minimum, and wash off any spilt fluid as soon as possible. Withdraw the valve.

Overhaul

4   Do not attempt to overhaul or 'repair' this unit; it must be renewed if faulty.

Refitting

5   Refitting is the reverse of the removal procedure, noting the following points.

(a) *Tighten the pipe unions securely, then tighten the valve mounting bolts to the specified torque wrench setting.*
(b) *Hook the valve spring on to the rear suspension torsion beam axle. With the vehicle parked on level ground and loaded to kerb weight, with a person weighing 75 kg in the driver's seat, check that dimension 'A', Fig. 9.13, is correct. If adjustment is required, slacken the locknut and screw the adjuster nut in or out until the setting is correct (photo), then bounce the suspension and recheck the setting before tightening the locknut securely.*

(c) *Bleed any air from the system (Section 9). Check for any fluid leaks which might subsequently appear.*
(d) *Check for satisfactory operation of the rear brakes. If in doubt, have the pressure-regulating valve adjustment checked by a Skoda dealer.*

20 Rear brake drum – removal, inspection and refitting

Note: *Before starting work, refer to the warning at the beginning of Section 21 concerning the dangers of asbestos dust.*

Removal

1   Jack up the rear of the vehicle, support it securely on axle stands, then remove the roadwheel (see 'Jacking, towing and wheel changing').

2   Use chalk or paint to mark the relationship of the drum to the hub.

3   With the handbrake firmly applied to prevent drum rotation, unscrew the drum securing screws (photo). Release the handbrake fully, and withdraw the drum.

4   If the drum will not pull away, first check that the handbrake is fully released, then insert a rod into one of the outermost holes in the drum, and depress the self-adjusting mechanism's toothed segment to allow the brake shoes to be retracted until the drum can be removed. If the drum still cannot be moved, it is probably stuck to the hub flange with corrosion; either use a soft-faced mallet to gently tap the drum off the hub, or screw two 8 mm (thread size) bolts into the holes tapped into the drum (but not into the hub) and tighten them evenly and carefully to jack the drum off the hub (photos).

Inspection

Note: *If either drum requires renewal, both should be renewed at the same time, to ensure even and consistent braking.*

5   Working carefully (see the warning in Section 21) remove all traces of brake dust from the drum.

6   Scrub clean the outside of the drum, and check it for obvious signs of wear or damage such as cracks around the roadwheel bolt holes; renew the drum if necessary.

7   Examine carefully the inside of the drum. Light scoring of the friction surface is permissible, but if heavy scoring is found, the drum must be renewed. It is usual to find a lip on the drum's inboard edge which consists of a mixture of rust and brake dust; this should be scraped away to leave a smooth surface which can be polished with fine (120 to 150 grade) emery paper. Provided that it does not enlarge the drum to beyond the specified maximum diameter, it may be possible to have the drum refinished by skimming or grinding to rectify slight wear or damage; if this is not possible, the drum must be renewed. If, however, the lip is due to the friction surface being recessed by wear, then the drum must be measured carefully as follows.

8   If the drum is thought to be excessively worn, or oval, its internal diameter must be measured, using an internal micrometer, at several points both on the inboard and outboard edges of the area swept by the

20.3 Removing rear brake drum securing screws (remaining screw arrowed)

20.4A If brake shoes must be retracted to release drum, insert rod through drum hole ...

20.4B ... to release self-adjusting mechanism

20.4C Using two bolts to jack drum off hub – tighten screws evenly to prevent risk of drum damage

20.9 Clean and prepare drum/hub mating surfaces (arrowed) before refitting drum

brake shoes. Take measurements in pairs, the second at right-angles to the first, and compare the two to check for signs of ovality; if any measurement differs from its counterpart by a significant amount, the drum is oval. If a drum is worn at any point to the specified maximum or beyond, or if it exceeds the maximum ovality allowed, it is worn out and both drums must be renewed.

Refitting

9   Refitting is the reverse of the removal procedure, noting the following points.

(a) On fitting a new brake drum, use a suitable solvent to remove any preservative coating that may have been applied to its interior.

(b) Use a clean wire brush to remove all traces of dirt, brake dust and corrosion from the mating surfaces of the drum and the hub flange (photo), then apply a thin smear of anti-seize compound (eg Holts Copaslip) to these surfaces.

(c) Align the marks made on removal (if applicable).

(d) Tighten the drum securing screws and the roadwheel bolts to their specified torque wrench settings (refer to Chapter 1 Specifications as necessary).

(e) Depress the brake pedal several times until the wheel cylinder(s) and brake shoes have taken up their correct working positions, and normal pedal travel is restored.

(f) Check and correct if necessary the handbrake adjustment (Chapter 1); ensure that the roadwheels rotate easily, with no (or only very slight) sound of brake shoe-to-drum contact.

---

21   Rear brake shoes – inspection and renewal

Warning: *Brake shoes must be renewed on both rear wheels at the same time – never renew the shoes on only one wheel, as uneven braking may result. Also, the dust created by wear of the shoes may contain asbestos, which is a health hazard. Never blow it out with compressed air, and don't*

inhale any of it. An approved filtering mask should be worn when working on the brakes. DO NOT use petroleum-based solvents to clean brake parts – use brake cleaner or methylated spirit only.

Inspection

1   Remove and check the brake drum (Section 20).

2   Working carefully (see warning above) remove all traces of brake dust from the brake drum, backplate and shoes. Ensure that the shoe friction material is not contaminated with oil or grease from careless handling; masking tape or similar can be used to protect the friction material from such contamination, providing its adhesive does not itself foul the material, and providing care is taken to remove it before the drum is refitted.

3   Measure at several points the thickness of friction material remaining on each brake shoe (photo). If either shoe is worn at any point to the specified minimum thickness or less, all four shoes must be renewed as an axle set (see warning above) as described later. Also, the shoes should be renewed if any are fouled with oil or grease; there is no truly satisfactory way of degreasing friction material.

4   If any of the brake shoes are worn unevenly or fouled with oil or grease, trace and rectify the cause before reassembly.

5   Carefully lifting each rubber protective cap, check the wheel cylinders for signs of leaks or corrosion, and ensure that both plungers and pistons are free to move (Section 22).

6   Apply a light smear of brake lubricant (paragraph 17) to the pivot points and bearing surfaces of the handbrake operating/shoe self-adjusting mechanism, then check that the mechanism operates correctly.

7   Refit the brake drum (Section 20).

8   Repeat the procedure on the opposite brake.

Renewal

Note: *The leading brake shoe of each rear brake assembly is the shoe immediately following the wheel cylinder in the direction of normal (ie forwards) drum rotation – these shoes are 'handed'. The remaining shoe (of each assembly) is the trailing shoe – these are the same for both left- and right-hand brakes.*

21.3 Measuring thickness of brake shoe friction material

21.14A Removing brake shoe assembly ...

21.14B ... note elastic band around wheel cylinder to retain plungers and pistons

21.18A Showing brake shoes and handbrake operating/shoe self-adjusting mechanism correctly reassembled ...

21.18B ... and secured by spring and spring clips

21.18C Needle-nosed pliers or similar will be required to remove/refit shoe return springs

9   Remove and check the brake drum (Section 20).
10   Working carefully (see warning above) remove all traces of brake dust from the brake drum, backplate and shoes. Depress the self-adjusting mechanism's toothed segment to allow the mechanism to retract.
11   Compressing its spring, unhook the handbrake cable inner wire from the operating lever on the trailing shoe.
12   Using needle-nosed pliers or similar, unhook the shoe bottom return spring.
13   Pressing in their spring clip free ends to release them, withdraw the shoe retainer pins.
14   Disengaging as necessary the components of the handbrake operating/shoe self-adjusting mechanism, withdraw the brake shoes. Do not depress the brake pedal until the brakes are reassembled; wrap an elastic band or similar around the wheel cylinder to prevent the plungers and pistons from being ejected (photos).
15   With the assembly placed on a clean work surface, unhook the shoe top return spring. Extracting the retaining spring clips and C-clips as required, dismantle the brake shoes and handbrake operating/shoe self-adjusting mechanism. Clean all components, check them for wear or damage, and renew any that are unfit for further use.
16   Peel back the rubber protective caps, check the wheel cylinder for fluid leaks or other damage, and ensure that both plungers and pistons are free to move (Section 22).
17   Clean the backplate, and apply a thin smear of high-temperature brake grease (silicone-based or PBC/Poly Butyl Cuprysil-based) or anti-seize compound (eg Holts Copaslip) to all bearing surfaces or pivots, and to those surfaces of the backplate which bear on the shoes, particularly the wheel cylinder plungers and the bottom anchor points. Do not allow any lubricant to foul the friction material; masking tape or similar can be used to protect the friction material from such contamination, providing its adhesive does not itself foul the material, and providing care is taken to remove it before the drum is refitted.
18   On refitting, assemble the shoes and handbrake operating/shoe self-adjusting mechanism on a clean work surface (photos). Note that the shoe top return spring is fitted so that the end with the shorter tag is hooked on to the leading shoe.
19   Fit the assembly to the backplate, being careful not to get grease on to the friction material. Ensure that the shoe ends engage properly

with the wheel cylinder plungers and the bottom anchor points, then refit the shoe retainer pins and spring clips (photos). Tap the shoes to centralise them on the backplate.
20   Ensuring that it runs correctly through the guide provided in the backplate, compress its spring and reconnect the handbrake cable inner wire to the operating lever.
21   Hook on the shoe bottom return spring. Check that all components are correctly refitted and securely fastened (photo).

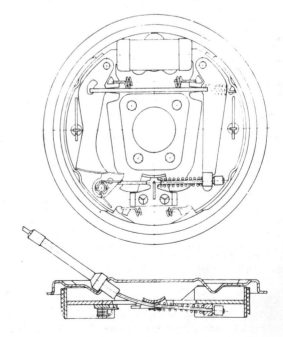

Fig. 9.14 Rear brake backplate, showing installation of brake shoes and handbrake cable (Sec 21)

21.19A Locating shoe ends with bottom anchor points

21.19B Brake shoe retainer pins are secured by spring clips fitted as shown (arrowed)

21.21 Check that all components are correctly refitted and securely fastened

22   Remove the masking tape (if used) from the brake shoes and the elastic band from the wheel cylinder, then refit the brake drum (Section 20).
23   Repeat the procedure on the opposite brake.
24   Be prepared for reduced braking efficiency for a few hundred miles until the new linings have bedded-in. Avoid harsh braking as far as possible during this period.

22   Rear wheel cylinder – removal, overhaul and refitting

Note: *Before starting work, refer to the note at the beginning of Section 9 concerning the dangers of hydraulic fluid, and to the warning at the beginning of Section 21 concerning the dangers of asbestos dust.*

Removal

1   Remove the brake drum (Section 20).
2   Remove the brake shoes (Section 21, paragraphs 10 to 14).
3   Minimise fluid loss by removing the master cylinder reservoir cap and then tightening it down on to a piece of polythene to obtain an airtight seal (taking care not to damage the sender unit), by using a brake hose clamp, a G-clamp or a similar tool to clamp the flexible hose, or by capping or plugging the metal brake pipe as it is disconnected from the cylinder (Section 10). Unscrew the bleed nipple, and plug both cylinder orifices; take great care not to allow dirt into the system.
4   Unbolt the cylinder from the backplate (photo).

Overhaul

Note: *Before attempting to overhaul the unit, check the price and availability of individual components, and the price of a new or reconditioned unit, as overhaul may not be viable on economic grounds alone.*

5   Remove the wheel cylinder from the vehicle, and clean it thoroughly.
6   Mount the wheel cylinder in a soft-jawed vice, then remove the rubber protective caps and plungers. Extract the piston assemblies and spring.
7   Thoroughly clean all components using as a cleaning medium only methylated spirit, isopropyl alcohol or clean hydraulic fluid. Never use mineral-based solvents such as petrol or paraffin, which will attack the hydraulic system's rubber components. Dry the components immediately using compressed air or a clean, lint-free cloth.
8   Check all components, and renew any that are worn or damaged. Check particularly the cylinder bore and pistons; the complete assembly must be renewed if these are scratched, worn or corroded. If there is any doubt about the condition of the assembly or of any of its components, renew it. Check that the fluid entry port and bleed nipple passage are clear.
9   If the assembly is fit for further use, obtain the components required to reassemble it. Renew as a matter of course the rubber protective caps, dust cap and seals disturbed on dismantling; these should never be re-used.
10   On reassembly, soak the pistons and the new seals in clean hydraulic fluid. Smear clean fluid into the cylinder bore.

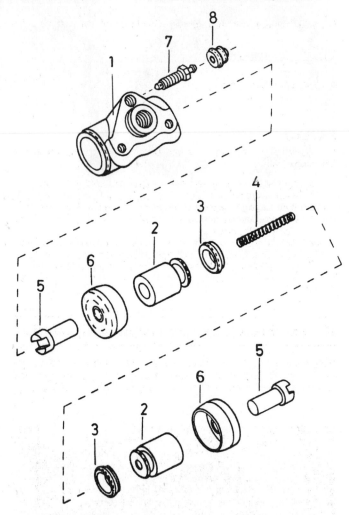

Fig. 9.15 Exploded view of rear wheel cylinder (Sec 22)

1 Body	5 Plunger
2 Piston	6 Rubber protective cap
3 Piston seal	7 Bleed nipple
4 Spring	8 Dust cap

11   Fit the new seals to their pistons, using only the fingers to manipulate them into the grooves. Ensure that all components are refitted in the correct order and the right way round.
12   Insert the pistons into the bore, using a twisting motion to avoid trapping the seal lips. Apply a smear of rubber lubricant to each piston before fitting the new rubber protective caps and the plungers.
13   Refit the wheel cylinder.

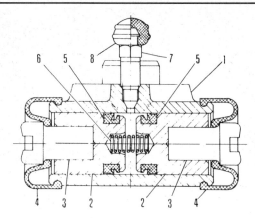

Fig. 9.16 Cross-section through rear wheel cylinder (Sec 22)

1 Body	5 Piston seal
2 Piston	6 Spring
3 Plunger	7 Bleed nipple
4 Rubber protective cap	8 Dust cap

Refitting

14   Refitting is the reverse of the removal procedure, noting the following points.

   (a) Tighten the cylinder mounting bolts to the specified torque wrench setting.

   (b) Refit the bleed nipple, then connect the metal brake pipe to the cylinder (Section 10) and refit the brake shoes and drum (Sections 21 and 20).

   (c) Bleed any air from the system (Section 9) and check for leaks while an assistant applies full pressure to the brake pedal, then wash off any spilt fluid and check for any fluid leaks which might subsequently appear.

23 Rear brake backplate – removal and refitting

Note: *Before starting work, refer to the note at the beginning of Section 9 concerning the dangers of hydraulic fluid, and to the warning at the beginning of Section 21 concerning the dangers of asbestos dust.*

23.4 Brake backplate mounting bolts (arrows)

22.4 Rear brake wheel cylinder mounting bolts (A) and bleed nipple (B)

Removal

1   Remove the rear hub (Chapter 10).
2   Compressing its spring, unhook the handbrake cable inner wire from the operating lever on the trailing shoe. Disconnect the handbrake cable from the backplate by releasing the inner wire from its guide, then tap out the cable outer bush.
3   Minimise fluid loss by removing the master cylinder reservoir cap and then tightening it down on to a piece of polythene to obtain an airtight seal (taking care not to damage the sender unit), by using a brake hose clamp, a G-clamp or a similar tool to clamp the flexible hose, or by capping or plugging the metal brake pipe as it is disconnected from the wheel cylinder (Section 10). Plug the cylinder orifice; take great care not to allow dirt into the hydraulic system.
4   Unbolt the backplate and withdraw it (photo).

Refitting

5   Refitting is the reverse of the removal procedure, but apply a smear of sealant to the backplate/trailing arm mating surfaces. Tighten all nuts and bolts to their specified torque wrench settings. Refer to the relevant Sections of Chapters 1 and 10 as well as this Chapter for detailed instructions.

24 Handbrake lever – removal and refitting

Removal

1   With the car parked on level ground, switch off the ignition, select first or reverse gear, and chock the roadwheels so that the car cannot move when the handbrake is released.
2   Unclip the handbrake lever trim, then unscrew the adjustment nut and locknut to disconnect each cable from the lever (Chapter 1).
3   If the lever pivot is secured on one side by a circlip, extract the circlip and drive out the pivot to release the lever assembly. If no circlip is fitted, cut the pivot with a hacksaw to remove it, and obtain a new pivot (with circlip) for reassembly.

Refitting

4   Refitting is the reverse of the removal procedure. Apply a smear of grease to all pivots, the cable compensator fittings and the adjuster threads. Adjust the handbrake (Chapter 1).

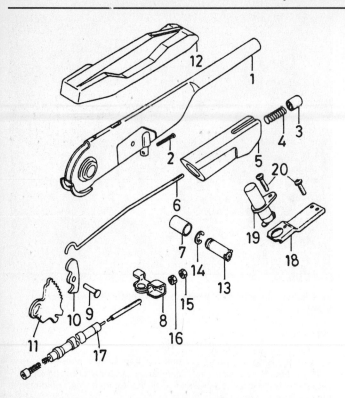

Fig. 9.17 Handbrake components (Sec 24)

1 Handbrake lever	11 Toothed quadrant
2 Split pin	12 Plastic trim
3 Release knob	13 Lever pivot
4 Spring	14 Circlip (where fitted)
5 Handgrip	15 Locknut
6 Link rod	16 Adjustment nut
7 Pivot bush	17 Handbrake cable
8 Cable compensator	18 Mounting bracket
9 Pivot pin (rivet)	19 Handbrake warning light switch
10 Lever pawl	20 Screw – 3 off

25   Handbrake cables – removal, inspection and refitting

Removal

1   With the vehicle parked on level ground, switch off the ignition, select first or reverse gear, and chock the front roadwheels so that the vehicle cannot move when the handbrake is released.

2   Unclip the handbrake lever trim, then unscrew the adjustment nut and locknut to disconnect the cable from the lever (Chapter 1). Tie a length of string to the cable end.

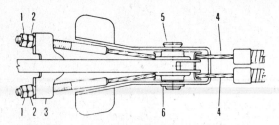

Fig. 9.18 Handbrake cable routing at lever pivot (Sec 25)

1 Locknut	4 Cable
2 Adjustment nut	5 Lever pivot
3 Cable compensator	6 Circlip (where fitted)

3   Jack up the rear of the vehicle, and support it securely on axle stands (see 'Jacking, towing and wheel changing').

4   Release the cable from the clips securing it to the fuel tank (photo), and from the cable tie securing it to the trailing arm of the rear suspension torsion beam axle.

5   Unfasten the nut securing the cable guide to the rear suspension torsion beam axle (photo), then pull the cable down clear of the underbody; untie the string, leaving it in place for reassembly.

6   Remove the brake drum (Section 20).

7   Compressing its spring, unhook the cable inner wire from the operating lever on the trailing shoe. Disconnect the cable from the backplate by releasing the inner wire from its guide, then tap out the cable outer bush (photo).

Inspection

8   Check the cable for wear or damage, and renew it if necessary; do not forget to transfer the cable guide and any other fittings to the new cable.

Refitting

9   Refitting is the reverse of the removal procedure, noting the following points.

(a)   Use the string to draw the cable front end into the passenger compartment, refit the adjustment nut and locknut, and fasten the clips securing the cable to the fuel tank.

(b)   Route the cable back along the underbody, tightening the nut securing the cable guide to the rear suspension torsion beam axle to its specified torque wrench setting, and passing the cable end through the backplate. Use a hammer and drift to gently tap the cable outer bush into the backplate.

(c)   Ensuring that it runs correctly through the guide provided in the backplate, compress its spring and reconnect the cable inner wire to the operating lever.

(d)   Refit the brake drum (Section 20).

(e)   Adjust the handbrake (Chapter 1).

(f)   Use new cable ties to secure the cables to the trailing arms, then lower the vehicle to the ground.

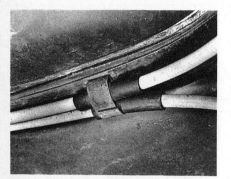

25.4 Handbrake cables clipped to underside of fuel tank ...

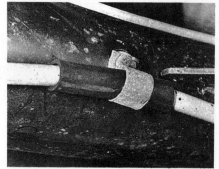

25.5 ... and secured by a guide to rear suspension torsion beam axle

25.7 Handbrake cable outer secured by bush (arrowed) to brake backplate

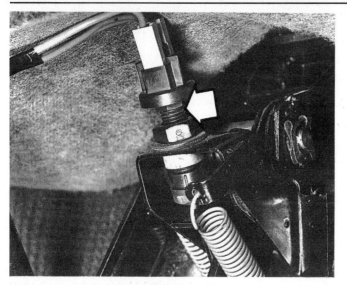

27.1 Location of stop-light switch (arrowed)

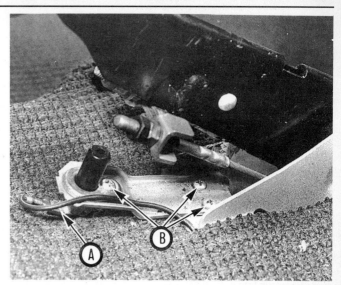

27.6 Handbrake switch connection (A) and mounting screws (B)

26 Stop-light switch – adjustment

1 The stop-light switch should be set so that the lights come on when the brake pedal is depressed by 10 to 15 mm from its normal at-rest position.
2 To adjust the switch setting, remove the steering column lower shroud if necessary (Chapter 10) and press back the carpet/insulating material as required to reach the switch (see photo 27.1).
3 Disconnect the switch wires to avoid damage through twisting them. Slacken the locknut securing the switch, and re-position the switch until the lights come on at the correct moment; either reconnect the wires and have an assistant check the stop-lights for you, or use a multi-meter to check when the switch contacts close, allowing current to flow. Tighten the locknut securely and reconnect the wires, then switch on the ignition and check the stop-light operation.
4 Refit any components removed for access.

27 Braking system warning lights and switches – general

Stop-light

1 The stop-light circuit is controlled by a plunger-type switch mounted on the brake pedal bracket (photo).
2 Check and adjust the switch setting as described in Section 26 of this Chapter.
3 If the switch is thought to be faulty, it can be tested by disconnecting its wires and connecting either a multi-meter (set to the resistance function) or a battery-and-bulb test circuit across the switch terminals. The switch should allow current to flow only when it is extended; if the switch is faulty, it must be renewed.

4 To remove the switch, disconnect its wires and slacken the locknut, then prise off the rubber seals as necessary to release the switch from the pedal bracket.
5 Refitting is the reverse of the removal procedure; adjust the switch setting on completion (Section 26).

Handbrake warning light

6 The instrument panel handbrake warning light is activated by a plunger switch mounted at the base of the handbrake lever, so that the light comes on whenever the handbrake is applied (photo).
7 Unclip the handbrake lever trim to reach the switch (Chapter 1).
8 The switch is not adjustable, and is secured by one screw to its mounting bracket, which is secured itself by two screws; to remove it, undo the screws and disconnect the wiring.
9 To test the switch, use the equipment described in paragraph 3 to check that current can flow between the switch's terminal and its earth only when the plunger is extended; if the switch is faulty, it must be renewed.
10 Refitting is the reverse of the removal procedure; position the switch plunger squarely under the handbrake lever, then tighten the mounting screws.

Brake (low fluid level) warning light

11 The instrument panel brake (low fluid level) warning light is activated by a float-type sender unit in the master cylinder reservoir filler cap, so that the light comes on whenever the fluid level falls to a dangerously-low level.
12 As a check of its function, the light should come on whenever the ignition switch is in position 'II' (engine starting); if the light does not come on at any time, first check the bulb, then test the circuit until the fault is found and cured (Chapter 12).
13 To test the sender unit, remove it and use the equipment described in paragraph 3 to check that current can flow between the unit's terminals only when the float is at the bottom of its travel.
14 The sender unit is only available with the master cylinder reservoir filler cap; if the sender unit is faulty, the assembly must be renewed.

Chapter 10 Suspension and steering

Contents

Front hub and bearing – removal and refitting 3
Front hub carrier – removal and refitting... 2
Front suspension and steering check................................. See Chapter 1
Front suspension lower arm and pivot bushes – removal,
overhaul and refitting 5
Front suspension lower arm balljoint – removal and refitting 6
Front suspension strut – removal, overhaul and refitting 4
Front suspension subframe – removal and refitting 7
General information.. 1
Rear hub and bearings – removal and refitting.............................. 8
Rear hub bearing check and adjustment............................... See Chapter 1
Rear stub axle – removal and refitting 9
Rear suspension check .... See Chapter 1
Rear suspension torsion beam axle pivot brackets – removal and
refitting... 12

Rear suspension torsion beam axle – removal and refitting 11
Rear suspension unit – removal, overhaul and refitting 10
Steering column – dismantling and reassembly 15
Steering column – removal and refitting............................... 14
Steering gear – overhaul.. 19
Steering gear – removal and refitting................................... 18
Steering gear rubber gaiters – renewal................................ 17
Steering lock/ignition switch – removal and refitting......................... 16
Steering wheel – removal and refitting 13
Suspension strut/shock absorber check............................ See Chapter 1
Track rod balljoint – removal and refitting 20
Wheel and tyre maintenance and tyre pressure checks ... See Chapter 1
Wheel alignment and steering angles – general information........... 21

Specifications

Front suspension

Type..	Independent, with MacPherson struts
Coil spring free length	350 mm

Rear suspension

Type..	Semi-independent, with torsion beam axle
Coil spring free length	410 mm

Steering

Type..	Rack-and-pinion
Turns lock-to-lock	3.7
Steering gear lubricant:	
Original type...	Kluber GLK 91 grease
Replacement type*..	Duckhams Hypoid 90S Gear Oil
Quantity	130 cc

*Note: To be used only if original lubricant is not available – steering gear must be dismantled and all grease cleaned out before refilling with oil.

Wheel alignment and steering angles

Note: *All measurements are with vehicle at normal kerb weight, and unladen.*

Toe-out in turns – full-lock	Inside roadwheel 36° 33', outside roadwheel 31° 30'
Camber angle:	
Front*..	0° 20' ± 30' positive
Rear*...	1° 24' ± 30' negative
Castor angle*...	1° 30' ± 45'
Toe setting:	
Front...	1.0 ± 1.0 mm toe-in
Rear*...	1.2 ± 1.4 mm toe-in

***Note:** *Given for reference (checking purposes) only – not adjustable.*

Roadwheels

Type...	Pressed-steel or light alloy
Size:	
Pressed-steel	4.5BH x 13
Light alloy..	5J x 13

Tyres

Type...	Tubeless steel-braced radial
Size..	165/70 R 13 79T
Pressures	See Chapter 1

Torque wrench settings

	Nm	lbf ft
Front suspension		
Strut top mounting nuts	17 to 22	13 to 16
Strut piston rod nut	45 to 50	33 to 37
Strut-to-hub carrier pinch-bolt and nut..............................	60 to 68	44 to 50
Lower arm balljoint-to-hub carrier pinch-bolt and nut	60 to 68	44 to 50
Lower arm balljoint-to-lower arm bolts and nuts – service replacement component only..	23	17
Lower arm front pivot bolt and nut.......................................	70 to 90	52 to 66
Lower arm rear pivot clamp fasteners:		
6 mm (thread size) nut and bolt.................................	10 to 15	7 to 11
10 mm (thread size) bolts..	39 to 45	29 to 33
Suspension subframe mounting bolts...................................	39 to 45	29 to 33
Earth strap bolts..	15 to 20	11 to 15
Driveshaft nut..	See Chapter 8	
Rear suspension		
Suspension unit top mounting nut	25 to 30	18 to 22
Suspension unit piston rod nut...	40 to 45	30 to 33
Suspension unit bottom mounting bolt and nut	50 to 55	37 to 41
Torsion beam axle pivot bolt and nut..................................	70 to 80	52 to 59
Torsion beam axle pivot bracket mounting bolts	60 to 65	44 to 48
Stub axle mounting bolts	50 to 55	37 to 41
Rear hub/stub axle nut	See Chapter 1	
Steering		
Steering wheel nut...	30 to 35	22 to 26
Steering column upper mounting bolts................................	20 to 25	15 to 18
Steering column lower mounting bolts	25 to 30	18 to 22
Steering column universal joint pinch-bolts	20 to 25	15 to 18
Steering gear mounting bolts...	20 to 25	15 to 18
Steering gear pinion cover bolts	7	5
Steering gear slipper cover bolts...	7	5
Steering gear reducing sleeves-to-rack	50 to 60	37 to 44
Track rod inboard joint locknut-to-coupling sleeve	50 to 60	37 to 44
Track rod balljoint locknut..	50 to 60	37 to 44
Track rod balljoint-to-hub carrier steering arm nut.........	50 to 60	37 to 44
Roadwheels		
Roadwheel bolts..	60 to 90	44 to 66

1 General information

The front suspension is fully independent, using MacPherson struts, and the rear suspension is semi-independent, using a torsion beam axle. Steering is by rack-and-pinion.

On the front suspension, the roadwheel hub carriers are clamped to the bottom of each strut, and are located both transversely and fore-and-aft, via a balljoint, by the suspension lower arms. The lower arms pivot on rubber bushes, and are secured via a subframe that is bolted direct to the body.

On the rear suspension, two trailing arms are pivoted, via rubber bushes, from brackets fastened to the vehicle's underbody, and are linked by a transverse beam to form a single unit – the torsion beam axle. This is designed to allow enough twisting to permit each roadwheel a measure of independent movement while being braced laterally to prevent side-to-side movement. Suspension is provided by a telescopic, hydraulically-damped suspension unit, with a concentric coil spring that is mounted between the body and the rear end of each trailing arm. Estate, Van and Pick-up models are fitted with stronger springs and units which give stiffer damping than those fitted to Hatchbacks. The roadwheel stub axles are bolted, with the brake backplates, to the rear ends of the trailing arms.

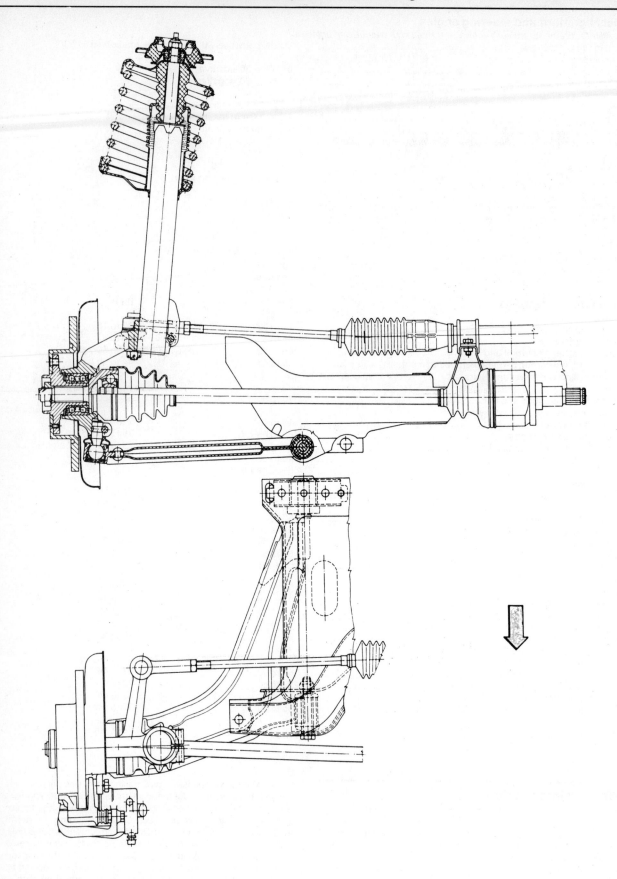

Fig. 10.1 Cross-section through front suspension (Sec 1)

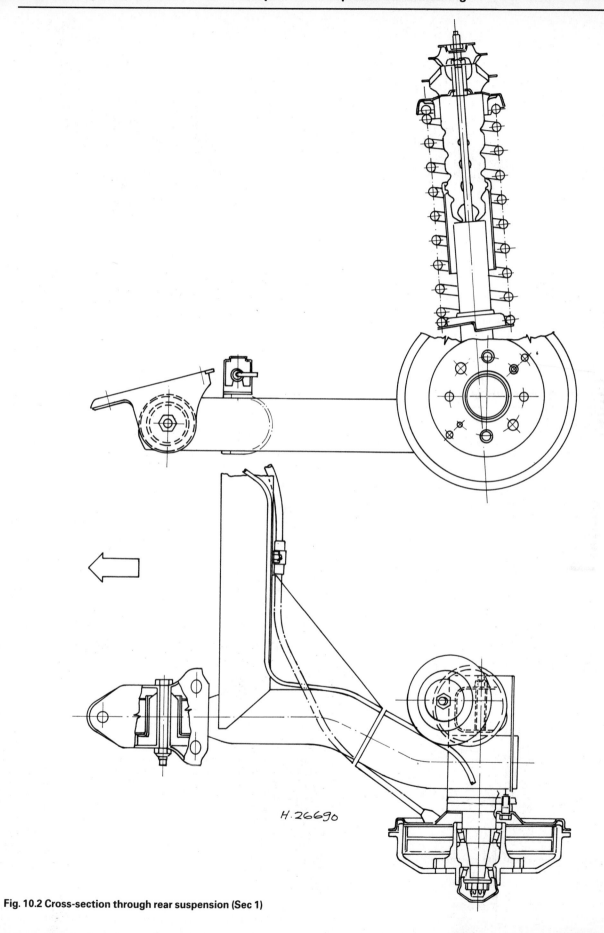

H.26690

Fig. 10.2 Cross-section through rear suspension (Sec 1)

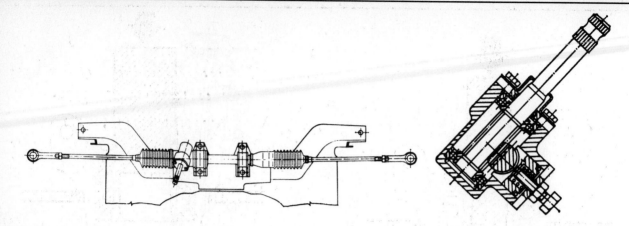

Fig. 10.3 Steering gear and front suspension subframe – cross-section through pinion, rack and slipper adjuster (Sec 1)

The steering column is of the collapsible, energy-absorbing type, to protect the driver in the event of an accident. The steering gear is clamped in two rubber bushes to the front suspension subframe, and is connected by two track rods to the steering arms projecting rearwards from the hub carriers. The track rods are fitted with balljoints at their outer ends; and are threaded so that the assembly's length can be adjusted, when required.

2   Front hub carrier – removal and refitting

Removal

1   Separate the hub carrier from the driveshaft, as described in Chapter 8, Section 2, paragraphs 1 to 8 (disregarding paragraph 4).
2   Unbolt the brake caliper mounting bracket from the hub carrier, then withdraw the caliper assembly and secure it out of harm's way without stretching or kinking the brake hose. Place a clean spacer (of the same thickness as the brake disc) between the pads, to prevent them being dislodged (Chapter 9, Section 14).

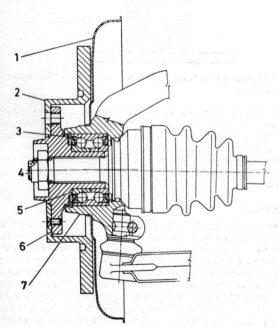

Fig. 10.4 Cross-section through front hub assembly (Sec 2)

1 Brake disc shield	5 Hub bearing
2 Brake disc	6 Hub
3 Circlip	7 Hub carrier
4 Driveshaft nut	

3   If the hub carrier is to be dismantled, remove the brake disc (Chapter 9, Section 16).
4   Unfasten the pinch-bolt and nut clamping the hub carrier to the strut lower end, tap out the bolt and remove the hub carrier from the vehicle.

Refitting

5   Refitting is the reverse of the removal procedure, noting the following points.

    (a)   Clean and grease the strut-to-hub carrier pinch-bolt and nut, then clean the mating surfaces of the hub carrier and strut.
    (b)   Offer up the hub carrier to the strut, then refit the pinch-bolt and nut, tightening them to the specified torque wrench setting.
    (c)   Refit the brake disc and caliper (Chapter 9).
    (d)   Reassemble the front suspension as described in Chapter 8, Section 2, paragraphs 16 to 21. Tighten all nuts and bolts securely, to the specified torque settings where given.

3   Front hub and bearing – removal and refitting

Note: *The bearing is sealed, of the (non-adjustable) double-row ball journal type, and is intended to last the vehicle's entire service life without maintenance or attention. Do not attempt to remove the bearing unless absolutely necessary, as it probably will be damaged during the removal operation. Never overtighten the driveshaft nut beyond the specified torque wrench setting in an attempt to 'adjust' the bearing.*

The bearing inner race is an interference fit on the hub, therefore a press will be required to dismantle and rebuild the assembly; if a press is not available, a large bench vice and suitable spacers may serve as an adequate substitute.

Removal

1   Remove the hub carrier from the vehicle (Section 2).
2   The brake disc shield can be removed if required (Chapter 9, Section 17).
3   Press the hub out of the hub carrier assembly. If the bearing's outboard inner race remains on the hub, use a proprietary general-purpose bearing puller to remove it.
4   Extract the circlip from the hub carrier, and press out the bearing.
5   Thoroughly clean the bearing, the hub carrier and the hub. Check all components for signs of wear or damage, and renew them if necessary. Check the roadwheel bolt threads with particular care. The bearing should be renewed as a matter of course whenever it is disturbed (see the note at the beginning of this Section), but if it appears fit for further service it can be examined as follows. Check that it rotates smoothly and easily, with no signs of noise or roughness. If the races and balls can be seen, check them for signs of scoring, pitting or flaking. Check that the circlip is fit for re-use.

Refitting

6   On reassembly, check (as far as possible) that the bearing is packed with grease, then press in the bearing as shown in Fig. 10.7 until it seats

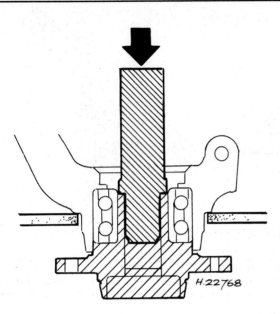

Fig. 10.5 Pressing out hub from hub carrier (Sec 3)

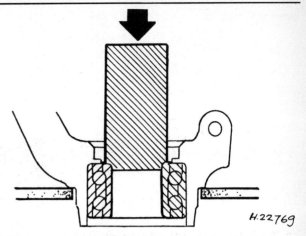

Fig. 10.6 Pressing hub bearing out of hub carrier (Sec 3)

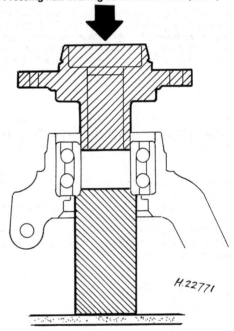

Fig. 10.8 Pressing hub into hub carrier – note support for bearing inner race (Sec 3)

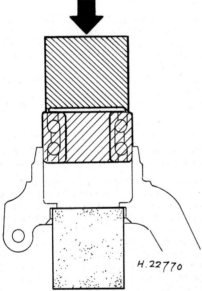

Fig. 10.7 Pressing new bearing into hub carrier (Sec 3)

against the locating shoulder; ensure that pressure is applied only to the bearing's outer race, or the bearing may be damaged.

7   Refit the circlip to the hub carrier groove.

8   Ensuring that the bearing's inner race is fully supported as shown in Fig. 10.8, press the hub into the hub carrier. Temporarily refit the hub carrier to the driveshaft, tighten the (used) driveshaft nut to the specified torque setting, and check that the bearing rotates smoothly and easily, with no trace of free play.

9   Refit, if removed, the brake disc shield (Chapter 9, Section 17).

10   Refit the hub carrier to the vehicle (Section 2).

4   Front suspension strut – removal, overhaul and refitting

Removal

1   Jack up the front of the vehicle, support it securely on axle stands, then remove the roadwheel (see 'Jacking, towing and wheel changing').

2   Unfasten the pinch-bolt and nut clamping the hub carrier to the strut lower end, tap out the bolt and pull the hub carrier downwards off the strut. Place a support under the hub carrier/lower arm to prevent the brake hose being stretched or damaged.

3   Open the bonnet and unscrew the two suspension strut top mounting nuts, then withdraw the strut from under the front wing (photos).

Overhaul

Warning: *Before attempting to dismantle the suspension strut, a suitable tool must be obtained to hold safely the coil spring in compression. Adjustable coil spring compressors are readily available, and are recommended for this operation. Any attempt to dismantle the strut without such a tool is likely to result in damage or personal injury; do not attempt to undo the piston rod nut with the strut in place on the vehicle.*

Note: *If either of the front springs requires renewal, it is good practice to renew both together as a matched pair. Check the spring upper end for signs of colour-coding indicating the spring's rating. Both springs should have the same marking; see a Skoda dealer for details.*

Similarly, if either of the front struts requires renewal, it is good practice to renew both together as a matched pair.

Always store suspension struts in an upright position. If a strut is to be fitted after a long period of storage, mount it upright in a vice, and move the piston rod fully up and down several times to prime the damper passages and restore full damping action.

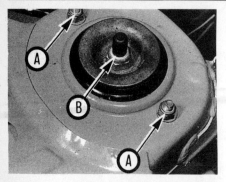

4.3A Front suspension strut top mounting nuts (A) and piston rod nut (B)

4.3B Removing a front suspension strut

4.6 Spring compressors must be used to compress spring safely

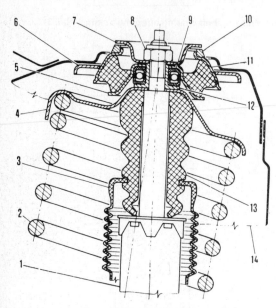

Fig. 10.9 Cross-section through front suspension strut top mounting (Sec 4)

1 Strut	8 Piston rod nut
2 Spring	9 Ball-bearing
3 Dust cover	10 Thrust ring
4 Spring upper seat	11 Mounting rubber
5 Bearing plate	12 Bearing insert
6 Seat plate	13 Rubber buffer
7 Upper plate	14 Vehicle bodywork

4   Remove the suspension strut from the vehicle, and thoroughly clean the assembly.

5   Using an open-ended spanner or similar (applied to the flats at its upper end) to prevent the piston rod from rotating, slacken the piston rod nut **but do not unscrew it fully yet.**

6   Fit spring compressors (available from most motor accessory shops) to each side of the spring, and tighten them evenly to compress the spring until there is no pressure on the spring upper seat or the strut top mounting (photo).

7   Unscrew the piston rod nut, and remove the top mounting components, the spring upper seat, the rubber buffer, the dust cover and the spring.

8   Visually inspect all components of the strut, and renew any that are showing obvious signs of wear or damage. Check particularly the top mounting components, looking for cracks, distortion or deterioration of the rubber itself.

9   Check the top mounting's ball-bearing, which should rotate smoothly and easily with no signs of free play. If it shows signs of stiffness, corrosion or free play, the bearing must be renewed. Press the insert out of the bearing plate, then tap out the bearing itself. The new bearing can be installed using either a press or a strong bench vice, and a

socket or piece of tubing which bears only on the bearing's outer race. When the bearing is securely seated, press in the insert; check that the bearing is securely fixed, with no free play evident.

10   If either of the top mounting studs require renewal, ensure that the mounting plate is securely supported so that it does not distort as the stud is tapped in or out; a suitable socket is ideal.

11   If the spring is obviously broken or damaged it must of course be renewed; also if it has sagged to significantly less than the specified free length.

12   Check the strut's damping action by mounting it upright in a vice and moving the piston rod fully up and down; firm, even resistance should be felt in both directions. If the damping is weak, if the strut shows signs of oil leaks at any point, or if the piston rod is bent, scored or damaged, the suspension strut must be renewed; individual components are not available to permit repairs.

13   Reassembly is the reverse of the dismantling procedure, noting the following points:

(a)   Pull out the piston rod to its full extent, and ensure that the spring is correctly compressed before refitting it. Locate its upper seat correctly on the spring, and ensure that the top mounting components are refitted in the correct order and the right way up.

(b)   To tighten the piston rod nut to the specified torque wrench setting, use a spring balance or similar to apply to the spanner handle a measured force at a corresponding distance from the nut's centre (for example, applying a pull of 33 to 37 lb at a distance of 1 ft is the same as 16.5 to 18.5 lb at 2 ft).

(c)   When the nut is correctly tightened, slacken the spring compressors evenly until they can be disengaged from the spring, then check that the top mounting is free to rotate.

(d)   Refit the strut assembly to the vehicle.

4.14 Tighten all nuts and bolts to specified torque wrench setting – strut-to-hub carrier pinch-bolt and nut shown

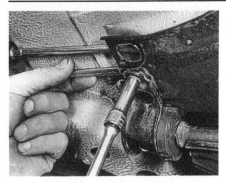

5.3A Wedge down front suspension subframe to permit unscrewing of smaller lower arm clamp bolts

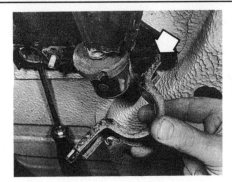

5.3B Note tag (arrowed) locating rear pivot clamp in subframe

5.3C Unscrewing the front pivot bolt and nut

Refitting

14 Refitting is the reverse of the removal procedure, noting the following points.

    (a) *Thoroughly clean the underwing area and all mounting points.*
    (b) *Tighten all nuts and bolts securely, to the specified torque wrench settings where given (photo).*
    (c) *Remember that it may be necessary to check the wheel alignment and steering angles (Section 21).*

5 Front suspension lower arm and pivot bushes – removal, overhaul and refitting

Removal

1 Jack up the front of the vehicle, and support it securely on axle stands (see *'Jacking, towing and wheel changing'*).
2 Separate the balljoint either from the lower arm or from the hub carrier (Section 6).
3 Unbolt and remove the lower arm rear pivot clamp, noting its locating tag. Unscrew first the two larger clamp bolts, then pull down the subframe and wedge it so that a spanner can be applied to the head of the smaller clamp bolt and the nut unscrewed. With the arm's rear mounting unfastened, unscrew the front pivot bolt nut and remove the bolt (photos).
4 Withdraw the arm.

Overhaul

5 Thoroughly clean the arm and the subframe/underbody areas around its mountings, removing all traces of dirt (and of underseal if necessary) then check it carefully for cracks, distortion or any other signs of wear or damage; do not forget the pivot and clamp fasteners. Renew any worn or damaged components.
6 Check the pivot bushes and renew them if they are cracked, worn, split or perished. While the rear pivot bush can be removed and refitted by hand, the front bush must be removed and refitted using a press, although it may be possible to achieve the required result using a strong bench vice and sockets or pieces of tubing; soak the old bush in penetrating fluid before attempting removal, and use liquid soap (washing-up liquid) or petroleum jelly as a lubricant when pressing in the new bush.

Refitting

7 Refitting is the reverse of the removal procedure, noting the following points.

    (a) *All fasteners should be tightened only lightly at first until the suspension is reassembled and the vehicle is lowered to the ground.*
    (b) *When all the vehicle's weight is back on its wheels, rock it to settle the suspension, then tighten all disturbed nuts and bolts to the specified torque wrench settings (photo).*
    (c) *It will be necessary to have the wheel alignment and steering angles checked (Section 21).*

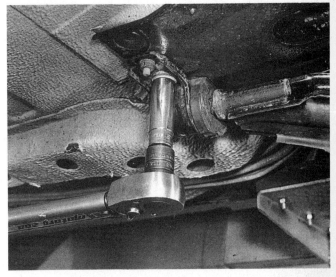

5.7 Tightening a rear pivot clamp bolt

6 Front suspension lower arm balljoint – removal and refitting

Note: *The original balljoint is riveted to the suspension lower arm; when it is renewed, the rivets are replaced by nuts and bolts. Proceed as described in the relevant sub-Section below.*
The balljoint dust cover is available separately, and can be renewed (by extracting both retaining circlips) once the balljoint pin has been disconnected from the hub carrier (see below). Note, however, that it is usually considered good working practice to renew as a matter of course any balljoint that is found to have a damaged dust cover (on the basis that dirt or other foreign matter will have entered and will soon damage the joint regardless of its present condition). Owners who discover a damaged balljoint dust cover are advised to check the joint very carefully for signs of wear or of contamination before considering renewing the dust cover alone; if there is the slightest doubt about the joint's condition, it must be renewed complete.

Removal

Riveted balljoint

1 Jack up the front of the vehicle, and support the body securely on axle stands (see *'Jacking, towing and wheel changing'*).
2 Unscrew the nut and remove completely the pinch-bolt securing the balljoint to the hub carrier. Pull down the lower arm to disconnect the balljoint pin from the hub carrier (photos).
3 Remove the suspension lower arm (Section 5).
4 Extract the rivets; it is best to use a pedestal drill (for accuracy) to drill out the rivet heads, so that a press can be used to remove the rivet studs.
5 Remove the old balljoint from the lower arm.

6.2A Remove the pinch-bolt ...

6.2B ... to separate the balljoint pin from the hub carrier

6.9 Tightening front suspension lower arm balljoint-to-hub carrier pinch-bolt and nut

Bolted balljoint

6   Jack up the front of the vehicle, and support the body securely on axle stands (see *'Jacking, towing and wheel changing'*).
7   Unscrew the nut and remove completely the pinch-bolt securing the balljoint to the hub carrier. Pull down the lower arm to disconnect the balljoint pin from the hub carrier.
8   Unbolt the balljoint from the lower arm.

Refitting

9   Refitting is the reverse of the removal procedure, noting the following points.

(a)   Tighten all disturbed nuts and bolts to their specified torque wrench settings (photo).
(b)   Depending on the reason for the work, it may be advisable to check the wheel alignment (Section 21) on completion.

7   Front suspension subframe – removal and refitting

Removal

1   Jack up the front of the vehicle, and support the body securely on axle stands (see *'Jacking, towing and wheel changing'*).
2   Unbolt the engine rear mounting from the subframe.
3   Unbolt the engine/transmission earth strap from the subframe.
4   Remove the exhaust downpipes (Chapter 4).
5   Disconnect the gearchange linkage from the transmission (Chapter 7).
6   Unscrew the steering gear mounting bolts from the top of the subframe, and support the steering gear (Section 18).

7   Unbolt the front suspension lower arm rear pivot clamps, then unscrew the front pivot bolt nuts and remove the bolts; wedge the arms clear of the subframe.
8   Unscrew the subframe front mounting bolts (photo), and lower the subframe from the vehicle.

Refitting

9   Refitting is the reverse of the removal procedure, noting the following points.

(a)   Offer up the subframe, locating it on the large pegs protruding from the underbody (photo), then refit the front mounting bolts to secure it in place.
(b)   All fasteners should be tightened only lightly at first until the suspension is reassembled and the vehicle is lowered to the ground.
(c)   When all the vehicle's weight is back on its wheels, rock it to settle the suspension, then tighten all disturbed nuts and bolts to the specified torque wrench settings.
(d)   It will be necessary to have the wheel alignment and steering angles checked (Section 21).

8   Rear hub and bearings – removal and refitting

Note: *Do not attempt to remove either bearing unless absolutely necessary, as it will probably be damaged during the removal operation. A press will be required to rebuild the assembly; if such is not available, a large bench vice and suitable spacers (such as large sockets) will serve as an adequate substitute.*

7.8 Front suspension subframe front mounting bolt (arrowed)

7.9 Front suspension subframe is located on large pegs (arrowed)

8.3 Removing rear hub from stub axle

8.13 Tang on washer must align with stub axle groove

8.15 Adjusting rear hub bearings – for details see Chapter 1

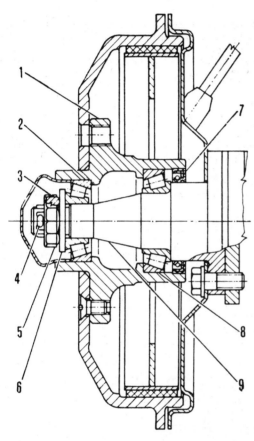

Fig. 10.10 Cross-section through rear hub and bearings (Sec 8)

1	*Rear hub*	*6*	*Washer*
2	*Outboard bearing*	*7*	*Oil seal*
3	*Rear hub/stub axle nut*	*8*	*Inboard bearing*
4	*Split pin*	*9*	*Stub axle*
5	*Retainer*		

Removal

1   Remove and inspect the brake drum (Chapter 9).
2   Prise off the hub cap and extract the split pin, withdraw the nut retainer, then unscrew the nut and remove the washer (Chapter 1).
3   Withdraw the hub from the stub axle (photo). If the bearings are to be renewed, remove their inner races now; if not, keep the hub assembly clean so that dirt cannot enter the bearings, and do not allow the inner races to drop out.
4   If the stub axle is worn or damaged, it must be renewed (Section 9).
5   Taking care not to scratch or damage the seal housing, prise the oil seal out of the hub inboard end and discard it; the seal must be renewed whenever it is disturbed.

6   Drive the outboard bearing outer race out of the hub, using a hammer and a suitable punch.
7   Drive the inboard bearing outer race out of the hub.
8   Thoroughly clean the hub, removing all traces of dirt and grease, and polishing away any burrs or raised edges which might hinder reassembly. Check for cracks or any other signs of wear or damage, particularly to the threads for the roadwheel bolts, and renew the hub if necessary.

Refitting

9   On reassembly, pack the new bearings with good-quality lithium-based grease. Apply a light film of grease to the bearing outer races and to the hub bores to aid installation. Note that both bearings must be installed with their marked faces outwards.
10   Supporting the hub outboard end, press in the new inboard bearing outer race until it seats against the shoulder.
11   Similarly, support the hub inboard end and press in the new outboard bearing outer race.
12   Press the new oil seal into the hub, ensuring that it is fitted with its sealing lips pointing outboard (towards the bearings). Apply a thin smear of grease to the seal lips; wipe off any surplus grease.
13   Refit the hub to the stub axle, followed by the washer and the nut (photo).
14   Refit the brake drum (Chapter 9).
15   Adjust the bearing and refit the roadwheel as described in Chapter 1 (photo).

9   Rear stub axle – removal and refitting

Removal

1   Remove the rear brake backplate (Chapter 9); the handbrake cables and brake hydraulic pipes need not be disturbed unless required. Withdraw the stub axle.

Refitting

2   Refitting is the reverse of the removal procedure, noting the following points.

  (a)   *Tighten the various nuts and bolts to the specified torque wrench settings.*
  (b)   *Refer to the relevant Sections of Chapter 9 to ensure that the rear brake components are correctly reassembled.*

10   Rear suspension unit – removal, overhaul and refitting

Removal

1   With the vehicle parked on smooth, level ground, select first or reverse gear and chock the front wheels.

10.2 Rear suspension unit top mounting nut is reached via luggage compartment

10.4A Unbolt rear suspension unit bottom mounting ...

10.4B ... and withdraw unit from vehicle

2   Working inside the vehicle, unscrew the top mounting nut (photo). Withdraw the nut and its washer, followed by the upper cup, mounting rubber and lower cup.

3   Jack up the rear of the vehicle, and support it securely on axle stands so that both roadwheels are clear of the ground (see 'Jacking, towing and wheel changing'); remove the roadwheel only if better access is required.

4   Unbolt the bottom mounting, and carefully withdraw the suspension unit (photos).

Overhaul

Warning: *Before attempting to dismantle the suspension unit, a suitable tool must be obtained to hold safely the coil spring in compression. Adjustable coil spring compressors are readily available, and are recommended for this operation. Any attempt to dismantle the unit without such a tool is likely to result in damage or personal injury; do not attempt to undo the piston rod nut with the spring unrestrained.*

Note: *If either of the rear springs requires renewal, it is good practice to renew both together as a matched pair. Check the spring upper end for signs of colour-coding indicating the spring's rating. Both springs should have the same marking; see a Skoda dealer for details.*

Similarly, if either of the rear units requires renewal, it is good practice to renew both together as a matched pair.

Always store suspension units in an upright position. If a unit is to be fitted after a long period of storage, mount it upright in a vice, and move the piston rod fully up and down several times to prime the damper passages and restore full damping action.

5   Remove the suspension unit from the vehicle and clean the assembly thoroughly.

6   Using an open-ended spanner or similar (applied to the flats at its upper end) to prevent the piston rod from rotating, slacken the piston rod nut **but do not unscrew it fully yet.**

7   Fit spring compressors (available from most motor accessory shops) to each side of the spring, and tighten them evenly to compress the spring until there is no pressure on the spring upper seat or the strut top mounting.

8   Unscrew the piston rod nut, and remove the top mounting components, the spring upper seat, the rubber buffer, the dust cover and the spring.

9   Visually inspect all components of the unit, and renew any that are showing obvious signs of wear or damage. Check particularly the top mounting components, looking for cracks, distortion or deterioration of the rubber itself.

10   Check the bottom mounting bush, and renew it if it is cracked, worn, split or perished. It must be removed and refitted using a press, although it may be possible to achieve the required result using a strong bench vice and sockets or pieces of tubing; soak the old bush in penetrating fluid before attempting removal, and use liquid soap (washing-up liquid) or petroleum jelly as a lubricant on pressing in the new bush.

11   If the spring is obviously broken or damaged, it must of course be renewed. The same applies if it has weakened so that its free length is significantly less than specified.

12   Check the unit's damping action by mounting it upright in a vice, and moving the piston rod fully up and down; firm, even resistance should be felt in both directions. If the damping is weak, if the unit shows signs of oil leaks at any point, or if the piston rod is bent, scored or

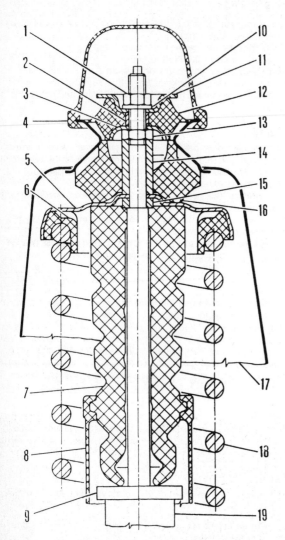

Fig. 10.11 Cross-section through rear suspension unit top mounting (Sec 10)

1 Top mounting nut	11 Upper cup
2 Spacer	12 Mounting rubber
3 Lower cup	13 Piston rod nut
4 Cover (where fitted)	14 Spacer
5 Spring upper seat	15 Spacer
6 Spring washer	16 Lower mounting rubber
7 Rubber buffer	17 Vehicle bodywork
8 Dust cover	18 Spring
9 Cover (where fitted)	19 Unit
10 Washer	

damaged, the unit must be renewed; individual components are not available to permit repairs.

13   Reassembly is the reverse of the dismantling procedure, noting the following points:

   (a)   *Pull out the piston rod to its full extent, and ensure that the spring is correctly compressed before refitting it. Locate its upper seat correctly on the spring, and ensure that the top mounting components are refitted in the correct order and the right way up.*

   (b)   *To tighten the piston rod nut to the specified torque wrench setting, use a spring balance or similar to apply to the spanner handle a measured force at a corresponding distance from the nut's centre (for example, applying a pull of 30 to 33 lb at a distance of 1 ft is the same as 15 to 16.5 lb at 2 ft).*

   (c)   *When the nut is correctly tightened, slacken evenly the spring compressors until they can be disengaged from the spring.*

   (d)   *Refit the unit to the vehicle.*

Refitting

14   Refitting is the reverse of the removal procedure, noting the following points.

   (a)   *Thoroughly clean the wheel arch area and all mounting points.*

   (b)   *Tighten all nuts and bolts securely, to the specified torque wrench settings where given.*

11   Rear suspension torsion beam axle – removal and refitting

Removal

1   With the vehicle parked on smooth, level ground, select first or reverse gear and chock the front wheels.

2   Jack up the rear of the vehicle evenly, and support it securely on axle stands so that both roadwheels are clear of the ground (see '*Jacking, towing and wheel changing*') then remove the roadwheels.

3   Working as described in the relevant Sections of Chapter 9, remove the brake drums and disconnect the handbrake cables from the brake backplates; on Pick-up models only, unhook the brake pressure-regulating valve spring from the torsion beam axle.

4   Either disconnect the brake pipes from the wheel cylinders (Chapter 9) so that the brake and hub assemblies can be removed with the torsion beam axle, or remove the rear stub axle (Section 9) so that the brake backplate can be detached and moved out of the way, thus avoiding the need to disturb the brake hydraulic system.

5   Removing bolts where necessary, release the handbrake cables and brake pipes from the torsion beam axle and its pivots. Move them clear of the working area, taking care not to kink or damage them, and secure them safely.

6   Remove the suspension unit bottom mounting bolts.

7   Unscrew the torsion beam axle pivot bolt nuts (photo). With an assistant working on the opposite side, tap out the bolts and lower the axle assembly to the ground.

8   Do not disturb the pivot brackets; see Section 12.

9   Thoroughly clean the axle and the underbody areas around its mountings, removing all traces of dirt (and of underseal if necessary) then check it carefully for excessive corrosion, cracks, distortion or any other signs of wear or damage; do not forget the pivot bolts and nuts. Renew any worn or damaged component.

10   If either the axle, its pivot brackets or the underbody show signs of rusting, the affected area must be cleaned back to bare metal and treated before being repainted. If the underbody is seriously rusted or if any of the pivot bracket captive nut threads are damaged, seek professional advice.

11   Check the pivot bushes, and renew them if they are cracked, worn, split or perished. Both must be removed and refitted using a press, although it may be possible to achieve the required result using a strong bench vice and sockets or pieces of tubing; soak the old bush in penetrating fluid before attempting removal, and use liquid soap (washing-up liquid) or petroleum jelly as a lubricant when pressing in the new bush.

Refitting

12   Refitting is the reverse of the removal procedure, noting the following points.

   (a)   *All fasteners should be tightened only lightly at first until the suspension is reassembled and the vehicle is lowered to the ground. When all the vehicle's weight is back on its wheels, rock it to settle the suspension, then tighten all disturbed nuts and bolts to the specified torque wrench settings.*

   (b)   *Refer to the relevant Sections of Chapter 9 to ensure that the brake components are correctly reassembled and adjusted.*

12   Rear suspension torsion beam axle pivot brackets – removal and refitting

Note: *This procedure is not recommended for the home mechanic, as the rear wheel alignment will be lost and cannot be restored accurately without special jigs.*

   If the brackets must be disturbed, a possible alternative is to remove them one at a time so that their original position will be shown by the axle itself, as well as by the marks made on removal. If this approach is adopted, support the vehicle's body carefully on axle stands, then unbolt one axle pivot and remove that pivot bracket (as described below). When the first bracket has been refitted, repeat the procedure on the remaining bracket.

11.7 Rear suspension torsion beam axle pivot bolt nut

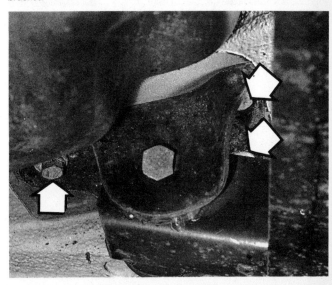

12.2 Rear suspension axle pivot bracket mounting bolts (arrows)

Removal

1   Remove the torsion beam axle (Section 11).
2   Using a heavy pencil, felt marker or similar, mark the underbody all around the bracket (as closely as possible, to minimise room for error) before unbolting the bracket (photo).

Refitting

3   On refitting, align the bracket exactly with the marks made on removal, then tighten the mounting bolts to their specified torque wrench setting.
4   Refit the torsion beam axle (Section 11).
5   Have the front and rear wheel alignment checked by a Skoda dealer.

13   Steering wheel – removal and refitting

Removal

1   Disconnect the battery negative terminal.
2   With the vehicle parked on level ground, check that the roadwheels are in the straight-ahead position; the steering wheel centre pad should be horizontal.
3   Prise out the cover from the wheel centre (photo).
4   Unscrew the steering wheel nut.
5   Check for alignment marks between the steering wheel and the steering column; if none can be seen, make your own (photo).
6   Grasp the steering wheel firmly and rock it to jar it free, then pull it off the steering column splines (photo). It is permissible to thump the wheel from behind with the palms of the hands, but do not hammer the wheel or column, or use excessive force.

Refitting

7   On refitting, check that the steering column splines are clean, and

also that the direction indicator self-cancelling tab is clamped on the underside of the column, with the clamp screw horizontal (photo).
8   Refit the wheel, aligning the marks made or noted on dismantling; this should leave the wheel positioned as described in paragraph 2 above.
9   Tighten the steering wheel nut to the specified torque setting (photo).
10   Refit the centre cover and reconnect the battery.

14   Steering column – removal and refitting

Removal

1   Check that the steering is unlocked, then disconnect the battery negative terminal.
2   Remove the single retaining screw and withdraw the steering column lower shroud, unclipping its bottom end and releasing it from the upper shroud at its top end, behind the steering wheel boss. Remove its two retaining screws and remove the upper shroud, unclipping it from the facia, then prise out the ignition switch surround (photos).
3   Either remove the multi-function switches (Chapter 12) or disconnect their wiring. Make careful notes of the connections, using the identifying labels on the switches themselves (as well as on the individual connector blocks) before disturbing any of the wiring. **Do not** disturb the position of the direction indicator self-cancelling tab on the underside of the column (photos).
4   Unscrewing its retaining nut and self-tapping screw, remove (if fitted) the shield from the bulkhead at the steering column's bottom end (photo).
5   Unscrew and remove the pinch-bolt securing the steering column bottom universal joint to the steering gear pinion shaft (photo).
6   Unscrew the two upper mounting bolts (and remove the clamp and rubber bushes), followed by the lower mounting bolts (photo), then

13.3 Prise out cover from steering wheel centre

13.5 Mark alignment of steering wheel to column as shown ...

13.6 ... before removing wheel

13.7 Check direction indicator self-cancelling tab is clamped as shown before refitting steering wheel

13.9 Tightening steering wheel nut to specified torque wrench setting

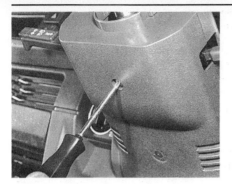

14.2A Remove single retaining screw ...

14.2B ... and unclip steering column lower shroud

14.2C Withdrawing steering column upper shroud ...

14.2D ... and ignition switch surround

14.3A Note connections before disturbing multi-function switch wiring

14.3B Do not disturb position of direction indicator self-cancelling tab on column (arrowed)

lower the steering column until the steering wheel rests on the driver's seat.

7   Making careful notes of the connections, disconnect the ignition switch wiring.

8   Remove the steering column.

Refitting

9   Refitting is the reverse of the removal procedure, noting the following points.

(a)   *Loosely assemble the column mountings and bottom universal joint, ensuring that the joint is positioned on the steering gear pinion shaft so that the pinch-bolt bore is aligned exactly with the pinion shaft groove. Refit the pinch-bolt and tighten it to the specified torque wrench setting.*

(b)   *Reconnect the ignition switch wires, using the notes made on dismantling to ensure correct connections.*

(c)   *Check that the column is seated without stress on its mountings, then tighten the bolts to their specified torque wrench settings; refit the shield, where applicable.*

(d)   *Reconnect the multi-function switch wiring, then refit the ignition switch surround and the steering column upper and lower shrouds (photo).*

(e)   *When reassembly is complete, raise the front of the vehicle and turn the steering from lock to lock to ensure that it is functioning correctly.*

Fig. 10.12 Cross-section through steering column (Sec 14)

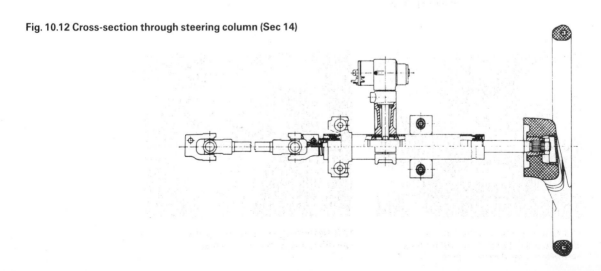

14.4 Shield at bottom end of steering column is secured by a nut and screw (arrows)

14.5 Remove the pinch-bolt (arrowed) to separate steering column bottom joint from steering gear pinion shaft

14.6 Steering column upper mounting (clamp) bolts (A), lower mounting bolts (B)

14.9 Note how steering column upper and lower shrouds are clipped together behind steering wheel boss

15.3 Steering column upper and intermediate shafts are secured by a pinch-bolt – note coil spring (A) and spacer (B)

15   Steering column – dismantling and reassembly

1   Remove the steering wheel (Section 13).
2   Remove the steering column from the vehicle (Section 14).
3   Unscrew and remove the pinch-bolt, then pull the intermediate shaft off the splines of the column's upper shaft; note the presence of the coil spring and spacer (photo).
4   Using suitable pliers, extract the retaining circlip from the upper end of the steering column jacket tube, withdraw the spacer, and drive out the column's upper shaft with the lower bearing; refit the steering wheel nut temporarily to protect it.
5   If it is worn, the bearing at the tube's upper end can be removed using an internally-expanding bearing puller. Note its installed depth before removing it; on refitting, use a hammer and a drift such as a socket which bears only on the bearing's outer race, and tap the bearing in to the position recorded on removal. The lower bearing can be tapped off the column's upper shaft if required; fit the new bearing using a hammer and a drift such as a socket which bears only on the bearing's inner race.
6   Check the universal joints carefully; if there are any signs of free play or of wear in the joints, the complete intermediate shaft must be renewed.
7   Check the splines at the ends of the upper shaft; renew the shaft if these are worn or damaged.
8   Reassembly is the reverse of the dismantling procedure. Apply a thin coat of grease to the column before refitting it to the jacket tube.

16   Steering lock/ignition switch – removal and refitting

Note: *The steering lock/ignition switch is secured by shear-head bolts; ensure that new bolts are available before beginning work.*

Removal

1   Check that the steering is unlocked, then disconnect the battery negative terminal.
2   Remove the single retaining screw and withdraw the steering column lower shroud, unclipping its bottom end and releasing it from the upper shroud at its top end, behind the steering wheel boss. Remove its two retaining screws and remove the upper shroud, unclipping it from the facia, then prise out the ignition switch surround.
3   Making careful notes of the connections (using the identifying labels on the switches and on the individual connector blocks) before disturbing any of the wiring, disconnect the multi-function switches.
4   Unscrewing its retaining nut and self-tapping screw, remove (if fitted) the shield from the bulkhead at the steering column's bottom end.
5   Unscrew the two upper mounting bolts (and remove the clamp and rubber bushes), followed by the lower mounting bolts, then lower the steering column until the steering wheel rests on the driver's seat.
6   Making careful notes of the connections, disconnect the ignition switch wiring. The ignition switch can now be separated (if required) from the steering lock by unscrewing the two retaining grub screws;

16.6A Remove grub screws ...

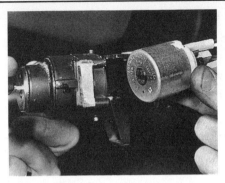

16.6B ... to separate ignition switch from steering lock

16.7 Steering lock/ignition switch-to-steering column shear-head bolts (A), assembly-to-mounting bracket shear-head bolt (B)

mark carefully the relationship of the switch to the lock before separating them (photos).

7 Centre-punch the shear-head bolts, then drill off the bolt heads (photo). New bolts will be required on refitting.

8 Withdraw the steering lock/ignition switch, then unscrew the remains of the shear-head bolts using a self-locking wrench or similar on the exposed ends. The lock/switch assembly can be separated, if required, from its mounting bracket by extracting the retaining shear-head bolt (as described above); a new bolt will be required on reassembly.

Refitting

9 Refitting is the reverse of the removal procedure, noting the following points.

(a) Align the assembly carefully on the steering column, then reconnect the ignition switch wiring. Tighten the shear-head bolts lightly, and check that the steering lock and ignition switch work smoothly.

(b) Locate the steering column on its mountings, and tighten the bolts to their specified torque wrench settings (Section 14).

(c) Raise the front of the vehicle and turn the steering from lock to lock to ensure that it is functioning correctly, check again the function of the steering lock and ignition switch, then tighten the shear-head bolts evenly until their heads shear off.

(d) Reconnect the (multi-function) switch wiring, then refit the ignition switch surround and steering column upper and lower shrouds.

17 Steering gear rubber gaiters – renewal

1 Remove the track rod balljoint and locknut (Section 20) and release the gaiter outboard clip.

2 Release the gaiter inboard clip, and slide the gaiter off the steering gear (photo).

3 Check the gaiter for any signs of splits, tears or perishing; renew it if any such damage is found, or if it is not a tight fit on the steering gear or track rod. The clips should be renewed if they are found to be damaged, or if they no longer fasten correctly.

4 Thoroughly clean the track rod and the steering gear housing, using fine abrasive paper to polish off any corrosion, burrs or sharp edges which might damage the new gaiter's sealing lips on installation.

5 If the steering gear is lubricated with grease, any lost lubricant must be replaced by **only** the specified type; if this is not available, Skoda state that the steering gear must be removed from the vehicle and dismantled so that all traces of grease can be removed and replaced by the specified amount and type of oil on reassembly (refer to Sections 18 and 19).

6 If the steering gear is lubricated with oil and a significant amount has been lost, move the steering from lock to lock several times until as much old oil as possible has been ejected from the steering gear. Measure the specified amount of oil into a spout-type can, install the gaiter and fasten one clip as described below, then inject the full amount of oil under the gaiter's sealing lip and into the steering gear before fastening the second clip.

7 On refitting, grease the gaiter's lips and slide it on, then fasten the first clip to secure it and replace any lost lubricant as noted above.

Fig. 10.13 Cross-section through steering column, showing steering lock/ignition switch mountings (Sec 16)

1 Steering column jacket tube
2 Steering lock/ignition switch mounting bracket
3 Steering lock/ignition switch
4 Shear-head bolt
5 Shear-head bolt

17.2 Steering gear rubber gaiter clips (arrows)

8   Settle the gaiter evenly on the track rod and fasten the remaining clip.
9   Refit the track rod balljoint and locknut (Section 20).
10   When checking the steering's operation, ensure that the gaiter does not snag or bulge at any point in the steering gear travel; if necessary, slacken the clip(s) and reposition the gaiter, then fasten the clip(s), losing as little lubricant as possible.

18   Steering gear – removal and refitting

Removal

1   Working inside the passenger compartment, remove the shield (if fitted) from the bulkhead at the steering column's bottom end, then unscrew and remove the pinch-bolt securing the steering column bottom universal joint to the steering gear pinion shaft (Section 14).
2   Disconnect both track rod balljoints from their respective hub carrier steering arms (Section 20).
3   Working inside the engine compartment, unbolt the steering gear (photo). Remove the air cleaner assembly (Chapter 4) if better access is required.
4   Manoeuvre the steering gear out of the vehicle.
5   Check the mounting bushes for signs of splitting, wear or damage, and renew them if necessary.

Refitting

6   Refitting is the reverse of the removal procedure, noting the following points.

(a) Ensure that the steering gear rack is at the exact mid-point of its travel, and that the components are correctly lubricated (Section 19).
(b) Use liquid soap (washing-up liquid) or petroleum jelly as a lubricant to ensure that the mounting rubber bushes are correctly seated when the steering gear is refitted. Tighten the mounting bolts evenly to the specified torque wrench setting.
(c) The remainder of the reassembly procedure is a reversal of removal. Tighten all disturbed nuts and bolts to the specified torque wrench settings.
(d) Have the wheel alignment and steering angles checked as soon as possible (Section 21).

19   Steering gear – overhaul

Note: *Before attempting to overhaul the steering gear, check the price and availability of individual components and the price of a new or reconditioned unit, as overhaul may not be viable on economic grounds alone. Also, read through the procedure and check that the tools and facilities required are available.*

Dismantling

1   Remove the steering gear from the vehicle (Section 18).
2   Thoroughly clean the assembly, prepare a clean working area, and observe scrupulous cleanliness throughout the overhaul. Clamp the steering gear carefully (so as not to distort the housing) in a soft-jawed vice. Pull the dust cover off the pinion shaft, then unfasten their clips and slide the rubber gaiters off the housing.
3   First establish for future reference the exact mid-point of the steering gear rack travel, which will correspond to the roadwheel straight-ahead position when the gear is installed. Proceed as follows.
4   Rotate the pinion until the rack is at full lock on one side, and measure the distance between one track rod balljoint and a fixed point on the housing. Move the rack across to the (full) opposite lock, and measure again the distance between the same two points. The difference between the two measurements is the total rack movement; halve this, and return the rack to that point – note that this should be when the rack is centred in the housing. For ease of reference, use a straight edge and a scriber to mark a line across the rack at each housing end face, so that the rack can be quickly and accurately positioned when required. Check also for reference the dimensions shown in Fig. 10.16.
5   Remove both track rod balljoints and their locknuts (Section 20), then slide off the rubber gaiters; allow any oil to drain off. Keep all left- and right-hand side components in separate, clearly-marked containers. It is good working practice to ensure that these components are refitted only in their original locations (some are physically interchangeable, but none may be swapped over during overhaul).
6   Use an electric drill or similar to relieve the staking of the reducing sleeve at each end of the rack. Applying a spanner to the coupling sleeve locknut, unscrew the reducing sleeves to separate each track rod assembly from the rack.
7   Prise up the lockwasher tabs and unscrew each coupling sleeve from its locknut, then dismantle all components of each track rod assembly.
8   Unbolt the slipper cover from the housing, noting the presence of any shims between the cover and its gasket. Withdraw the coil spring, dislodge the slipper, and extract it using circlip pliers or similar which fit into the slipper's spring recess. Remove and discard the slipper's sealing O-ring.
9   Unbolt the pinion cover from the housing. Withdraw the cover, noting the presence of the gasket and of any shims beneath it. On early models, the cover consists of a retaining plate and a lid with an O-ring between them; on later models, the cover is in one piece, with an oil seal.
10   Extract the pinion shaft with its upper bearing by clamping the pinion shaft in the soft-jawed vice and gently tapping the housing upwards.
11   The pinion shaft lower bearing can be extracted using an internally-expanding bearing puller. If the upper bearing is to be renewed, a suitable bearing puller must be used to draw it off the pinion shaft.
12   Withdraw the rack, then extract the circlip and withdraw the rack supporting bush from the housing's left-hand end, noting that it has locating lugs which engage in the gear housing.

Examination

13   Thoroughly clean all components, removing all traces of dirt and old lubricant, and renew any that show obvious signs of wear or damage. Roll the rack on a known flat surface to check that it is not bent or distorted, then check the teeth of both the rack and of the pinion. Check all bearings, bushes and bearing surfaces for wear. Whenever they are disturbed, renew as a matter of course all gaskets, O-rings or seals, lockwashers and the reducing sleeves.
14   On reassembly, thoroughly coat all components with the specified lubricant; if the grease is used, measure out the specified amount and ensure that as much as possible is packed into the steering gear during the course of work – any surplus can be packed into the gaiters. Skoda specify that if the grease originally used by the factory on manufacture is not available, it must be removed completely from all steering gear components and replaced by the specified type of oil on assembly.

Reassembly

15   Refit the rack bush, and secure it with a new circlip.

18.3 Steering gear mounting bolts (arrows)

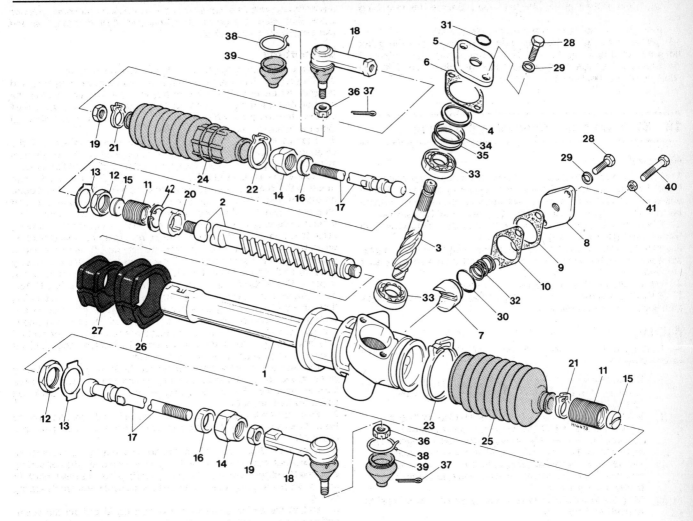

Fig. 10.14 Exploded view of steering gear (Sec 19)

1	Steering gear housing	13 Lockwasher	24 Steering gear left-hand
2	Rack	14 Coupling sleeve	rubber gaiter
3	Pinion	15 Socket	25 Steering gear right-hand
4	Spacer (where fitted)	16 Insert	rubber gaiter
5	Pinion cover	17 Track rod	26 Steering gear mounting
6	Gasket	18 Track rod balljoint	rubber bush
7	Slipper	19 Balljoint locknut	27 Steering gear mounting
8	Slipper cover	20 Rack bush	rubber bush
9	Gasket	21 Gaiter outboard clip	28 Bolt
10	Shim (as required)	22 Gaiter inboard clip (left-hand)	29 Washer
11	Reducing sleeve	23 Gaiter inboard clip	30 O-ring
12	Locknut	(right-hand)	

31 Oil seal (O-ring, early models)	
32 Coil spring	
33 Bearing	
34 Shim (as required)	
35 Shim (as required)	
36 Nut	
37 Split pin	
38 Circlip	
39 Dust cover	
40 Slipper adjuster	
41 Locknut	
42 Circlip	

16   To refit the pinion and bearings accurately, Skoda specify the use of a special service tool – a stepped tubular drift available under number MP 7-108. If this is not available, the procedure given in paragraphs 17, 18 and 19 below will serve as an acceptable alternative; note that if the housing is first heated gently and evenly, the bearings will enter more easily into their recesses and settle correctly with the minimum risk of damage. Excessive force will not be required.

17   Using a hammer and a tubular drift such as a socket which bears only on the bearing's outer race, tap the new pinion lower bearing into the housing until it seats in the bottom of its recess.

18   Applying pressure only to its inner race, press the new pinion upper bearing on to the pinion shaft until the inner race contacts the pinion teeth.

19   Applying pressure only to the upper bearing's outer race and ensuring that the pinion's lower end enters squarely into the lower bearing, press or tap the pinion and upper bearing into the housing until the lower bearing's inner race contacts the pinion teeth. Lubricate the pinion components.

20   Lubricate the rack and refit it, ensuring that the rack and pinion teeth mesh properly; centre the rack in the housing to position it at the mid-point of its travel (see paragraph 4 above).

21   Use a smear of lubricant to stick a new gasket to the pinion cover mating surface, then measure the distance from the upper bearing's inner race to the gasket's top surface. Select shims of a total thickness (including the spacer, where fitted) equal to the measured distance (maximum permissible tolerance of + 0.10 mm) – shims are available in thicknesses of 0.10 and 0.20 mm.

22   Fit the shims (with the spacer above them, where fitted), install the cover components, and apply a few drops of sealant to the threads of the cover bolts. Tighten the bolts to their specified torque wrench setting.

23   Move the rack from one lock to the other, checking that it moves smoothly and easily, with no signs of free play at the pinion. Return the rack to the mid-point of its travel.

24   Lubricating the housing bore and slipper, refit the slipper, pressing it firmly against the rack; there must be no free play between the rack

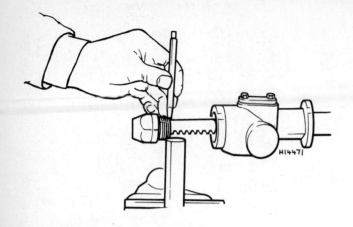

Fig. 10.15 Staking reducing sleeve to rack (Sec 19)

and the slipper. Fit a new O-ring to the slipper groove, then refit the coil spring. Using a new gasket (but omitting any shims at first, while measurements are made) refit the cover. Slacken the adjuster locknut, and unscrew the adjuster so that there is no pressure on the rack except that provided by the slipper and spring.

25   Using a spring balance or similar, measure the amount of force required to slide the rack back and forth. Repeat the measurement three times, taking the average of the three results for accuracy; the specified value is 110 to 130 N. If the measured value is less than 110 N, renew the coil spring and repeat the measurement; if it is more than 130 N, fit shims as required between the cover gasket and the housing – the shims are 0.2 mm thick, one shim reducing the force required by 20 N.

26   Lubricate the slipper components and refit the slipper cover, together with any shims selected. Tighten the cover bolts to their specified torque wrench setting.

27   With the rack at the mid-point of its travel, carefully tighten the adjuster by hand only until firm pressure is felt; at this point all free play should be eliminated between the slipper, the rack and the pinion. Slacken the adjuster through an angle of 30°, apply a few drops of sealant to its threads, and prevent it from rotating while the locknut is tightened securely. Again check that the rack moves smoothly and easily from one lock to the other, then return it to the mid-point of its travel.

28   Screw a new reducing sleeve on to each end of the rack, then temporarily tighten its coupling sleeve and locknut onto each reducing sleeve. Clamping one end's coupling sleeve and locknut in the vice, tighten both reducing sleeves (by means of a socket fitted to the opposite coupling sleeve) to the specified torque wrench setting. Supporting carefully the rack ends, stake each reducing sleeve in turn into the slot in the rack end.

29   Unscrew the coupling sleeves and refit the track rod assemblies, fitting new lockwashers and applying a smear of lithium-based grease to the mating surfaces of the ball ends, their sockets and inserts. Tighten the coupling sleeve by hand only at first to secure each track rod to the rack.

30   Slide both rubber gaiters on to the track rods, then refit the locknuts and the track rod balljoints.

31   Screw each balljoint onto its track rod until the distance from the

outboard edge of the track rod's gaiter groove to the centre of the balljoint is as shown in Fig. 10.16, then tighten lightly its locknut against each balljoint; check that the distance from the outboard edge of the track rod's gaiter groove to the locknut's inboard edge is as shown in Fig. 10.16. Note that the alignment marks made (where applicable) on removal should now line up.

32   Check that the distance between the centres of the two track rod balljoints is as shown in Fig. 10.16. If the position of the balljoints has to be altered to correct this dimension, ensure that each is screwed in or out by **exactly** the same amount, to preserve the symmetry of the steering geometry; the final track rod-to-balljoint centre/locknut dimensions must always be exactly the same on both sides, but may vary by a permissible tolerance of up to 3 mm from the values shown.

33   **Note:** *This is a basic setting only, to be set finally on checking the wheel alignment and steering angles when the steering gear is refitted to the vehicle.* If the vehicle is to be driven to have the wheel alignment checked, tighten the balljoint locknuts securely; otherwise, refer to Section 21.

34   With the housing clamped in the soft-jawed vice, and a spring balance or similar applied to the balljoint's dust cover recess, tighten the coupling sleeve until the force required to move the corresponding track rod from its at-rest position (projecting in a straight line from the rack) is between 12.5 and 20.5 N. When the setting is correct, hold steady the coupling sleeve and tighten the locknut securely onto it (apply the specified torque wrench setting if the necessary tools are available). Secure the assembly by bending down the lockwasher tabs over both the locknut and coupling sleeve, then repeat the procedure on the remaining track rod assembly.

35   Check that the rack is at the mid-point of its travel (centred in the housing, with the alignment marks lined up that were made on removal), then use white paint or similar to mark the relationship of the pinion shaft to the housing, so that the mid-point of the rack's travel can be easily identified on refitting the steering gear to the vehicle. Refit the dust cover to the pinion shaft, and ensure that the pins of both balljoints are pointing downwards (ie, in the correct position for refitting to the vehicle).

36   If the steering gear is lubricated with grease, locate the rubber gaiters in their track rod grooves and fasten the outboard clips, then pack the remaining grease into the gaiters, settle them in the housing grooves, and fasten the inboard clips to secure them.

37   If the steering gear is lubricated with oil, refit first one rubber gaiter and fasten its clips, then locate the remaining gaiter in its housing groove and fasten the inboard clip. Using a spout-type oil can, inject the remaining oil under the gaiter's sealing lip and into the steering gear before fastening the outboard clip.

38   Refit the steering gear to the vehicle (Section 18). If it is necessary to rotate either track rod, slacken the clip(s) and reposition the gaiter, then fasten the clip(s), losing as little lubricant as possible.

Rack slipper final adjustment

39   **Note:** *The rack slipper setting should be checked as follows whenever it has been disturbed, or if a steering fault has arisen.* Proceed as follows.

40   First check that the tyres are in good condition and inflated to the correct pressure, and also that the brakes are not binding.

41   Drive the vehicle along a flat, level road, and check that it continues to move in a straight line when the steering wheel is released from the straight-ahead position (centre pad horizontal).

42   Carefully check that the steering wheel returns to the straight-ahead position when released from a slightly (approx 20°) rotated position on each side of straight-ahead.

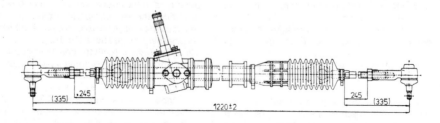

Fig. 10.16 Steering gear track rod setting dimensions – in mm (Sec 19)

19.43 Steering gear rack slipper adjuster (arrowed) seen from beneath

20.4 Using a universal balljoint separator tool to disconnect track rod balljoint from hub carrier steering arm

43   If the self-centring action and response is slow or stiff, the slipper adjustment must be reset, as described above. Note however that this may mean removing the steering gear from the vehicle, as the adjuster is very difficult to reach when the gear is in place (photo).

20   Track rod balljoint – removal and refitting

Note: *The balljoint dust cover is available separately, and can be renewed (by extracting the retaining circlip) once the balljoint has been separated from the hub carrier steering arm (see below). Note, however, that it is usually considered good working practice to renew as a matter of course any balljoint that is found to have a damaged dust cover (on the basis that dirt or other foreign matter will have entered, and will soon damage the joint regardless of its present condition). Owners who discover a damaged balljoint dust cover are advised to check the joint very carefully for signs of wear or of contamination before considering renewing the dust cover alone; if there is the slightest doubt about the joint's condition, it must be renewed complete.*

Removal

1   Jack up the front of the vehicle, support it securely on axle stands, then remove the roadwheel (see *'Jacking, towing and wheel changing'*).
2   If the balljoint is to be re-used, use a straight edge and a scriber or similar to mark its relationship to the track rod.
3   Holding the balljoint, unscrew its locknut by one quarter of a turn.
4   Extract its split pin and unscrew the balljoint-to-steering arm nut until it is flush with the end of its thread. Using a universal balljoint separator tool if necessary, separate the balljoint from the hub carrier steering arm (photo).
5   Counting the **exact** number of turns necessary to do so, unscrew the balljoint from the track rod. If the locknut is to be removed, mark its position on the track rod, and count the number of turns required to remove it, so that it can be returned to exactly its original position on reassembly.
6   Carefully clean the balljoint and the threads. Renew the balljoint if its movement is sloppy or if it is too stiff, if it is excessively worn, or if it is damaged in any way; check carefully the stud taper and threads. No grease leakage should be visible – the dust cover is available separately (see note at the beginning of this Section). Renew the retaining nut split pin as a matter of course whenever it is disturbed.

Refitting

7   On refitting, screw the balljoint on to the track rod by the number of turns noted on removal. This should bring the balljoint to within a quarter of a turn from the locknut, with the alignment marks that were made on removal (if applicable) lined up.
8   Degrease the tapers of the balljoint stud and of the hub carrier

steering arm, then press the balljoint firmly into the steering arm while the nut is refitted and tightened to its specified torque wrench setting. Fit a new split pin, spreading its ends securely; the nut may be slackened slightly, if necessary, to align the nearest nut slots with the stud's split pin hole.
9   If the vehicle is to be driven to have the wheel alignment checked, hold the balljoint and tighten the locknut securely (apply the specified torque wrench setting if the necessary tools are available); otherwise, refer to Section 21.
10   Where applicable, refit the roadwheel and lower the vehicle to the ground.

21   Wheel alignment and steering angles – general information

Wheel alignment and steering angles – general

1   A vehicle's steering and suspension geometry is defined in five basic settings – all angles are expressed in degrees, and the steering axis is defined as an imaginary line drawn through the centres of the front suspension strut top mounting and of the lower arm balljoint, extended where necessary to contact the ground.
2   **Camber** is the angle between each roadwheel and a vertical line drawn through its centre and tyre contact patch, when viewed from the front or rear of the vehicle. Positive camber is when the roadwheels are tilted outwards from the vertical at the top; negative camber is when they are tilted inwards.
3   Camber is not adjustable, and is given for reference only; while it can be checked using a camber checking gauge, if the figure obtained is significantly different from that specified, the vehicle must be taken for careful checking by a professional, as the fault can only be caused by wear or damage to the body or suspension components.
4   **Castor** is the angle between the steering axis and a vertical line drawn through each roadwheel's centre and tyre contact patch, when viewed from the side of the vehicle. Positive castor is when the steering axis is tilted so that it contacts the ground ahead of the vertical; negative castor is when it contacts the ground behind the vertical.
5   Castor is not adjustable, and is given for reference only; while it can be checked using a castor checking gauge, if the figure obtained is significantly different from that specified, the vehicle must be taken for careful checking by a professional, as the fault can only be caused by wear or damage to the body or suspension components.
6   **Steering axis inclination/SAI** – also known as **kingpin inclination/KPI** – is the angle between the steering axis and a vertical line drawn through each roadwheel's centre and tyre contact patch, when viewed from the front or rear of the vehicle.
7   SAI/KPI is not adjustable, and is given for reference only.

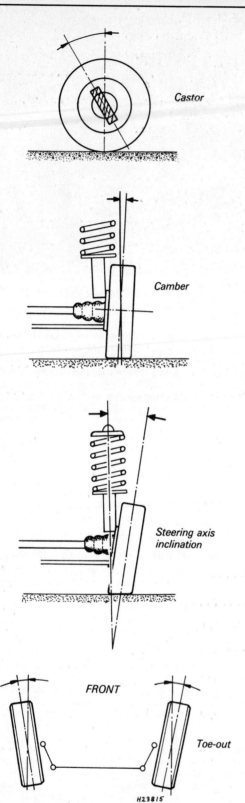

Fig. 10.17 Wheel alignment and steering angles (Sec 21)

8   Toe is the difference, viewed from above, between lines drawn through the roadwheel centres and the vehicle's centre-line. 'Toe-in' is when the roadwheels point inwards, towards each other at the front, while 'toe-out' is when they splay outwards from each other at the front.
9   At the front, the toe setting is adjusted by screwing the track rods in or out of their balljoints to alter the effective length of the track rod assemblies.

10   At the rear, the toe setting is not adjustable, and is given for reference only; while it can be checked as described below, if the figure obtained is significantly different from that specified, the vehicle must be taken for careful checking by a professional, as the fault can only be caused by wear or damage to the body or suspension components.
11   **Toe-out on turns** - also known as 'turning angles' or 'Ackermann angles' - is the difference, viewed from above, between the angles of rotation of the inside and outside front roadwheels when they have been turned through a given angle.
12   Toe-out on turns is set in production, and is not adjustable as such, but can be upset by altering unequally the length of the track rods. It is essential, therefore, to ensure that the track rod lengths are exactly the same, and that they are turned by the same amount whenever the toe setting is altered.

Checking – general

13   Due to the special measuring equipment necessary to check the wheel alignment, and the skill required to use it properly, the checking and adjustment of these settings is best left to a Skoda dealer or similar expert; note that most tyre-fitting centres now possess sophisticated checking equipment.
14   For accurate checking, the vehicle must be at normal kerb weight, and unladen. Before starting work, always check first that the tyre sizes and types are as specified, then check the pressures and tread wear, the roadwheel run-out, the condition of the hub bearings, the steering wheel free play and the condition of the front suspension components (Chapter 1). Correct any faults found.
15   Park the vehicle on level ground. Check that the front roadwheels are in the straight-ahead position, then rock the rear and front ends to settle the suspension. Release the handbrake and roll the vehicle backwards approximately 1 metre, then forwards again to relieve any stresses in the steering and suspension components.

Toe-out on turns – checking and adjusting

16   As far as the home mechanic is concerned, this can be checked only using a pair of scuff plates.
17   Prepare the vehicle as described in paragraphs 14 and 15 above. Roll the vehicle backwards, check that the front roadwheels are in the straight-ahead position, then roll it forwards onto the scuff plates until each front roadwheel is seated squarely on the centre of each plate.
18   Turn the steering wheel first one way until the outside roadwheel is at the specified angle; record the angle of the inside roadwheel. Next turn the steering wheel back through the straight-ahead position, and repeat the check on that side.
19   If, in either check, the inside roadwheel is not at the angle specified, check that both track rod assemblies are exactly the same length by counting the exposed threads inboard of the locknuts. If the lengths are different, this can be corrected by screwing the track rods in or out of the balljoints, but this will affect the toe setting (see below) and the steering wheel position.
20   If the angles are incorrect but the track rods are the same length and the steering mechanism components are known from the preliminary checks to be unworn, then there is damage to, or distortion of, part of the steering mechanism, the front suspension or the body itself. This will require careful checking, preferably by an expert such as a Skoda dealer, as soon as possible.

Toe setting – checking and adjusting

21   The procedure given below refers specifically to the front toe setting. As noted in paragraph 10 above, while the rear toe setting can be checked using a similar procedure, it is not adjustable, and any variation from the specified setting must be caused by wear or damage of the suspension or body.
22   Toe can be checked only using a toe checking gauge (sometimes known as a tracking gauge) which can measure the distance between the front and rear inside edges of the roadwheels. While such gauges are available in relatively inexpensive form from accessory outlets, a home-made version can be fabricated from a length of steel tubing, cranked to clear the engine/transmission or suspension components, with a long bolt and locknut at one end.
23   Prepare the vehicle as described in paragraphs 14 and 15 above.
24   First measure the distance between the inside edges of the front roadwheel rims, at hub centre height at the rear of the roadwheels; call this dimension 'A'.

25   Push the vehicle forwards so that the roadwheels rotate exactly 180° (half a turn) and measure the distance again, but now at hub centre height at the front of the roadwheels; call this dimension 'B'.

26   To ensure absolute accuracy, repeat the measurements twice more, at points spaced 120° apart around the roadwheel rims, and take the average of the three readings.

27   To calculate toe-in, subtract 'B' from 'A'; the result should be within the specified tolerance.

28   If adjustment is required, jack up the front of the vehicle and support it securely on axle stands if the working clearance is required (see 'Jacking, towing and wheel changing'). First clean the track rod threads; if they are corroded, apply penetrating fluid before starting adjustment. Release the rubber gaiter outboard clips, lift the gaiters slightly and apply a smear of grease, so that both are free and will not be twisted or strained as their respective track rods are rotated; try to lose as little lubricant as possible from the steering gear during adjustment.

29   Use a straight edge and a scriber or similar to mark the relationship of each track rod to its balljoint then, holding each balljoint in turn, slacken its locknut.

30   Alter the length of both track rods (by exactly the same amount) by screwing them into or out of the balljoints one-quarter of a turn at a time and rechecking the toe setting until it is correct; shortening the track rods (screwing them into their balljoints) will reduce toe-in/increase toe-out. If the track rods are not provided with flats permitting the use of a spanner (photo), they must be rotated using a self-locking wrench.

31   To ensure that the track rod lengths remain equal, always rotate them in the same direction (viewed from the centre of the vehicle).

32   When the setting is correct, hold the balljoints and tighten the locknuts securely (apply the specified torque wrench setting if the necessary tools are available). Check that the balljoints are seated correctly in their sockets, and count the exposed threads to check the length of both track rods. If they are not the same, then the adjustment has not been made equally, and problems will be encountered with tyre

21.30 Use flats on track rod (where applicable) to adjust toe setting

scrubbing in turns; also, the steering wheel will no longer be in the straight-ahead position.

33   If the track rod lengths are the same, check that the toe setting has been correctly adjusted by lowering the vehicle to the ground and preparing it (paragraphs 14 and 15 above), then re-checking the toe setting (paragraphs 24 to 27); re-adjust if necessary. If the setting is correct, ensure that the rubber gaiters are seated correctly and are not twisted or strained, then fasten their clips.

Chapter 11 Bodywork and fittings

Contents

Body exterior fittings – removal and refitting 11
Bonnet – removal, refitting and adjustment............................... 9
Bonnet lock and release mechanism – removal, refitting and
adjustment.. 10
Bumpers – removal and refitting.. 8
Door lock and handle components – removal and refitting 17
Door window glass and regulator – removal and refitting 18
Doors and hinges – removal, refitting and adjustment 16
Facia – removal and refitting... 24
Front-end panel – removal and refitting.. 7
Front wings – removal and refitting 6
General information... 1
Glovebox – removal and refitting.. 23
Hinges and locks – check and lubrication .... See Chapter 1

Interior trim – general information... 22
Maintenance – bodywork and underframe...................................... 2
Maintenance – upholstery and carpets 3
Major body damage – repair 5
Minor body damage – repair 4
Mirrors – removal and refitting 19
Seat belt check... See Chapter 1
Seat belts – removal and refitting 21
Seats – removal and refitting 20
Tailgate – removal, refitting and adjustment 13
Tailgate lock components – removal and refitting 15
Tailgate support struts – removal and refitting 14
Windscreen, rear quarterlight and tailgate glass – general
information... 12

Specifications

Torque wrench settings

	Nm	lbf ft
Tailgate hinge nuts	14 to 16	10 to 12
Tailgate strut retaining nuts	11 to 15	8 to 11
Tailgate hinge bolts	11 to 15	8 to 11
Tailgate lock screws	14 to 16	10 to 12
Tailgate latch screws	14 to 16	10 to 12
Bonnet hinge bolts	6 to 7	4 to 5
Bonnet lock bolts	6 to 7	4 to 5
Door hinge bolts	11 to 15	8 to 11
Door lock screws	14 to 16	10 to 12
Door latch screws	14 to 16	10 to 12
Front wing bolts	6 to 7	4 to 5
Front and rear bumper bolts	6 to 7	4 to 5
Seat belt anchorage bolts	40	30

1 General information

The bodyshell is made of pressed-steel sections in five-door Hatchback and Estate, three-door Van and two-door Pick-up configurations. Most components are spot-welded together, but the front wings are bolted on, for easier replacement in the event of an accident. Childproof locks are fitted to the rear doors.

Once assembled, the entire body is given a four-stage pre-treatment process. The first coat of primer is applied by cathodic electro-deposition, followed by a coat of sanding filler, and finally a coat of paint and a coat of lacquer. A PVC coating is applied to the underbody, followed by a coating of protective wax; all chassis members, box-sections and sills are injected with liquid cavity wax.

Extensive use is made of plastic materials, mainly on the interior, but also in exterior components such as the bumpers.

2 Maintenance – bodywork and underframe

Cleaning the vehicle's exterior

1 The general condition of a vehicle's bodywork is the one thing that significantly affects its value. Maintenance is easy but needs to be regular. Neglect, particularly after minor damage, can lead quickly to further deterioration and costly repair bills. It is important also to keep watch on those parts of the vehicle not immediately visible, for instance the underbody, inside all the wheel arches and the lower part of the engine compartment.

2 The basic maintenance routine for the bodywork is washing – preferably with a lot of water, from a hose. This will remove all the loose solids which may have stuck to the vehicle. It is important to flush these off in such a way as to prevent grit from scratching the finish. The wheel arches and underbody need washing in the same way to remove any

accumulated mud which will retain moisture and tend to encourage rust, particularly in winter when it is essential that any salt (from that put down on the roads) is washed off. Paradoxically enough, the best time to clean the underbody and wheel arches is in wet weather when the mud is thoroughly wet and soft. In very wet weather, the underbody is usually cleaned automatically of large accumulations; this is therefore a good time for inspection.

3   If the vehicle is very dirty, especially underneath or in the engine compartment, it is tempting to use one of the pressure washers or steam cleaners available on garage forecourts; while these are quick and effective, especially for the removal of the accumulation of oily grime which sometimes is allowed to become thick in certain areas, their usage does have some disadvantages. If caked-on dirt is simply blasted off the paintwork, its finish soon becomes scratched and dull and the pressure can allow water to penetrate door and window seals and the lock mechanisms; if the full force of such a jet is directed at the vehicle's underbody the wax-based protective coating can easily be damaged and water (with whatever cleaning solvent is used) could be forced into crevices or components that it would not normally reach. Similarly, if such equipment is used to clean the engine compartment water can be forced into the components of the fuel and electrical systems and the protective coating can be removed that is applied to many small components during manufacture; this may therefore actually promote corrosion (especially inside electrical connectors) and initiate engine problems or other electrical faults. Also, if the jet is pointed directly at any of the oil seals, water can be forced past the seal lips and into the engine or transmission. Great care is required, therefore, if such equipment is used and, in general, regular cleaning by such methods should be avoided.

4   A much better solution in the long term is just to flush away as much loose dirt as possible using a hose alone, even if this leaves the engine compartment looking 'dirty'. If an oil leak has developed, or if any other accumulation of oil or grease is to be removed, there are one or two excellent grease solvents available, such as Holts Engine Cleaner or Holts Foambrite, which can be brush applied. The dirt can then be simply hosed off. Take care to replace the wax-based protective coat, if this was affected by the solvent.

5   Normal washing of the vehicle's bodywork is best carried out using cold or warm water with a proprietary vehicle shampoo such as Holts Turtle Wax Zipwax or Turtle Extra Car Wash and Wax. Remove dead insects with products such as Holts Fly Squash Remover; tar spots can be removed either by using white spirit, followed by soapy water to remove all traces of spirit, or by using Holts Body + Plus Tar Remover. Try to keep water out of the bonnet air intakes, and check afterwards that the heater air inlet box drain tube is clear so that any water has drained out of the box.

6   After washing the paintwork, wipe off with a chamois leather to give an unspotted clear finish. A coat of clear protective wax polish, such as one of the many excellent Turtle Wax polishes, will give added protection against chemical pollutants in the air. If the paintwork sheen has dulled or oxidised, use a cleaner/polisher combination such as Turtle Extra to restore the brilliance of the shine. This requires a little effort, but such dulling is usually caused because regular washing has been neglected. Care needs to be taken with metallic paintwork, as special non-abrasive cleaner/polisher is required to avoid damage to the finish.

7   Brightwork should be treated in the same way as paintwork.

8   Windscreens and windows can be kept clear of the smeary film which often appears, by the use of proprietary glass cleaner like Holts Mixra. Never use any form of wax or other body or chromium polish on glass.

Exterior paintwork and body panels check

9   Once the vehicle has been washed and all tar spots and other surface blemishes have been cleaned off, check carefully all paintwork, looking closely for chips or scratches; check with particular care vulnerable areas such as the front (bonnet and spoiler) and around the wheel arches. Any damage to the paintwork must be rectified as soon as possible to comply with the terms of the manufacturer's cosmetic and anti-corrosion warranties; check with a Skoda dealer for details.

10   If a chip or (light) scratch is found that is recent and still free from rust, it can be touched-up using the appropriate touch-up pencil; these can be obtained from Skoda dealers or from the Holts Dupli-Color Color Touch range. Any more serious damage, or rusted stone chips, can be repaired as described in Section 4, but if damage or corrosion is so severe that a panel must be renewed, seek professional advice as soon as possible.

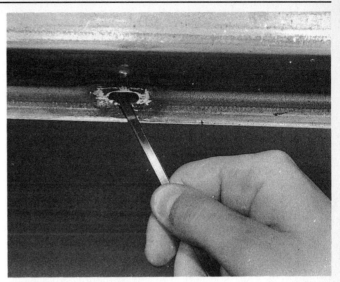

2.11 Clearing a door drain hole

11   Always check that the door and ventilator opening drain holes and pipes are completely clear, so that water can drain out (photo).

Underbody sealer check

12   The wax-based underbody protective coating should be inspected annually, preferably just prior to Winter, when the underbody should be washed down as thoroughly but gently as possible (see paragraph 3 above concerning steam cleaners, etc) and any damage to the coating repaired using Holts Undershield; if any of the body panels are disturbed for repair or renewed, do not forget to replace the coating and to inject wax into door panels, sills, box sections etc, to maintain the level of protection provided by the vehicle's manufacturer.

3   Maintenance – upholstery and carpets

Mats and carpets should be brushed or vacuum-cleaned regularly to keep them free of grit. If they are badly stained remove them from the vehicle for scrubbing or sponging and make quite sure they are dry before refitting.

Fabric-trimmed seats and interior trim panels can be kept clean by wiping with a damp cloth and Turtle Wax Carisma. If they do become stained (which can be more apparent on light coloured upholstery) use a little liquid detergent and a soft nail brush to scour the grime out of the grain of the material. Do not forget to keep the headlining clean in the same way as the (fabric) upholstery.

When using liquid cleaners of any sort inside the vehicle, do not over-wet the surfaces being cleaned. Excessive damp could get into the seams and padded interior causing stains, offensive odours or even rot. If the inside of the vehicle gets wet accidentally, it is worthwhile taking some trouble to dry it out properly, particularly where carpets are involved. *Do not leave oil or electric heaters inside the vehicle for this purpose.*

4   Minor body damage – repair

Note: *The photographic sequence between pages 32 and 33 illustrates the operations detailed in the following sub-Sections.*
Note: *For more detailed information about bodywork repair, the Haynes Publishing Group publish a book by Lindsay Porter called 'The Car Bodywork Repair Manual'. This incorporates information on such aspects as rust treatment, painting and glass-fibre repairs, as well as details on more ambitious repairs involving welding and panel beating.*

Repair of minor scratches in bodywork

If the scratch is very superficial and does not penetrate to the metal of the bodywork, repair is very simple. Lightly rub the area of the scratch with a paintwork renovator, such as Turtle Wax New Color Back, or a very fine cutting paste, like Holts Body + Plus Rubbing Compound, to remove loose paint from the scratch and to clear the surrounding bodywork of wax polish. Rinse the area with clean water.

Apply touch-up paint, such as Holts Dupli-Color Color Touch, or a paint film, such as Holts Autofilm, to the scratch using a fine paint brush; continue to apply fine layers of paint until the surface of the paint in the scratch is level with the surrounding paintwork. Allow the new paint at least two weeks to harden, then blend it into the surrounding paintwork by rubbing the scratch area with a paintwork renovator, such as Turtle Wax New Color Back, or a very fine cutting paste, like Holts Body + Plus Rubbing Compound. Finally apply wax polish from one of the Turtle Wax range of wax polishes.

Where the scratch has penetrated right through to the metal of the bodywork, causing the metal to rust, a different repair technique is required. Remove any loose rust from the bottom of the scratch with a penknife, then apply rust inhibiting paint, such as Turtle Wax Rust Master, to prevent the formation of rust in the future. Using a rubber or nylon applicator fill the scratch with bodystopper paste, such as Holts Body + Plus Knifing Putty. If required, this paste can be mixed with cellulose thinners, such as Holts Body + Plus Cellulose Thinners, to provide a very thin paste which is ideal for filling narrow scratches. Before the stopper-paste in the scratch hardens, wrap a piece of smooth cotton rag around the top of a finger. Dip the finger in cellulose thinners, such as Holts Body + Plus Cellulose Thinners, and quickly sweep it across the surface of the stopper-paste in the scratch; this will ensure that the surface of the stopper-paste is slightly hollowed. The scratch can now be painted over as described earlier in this Section.

Repair of dents in bodywork

When deep denting of the vehicle's bodywork has taken place, the first task is to pull the dent out, until the affected bodywork almost attains its original shape. There is little point in trying to restore the original shape completely, as the metal in the damaged area will have stretched on impact and cannot be reshaped fully to its original contour. It is better to bring the level of the dent up to a point which is about 3 mm below the level of the surrounding bodywork. In cases where the dent is very shallow anyway, it is not worth trying to pull it out at all. If the underside of the dent is accessible, it can be hammered out gently from behind, using a mallet with a wooden or plastic head. Whilst doing this, hold a suitable block of wood firmly against the outside of the panel to absorb the impact from the hammer blows and thus prevent a large area of the bodywork from being 'belled-out'.

Should the dent be in a section of the bodywork which has a double skin or some other factor making it inaccessible from behind, a different technique is called for. Drill several small holes through the metal inside the area – particularly in the deeper section. Then screw long self-tapping screws into the holes just sufficiently for them to gain a good purchase in the metal. Now the dent can be pulled out by pulling on the protruding heads of the screws with a pair of pliers.

The next stage of the repair is the removal of the paint from the damaged area and from an inch or so of the surrounding 'sound' bodywork. This is accomplished most easily by using a wire brush or abrasive pad on a power drill, although it can be done just as effectively by hand using sheets of abrasive paper. To complete the preparation for filling, score the surface of the bare metal with a screwdriver or the tang of a file, or alternatively, drill small holes in the affected area. This will provide a really good 'key' for the filler paste.

To complete the repair see the Section on filling and respraying.

Repair of rust holes or gashes in bodywork

Remove all paint from the affected area and from an inch or so of the surrounding 'sound' bodywork, using an abrasive pad or a wire brush on a power drill. If these are not available a few sheets of abrasive paper will do the job most effectively. With the paint removed you will be able to judge the severity of the corrosion and therefore decide whether to renew the whole panel (if this is possible) or to repair the affected area. New body panels are not as expensive as most people think and it is often quicker and more satisfactory to fit a new panel than to attempt to repair large areas of corrosion.

Remove all fittings from the affected area except those which will act as a guide to the original shape of the damaged bodywork (eg headlamp shells etc). Then, using tin snips or a hacksaw blade, remove all loose metal and any other metal badly affected by corrosion. Hammer the edges of the hole inwards in order to create a slight depression for the filler paste.

Wire brush the affected area to remove the powdery rust from the surface of the remaining metal. Paint the affected area with rust inhibiting paint, such as Turtle Wax Rust Master; if the back of the rusted area is accessible treat this also.

Before filling can take place it will be necessary to block the hole in some way. This can be achieved by the use of aluminium or plastic mesh, or aluminium tape.

Aluminium or plastic mesh or glass-fibre matting, such as Holts Body + Plus Glass-Fibre Matting, is probably the best material to use for a large hole. Cut a piece to the approximate size and shape of the hole to be filled, then position it in the hole so that its edges are below the level of the surrounding bodywork. It can be retained in position by several blobs of filler paste around its periphery.

Aluminium tape should be used for small or very narrow holes. Pull a piece off the roll and trim it to the approximate size and shape required, then pull off the backing paper (if used) and stick the tape over the hole; it can be overlapped if the thickness of one piece is insufficient. Burnish down the edges of the tape with the handle of a screwdriver or similar, to ensure that the tape is securely attached to the metal underneath.

Bodywork repairs – filling and respraying

Before using this Section, see the Sections on dent, deep scratch, rust holes and gash repairs.

Many types of bodyfiller are available, but generally speaking those proprietary kits are best for this type of repair which contain a tin of filler paste and a tube of resin hardener, such as Holts Body + Plus, or Holts No Mix which can be used directly from the tube. A wide, flexible plastic or nylon applicator will be found invaluable for imparting a smooth and well contoured finish to the surface of the filler.

Mix up a little filler on a clean piece of card or board – measure the hardener carefully (follow the maker's instructions on the pack) otherwise the filler will set too rapidly or too slowly. Alternatively, Holts No Mix can be used straight from the tube without mixing, but daylight is required to cure it. Using the applicator apply the filler paste to the prepared area; draw the applicator across the surface of the filler to achieve the correct contour and to level the surface. As soon as a contour that approximates to the correct one is achieved, stop working the paste – if you carry on too long the paste will become sticky and begin to 'pick-up' on the applicator. Continue to add thin layers of filler paste at twenty minute intervals until the level of the filler is just proud of the surrounding bodywork.

Once the filler has hardened, excess can be removed using a metal plane or file. From then on, progressively finer grades of abrasive paper should be used, starting with a 40 grade production paper and finishing with a 400 grade wet-and-dry paper. Always wrap the abrasive paper around a flat rubber, cork, or wooden block – otherwise the surface of the filler will not be completely flat. During the smoothing of the filler surface the wet-and-dry paper should be periodically rinsed in water. This will ensure that a very smooth finish is imparted to the filler at the final stage.

At this stage the 'dent' should be surrounded by a ring of bare metal, which in turn should be encircled by the finely 'feathered' edge of the good paintwork. Rinse the repair area with clean water, until all of the dust produced by the rubbing-down operation has gone.

Spray the whole area with a light coat of primer, either Holts Body + Plus Grey or Red Oxide Primer – this will show up any imperfections in the surface of the filler. Repair these imperfections with fresh filler paste or bodystopper and once more smooth the surface with abrasive paper. If bodystopper is used, it can be mixed with cellulose thinners to form a really thin paste which is ideal for filling small holes. Repeat this spray and repair procedure until you are satisfied that the surface of the filler and the feathered edge of the paintwork are perfect. Clean the repair area with clean water and allow to dry fully.

The repair area is now ready for final spraying. Paint spraying must be carried out in a warm, dry, windless and dust free atmosphere. This condition can be created artificially if you have access to a large indoor working area, but if you are forced to work in the open, you will have to pick your day very carefully. If you are working indoors, dousing the floor in the work area with water will help to settle the dust which would otherwise be in the atmosphere. If the repair area is confined to one body panel, mask off the surrounding panels; this will help to minimise the effects of a slight mis-match in paint colours. Bodywork fittings (eg chrome strips, door handles etc) will also need to be masked off. Use genuine masking tape and several thicknesses of newspaper for the masking operations.

Before commencing to spray, agitate the aerosol can thoroughly, then spray a test area (an old tin, or similar) until the technique is mastered. Cover the repair area with a thick coat of primer; the thickness should be built up using several thin layers of paint rather than one thick one. Using 400 grade wet-and-dry paper, rub down the surface of the primer until it is really smooth. While doing this, the work area should be thoroughly doused with water and the wet-and-dry paper periodically rinsed in water. Allow to dry before spraying on more paint.

Spray on the top coat using Holts Dupli-Color Autospray, again building up the thickness by using several thin layers of paint. Start spraying in the centre of the repair area and then, with a side-to-side motion, work outwards until the whole repair area and about 50 mm of the surrounding original paintwork is covered. Remove all masking material 10 to 15 minutes after spraying on the final coat of paint.

Allow the new paint at least two weeks to harden, then, using a paintwork renovator, such as Turtle Wax New Color Back, or a very fine cutting paste, like Holts Body + Plus Rubbing Compound, blend the edges of the paint into the existing paintwork. Finally, apply wax polish from one of the Turtle Wax range of wax polishes.

Plastic components

With the use of more and more plastic body components by the vehicle manufacturers (eg bumpers, spoilers and in some cases major body panels), rectification of more serious damage to such items has become a matter of either entrusting repair work to a specialist in this field, or renewing complete components. Repair of such damage by the DIY owner is not really feasible owing to the cost of the equipment and materials required for effecting such repairs. The basic technique involves making a groove along the line of the crack in the plastic using a rotary burr in a power drill. The damaged part is then welded back together by using a hot air gun to heat up and fuse a plastic filler rod into the groove. Any excess plastic is then removed and the area rubbed down to a smooth finish. It is important that a filler rod of the correct plastic is used, as body components can be made of a variety of different types (eg polycarbonate, ABS, polypropylene).

Damage of a less serious nature (abrasions, minor cracks etc) can be repaired by the DIY owner using a two-part epoxy filler repair material such as Holts Body + Plus, or Holts No Mix which can be used directly from the tube. Once mixed in equal proportions (or applied direct from the tube in the case of Holts No Mix), this is used in similar fashion to the bodywork filler used on metal panels. The filler is usually cured in twenty to thirty minutes, ready for sanding and painting.

If the owner is renewing a complete component himself, or if he has repaired it with epoxy filler, he will be left with the problem of finding a suitable paint for finishing which is compatible with the type of plastic used. At one time the use of a universal paint was not possible owing to the complex range of plastics encountered in body component applications. Standard paints, generally speaking, will not bond satisfactorily to plastic or rubber, but Holts Professional Spraymatch paints to match any plastic or rubber finish can be obtained from dealers. However, it is now possible to obtain a plastic body parts finishing kit which consists of a pre-primer treatment, a primer and coloured top coat. Full instructions are normally supplied with a kit, but basically the method of use is to first apply the pre-primer to the component concerned and allow it to dry for up to 30 minutes. Then the primer is applied and left to dry for about an hour before finally applying the special coloured top coat. The result is a correctly-coloured component where the paint will flex with the plastic or rubber, a property that standard paint does not normally possess.

5 Major body damage – repair

Where serious damage has occurred, or large areas need renewal due to neglect, it means that complete new panels will need welding in; this is best left to professionals. If the damage is due to impact, it will also be necessary to check completely the alignment of the bodyshell; this can only be carried out accurately by a Skoda dealer using special jigs. If the body is left misaligned, it is primarily dangerous as the vehicle will not handle properly and secondly, uneven stresses will be imposed on the steering, suspension and possibly transmission, causing abnormal wear or complete failure, particularly to items such as the tyres.

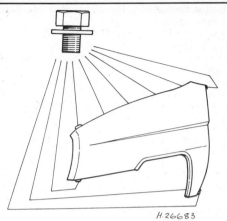

H.26683

Fig. 11.1 Location of front wing mountings (Sec 6)

6 Front wings – removal and refitting

Removal

1 Remove the direction indicator side repeater lamp (Chapter 12, Section 13).
2 Remove the front bumper (Section 8).
3 Remove the bonnet (Section 9).
4 Remove the front door (Section 16).
5 Unscrew the nine bolts securing the wing.
6 Cut along the joints and remove the wing.

Refitting

7 Before fitting the new wing, clean the body mating surfaces and apply new sealant.
8 Fit the wing and adjust its position before refitting the bolts, then tighten them securely.
9 Refit all remaining components using the reverse of the removal procedure.

7 Front-end panel – removal and refitting

Removal

1 Remove the headlight units (Chapter 12, Section 15).
2 Unscrew the four securing bolts and remove the front-end panel (photo).

7.2 Front-end panel securing bolts – right-hand bolts shown (arrowed)

8.3 Bumper reinforcement bar securing bolts (arrowed) – right-hand bolts shown

Refitting

3   Refitting is the reverse of the removal procedure.

---

8   Bumpers – removal and refitting

Removal

Front

1   Remove the front-end panel (Section 7).
2   Taking care to support the bumper as necessary, unscrew the six securing nuts and bolts, and remove the bumper.
3   The bumper reinforcement bar can then be removed by unscrewing the four retaining bolts (photo).

Rear

4   Open the tailgate (as applicable).

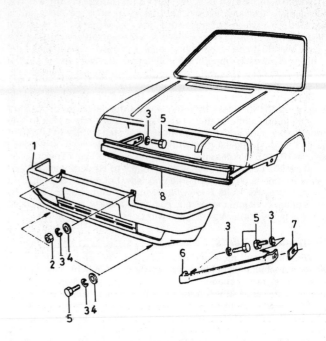

Fig. 11.2 Front bumper mounting points (Sec 8)

1	Front bumper	5	Bolt
2	Nut	6	Support strut
3	Spring washer	7	Captive nut (held in bumper)
4	Washer	8	Bumper reinforcement bar

5   Taking care to support the bumper as necessary, unscrew the seven securing bolts and remove the bumper.

Refitting

6   Refitting for front and rear bumpers is the reverse of the removal procedure, ensuring that the bumper is correctly aligned with the rest of the body.

Fig. 11.3 Rear bumper mounting points (Sec 8)

1   Rear bumper
2   Bolt
3   Spring washer
4   Washer
5   Captive nut (held in bumper)

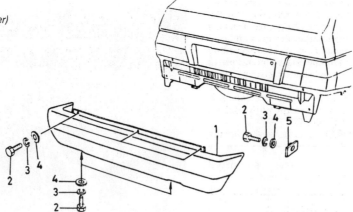

9.2 Bonnet-to-hinge arm bolts (arrowed)

9.3 Always have an assistant to help with bonnet removal

9 Bonnet – removal, refitting and adjustment

Removal

Note: *The aid of an assistant will be required for this operation.*

1   First, with the bonnet propped open, place a thick pad of cloth beneath each rear corner of the bonnet, to protect the paintwork.
2   Mark with a pencil around the hinge arms where they meet the bonnet, then slacken the bonnet-to-hinge arm bolts (photo).
3   Working with one person at each side, support the bonnet on the shoulders, lower the stay and unscrew the bolts. Remove the bonnet (photo).
4   The bonnet stay can be removed by working it out of its locating rubber bush in the bonnet lock platform.

Refitting

5   Refitting is the reverse of the removal procedure. If the original bonnet is being refitted, align the marks made on removal; if a new bonnet is being fitted, centre the bolt holes on the hinge arms. Tighten the bonnet-to-hinge arm bolts only lightly at first, then gently close the bonnet and check that it aligns evenly with the surrounding bodywork.
6   When the fit of the bonnet is correctly adjusted (see below), tighten the bolts to the specified torque wrench setting.

Adjustment

7   If the bonnet is not aligned correctly with the front wings, slacken the bonnet-to-hinge arm bolts, and reposition the bonnet on the hinge arms until the gaps are equal between each side of the bonnet and each wing, then tighten the bolts to their specified torque wrench setting.
8   If, when closed, the bonnet stands proud of, or is lower than, either front wing, screw both bonnet rubber buffers fully down into the bonnet lock platform, then close the bonnet and check its height relative to each wing. Screw the striker pin into the bonnet to lower its height, outwards to raise it; when the height is correct (ie when closed, the bonnet is exactly flush with the adjacent wings) adjust the height of the buffers until they just contact the underside of the bonnet.
9   Refer to Section 10 for details of adjustments possible with the bonnet lock.

10 Bonnet lock and release mechanism – removal, refitting and adjustment

Note: *Releasing the bonnet lock if the cable has broken is not easy. Attempting to gain access from the front will probably result in damage*

to the radiator. The best approach is to remove the engine undershield and to work from below, using a length of stiff wire such as a coat-hanger.

Removal

Lock

1   Open the bonnet and mark with a pencil around the bonnet lock, then unscrew the three mounting bolts (photo) and withdraw the lock and guide plate until the release cable can be disconnected.

Striker

2   Open the bonnet and mark with a pencil around the assembly's mounting plate, then unscrew the mounting bolts and withdraw the striker and safety catch assembly.

Release cable and lever

3   Disconnect the cable from the lock, by deforming the metal clamping tag, and release it from the clips or ties securing it to the body (photo).
4   The release lever is located on the left-hand side of the passenger footwell, beneath the glovebox. Drive out the lever pivot pin from the lever, withdraw the lever and disconnect the cable.
5   Withdraw the cable into the engine compartment.

10.1 Bonnet lock mounting bolts

10.3 Disconnect cable from bonnet lock by deforming metal clamping tag (arrowed)

Refitting

6   Refitting is the reverse of the removal procedure, noting the following points.

   (a)   *Align (where applicable) the component on the marks made on removal; if a new bonnet or bonnet lock platform has been fitted, centre the component on its bolt holes.*
   (b)   *Tighten the component's fasteners lightly, then check carefully the operation and adjustment of all disturbed components; if adjustment is required, proceed as described below.*
   (c)   *Tighten the bolts securely, or to the specified torque wrench settings (where given).*

Adjustment

7   If the operation of any part of the bonnet release mechanism requires adjustment, check first the fit of the bonnet on the body (Section 9); while some adjustments are interdependent (the bonnet height adjustment being made using the lock's striker pin), the lock cannot function correctly if the bonnet is not aligned properly with the bodywork.
8   To adjust the lock and/or striker assembly, first slacken their mounting bolts, then move them as necessary until the striker pin and safety catch hook engage squarely in the centre of their respective lock apertures; tighten the bolts securely, or to the specified torque wrench settings (where given).
9   When the lock and striker are correctly aligned, check that the bonnet closes securely when dropped from a height of approximately 6 inches (150 mm); there should be no trace of movement when attempting to lift the front edge of the bonnet.
10   If the bonnet does not lock when dropped, check first that the striker pin is properly lubricated (Chapter 1); some adjustment may be made by screwing the striker pin in or out, but take care that this does not alter the bonnet height (Section 9). Renew the striker or the lock assembly as necessary if the fault is due to wear or damage of either component.
11   If there is any doubt about the safety catch's performance, the striker assembly must be renewed.
12   There is no adjustment as such of the release cable, but the cable outer stops can be bent slightly to effect minor alterations if required; renew the cable if the bonnet release is ineffective.

11   Body exterior fittings – removal and refitting

Removal

Mudflaps

1   The mudflaps are secured by bolts and captive nuts. Undo the bolts to remove the mudflaps.

Roof drip channel

2   The drip channel moulding along the roof edges is clipped in place and can be prised off, taking care not to break it or to damage the paintwork.

Side rubbing strips

3   Apply masking tape along the edge of the strip to be removed, as an aid to correct location on refitting.
4   Using a hot air gun, heat the strip until the adhesive softens enough for the strip to be peeled off. Take care not to damage the surrounding paintwork with the hot air gun.

Front badge

5   The front badge is held in place by several integrally-moulded plastic tags.
6   To remove the front badge, use a slim-bladed knife to prise it off gently, taking care not to break it.

Rear badges

7   The various rear badges are secured with adhesives. To remove them, either soften the adhesive using a hot air gun (taking care to avoid damage to the paintwork) or separate the badge from the bodywork by 'sawing' through the adhesive bond using a length of nylon cord.

Refitting

Mudflaps

8   Refitting is a reversal of removal.

Roof drip channel

9   Refitting is a reversal of removal, but make sure that the channel is pressed securely into place.

Side rubbing strips

10   Clean off all traces of adhesive using white spirit, then wash the area with warm soapy water to remove all traces of spirit. Ensure that the surface to which the new strip is to be fastened is completely clean, and free from grease or dirt.
11   Use the hot air gun to soften the adhesive on the new strip, then press it firmly into position, using the masking tape as a guide. Remove the masking tape when the strip is secured.

Front badge

12   To refit, simply ease the tags into the body aperture, and press the badge firmly into place.

Rear badges

13   Clean off all traces of adhesive using white spirit, then wash the area with warm soapy water to remove all traces of spirit. Ensure that the surface to which the new badge is to be fastened is completely clean, and free from grease or dirt.
14   Use the hot air gun to soften the adhesive on the new badge, then press it firmly into position.

12   Windscreen, rear quarterlight and tailgate glass – general information

These areas of glass are secured by the tight fit of the weatherstrip in the body aperture; although they are not fixed by the direct-bonding method used on many modern vehicles, the removal and refitting of these areas of fixed glass is still difficult, messy and time-consuming for the inexperienced. It is also difficult, unless one has plenty of practice, to obtain a secure, waterproof fit. Furthermore, the task carries a high risk of breakage; this applies especially to the laminated glass windscreen. In view of this, owners are strongly advised to have this sort of work carried out by one of the many specialist windscreen fitters.

13.3 Disconnecting the tailgate washer system tube

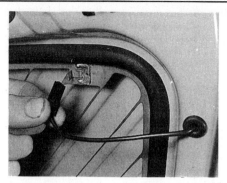

13.5 Disconnect the wiring from the heated rear window element

13.8 Tailgate hinge bolts

13 Tailgate – removal, refitting and adjustment

Removal

Note: *The aid of an assistant will be required for this operation.*

1 Open the tailgate, and remove the rear parcel shelf.
2 Remove the interior trim panel (Section 22) and the plastic membrane.
3 Where fitted, disconnect the washer system tube from the top edge of the tailgate (photo), and plug it to prevent loss of water.
4 On early Hatchback models, the wiring to the tailgate electrical components is made by means of one or two spring-loaded contact plates. On such models, the next paragraph can be ignored.
5 On Estate and later Hatchback models, disconnect the wiring from the heated rear window element, wiper motor and tailgate lights as applicable (photo). Tie a strong cord to the end of each separate wiring loom. Pull out any sealing grommets, and withdraw the wiring looms until the cords appear. Untie the looms, leaving the cords in the tailgate.
6 On all models, mark with a pencil around the hinges where they meet the tailgate, and place a thick pad of cloth beneath each tailgate top corner, to protect the paintwork.
7 Support the tailgate and remove the struts (Section 14).
8 Unscrew the two bolts securing each tailgate hinge to the tailgate (photo), then remove the tailgate.

Refitting

9 Refitting is the reverse of the removal procedure, noting the following points.

(a) If the original tailgate is being refitted, align the marks made on removal; if a new tailgate is being fitted, centre the hinges across the bolt holes. Tighten the bolts only lightly at first, then gently close the tailgate and check that it fits correctly.
(b) When the fit of the tailgate is correct (see below), tighten the bolts to the specified torque wrench setting.

Adjustment

10 When the tailgate is closed, check that it sits squarely on its weatherstrip, with no sign of gaps, and also that it is aligned evenly with the surrounding bodywork.
11 If the fit is not correct, open the tailgate and slacken the hinge bolts.
12 Adjust the position of the tailgate until the gaps are equal between it and the surrounding bodywork, and it sits correctly on the weatherstrip; tighten the hinge bolts to their specified torque wrench setting.
13 Refer to Section 15 for details of adjustments possible with the tailgate striker.

14 Tailgate support struts – removal and refitting

Removal

1 Open the tailgate and support it with a piece of wood.
2 Release the spring clips at both ends (photo), and pull the strut off each of its mountings.

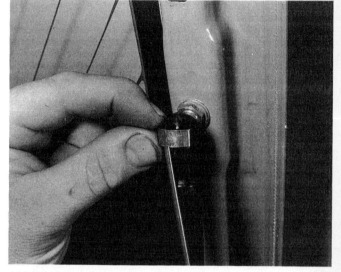

14.2 Releasing tailgate support strut spring clip

3 The struts are sealed, containing gas under pressure; **do not** attempt to dismantle them, or to apply any heat. If failed or damaged, the struts must be renewed; dispose of the old struts safely.

Refitting

4 Refitting is the reverse of the removal procedure; ensure that each end of the strut snaps securely home on its mounting.

15 Tailgate lock components – removal and refitting

Removal

Lock

1 Open the tailgate, and remove the interior trim panel (Section 22) and the plastic membrane.
2 By carefully levering apart the ball-and-socket joint, release the lock-to-latch connecting rod from the lock lever (photo).
3 Slide the lock-to-tailgate securing clip to the right (looking at the lock from inside the vehicle), and then remove the lock.

Latch

4 Open the tailgate, and remove the interior trim panel (Section 22) and the plastic membrane.
5 By carefully levering apart the ball-and-socket joint, release the lock-to-latch connecting rod from the latch.
6 Remove the two screws securing the latch to the tailgate (photo), and withdraw the two halves of the latch.

Striker

7 Open the tailgate and mark with a pencil around the striker, then undo the two screws and withdraw the striker (photo).

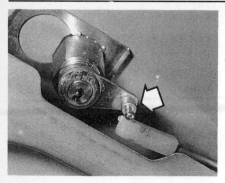

15.2 Release the lock-to-latch connecting rod from the ball-and-socket joint (arrowed)

15.6 Latch securing screws

15.7 Tailgate striker

Refitting

Lock

8   Refitting is the reverse of the removal procedure.

Latch

9   Refitting is the reverse of the removal procedure; lubricate all moving parts and the striker (Chapter 1).

Striker

10   On refitting, align the striker on the marks made on removal; if new components have been fitted, centre the striker on the screw holes, then tighten the screws lightly and check the fit of the tailgate on the body (see below). When the fit is correct, tighten the screws fully.
11   When the tailgate is closed, check that it sits squarely on its weatherstrip, with no sign of gaps, and that it is aligned evenly with the surrounding bodywork.
12   If the fit is not correct, open the tailgate and slacken the striker screws, then adjust the position of the striker until the tailgate aligns with the surrounding bodywork and the gaps are equal at all points between the tailgate and the body panels.
13   When the fit is correct, tighten the striker screws and check the operation of the tailgate lock.

---

16   Doors and hinges – removal, refitting and adjustment

Removal

Door

1   Support the door using a block of wood or a trolley jack; ensure that the paintwork is protected with a wad of clean rag.

2   Disconnect the check link by levering out the pin, taking care not to lose the protective end cap.
3   Using a suitable punch, drive out the roll pins from the upper and lower door hinges (photo), and remove the door.

Hinges

4   To remove the hinge-to-body hinge plates, remove the door (see above). In the case of the front door, also remove the front wing (Section 6).
5   Mark with a pencil around the hinge plates where they meet the body, then unscrew the bolts securing the upper and lower hinge plates to the body (photo).
6   To remove the hinge-to-door hinge plates, remove the door, the interior door handle (Section 17), the door trim panel (Section 22) and the plastic membrane.
7   Mark with a pencil around the hinge plates where they meet the door, then unscrew the bolts securing the upper and lower hinge plates to the door.

Refitting

8   Refitting is the reverse of the removal procedure, noting the following points.

(a)   If the original door is being refitted, align the marks made on removal; if a new door is being fitted, centre the hinges across the bolt holes. Tighten the bolts only lightly at first, then gently close the door and check that it fits correctly.
(b)   When the fit of the door is correct (see below), tighten the bolts to the specified torque wrench setting.

Adjustment

Note: If the door hinges have not been disturbed, it is most probable that the required adjustment can be carried out using just the door striker (Section 17).

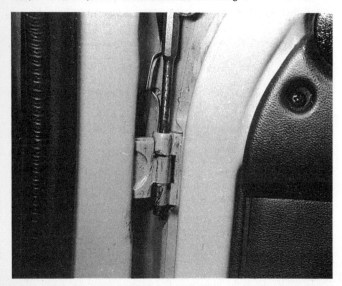

16.3 Driving out the door hinge roll pins

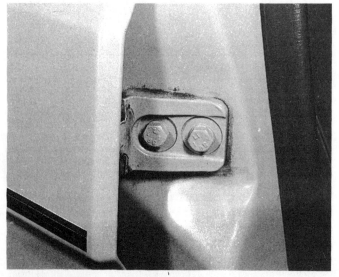

16.5 Rear door hinge-to-body hinge plate

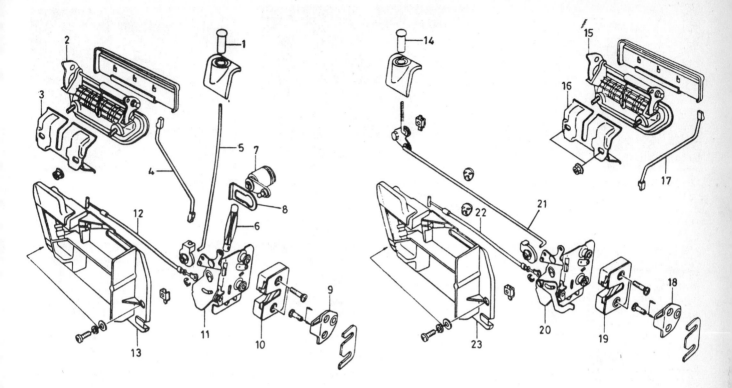

Fig. 11.4 Door lock and handle components (Sec 17)

Front door – items 1 to 13
1 Interior lock button
2 Exterior handle
3 Exterior handle retainer
4 Latch operating
   mechanism-to-exterior
   handle connecting rod
5 Latch operating
   mechanism-to-interior lock
   button connecting rod

6 Latch operating
   mechanism-to-lock
   connecting rod
7 Lock
8 Lock-to-door securing clip
9 Striker plate
10 Latch
11 Latch operating mechanism
12 Latch operating cable
13 Interior handle assembly

Rear door – items 14 to 23
14 Interior lock button
15 Exterior handle
16 Exterior handle retainer
17 Latch operating
   mechanism-to-exterior
   handle connecting rod
18 Striker plate

19 Latch
20 Latch operating
   mechanism
21 Latch operating
   mechanism-to-interior
   lock button connecting rod
22 Latch operating cable
23 Interior handle assembly

9   When the door is closed, check that it fits flush with the surrounding bodywork, and centrally in the body aperture.
10   If the fit is not correct, open the door, remove the interior door handle (Section 17), the interior trim panel (Section 22) and the plastic membrane, then slacken the hinge bolts.
11   Adjust the position of the door until it fits correctly, then tighten the hinge bolts to their specified torque wrench setting.

17 Door lock and handle components – removal and refitting

Removal

Front door lock

1   Open the door and fully raise the window glass. Remove the interior door handle (see below), the door trim panel (Section 22) and the plastic membrane (photo). Also remove the plastic shield, when fitted.
2   By carefully levering the ball-and-socket joint apart, disconnect the latch operating mechanism connecting rod from the lock.
3   Slide the lock-to-door securing clip towards the exterior handle, and then remove the lock.

Exterior handle

4   Open the door and fully raise the window glass. Remove the interior door handle (see below), the door trim panel (Section 22) and the plastic membrane.

5   By carefully levering the ball-and-socket joint apart, disconnect the latch operating mechanism-to-exterior handle connecting rod (photo).
6   Undo the two securing nuts, and remove the handle retainer (photo).
7   From the outside of the door, withdraw the exterior handle (photo). Take care not to damage the surrounding paintwork.

Latch and latch operating mechanism

8   Open the door and fully raise the window glass. Remove the interior door handle (see below), the interior lock button (see below), the door trim panel (Section 22) and the plastic membrane.
9   By carefully levering the ball-and-socket joints apart, disconnect the latch operating mechanism-to-exterior handle connecting rod, and the latch operating mechanism-to-interior lock button connecting rod.
10   Undo the two screws securing the latch to the door, and remove the latch from the door (photo).
11   Carefully withdraw the latch operating mechanism from within the door (photo).

Interior handle

12   Remove the door pockets.
13   Gently prise the armrest away from the interior handle assembly, and undo the screws that secure the interior handle assembly to the door.
14   Disconnect the latch operating cable from the interior handle, and thread it back through the interior handle assembly, noting its routing (photo).

Interior lock button

15   Unscrew the button from the top of its link rod.

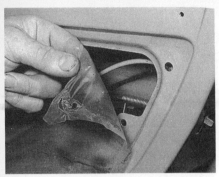

17.1 Removing the plastic membrane

17.5 Disconnect the latch operating mechanism-to-exterior handle connecting rod from the ball-and-socket joint (arrowed) ...

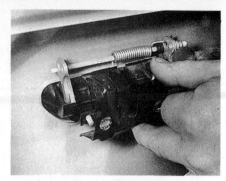

17.6 ... remove the handle retainer ...

17.7 ... and withdraw the exterior handle

17.10 Remove the latch from the door ...

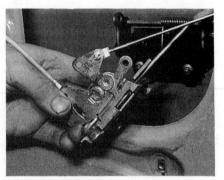

17.11 ... before withdrawing the latch operating mechanism

17.14 Disconnecting the latch operating mechanism cable from the interior door handle

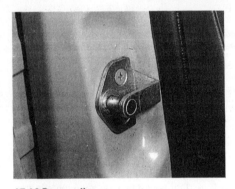

17.16 Door striker

Striker

16   Open the door and mark with a pencil around the striker, then undo the two retaining screws (photo) and withdraw the striker.

Refitting

Front door lock

17   Refitting is the reverse of the removal procedure. Ensure that the ball-and-socket joints snap together firmly.

Exterior handle

18   Refitting is the reverse of the removal procedure. Ensure that the ball-and-socket joints snap together firmly, and that the handle is positioned squarely on the door.

Latch

19   Refitting is the reverse of the removal procedure. Ensure that the ball-and-socket joints snap together firmly.

Interior handle

20   Refitting is the reverse of the removal procedure. Ensure that the operating cable is correctly routed through the handle, and is not trapped or kinked.

Interior lock button

21   Refitting is the reverse of the removal procedure.

Striker

22   On refitting, align the striker with the marks made on removal. If new components have been fitted, centre the striker on its mounting holes, tighten the striker/screws lightly, and check the fit of the door in the body (see below). When the fit is correct, tighten the striker/screws securely.

23   The striker can only be positioned accurately when the door is properly located in its aperture (Section 16).

24   When the door is closed, check that it sits squarely on its weatherstrip, with no sign of gaps, so that it is flush with the surrounding bodywork and so that the door lock closes securely, with no sign of rattles.

25   If the fit is not correct, open the door and slacken the striker/screws, then adjust the position of the striker by closing the door

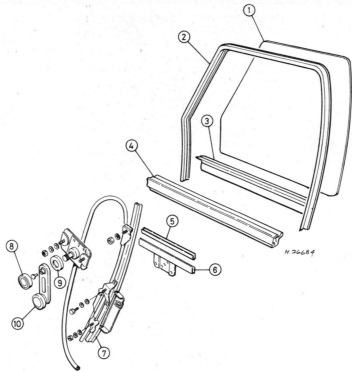

H.26684

Fig. 11.5 Door window glass and regulator components – front shown, rear similar (Sec 18)

1 Window glass	4 Inner weatherstrip	6 Regulator channel	9 Collar
2 Weatherstrip	5 Regulator channel	7 Regulator mechanism	10 Regulator handle
3 Outer weatherstrip	weatherstrip	8 Cover	

as gently as possible, then opening it again without disturbing the position of the striker.

26 When the fit is correct, tighten the striker/screws securely, and check the operation of the door lock.

18 Door window glass and regulator – removal and refitting

Removal

Window glass

1 Open the door and fully raise the window glass, then remove the interior door handle (Section 17), the door trim panel (Section 22) and the plastic membrane.

2 Pull off the outer and inner weatherstrips, then pull out the plastic water-deflecting strip.

3 Lower the window glass halfway, and mark the relationship of the

regulator channel to the regulator before unscrewing the two regulator channel-to-regulator bolts (photo).

4 Manoeuvre the glass out of the door (photo).

Regulator

5 Open the door and fully raise the window glass, then remove the interior door handle (Section 17), the door trim panel (Section 22) and the plastic membrane.

6 Lower the window glass halfway, and mark the relationship of the regulator channel to the regulator before unscrewing the two regulator channel-to-regulator bolts.

7 Wind the window glass fully up and secure it with adhesive tape, then wind the regulator halfway down again.

8 Unscrew the regulator retaining nuts (photo) and withdraw the regulator.

Refitting

Window glass

9 Refitting is the reverse of the removal procedure, but apply a little grease to the regulator mechanism, and align the marks that were made

18.3 Regulator channel-to-regulator retaining bolts (arrowed)

18.4 Manoeuvring window glass out of door

18.8 Regulator retaining nuts (arrowed)

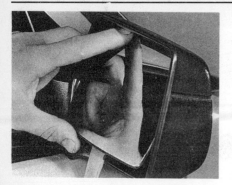

19.1A Carefully prise the mirror glass ...

19.1B ... from the bezel inside the mirror casing

19.2 Pulling off the mirror adjuster knob – note adjuster retaining ring (arrowed)

on removal before tightening the two bolts. Check that the glass moves smoothly and easily through its travel.

Regulator

10   Refitting is the reverse of the removal procedure, but apply a little grease to the regulator and refit it, tightening the mounting bolts only loosely at first. Move the window glass several times through its full travel, to check that the glass moves smoothly and easily. If necessary, slacken the mounting nuts and bolts to adjust the fit of those components that require it.

19   Mirrors – removal and refitting

Removal

Exterior mirror glass

1   Taking care not to mark the plastic, and wearing gloves and suitable eye protection, carefully prise the mirror glass from the bezel inside the mirror casing (photos).

Exterior mirror assembly

2   Pull off the adjusting knob, and unscrew the mirror adjuster retaining ring (photo).
3   Unscrew the inner trim panel and remove it (photo).
4   Remove the retaining screws, and withdraw the mirror, the adjuster mechanism and the outer trim panel. Remove and discard the sealing pad, if fitted.

Interior mirror

5   The mirror mounting is accessible after removal of the roof console – refer to Section 22.

Refitting

Exterior mirror glass

6   Refitting is the reverse of the removal procedure; ensure the bezel is clipped securely into the casing.

Exterior mirror assembly

7   Refitting is the reverse of the removal procedure; where applicable, fit a new sealing pad to the mirror.

Interior mirror

8   Refitting is the reverse of the removal procedure.

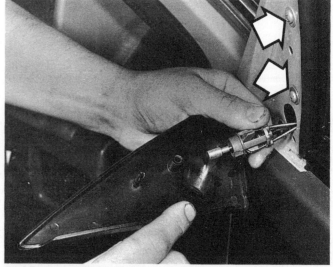

19.3 Removing the inner trim panel – note mirror assembly retaining screws (arrowed)

20.1 Removing a seat front mounting screw ...

20.2 ... and a rear mounting screw

20.5 Align flats on pivot pin and hinge bracket for rear seat removal

21.3 Unbolting the seat belt retractor

21.4 Front seat belt stalk mountings and cover

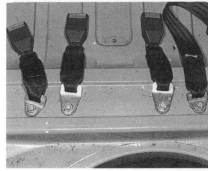

21.6 Rear seat belt buckle mounting points

21.7 Rear seat belt top anchorage and retractor

21.8 Rear seat belt bottom anchorage

21.9 Rear seat belt retractor mounting

20 Seats – removal and refitting

Removal

Front

1 Operate the adjuster and move the seat fully backwards, then undo the front mounting screws (photo).
2 Move the seat fully forwards, and undo the rear mounting screws (photo).
3 Remove the seat.

Rear

4 Release the seat belts from the seat.
5 Tip the backrest down to the seat cushion. Tilt the backrest and cushion forwards until the flat on the left-hand pivot pin corresponds with the flat in the left-hand hinge bracket, then pull the complete seat towards the right-hand side of the vehicle and remove it (photo).

Refitting

Front and rear

6 Refitting is the reverse of the removal procedure.

21 Seat belts – removal and refitting

Warning: *Seat belts which have been subjected to accident loads must be renewed. Do not attempt to repair or modify seat belt components. When removing belt anchorages and mountings, note the fitted sequence of spacers, washers etc, and follow the same sequence on refitting.*

Removal

Front

1 Prise off the plastic cover, and unbolt the belt top anchorage.
2 Unbolt the belt bottom anchorage.
3 Remove the B-pillar trim panel (Section 22), and unbolt the retractor from the body (photo).
4 Prise off the cover, then unbolt the stalks from their mounting bracket (photo).

Rear

5 Remove the parcel shelf. Release the belts from the seat, then fold the seat fully forwards.
6 Remove the load area carpet, and unbolt the belt buckle from the floor. Note that the centre two-point belt can be unbolted completely (photo).
7 Prise off the plastic cover, and unbolt the belt top anchorage (photo).
8 Unbolt the belt bottom anchorage from the body (photo).
9 Unbolt the retractor from the body (photo).
10 Feed the belt through the slot in the parcel shelf support until it can be removed, taking care not to fray or cut the belt material on the plastic trim.

Refitting

Front and rear

11 Refitting is the reverse of the removal procedure, tightening the mounting and anchorage bolts to the specified torque. Ensure that the anchorages are free to move when the bolts have been securely tightened.

22 Interior trim – general information

Interior trim panels

1 The interior trim panels are all secured using either screws or various types of trim fasteners, usually either studs or clips.

22.2A Remove the cover ...

22.2B ... and remove the screw to release window regulator handle

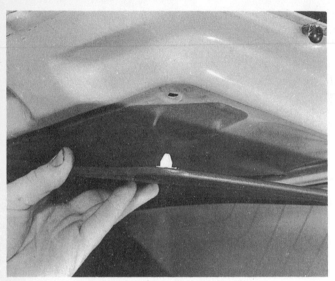

22.4A Trim panels are often secured with hidden clips

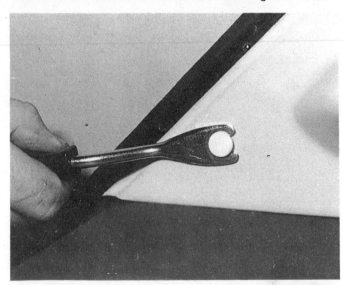

22.4B Using the correct tool to release a C-pillar trim panel securing clip

2   To remove a panel, study it carefully, noting how it is secured; usually there are some ancillary components which must be removed first such as (on door trim panels) the front door pockets, the armrests/door pulls and the window regulator handles (photos).

3   Once any such components have been removed, check that there are no other panels overlapping the one to be removed; usually there is a sequence that has to be followed that will become obvious on close inspection. For example, when removing two-piece door interior trim panels, the upper panel must be removed first.

4   Remove all obvious fasteners, such as screws. If the panel will not come free, it is held by hidden clips or fasteners. These are usually situated around the edge of the panel, and can be prised up to release them; note, however, that they can break quite easily, so replacements should be available. The best way of releasing such clips is to use the correct type of tool (photos); if this is not available, an old, broad-bladed screwdriver with the edges rounded-off and wrapped in insulating tape will serve as a good substitute.

5   When removing a panel, **never** use excessive force, or the panel may be damaged; always check carefully that all fasteners have been removed or released before attempting to withdraw a panel.

6   Refitting is the reverse of the removal procedure; secure the fasteners by pressing them firmly into place, and ensure that all disturbed components are correctly secured to prevent rattles. If adhesives were found at any point on removal, use white spirit to

remove all traces of old adhesive, then wash off all traces of spirit using soapy water; use a suitable trim adhesive (a Skoda dealer should be able to recommend a proprietary product) on reassembly.

Carpets

7   The passenger compartment floor carpet is in one piece, and is secured at its edges by screws or clips – usually the same fasteners used to secure the various adjoining trim panels.

8   Carpet removal and refitting is reasonably straightforward, but very time-consuming, due to the fact that all adjoining trim panels must be removed first, as must components such as the seats and their mountings, the gearchange lever gaiters and seat belt lower anchorages.

Headlining

9   The headlining is clipped to the roof, and can be withdrawn only once all fittings such as the grab handles, sunvisors, roof console, sunroof, windscreen and related trim panels have been removed, and the door, tailgate and sunroof aperture weatherstrips have been prised clear.

10   Note that headlining removal requires considerable skill and experience if it is to be carried out without damage, and is therefore best entrusted to an expert.

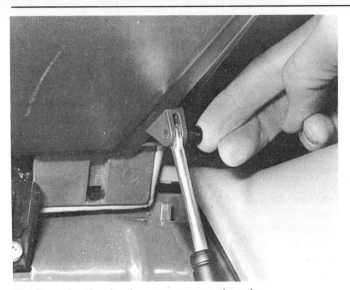

23.1 Removing the glovebox support strut pivot pin

23.2 Undo the glovebox lid securing screws

23 Glovebox – removal and refitting

Removal

1   Open the glovebox lid, and remove the support strut by pulling out the pivot pin (photo).

2   Undo the two screws securing the lid to the glovebox (photo), and withdraw the lid.
3   Undo the screws securing the front edge of the glovebox, then carefully prise the glovebox from the facia (photos).

Refitting

4   Refitting is the reverse of the removal procedure.

23.3A Undo the glovebox securing screws ...

23.3B ... and prise the glovebox from the facia

Fig. 11.6 Location of facia mounting screws (Sec 24)

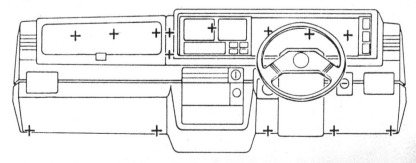

Fig. 11.7 The facia and its components (Sec 24)

1   Facia
2   Heating/ventilation ducts
3   Sideplate
4   Air vent
5   Ashtray
6   Radio aperture
7   Instrument panel-to-facia retaining bracket
8   Steering column upper shroud
9   Steering column lower shroud
10 Instrument cowl
11 Central switch panel
12 Instrument cowl lower trim panel
13 Auxiliary switch panel
14 Instrument panel
15 Glovebox
16 Glovebox lid
17 Glovebox lid support strut

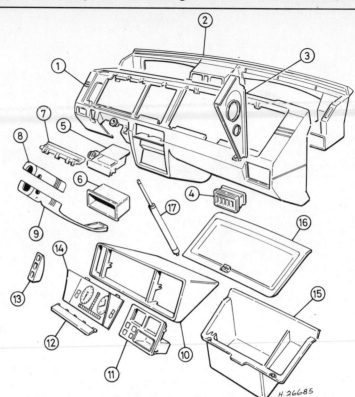

H.26685

24   Facia – removal and refitting

Removal

1   Disconnect the battery negative lead.
2   Remove the steering wheel and steering column upper and lower shrouds (Chapter 10).
3   Remove the instrument panel (Chapter 12).
4   Remove the heater control panel (Chapter 3).
5   Remove the radio (Chapter 12).

6   Remove the fourteen screws securing the facia, and pull it slowly into the passenger compartment. Do not use excessive force; it is not necessary, and may damage the plastic components. If difficulty is encountered at any point, check carefully that all fasteners, electrical connections and other components have been removed or disconnected as required.

Refitting

7   Refitting is the reverse of the removal procedure. Refer where necessary to the relevant Sections of Chapters 3, 10 and 12.

Chapter 12 Electrical system

Contents

Alternator – removal and refitting	6
Alternator brushes and voltage regualtor – renewal	7
Alternator drivebelt check, adjustment and renewal	See Chapter 1
Battery – removal and refitting	4
Battery – testing and charging	3
Battery check and maintenance	See Chapter 1
Bulbs (exterior lights) – renewal	13
Bulbs (interior lights) – renewal	14
Charging system – testing	5
Dim-dip system – general information	18
Electrical fault-finding – general information	2
Exterior light units – removal and refitting	15
Fuses, relays and flasher unit – general information	11
General information and precautions	1
Headlight alignment control system – general information	17
Headlight beam alignment – general information	16
Heated rear window – general information	23
Horn – adjustment, removal and refitting	22
Instrument panel – removal and refitting	19
Instrument panel components – removal and refitting	20
Lights, horn and direction indicators operational check	See Chapter 1
Loudspeakers – removal and refitting	30
Radio aerial – general information	31
Radio/cassette unit – removal and refitting	29
Rear window wiper motor – removal and refitting	27
Seat belt warning system – general information	24
Speedometer drive cable – removal and refitting	21
Starter motor – brush and solenoid renewal	10
Starter motor – removal and refitting	9
Starting system – testing	8
Switches – removal and refitting	12
Washer system components – removal and refitting	28
Windscreen and rear window washer/wiper system check	See Chapter 1
Windscreen wiper motor and linkage – removal and refitting	26
Wiper arms – removal and refitting	25

Specifications

System type .... 12-volt, negative earth

Battery
Capacity .... 40 Amp-hours

Alternator
Type	PAL Kromeriz 443 113 516 631
Output – at 14 volts and 6000 rpm	55 amps
Regulated voltage	14.2 volts maximum
Voltage regulator	PAL Kromeriz 443 930 166 111
Drivebelt deflection	10 to 15 mm @ 2 kg pressure

Starter motor
Type	PAL Kromeriz 443 115 142 350
Rating	0.8 kW
Commutator minimum diameter	32.5 mm

Fuses – models from 1989 to 1992

Fuse No	Rating (amps)	Circuit(s) protected
1	15	Inspection light socket, courtesy lights, stop-lights, horn, hazard lights
2	8 or 15	Front and rear screen wiper motors, washer motors, reversing lights, carburettor
3	8	Direction indicators, instrument panel illumination and warning lights
4	15	Radiator cooling fan motor
5	15	Heated rear window
6	15	Heater blower motor
7	8	Left-hand sidelights, number plate light
8	8	Right-hand sidelights
9	8	Left-hand headlight dipped beam
10	8	Right-hand headlight dipped beam
11	15	Front and rear foglights
12	8	Right-hand headlight main beam
13	8	Left-hand headlight main beam
14	15	Spare

Fuses – models from 1992

Fuse No	Rating (amps)	Circuit(s) protected
1	15	Spare
2	15	Heated rear window
3	7.5	Left-hand headlight main beam and warning light
4	7.5	Right-hand headlight main beam
5	15	Front and rear screen wiper motors and reversing lights
6	15	Brake reservoir low warning system, hazard lights switch, heated rear window switch, instrument panel, seat belt warning system, digital clock
7	15	Radiator cooling fan motor and carburettor
8	15	Heater blower motor
9	15	Hazard lights switch, headlight dipped beam switch, stop-lights, courtesy light and instrument panel
10	7.5	Rear foglights and warning light
11	7.5	Left-hand front foglight and warning light
12	7.5	Right-hand front foglight
13	7.5	Left-hand headlight dipped beam
14	7.5	Right-hand headlight dipped beam and warning light
15	7.5	Left-hand sidelights and switch illumination
16	7.5	Right-hand sidelights and instrument panel illumination

Relays and control units – models from 1989 to 1992

Component or function	Location (see text)
Windscreen wiper delay unit	Fuse board
Rear foglights	Fuse board
Heated rear window	Fuse board
Front foglights	Fuse board
Relay for fuses 2, 3, 4	Fuse board
Headlight dipped beam	Fuse board
Headlight main beam	Fuse board
Direction indicator/hazard warning flasher unit	Behind central switch panel

Relays and control units – models from 1992

Component	Location (see text)
Windscreen wiper delay unit	Fuse board
Heated rear window	Fuse board
Headlight main beam	Fuse board
Relay for fuses 5, 6, 7	Fuse board
Rear foglights	Fuse board
Front foglights	Fuse board
Headlight dipped beam	Fuse board
Direction indicator/hazard warning flasher unit	Behind central switch panel

Bulbs

	Type	Wattage
Headlights	H4	55/60
Sidelights	T	4
Direction indicators – front and rear	P	21
Direction indicators – side repeater	T	4
Tail lights	R	10
Stop-lights	P	21
Reversing lights	P	21
Rear foglights	P	21
Front foglights	H3	55
Number plate light	T	4
Courtesy light	C	5
Instrument panel warning lights	R5	1.2
Switch illumination lights	R5	1.2
Instrument panel lights	R5	1.2

Torque wrench settings

	Nm	lbf ft
Starter motor-to-transmission nuts	40 to 50	30 to 37
Oil pressure switch	20 to 25	15 to 18
Alternator mounting bracket-to-cylinder block nut	20 to 28	15 to 21
Alternator pivot and clamp bolts:		
M8	16 to 24	12 to 18
M10	28 to 42	21 to 31

1 General information and precautions

Warning: *Before carrying out any work on the electrical system, read through the precautions given in 'Safety first!' at the beginning of this manual.*

The electrical system is of the 12-volt negative earth type, and consists of a 12-volt battery, an alternator with integral voltage regulator, a starter motor, and related electrical accessories, components and wiring.

The battery is charged by the alternator, which is belt-driven from a crankshaft-mounted pulley.

The starter motor is of the pre-engaged type, incorporating an integral solenoid. On starting, the solenoid moves the drive pinion into engagement with the flywheel ring gear before the starter motor is energised. Once the engine has started, a one-way clutch prevents the motor armature being driven by the engine until the pinion disengages from the flywheel.

Further details of the various systems are given in the relevant Sections of this Chapter. While some repair procedures are given, the usual course of action is to renew the component concerned. The owner whose interest extends beyond mere component renewal should obtain a copy of the *'Automobile Electrical & Electronic Systems Manual'*, available from the publishers of this manual.

It is necessary to take extra care when working on the electrical system to avoid damage to semi-conductor devices (diodes and transistors), and to avoid the risk of personal injury. In addition to the precautions given in *'Safety first!'* at the beginning of this manual, observe the following when working on the system.

Always remove rings, watches, etc., before working on the electrical system. Even with the battery disconnected, capacitive discharge could occur if a component's live terminal is earthed through a metal object. This could cause a shock or nasty burn.

Do not reverse the battery connections. Components such as the alternator or any other having semi-conductor circuitry could be irreparably damaged.

If the engine is being started using jump leads and a slave battery, connect the batteries *positive-to-positive* and *negative-to-negative* (see *'Booster battery (jump) starting'*). This also applies when connecting a battery charger.

Never disconnect the battery terminals, the alternator, any electrical wiring or any test instruments when the engine is running.

Do not allow the engine to turn the alternator when the alternator is not connected.

Never test for alternator output by 'flashing' the output lead to earth.

Never use an ohmmeter of the type incorporating a hand-cranked generator for circuit or continuity testing.

Always ensure that the battery negative lead is disconnected when working on the electrical system.

Before using electric-arc welding equipment on the vehicle, disconnect the battery, alternator and other such components to protect them.

2 Electrical fault-finding – general information

Note: *Refer to the precautions given in 'Safety first!' and in Section 1 of this Chapter before starting work. The following tests relate to testing of the main electrical circuits, and should not be used to test delicate electronic circuits.*

General

1   A typical electrical circuit consists of an electrical component, any switches, relays, motors, fuses, fusible links or circuit breakers related to that component, and the wiring and connectors which link the component to both the battery and the chassis. To help to pinpoint a problem in an electrical circuit, wiring diagrams are included at the end of this manual.

2   Before attempting to diagnose an electrical fault, first study the appropriate wiring diagram to obtain a complete understanding of the components included in the particular circuit concerned. The possible sources of a fault can be narrowed down by noting if other components related to the circuit are operating properly. If several components or circuits fail at one time, the problem is likely to be related to a shared fuse or earth connection.

3   Electrical problems usually stem from simple causes, such as loose or corroded connections, a faulty earth connection, a blown fuse, a melted fusible link, or a faulty relay (refer to Section 11 for details of testing relays). Visually inspect the condition of all fuses, wires and connections in a problem circuit before testing the components. Use the wiring diagrams to determine which terminal connections will need to be checked in order to pinpoint the trouble-spot.

4   The basic tools required for electrical fault-finding include a circuit tester or voltmeter (a 12-volt bulb with a set of test leads can also be used for certain tests); a self-powered test light (sometimes known as a continuity tester); an ohmmeter (to measure resistance); a battery and

set of test leads; and a jumper wire, preferably with a circuit breaker or fuse incorporated, which can be used to bypass suspect wires or electrical components. Before attempting to locate a problem with test instruments, use the wiring diagram to determine where to make the connections.

5   To find the source of an intermittent wiring fault (usually due to a poor or dirty connection, or damaged wiring insulation), a 'wiggle' test can be performed on the wiring. This involves wiggling the wiring by hand to see if the fault occurs as the wiring is moved. It should be possible to narrow down the source of the fault to a particular section of wiring. This method of testing can be used in conjunction with any of the tests described in the following sub-Sections.

6   Apart from problems due to poor connections, two basic types of fault can occur in an electrical circuit – open-circuit, or short-circuit.

7   Open-circuit faults are caused by a break somewhere in the circuit, which prevents current from flowing. An open-circuit fault will prevent a component from working, but will not cause the relevant circuit fuse to blow.

8   Short-circuit faults are caused by a 'short' somewhere in the circuit, which allows the current flowing in the circuit to 'escape' along an alternative route, usually to earth. Short-circuit faults are normally caused by a breakdown in wiring insulation, which allows a feed wire to touch either another wire, or an earthed component such as the bodyshell. A short-circuit fault will normally cause the relevant circuit fuse to blow.

Finding an open-circuit

9   To check for an open-circuit, connect one lead of a circuit tester or voltmeter to either the negative battery terminal or a known good earth.

10   Connect the other lead to a connector in the circuit being tested, preferably nearest to the battery or fuse.

11   Switch on the circuit, bearing in mind that some circuits are live only when the ignition switch is moved to a particular position.

12   If voltage is present (indicated either by the tester bulb lighting or a voltmeter reading, as applicable), this means that the section of the circuit between the relevant connector and the battery is problem-free.

13   Continue to check the remainder of the circuit in the same fashion.

14   When a point is reached at which no voltage is present, the problem must lie between that point and the previous test point with voltage. Most problems can be traced to a broken, corroded or loose connection.

Finding a short-circuit

15   To check for a short-circuit, first disconnect the load(s) from the circuit (loads are the components which draw current from a circuit, such as bulbs, motors, heating elements, etc).

16   Remove the relevant fuse from the circuit, and connect a circuit tester or voltmeter to the fuse connections.

17   Switch on the circuit, bearing in mind that some circuits are live only when the ignition switch is moved to a particular position.

18   If voltage is present (indicated either by the tester bulb lighting or a voltmeter reading, as applicable), this means that there is a short-circuit.

19   If no voltage is present, but the fuse still blows with the load(s) connected, this indicates an internal fault in the load(s).

Finding an earth fault

20   The battery negative terminal is connected to 'earth' – the metal of the engine/transmission unit and the car body – and most systems are wired so that they only receive a positive feed, the current returning via the metal of the car body. This means that the component mounting and the body form part of that circuit. Loose or corroded mountings can therefore cause a range of electrical faults, ranging from total failure of a circuit, to a puzzling partial fault. In particular, lights may shine dimly (especially when another circuit sharing the same earth point is in operation), motors (eg wiper motors or the radiator cooling fan motor) may run slowly, and the operation of one circuit may have an apparently-unrelated effect on another. Note that on many vehicles, earth straps are used between certain components, such as the engine/transmission and the body, usually where there is no metal-to-metal contact between components due to flexible rubber mountings, etc.

21   To check whether a component is properly earthed, disconnect the battery and connect one lead of an ohmmeter to a known good earth point. Connect the other lead to the wire or earth connection being tested. The resistance reading should be zero; if not, check the connection as follows.

22   If an earth connection is thought to be faulty, dismantle the connection and clean back to bare metal both the bodyshell and the wire terminal or the component earth connection mating surface. Be careful to remove all traces of dirt and corrosion, then use a knife to trim away any paint, so that a clean metal-to-metal joint is made. On reassembly, tighten the joint fasteners securely; if a wire terminal is being refitted, use serrated washers between the terminal and the bodyshell to ensure a clean and secure connection. When the connection is remade, prevent the onset of corrosion in the future by applying a coat of petroleum jelly or silicone-based grease or by spraying on (at regular intervals) a proprietary ignition sealer such as Holts Damp Start, or a water-dispersant lubricant such as Holts Wet Start.

---

3   Battery – testing and charging

General

1   In normal use, the battery should not require charging from an external source, unless very heavy use is made of electrical equipment over a series of journeys that are too short to allow the charging system to keep pace with demand. Otherwise, a need for regular recharging points to a fault either in the battery or in the charging system.

2   If, however, the vehicle is laid up for long periods (in excess of thirty days at a time) the battery will lose approximately 1% of its charge per week. This figure is for a disconnected battery; if the battery is left connected, circuits such as the clock and the radio tuning memory (where applicable) will drain it at a faster rate. To prevent this happening, always disconnect the battery negative lead whenever the vehicle is to be laid up for a long period. To keep the battery fully charged, it should be given regular 'refresher' charges every six weeks or so. This is particularly important on 'maintenance-free' batteries, which will suffer permanent reduction of charge capacity if allowed to become fully discharged.

Testing

3   If a discharged battery is suspected, the simplest test for most owners is as follows. Leave the battery disconnected for at least two hours, then measure the (open-circuit, or no-load) voltage using a sensitive voltmeter connected across the battery terminals. Compare the reading obtained with the following table.

Voltmeter reading	Charge condition
10.50 volts	Fully-discharged – scrap battery
12.30 volts	50% charged
12.48 volts	75% charged
12.66 volts or more	Fully-charged

4   Electrolyte level checking is described in Chapter 1. If frequent topping-up is required and the battery case is not fractured, the battery is being over-charged; the voltage regulator will have to be checked.

5   If the vehicle covers a very small annual mileage, it is worthwhile checking the specific gravity of the electrolyte every three months to determine the state of charge of the battery. Use a hydrometer to make the check, and compare the results with the following table.

	Normal climates	Tropics
Discharged	1.120	1.080
Half-charged	1.200	1.160
Fully-charged	1.280	1.230

6   If the battery condition is suspect, first check the specific gravity of electrolyte in each cell. A variation of 0.040 or more between any cells indicates loss of electrolyte, or deterioration of the internal plates.

7   A further test can be made only by a battery specialist, using a battery heavy-discharge meter. Alternatively, connect a voltmeter across the battery terminals and operate the starter motor with the ignition coil HT lead disconnected from the distributor and earthed, and with the headlights, heated rear window and heater blower switched on. If the voltmeter reading remains above approximately 9.5 volts, the battery condition is satisfactory. If the voltmeter reading drops below 9.5 volts and the battery has already been charged, it is proved faulty.

Charging

8   In Winter, when heavy demand is placed on the battery (starting from cold and using more electrical equipment), it is a good idea occasionally to have the battery fully charged from an external source. The battery's bench charge rate depends on its code (see a Skoda dealer for details); for most owners, the best method will be to use a trickle-charger overnight, charging at a rate of 1.5 amps. Rapid 'boost' charges which are claimed to restore the power of the battery in 1 to 2 hours are **not** recommended, as they can cause serious damage to the battery plates through overheating, and may cause a sealed battery to explode.

9   Ideally, the battery should be removed from the vehicle before charging, and moved to a well-ventilated area. As a minimum precaution, both battery terminal leads must be disconnected (disconnect the negative lead first) before connecting the charger leads (Section 1). **Warning:** *The battery will be emitting significant quantities of (highly-inflammable) hydrogen gas during charging and for approximately 15 minutes afterwards; do not allow sparks or naked flames near the battery, or it may explode.*

10   Continue to charge the battery until all cells are gassing vigorously, and no further rise in specific gravity or increase in no-load voltage is noted over a four-hour period. When charging is complete, turn the charger off **before** disconnecting the leads from the battery.

---

4   Battery – removal and refitting

Removal

1   First check that all electrical components are switched off, to avoid a spark occurring as the negative lead is disconnected.

2   Slacken the negative terminal clamp nut, then lift the clamp and negative lead from the terminal. This is the terminal to disconnect before working on any electrical component on the vehicle. If the terminal is tight, carefully ease it off by moving it from side to side (photo).

3   Slacken the positive terminal clamp nut, then lift the clamp and lead from the terminal.

4   Unscrew the clamp bolts (photo), and remove the clamp from the front of the battery.

5   Lift the battery from the tray, keeping it upright and taking care not to allow it to contact your clothing.

6   Clean the battery terminal posts, clamps, tray and battery casing. If the bodywork is rusted as a result of battery acid spilling onto it, clean it thoroughly and re-paint. See Chapter 1 for more details.

7   Whenever the battery is removed, check it for cracks and leakage.

4.2 Disconnecting the battery negative lead

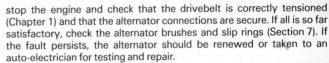

4.4 Battery clamp bolts (arrowed)

stop the engine and check that the drivebelt is correctly tensioned (Chapter 1) and that the alternator connections are secure. If all is so far satisfactory, check the alternator brushes and slip rings (Section 7). If the fault persists, the alternator should be renewed or taken to an auto-electrician for testing and repair.

3   If the alternator output is suspect even though the warning light functions correctly, the regulated voltage may be checked as follows.

4   Connect a voltmeter across the battery terminals and start the engine.

5   Increase engine speed until the voltmeter reading remains steady; this should be approximately 13 to 14 volts, and certainly no less than 12.5, nor more than 14.5 volts.

6   Switch on as many electrical accessories (eg the headlights, heated rear window and heater blower) as possible, and check that the alternator maintains the regulated voltage at around 13 to 14 volts. Increase the engine speed slightly if necessary to keep the voltage up.

7   If the regulated voltage is not as stated, the fault may be due to worn brushes, worn or damaged slip rings, weak brush springs, a faulty voltage regulator, a faulty diode or a severed phase winding. The brushes and slip rings may be checked and the voltage regulator renewed (Section 7), but if the fault persists, the alternator should be renewed or taken to an auto-electrician for testing and repair.

Refitting

8   Refitting is the reverse of the removal procedure. Ensure that the terminal posts and leads are cleaned before re-connection. Smear petroleum jelly on the terminals after reconnecting the leads. Always connect the positive terminal clamp first, and the negative terminal clamp last.

5 Charging system – testing

1   If the ignition warning light fails to come on when the ignition is switched on (and the battery is not dead), first check the alternator wiring connections for security. If satisfactory, check that the warning light bulb has not blown and is secure in its holder (Section 14). If the light still fails to come on, check the continuity of the warning light feed wire from the alternator to the bulbholder. If all is satisfactory, the alternator is at fault, and should be renewed or taken to an auto-electrician for testing and repair.

2   If the ignition warning light comes on when the engine is running,

6 Alternator – removal and refitting

Removal

1   Disconnect the battery negative lead.

2   Disconnect the wires from the rear of the alternator, noting their relative terminal positions (photo).

3   Remove the alternator drivebelt (Chapter 1).

4   Remove the oil filter (Chapter 1), having placed a suitable container under the filter adaptor to catch the spilt oil. Unless the filter was installed only recently, it should be discarded and a new filter should be installed on reassembly. Common sense suggests that the engine oil should be changed at the same time.

5   Unscrew the alternator clamp and pivot bolts (photo), and manoeuvre the alternator out of the vehicle.

6   The alternator mounting bracket can be unbolted from the cylinder block/crankcase if required.

7   If the alternator is to be renewed, the pulley may have to be transferred to the new unit. Clamp the pulley firmly in a vice with padded jaws and unscrew the pulley nut, taking care not to damage the pulley. Withdraw the pulley. On reassembly, apply a little thread-locking compound before tightening the pulley nut.

6.2 Alternator wiring connections (arrowed)

6.5 Removing the alternator pivot bolt

Refitting

8   Refitting is the reverse of the removal procedure, noting the following points.

   (a) Tighten the alternator clamp and pivot bolts loosely, then refit the drivebelt and adjust it (Chapter 1) before tightening the bolts to their specified torque wrench settings.
   (b) Connect the alternator wiring.
   (c) Fit the oil filter (see paragraph 4 above).
   (d) Refill the engine with oil, or check the oil level and top-up if necessary (Chapter 1).

7   Alternator brushes and voltage regulator – renewal

Note: The vast majority of actual alternator faults are due to the voltage regulator or to the brushes. If the renewal of either of these assemblies does not cure the fault, the advice of an expert should be sought as to the best approach; for most owners, the best course of action will be to renew the alternator as a complete unit. In many cases, overhaul will not be viable, on economic grounds alone.

1   While it is physically possible to remove the voltage regulator and brushbox assembly with the alternator in place on the vehicle, owners are advised to remove the alternator (Section 6) so that it can be serviced in clean working conditions.
2   Disconnect the voltage regulator/brushbox electrical lead (photo).
3   Unscrew the two screws securing the voltage regulator and brushbox assembly to the alternator, and remove the voltage regulator/brushbox from the alternator (photo).
4   In most cases, the brushes will have wear-limit marks in the form of a groove etched along one face of each brush; when these marks are erased by wear, the brushes are worn out. If no marks are provided, measure the protrusion of each brush from the brushbox end to the tip of the brush. No dimension is given by Skoda, but as a rough guide, 5 mm should be regarded as a minimum. If either brush is worn to or below this amount, renew the voltage regulator and brushbox assembly.
5   If the brushes are still serviceable, clean them with a solvent-moistened cloth. Check that the brush spring pressure is equal for both brushes, and holds the brushes securely against the slip rings. If in doubt about the condition of the brushes and springs, compare them with new components.
6   Inspect the slip rings through the brushbox window in the alternator. Clean the rings using a non-greasy solvent if they are dirty. If the rings are damaged or badly burnt, the alternator will have to be renewed or reconditioned.
7   Refitting is the reverse of the removal procedure. Note however

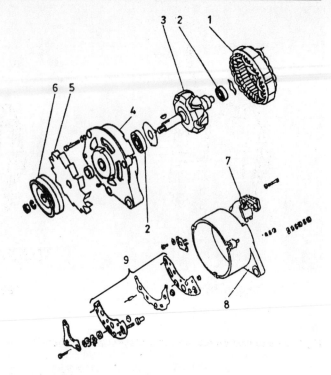

Fig. 12.1 Exploded view of alternator (Sec 7)

1	Stator assembly	6	Pulley
2	Bearing	7	Voltage regulator and
3	Rotor assembly		brushbox assembly
4	Body – front	8	Body – rear
5	Alternator cooling fan	9	Rectifier assembly

that if the voltage regulator has been renewed, repolarisation may be necessary as described in the following paragraphs.

Repolarisation after voltage regulator renewal

8   Three makes of voltage regulator have been used. Those fitted to early models (up to 1991) are marked 'DLR-2' or 'Tesla'. The type fitted to later models (1992-on) is marked 'PAL' (Fig. 12.2).
9   The 'DLR-2' and 'Tesla' regulators are interchangeable with no problems. If the 'PAL' regulator is to be fitted to an earlier alternator, or vice-versa, the alternator rotor must be repolarised as follows.

7.2 Disconnecting the voltage regulator/brushbox electrical lead

7.3 Removing the voltage regulator/brushbox from the alternator

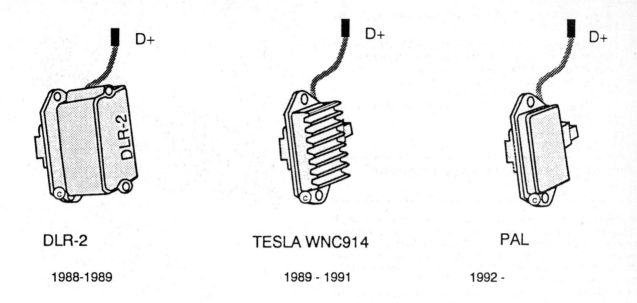

Fig. 12.2 Identification of alternator voltage regulators (Sec 7)

DLR-2	TESLA WNC914	PAL
1988-1989	1989 - 1991	1992 -

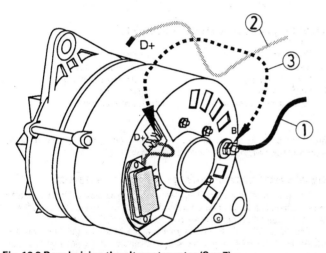

Fig. 12.3 Repolarising the alternator rotor (Sec 7)

1 *Main harness B + lead*	3 *Join for one second*
2 *Main harness D + lead*	

10   Having refitted the assembled alternator to the engine, reconnect the main alternator lead (B +) and reconnect the battery. Connect the regulator D + lead to the alternator, but do not reconnect the wiring harness D + lead yet.

11   Use a short length of insulated wire, bared at each end, to join the B + and D + terminals on the alternator for approximately one second (Fig. 12.3). Be careful not to touch the live end of the wire against any other metal. Remove the length of wire.

12   Reconnect the original D + lead to the alternator.

13   Run the engine, and check that the alternator is charging correctly.

14   If the repolarising process is not carried out, no harm will result, but the alternator will not produce a charge.

8   Starting system – testing

Note: *Refer to the warnings given in 'Safety first!' and in Section 1 of this Chapter before starting work.*

1   If the starter motor fails to operate when the switch is operated, the following may be the cause.

   (a)   The battery is faulty.
   (b)   The electrical connections between the switch, solenoid, battery and starter motor are somewhere failing to pass the necessary current from the battery through the starter to earth.
   (c)   The solenoid is faulty.
   (d)   The starter motor is mechanically or electrically defective.

2   To check the battery, switch on the headlights. If they dim after a few seconds, the battery is discharged; recharge (Section 3) or renew the battery. If the lights glow brightly, operate the ignition switch and see what happens to the lights. If they dim, then you know that power is reaching the starter motor; therefore the starter motor must be removed and renewed or overhauled to cure the fault. If the lights stay bright (and no clicking sound can be heard from the solenoid) there is a fault in the circuit or solenoid; see below. If the starter turns slowly when switched on, but the battery is in good condition, then either the starter must be faulty or there is considerable resistance in the circuit.

3   If the circuit is suspected, disconnect the battery terminals (including the earth connection to the body), the starter/solenoid wiring and the engine/transmission earth lead, thoroughly clean their connections and refit them, then use a meter or test light to check that full battery voltage is available at the solenoid battery positive terminal, and that the earth is sound. Smear petroleum jelly around the battery terminals to prevent corrosion. Corroded connections are the most frequent cause of electric system malfunctions.

4   If the battery and all connections are in good condition, check the circuit first by disconnecting the command (small) wire from the solenoid. Connect a meter or test light between the wire end and the terminal, and check that the wire is live when the ignition switch is operated. If it is, then the circuit is sound; if not, proceed to paragraph 7.

5   The solenoid contacts can be checked by putting a voltmeter or test light across the positive cable connection on the starter side of the solenoid and earth. When the switch is operated, there should be a reading or lighted bulb. If there is no reading or lighted bulb, the solenoid is faulty, and should be renewed.

6   If the circuit and solenoid are proved sound, the fault must be in the starter motor; remove it (Section 9) and check the brushes (Section 10). If the fault does not lie in the brushes, the motor windings must be faulty; in this event the motor must be renewed, unless an auto-electrical specialist can be found who will overhaul the unit at a cost significantly less than that of a new or exchange starter motor.

7   If the circuit is thought to be faulty, check it using the equipment and procedures outlined in Section 2 of this Chapter, referring to the wiring diagrams for full details.

9.2 Starter motor wiring connections (arrowed)

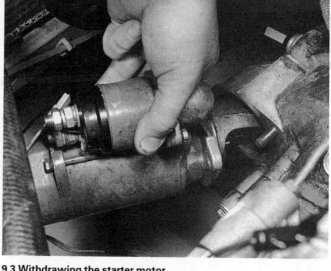

9.3 Withdrawing the starter motor

9   Starter motor – removal and refitting

Removal

1   Disconnect the battery negative lead.
2   Pull off the protective rubber boot and disconnect the wires from the rear of the starter solenoid, noting their relative terminal positions (photo).
3   While supporting the weight of the starter motor, unscrew the two starter motor-to-transmission nuts and withdraw the motor (photo).

Refitting

4   Refitting is the reverse of the removal procedure; tighten the nuts to the specified torque.

10   Starter motor – brush and solenoid renewal

General

1   While it is physically possible to remove the solenoid and brushes with the starter motor in place on the vehicle, owners are advised to remove the starter (Section 9) so that it can be serviced in clean working conditions.

Brushes

Removal

2   Remove the starter motor rear cover by undoing the small retaining bolt (photo).
3   To remove a brush for inspection, release the brush spring with a

10.2 Removing the starter motor end cover bolt

10.3A Releasing a brush spring

10.3B Withdrawing a brush

10.4 Measuring length of starter motor brushes

10.8 Removing the lower terminal nut

10.10 Removing the starter motor solenoid

Fig. 12.4 Exploded view of starter motor (Sec 10)

1 Starter solenoid plunger and spring
2 Starter solenoid coil assembly
3 Bridge
4 Spring
5 Starter solenoid switch and cover assembly
6 Lever
7 Motor drive end bracket
8 Pinion and freewheel assembly
9 Armature
10 Yoke and field coils
11 Bush
12 Brush
13 Brushbox assembly
14 End cover

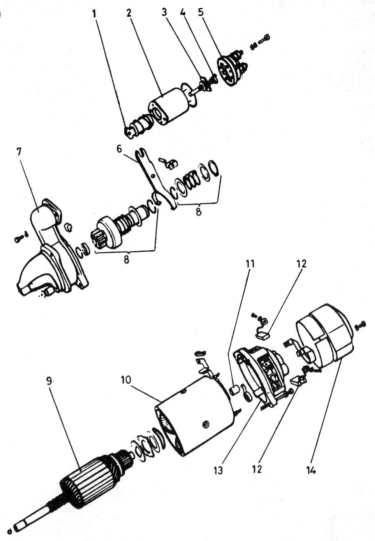

small screwdriver and unscrew the lead screw, then withdraw the brush from its guide (photos).
4   In most cases, the brushes will have wear-limit marks in the form of a groove etched along one face of each brush; when the brushes are worn down to these marks, they are worn out and must be renewed. If no marks are provided, measure the length of each brush. No dimension is given by Skoda, but as a rough guide, 10 mm should be regarded as a minimum (photo).
5   If the brushes are badly worn, they must be renewed as a set.
6   If the brushes are still serviceable, clean them with a solvent-moistened cloth. Check that the brush spring pressure is equal for all brushes, and holds the brushes securely against the commutator. If in doubt about the condition of the brushes and springs, compare them with new components.

Refitting

7   Refitting is the reverse of the removal procedure.

Solenoid

Removal

8   Undo the lower terminal nut on the back of the solenoid, and gently bend the conductor strap over the stud (photo).
9   Unscrew the two bolts securing the solenoid to the motor drive end bracket.
10   Release the solenoid plunger from the starter engaging lever, then withdraw the solenoid, noting the spring (photo).

Refitting

11   Refitting is the reverse of the removal procedure. Clean the

solenoid, its plunger and the motor/solenoid mating surfaces carefully, and lubricate the plunger/starter engaging lever surfaces with a very light smear of general-purpose grease (Duckhams LB10).

11   Fuses, relays and flasher unit – general information

Fuses

1   The main fuses are found in the fusebox located in the front passenger footwell, attached to the underside of the facia. Early models have ceramic fuses; later models have blade type fuses. Additional in-line fuses may be found in the wiring to certain items. The radio fitted by Skoda dealers is protected by its own fuse, which is found in a holder on the back of the radio.
2   Access to the fuses is gained by unclipping the cover (photo).
3   To remove a fuse, first switch off the circuit concerned (or the ignition), then pull the fuse from its terminals. The wire within the fuse is clearly visible; if the fuse has blown, it will be broken or melted.
4   Always renew a fuse with one of an identical rating; never use a fuse with a different rating from the original, or substitute anything else. Never renew a fuse more than once without tracing the source of the trouble. The fuse rating is stamped on top of the fuse; note that the fuses are also colour-coded for easy recognition.
5   If a new fuse blows immediately, find the cause before renewing it

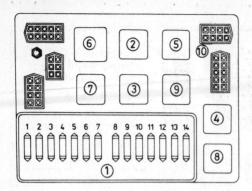

Fig. 12.5 Fusebox and relay board layout – models from 1989 to 1992 (Sec 11)

1 Fuses	6 Relay – front wiper intermittent
2 Relay – rear foglights	control
3 Relay – front foglights	7 Relay – heated rear window
4 Relay – headlight dipped	8 Relay – headlight main beam
beam	9 Relay – fuses 2, 3 & 4 (see
5 Relay – spare	Specifications)
	10 Terminal block

again; a short to earth as a result of faulty insulation is most likely. Where a fuse protects more than one circuit, try to isolate the defect by switching on each circuit in turn (if possible) until the fuse blows again.
6   If any of the spare fuses are used, always renew them immediately so that a spare of each rating is available.

Fusebox – removal and refitting
Removal
7   Disconnect the battery negative lead.

8   Remove the fuse cover.
9   Unscrew the two bolts securing the fusebox to the facia (photo), then lower it to the floor.
10   Unplug the connector plugs from the fusebox, making careful notes as to their relative positions.
11   Undo the terminal nut and remove the fusebox supply cable (photo). Remove the fusebox.

Refitting
12   Refitting is the reverse of the removal procedure; ensure that the wiring is correctly reconnected and routed.

Relays
13   The Specifications Section of this Chapter gives full information on the location and function of the various relays fitted; refer to the relevant wiring diagram for details of wiring connections.
14   A relay is an electrically-operated switch that is used for the following reasons.

(a)   A relay can switch a heavy current at a distance, thus allowing the use of lighter-gauge wiring and switch contacts.
(b)   A relay can receive more than one control input, unlike a mechanical switch.
(c)   A relay can have a 'timer' function – eg a windscreen intermittent wiper relay..

15   If a circuit or system controlled by a relay develops a fault and the relay is suspect, operate the system; if the relay is functioning, it should be possible to hear it click as it is energized. If this is the case, the fault lies with the components or wiring of the system. If the relay is not being energized, then either the relay is not receiving a main supply or a switching voltage, or the relay itself is faulty. (Do not overlook the relay socket terminals when tracing faults.) Testing is by the substitution of a known good unit, but be careful; while some relays are identical in appearance and in operation, others look similar but perform different functions.

11.2 Unclipping the fuse cover

11.9 Remove the two bolts securing the fusebox to the facia

11.11 Removing the fusebox supply cable

11.16 Fitting a relay

11.17 Direction indicator/hazard warning flasher unit (arrowed) behind central switch panel

Fig. 12.6 Fusebox and relay board layout – 1992 and later models (Sec 11)

1 *Fuses*
2 *Relay – rear foglights*
3 *Relay – front foglights*
4 *Relay – headlight dipped beam*
5 *Relay – spare*
6 *Relay – front wiper intermittent control*
7 *Relay – heated rear window*
8 *Relay – headlight main beam*
9 *Relay – fuses 5, 6 & 7 (see Specifications)*
10 *Terminal block*
11 *Diode*

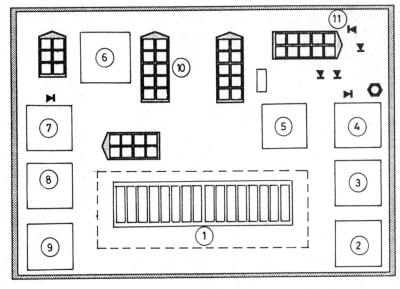

16   To renew a relay, disconnect the battery, then simply pull the old relay directly from the socket and press in the new relay (photo). **Caution:** *The relay socket terminals are easily damaged by clumsy handling.* Reconnect the battery on completion.

Flasher unit

17   The direction indicator/hazard warning flasher unit is accessible after removal of the central switch panel (Section 12) (photo).
18   Before renewing a suspect flasher unit, check that the problem is not a blown bulb or a poor earth.

12 Switches – removal and refitting

Note: *Disconnect the battery negative lead before removing any switch, and reconnect the lead after refitting the switch.*

Ignition switch

1   Refer to Chapter 10 for details of switch removal and refitting. A Skoda dealer will be able to tell you whether the switch can be obtained separately from the steering lock.

Steering column multi-function switches
Removal
2   Remove the steering column upper and lower shrouds (Chapter 10).

3   Unplug the switch wiring connectors (photo).
4   Unscrew the switch retaining screw (photo) and withdraw the switch.

Refitting
5   Refitting is the reverse of the removal procedure.

Instrument panel switches
Removal
6   The headlight, sidelight, heated rear window and hazard warning switches are housed in the central switch panel. The front foglight (where fitted) and rear foglight switches are housed in the auxiliary switch panel. All are removed as follows.
7   To remove a switch panel, unscrew the single retaining screw (photo), withdraw the panel from the facia and unplug the wiring connectors.
8   To remove a switch from the panel, pull the front cover from the switch, then carefully bend back the four metal tabs securing the switch to the switch panel, and withdraw the switch (photos).

Refitting
9   Refitting is the reverse of the removal procedure.

Interior light switches
10   The interior light is controlled by a switch mounted in each (front) door pillar, and by a switch in the light assembly itself.
11   To remove a door pillar switch, remove its retaining screw (photo) and ease the switch out of the pillar, then disconnect the switch wire,

12.3 Unplug the wiring connectors ...

12.4 ... and undo retaining screw to remove steering column switches

12.7 Removing a switch panel retaining screw

12.8A Pull the front cover from the switch ...

12.8B ... carefully bend back the metal retaining tabs ...

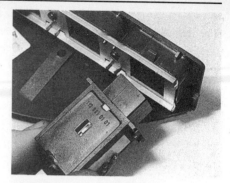

12.8C ... and withdraw the switch

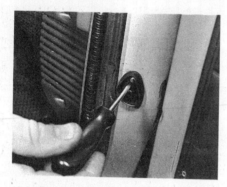

12.11 Removing a pillar-mounted interior light switch

12.13 Oil pressure switch

taking care not to allow the wire to drop back into the pillar – tape it to the pillar if in doubt. Refitting is the reverse of the removal procedure.
12   The roof-mounted switch is part of the light assembly; refer to Section 14 of this Chapter for details of removal and refitting.

Oil pressure switch

Removal

13   The switch is located on the engine block, adjacent to the oil filter (photo).
14   On removal, pull off the wiring connector, then unscrew the switch; use clean rag to pack the opening in the block, to minimise oil loss.

Refitting

15   On refitting, clean the switch threads and renew the sealing washer, if one is fitted; if a sealing washer is not fitted, apply a thin smear of suitable sealant to the threads.

16   Remove the packing rag, and screw in the switch; tighten it to the specified torque.

Radiator cooling fan thermostatic switch

17   Refer to Chapter 3 for details of switch removal, refitting and testing.

Reversing light switch

18   Refer to Chapter 7 for details of switch removal, refitting and testing.

Stop-light switch

19   Refer to Chapter 9 for details of switch removal, refitting and testing.

Handbrake switch

20   Refer to Chapter 9 for details of switch removal, refitting and testing.

13.3 Removing the headlight bulb retainer

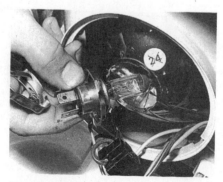

13.4 Removing a headlight bulb

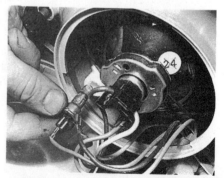

13.7 Removing front sidelight bulb from headlight unit

13.10 Removing a front direction indicator bulb

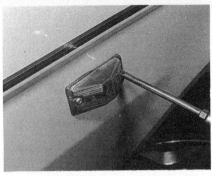

13.13 Removing a direction indicator side repeater lens

13.15 Removing a direction indicator side repeater bulb

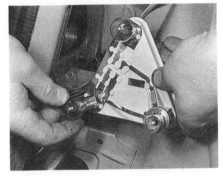

13.19 Removing a bulb from the rear light cluster

13.22 Remove the rear foglight lens ...

13.23 ... to renew the rear foglight bulb

13.26 To remove number plate light lens, depress plastic tab and slide lens towards number plate

13.27 Removing the number plate light bulb

13 Bulbs (exterior lights) – renewal

General

1 Whenever a bulb is renewed, note the following points.

(a) *Switch off the lights concerned before starting work.*
(b) *Remember that, if the light has just been in use, the bulb may be extremely hot.*
(c) *Always check the bulb contacts and holder, ensuring that there is clean metal-to-metal contact between the bulb and its live contact(s) and earth. Clean off any corrosion or dirt before fitting a new bulb.*
(d) *Wherever bayonet-type bulbs are fitted, ensure that the live contact(s) bear firmly against the bulb contact.*
(e) *Always ensure that the new bulb is of the correct rating, and that it is completely clean before fitting it; this applies particularly to headlight bulbs (see below).*

Headlight

2 Working in the engine compartment, unscrew the plastic cover from the rear of the light unit.
3 Unplug the wiring connector, then press in the retainer and twist it anti-clockwise (photo).
4 Withdraw the bulb (photo).
5 When handling the new bulb, use a tissue or clean cloth to avoid touching the glass with the fingers; moisture and grease from the skin can cause blackening and rapid failure of this type of bulb. If the glass is accidentally touched, wipe it clean using methylated spirit.
6 Refitting is the reverse of the removal procedure; ensure that the new bulb's locating tabs align with the reflector slots.

Front sidelight

7 Working in the engine compartment, pull the bulbholder from its rubber mounting on the headlight reflector (photo).
8 Press the bulb into the holder, twist anti-clockwise and remove.
9 Refitting is the reverse of the removal procedure.

14.2 Removing the interior light unit

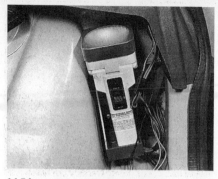

14.5 Luggage compartment light

14.7 Removing bulb from luggage compartment light

14.10 Instrument panel warning light bulb and holder

14.15 Heater panel illumination bulb and holder

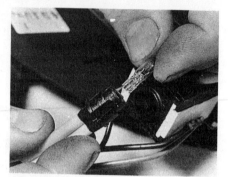

14.20 Removing a switch illumination bulb

Front direction indicator

10 Working in the engine compartment, rotate the bulbholder anti-clockwise and unclip it from the rear of the headlight unit. It may be necessary to unplug the wiring connector first (photo).
11 Press the bulb into the holder, twist anti-clockwise and remove.
12 Refitting is the reverse of the removal procedure.

Direction indicator side repeater

13 Working on the outside of the vehicle, remove the two screws securing the lens to the front wing (photo).
14 Depress the two tangs securing the bulbholder to the front wing and withdraw it.
15 Press the bulb into the holder, twist anti-clockwise and remove (photo).
16 Refitting is the reverse of the removal procedure, taking care not to overtighten the lens screws.

Rear light cluster

17 Open the tailgate (where applicable) and remove the wiring connector from the back of the rear light cluster bulbholder.
18 Lift the metal tang, and withdraw the light cluster bulbholder.
19 The three bulbs housed in the cluster are of the bayonet type, and can be removed by pushing the bulb into the holder and twisting anti-clockwise (photo).
20 Refitting is the reverse of the removal procedure.

Rear foglight

21 The rear foglight is housed in the light cluster attached to the tailgate, along with the reversing light.
22 Working on the outside of the vehicle, remove the two screws securing the lens (photo).
23 Press the bulb into its holder, twist anti-clockwise and remove (photo).
24 Refitting is the reverse of the removal procedure.

Reversing light

25 The procedure for renewing the reversing light bulb is identical to that of the rear foglight bulb (see above).

Number plate light

26 Working on the outside of the vehicle, depress the plastic tab securing the lens, and slide the lens towards the number plate to release (photo).
27 Press the bulb into its holder, twist anti-clockwise and remove (photo).
28 Refitting is the reverse of the removal procedure.

14　Bulbs (interior lights) – renewal

General

1 Refer to Section 13, paragraph 1. In the case of circuits which cannot be switched off (for instance the interior lights), remove the appropriate fuse or disconnect the battery earth lead before starting work.

Interior light

2 Remove the light unit by using a small flat-bladed screwdriver to prise it out of the roof console (photo).
3 The bulb is of the festoon type, which can be prised out of its contacts.
4 Refitting is the reverse of the removal procedure, but ensure that the contacts are sufficiently tensioned to hold the bulb firmly – bend them carefully if necessary.

Luggage compartment light

5 The luggage compartment light also doubles as a rechargeable torch. To renew the bulb, first unclip the torch from its holder (photo).
6 Remove the lens/reflector unit by prising it away from the body of the torch.
7 The bulb is a bayonet fitting; press the bulb into its holder, twist anti-clockwise and remove (photo).
8 Refitting is the reverse of the removal procedure.

Instrument panel illumination and warning lights

9 Remove the instrument panel (Section 19).

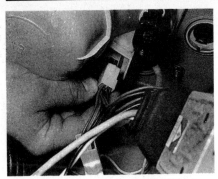

15.1 Disconnecting a headlight wiring connector

15.3 Removing a headlight unit – note retaining points (arrowed)

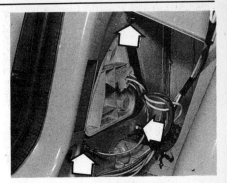

15.8 Rear light cluster retaining nuts (arrowed) – note earth lead under one nut

10   Remove the bulbholder from the rear of the instrument panel by twisting it anti-clockwise (photo).

11   The bulb is of the capless type; simply pull it from its holder.

12   Refitting is the reverse of the removal procedure.

Heater control panel illumination

13   Remove the central switch panel (Section 12).

14   Remove the bulbholder from the rear of the heater control panel by twisting it anti-clockwise.

15   The bulb is of the capless type; simply pull it from its holder (photo).

16   Refitting is the reverse of the removal procedure.

Switch illumination

17   The headlight, sidelight, heated rear window, hazard warning, front foglight (where fitted) and rear foglight switches are fitted with an illuminating bulb; some are also fitted with warning bulbs to show when the circuit concerned is operating.

18   Remove the appropriate switch panel as described in Section 12 of this Chapter.

19   Remove the bulbholder from the rear of the switch by twisting it anti-clockwise.

20   The bulb is of the capless type; simply pull it from its holder (photo).

21   Refitting is the reverse of the removal procedure.

15   Exterior light units – removal and refitting

Caution: *Switch off the lights concerned before starting work.*

Headlight unit

Removal

1   Working in the engine compartment, remove the wiring connectors from the headlight and the front direction indicator (photo).

2   Disconnect the headlight alignment control system actuator from the rear of the headlight unit (Section 17).

3   Undo the three retaining nuts and remove the headlight unit (photo).

Refitting

4   Refitting is the reverse of the removal procedure. Check the headlight beam alignment if necessary (Section 16).

Front direction indicator

5   The front direction indicator is an integral part of the headlight unit – for removal and refitting, see above.

Direction indicator side repeater

6   Refer to Section 13.

Rear light cluster

Removal

7   Remove the rear light cluster bulbholder (Section 13).

8   Undo the three retaining nuts, noting any earthing points, and remove the cluster (photo).

Refitting

9   Refitting is the reverse of the removal procedure.

Rear foglight and reversing light

Removal

10   Open the tailgate and remove the interior trim panel (Chapter 11) and the plastic membrane.

11   Remove the plastic covers from the securing nuts and undo the securing nuts, noting any earthing points.

12   Carefully pull the light units away from the tailgate, and disconnect the wiring connectors.

Refitting

13   Refitting is the reverse of the removal procedure.

Number plate lights

Removal

14   The number plate light units are housed in the tailgate exterior trim panel.

15   Remove the lens and bulb (Section 13), then use a small flat-bladed screwdriver to carefully prise the light unit from the tailgate trim panel.

16   Disconnect the light wiring connectors and remove.

Refitting

17   Refitting is the reverse of the removal procedure.

16   Headlight beam alignment – general information

1   It is advisable to have the headlight beam alignment checked and if necessary adjusted by a Skoda dealer using optical beam-setting equipment. Correct alignment of the headlight beams is most important, not only to ensure good vision for the driver, but also to protect other drivers from being dazzled.

2   The headlight alignment may be adjusted to compensate for the load being carried by turning a knob on the facia – see Section 17. The setting should be returned to the 'driver-only' position before any checks are made.

3   In an emergency, adjustment of the headlights may be made by turning the adjuster knobs on the rear of each headlight unit. The upper knob is for vertical adjustment, and the lower knob is for lateral adjustment (photo).

4   The vehicle should be at normal kerb weight, with no load in the boot. The headlight height-setting knobs should be in the normal-load position (as described above), and the tyres correctly inflated. Park the vehicle on level ground, approximately 5 metres (16 feet) in front of a flat wall or garage door, and bounce it to settle the suspension. Have an assistant sit in the driver's seat during the adjustment.

5   Draw a vertical line on the wall or door corresponding to the

16.3 Headlight beam adjustment knobs (arrowed)

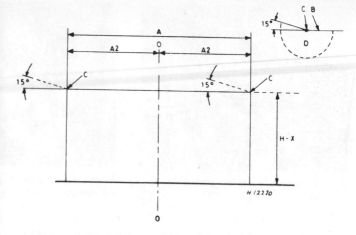

Fig. 12.7 Headlight beam alignment chart (Sec 16)

A   Distance between
     headlight centres
B   Light/dark boundary
C   Dipped beam centre
D   Dipped beam pattern

H   Height from ground to
     headlight centre
O   Car's centre-line
X   = 65 mm

centre-line of the vehicle. (This can be determined by marking with crayon the centres of the windscreen and rear window, then viewing the wall or door from the rear of the vehicle).

6   With the centre-line established, construct the other lines shown in Fig. 12.7.

7   Switch the headlights on to dipped beam. Cover one headlight with cloth. Working on the other light, use its two adjuster screws to bring the centre of the beam to the point 'C' on the appropriate side of the alignment chart.

8   Transfer the cloth to the adjusted headlight, and repeat the adjustment on the other.

9   While this will produce an acceptable setting, it is important to have accurate adjustments made at the earliest opportunity.

17   Headlight alignment control system – general information

1   The headlight beam alignment may be adjusted to compensate for the load being carried by turning a knob on the facia.

2   The system is hydraulically-operated using a special antifreezing solution, and comprises the facia-mounted control unit, an actuator

fitted to each headlight unit, and a pipe connecting each actuator with the control unit.

3   Note that the system is available only as a complete assembly. None of the component parts can be renewed separately.

4   The system can be checked by unclipping both actuators (see below) and comparing their range of movement. If they do not work together as a pair, the system is faulty and must be renewed. Similarly, if signs of fluid leaks appear on any part of the system, it must be renewed.

5   To remove the system, unclip each actuator from the rear of the headlight unit by rotating it anti-clockwise and pulling it sharply to release the balljoint, taking care not to damage the connecting pipe (photo).

6   Releasing them from any clamps or ties, trace the pipes back to the bulkhead, press in the large sealing grommet, and carefully pull the pipes and actuators into the passenger compartment.

7   Pull off the control knob, lever the scale panel from the facia (photo), then unscrew the control unit from the facia.

8   Remove the instrument panel (Section 19) and withdraw the system components.

9   Refitting is the reverse of the removal procedure.

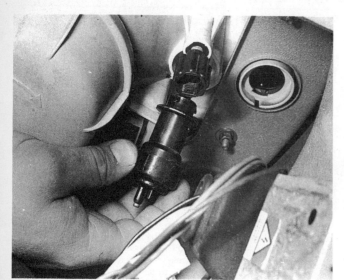

17.5 Unclipping a headlight alignment control system actuator

17.7 Removing the headlight alignment control system scale panel

18.1 Dim-dip unit

18 Dim-dip system – general information

Note: *The dim-dip system is not fitted to all models.*

1   The dim-dip unit is mounted on the forward face of the right-hand suspension turret, and controls the headlight circuit in such a way so as not to allow sidelights alone to be used while the ignition is switched on (photo).
2   With the ignition switched on, if the sidelights are also switched on, the dipped-beam headlights will come on too, at approximately one-sixth of their normal brightness (hence the term 'dim-dip').

3   The idea of the system is to prevent driving (in well-lit built-up areas) at night with only the sidelights on.
4   The dim-dip unit is a non-repairable item, and must be replaced if found to be faulty.

19 Instrument panel – removal and refitting

Removal
1   Disconnect the battery negative lead.
2   Remove the central and auxiliary switch panels (Section 12).
3   Lever the instrument cowl lower trim panel from its fixings (photo).
4   Undo the three screws securing the instrument cowl to the facia, and remove the instrument cowl (photo).
5   Undo the two screws securing the instrument panel to the facia (photo), and withdraw the instrument panel.
6   Unplug the wiring connectors, disconnect the speedometer drive cable (Section 21) and remove the instrument panel (photos).

Refitting
7   Refitting is the reverse of the removal procedure.

20 Instrument panel components – removal and refitting

General
1   Remove the instrument panel (Section 19), then proceed as described in the relevant sub-Section below.

Instruments
Testing
2   Refer to Chapter 3 for details of tests on the coolant temperature gauge circuit.

19.3 Removing the instrument cowl lower trim panel

19.4 Removing the instrument cowl

19.5 Instrument panel securing screws

19.6A Disconnecting instrument panel wiring connectors

19.6B Withdrawing the instrument panel

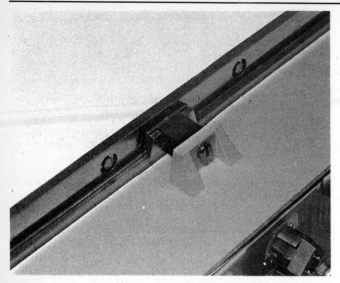

20.5 Securing screw on rear edge of instrument panel

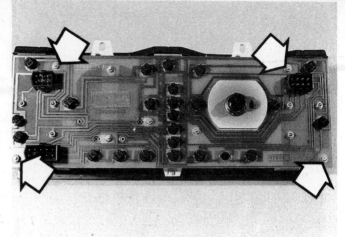

20.10 Printed circuit-to-instrument panel fixing nuts (arrowed)

3   Refer to Chapter 4 for details of tests on the fuel gauge circuit.

Removal
4   Undo the two securing screws, and remove the instrument panel top cover.
5   Undo the screws around the rear edge of the panel (photo), and separate the two halves. Note that at several points around the joint, adhesive has been used; carefully remove this using a sharp craft knife or scalpel.
6   Undo the nuts securing the particular instrument to the panel, and remove it.

Refitting
7   Refitting is the reverse of the removal procedure.

Printed circuit

Removal
8   Remove all panel illumination and warning bulbs from the rear of the panel (Section 14).
9   Undo the nuts securing the instruments to the panel.
10   Undo the nuts securing the printed circuit to the panel, and remove it (photo).

Refitting
11   Refitting is the reverse of the removal procedure.

21   Speedometer drive cable – removal and refitting

Removal
1   Remove the instrument panel (Section 19).
2   Unscrew the speedometer cable from the rear of the instrument panel, and withdraw the cable into the engine compartment (photo).
3   Working in the engine compartment, unscrew the cable from the speedometer drivegear, and remove it (photo).

Refitting
4   Refitting is the reverse of the removal procedure. Ensure that the cable is correctly routed, and be careful not to kink it.

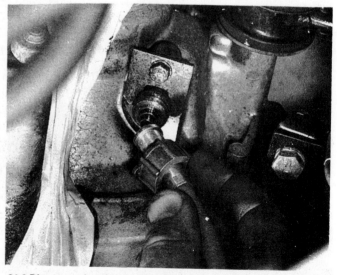

21.2 Disconnecting the speedometer cable from the instrument panel

21.3 Disconnecting the speedometer cable from the speedometer drive on the transmission

22.4 Horn and mounting bracket – adjuster screw (arrowed) is just visible

22 Horn – adjustment, removal and refitting

Adjustment

1   Unusually for a modern vehicle, the horn can be adjusted if its note is weak or unsatisfactory. Proceed on a trial-and-error basis, turning the adjuster screw on the rear of the horn a quarter-turn at a time in either direction and observing the effect (see photo 22.4).
2   When adjustment is satisfactory, lock the adjuster screw with a dab of paint.

Removal

3   Disconnect the battery negative lead.
4   Disconnect the horn positive feed wire, and unbolt the horn from its mounting bracket. Note the earth lead under one of the mounting nuts (photo).

Refitting

5   Refitting is the reverse of the removal procedure.

23 Heated rear window – general information

1   The rear window is heated by passing current through a resistive grid bonded to the inside of the glass.

2   The heater elements are fragile, and the following precautions should be observed.

   (a) *Do not allow luggage or other items to rub against the inside surface of the glass.*
   (b) *Do not stick labels over the elements.*
   (c) *Avoid scratching the elements when cleaning with rings on the fingers.*
   (d) *Clean the glass with water and detergent only, and rub in the direction of the elements using a soft cloth or chamois leather.*

3   Should an element be damaged so that the current is interrupted, a repair can be made using one of the conductive paints available from good motor accessory shops.
4   Note that the system draws a very high current, and therefore has its own relay. Operating the switch completes the circuit to energise the relay, and a supply is then drawn to feed the element and the switch warning light.

24 Seat belt warning system – general information

Note: *The seat belt warning system is not fitted to all models.*

1   When the ignition is switched to position 1, a buzzer will sound for approximately five seconds to remind you to fasten your seat belt.
2   The system is fed via the ignition switch. The buzzer is located underneath the driver's footwell panel, adjacent to the speaker – see photo 30.2.

25 Wiper arms – removal and refitting

Removal

1   Before removing a wiper arm, make sure that the motor is in the 'parked' position. To check this, operate the wipers as normal, then switch them off before they complete a sweep – the motor should return the wipers to the 'parked' position automatically. Stick a piece of masking tape on the glass, along the blade, to aid arm alignment on refitting.

Front

2   Pull the arm fully away from the glass until it locks; remove the blade only, if required (Chapter 1).
3   Prise off the cover to reveal the wiper-to-spindle nut (photo).

25.3 Prise off the cover to reveal the wiper-to-spindle nut

25.4 Removing a front wiper arm

25.7 Removing the rear wiper arm

7   Pull the arm from the spindle splines (photo). If necessary, use a wide-bladed screwdriver to prise off the arm.
8   Clean the splines of the arm, and of the spindle.

Refitting

9   Refitting is the reverse of the removal procedure; use the masking tape to ensure that the arm is refitted in its original position.

26   Windscreen wiper motor and linkage – removal and refitting

Motor
Removal

1   Make sure that the motor is in the 'parked' position (as described in Section 25 above), then disconnect the battery negative lead.
2   Undo the nut which connects the motor spindle to the wiper linkage crank arm (photo).
3   Undo the three bolts securing the wiper motor to the bracket (photo).
4   Disconnect the motor wiring connector and the motor earthing cable (photos).
5   Remove the motor.

Refitting

6   Refitting is the reverse of the removal procedure. Make sure that the motor is in the parked position before securing the linkage crank arm.

Motor and linkage
Removal

7   Make sure that the wipers are in the parked position, then remove both wiper arms (see Section 25).
8   Prise off their covers (photo), unscrew the linkage spindle housing nuts, then remove the rubber spacer under each.
9   Withdraw the motor and linkage assembly sufficiently to allow access to the motor wiring connector and earthing cable.
10   Disconnect the battery negative lead. Disconnect the motor wiring connector and the motor earthing cable.
11   Withdraw the motor and linkage assembly.
12   The assembly can now be dismantled, if required (photo).

Refitting

13   Refitting is the reverse of the removal procedure, noting the following points.

(a)   If the assembly was dismantled, refit the motor to the mounting bracket. With the motor in the parked position, the crank must be parallel to the main length of the mounting bracket, and pointing to the driver's side of the car.
(b)   Grease the bushes and spacer washers.
(c)   Ensure that the rubber spacers are correctly located.
(d)   Connect the motor wiring, and press the connector into its clip.
(e)   Check that the wipers operate correctly.

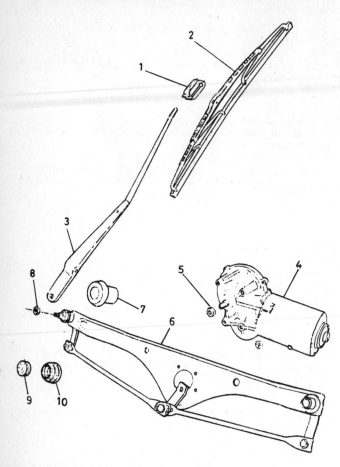

Fig. 12.8 Windscreen wiper motor and linkage (Secs 25 and 26)

1   Wiper blade swivel clip
2   Wiper blade
3   Wiper arm
4   Motor
5   Nut
6   Wiper linkage and motor mounting bracket
7   Upper rubber spacer
8   Wiper-to-spindle nut
9   Cover
10   Cover

4   Unscrew the wiper arm-to-spindle nut, and pull the arm from the spindle splines (photo). If necessary, use a wide-bladed screwdriver to prise off the arm.
5   Clean the splines of the arm, and of the spindle.

Rear

6   Pull the arm fully away from the glass until it locks; remove the blade only, if required (Chapter 1).

26.2 Wiper motor-to-linkage crank arm nut (arrowed)

26.3 Undoing the wiper motor-to-bracket bolts

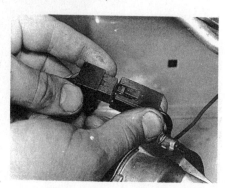

26.4A Disconnect the motor wiring connector ...

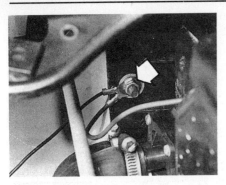

26.4B ... and the earthing point (arrowed)

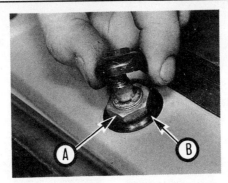

26.8 Removing linkage spindle housing nut cover – note linkage spindle housing nut (A) and rubber spacer (B)

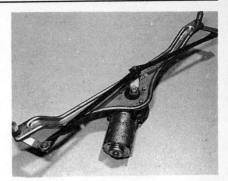

26.12 Windscreen wiper linkage and motor assembly. Note that the motor is not in the parked position

Fig. 12.9 Rear wiper motor (Secs 25 and 27)

1   Motor
2   Motor support bracket
3   End support bracket
4   Wheel box

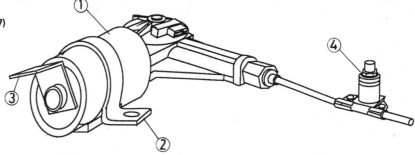

27   Rear window wiper motor – removal and refitting

Removal

1   Remove the tailgate interior trim panel (Chapter 11).
2   Disconnect the battery negative lead.
3   Remove the wiper arm and blade (Section 25).
4   Unscrew the spindle housing nut, then remove each washer and seal, noting their locations.
5   Unscrew the nut securing the motor end-support bracket, and the nuts and bolts securing the motor support bracket (photo).

6   Manoeuvre the motor out of the tailgate, and disconnect the motor wiring plug (photo).

Refitting

7   If a new motor is being fitted, note that changes in the wiring have been made for 1992 and later models. A later-type motor can be fitted to an early model without problems, but an early-type motor cannot be fitted to a later model without modifying the wiring. Consult a Skoda dealer if in doubt.
8   Refitting is the reverse of the removal procedure. If the nut or bolt securing the end-support bracket to the motor has been disturbed, do not overtighten it – it should be little more than finger-tight. Lock it using paint or thread-locking compound. Later models have a revised bracket which is a push fit on the motor end cover.

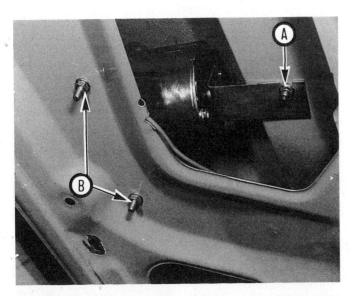

27.5 Rear wiper motor fixing points – end-support bracket (A) and support bracket (B)

27.6 Disconnecting the rear wiper motor wiring plug

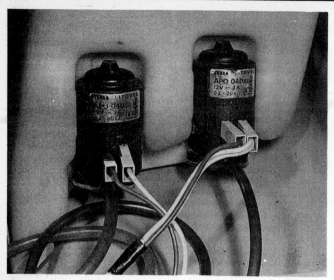

28.2 Washer system pumps

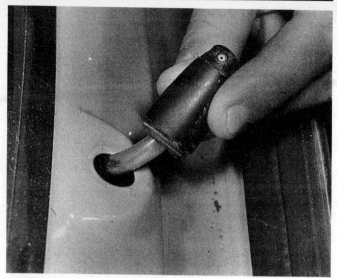

28.3 Removing a windscreen washer jet

28 Washer system components – removal and refitting

1   Refer to Chapter 1 for details of maintenance requirements.
2   The system comprises the reservoir, and either one or two pumps to direct flow to the windscreen and (if applicable) to the rear window, as required (photo).
3   The removal and refitting of all components is self-explanatory on examination (photo). Ensure that the tubes are not trapped when refitting the reservoir.
4   If the rear washer stops working, check that the problem is not caused by the blockage of the non-return valve, which is located in the rear washer tubing where it leaves the engine compartment.

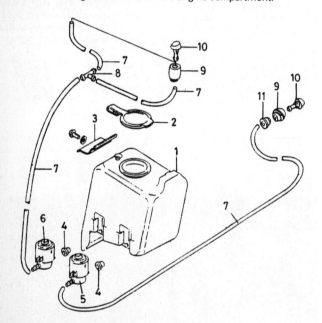

Fig. 12.10 Washer system components (Sec 28)

1   Reservoir
2   Filler cap
3   Reservoir-to-body retaining bracket
4   Washer pump-to-reservoir sealing grommet
5   Rear window washer pump
6   Windscreen washer pump
7   Tube
8   T-piece
9   Nozzle adaptor
10   Nozzle
11   Nozzle-to-body sealing grommet

29 Radio/cassette unit – removal and refitting

Removal
1   If the radio/cassette unit has a security code, de-activate the code temporarily and re-activate it when the battery is re-connected; refer to the instructions and code supplied with the unit.
2   Disconnect the battery negative lead.
3   Actual removal and refitting procedures will vary according to the type of radio fitted, but one of the following will be a reasonably representative procedure (photos).

(a)   If the unit has a finisher on each end of its faceplate, carefully prise these off, and remove the screw from the retaining clip underneath each finisher. Press the retaining clips towards each other to release the unit; reach behind the facia to push the unit out from behind. Disconnect the wiring plugs and aerial lead to remove the unit.

(b)   If the unit has two holes, one above the other, on each end of its faceplate, two standard DIN extraction tools are required to unlock and remove it. The tools may be obtained from an audio accessory outlet, or can be made out of 3 mm (0.12 in) wire rod such as welding rod. Using the tools, push back the clamps on the left and right-hand sides, withdraw the unit, and disconnect the wiring plugs and aerial.

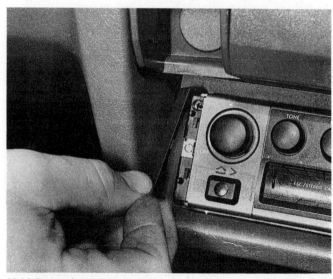

29.3A Remove the finishers from the radio/cassette faceplate ...

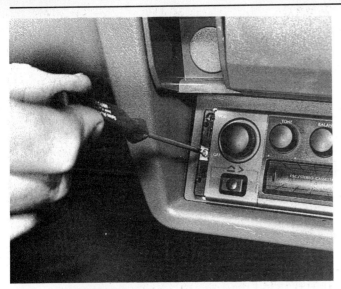

29.3B ... take out the screws ...

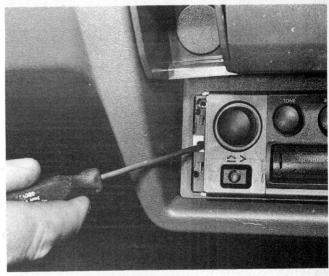

29.3C ... press in the retaining clips ...

29.3D ... and withdraw the unit

30.2 Right-hand loudspeaker – note seat belt warning buzzer
(arrowed)

Refitting
4   Refitting is the reverse of the removal procedure.

30   Loudspeakers – removal and refitting

Removal
1   Remove the footwell trim panel (Chapter 11).
2   Remove the two screws securing the loudspeaker to the footwell trim
panel and withdraw the loudspeaker, then disconnect its wiring (photo).

Refitting
3   Refitting is the reverse of the removal procedure.

31   Radio aerial – general information

1   On models with a factory-fitted sunroof, the radio aerial is a
conductive grid bonded to the inside of the sunroof glass (photo).
2   The aerial is not removable, and if a fault is suspected, rectification
can only be carried out by a Skoda dealer.
3   On models without a sunroof, a conventional roof-mounted aerial
may be fitted. No information on this type of aerial was available at the
time of writing.

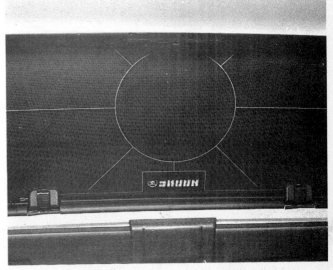

31.1 Radio aerial is bonded to inside of sunroof glass

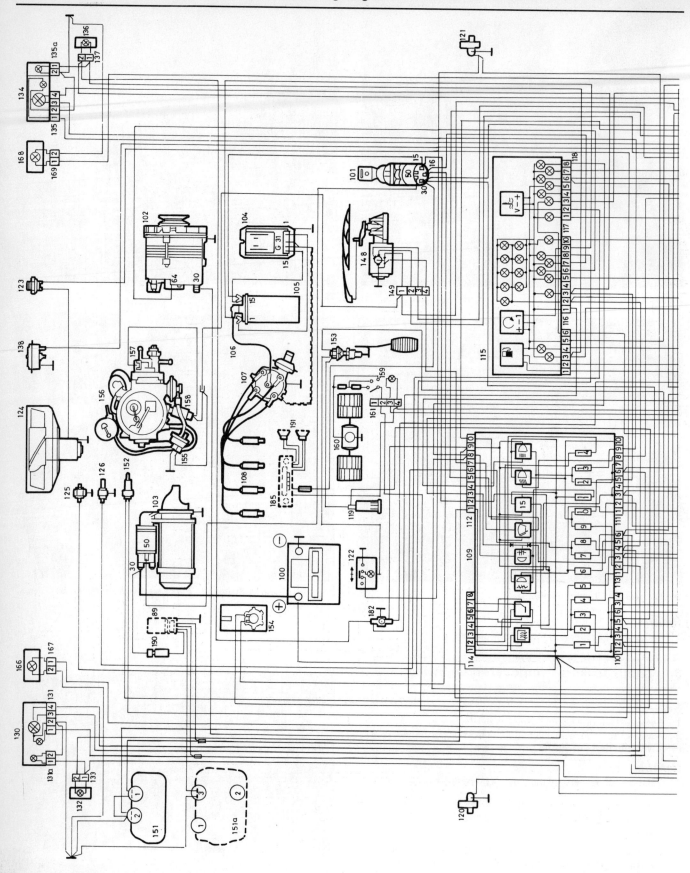

Wiring diagram – all models

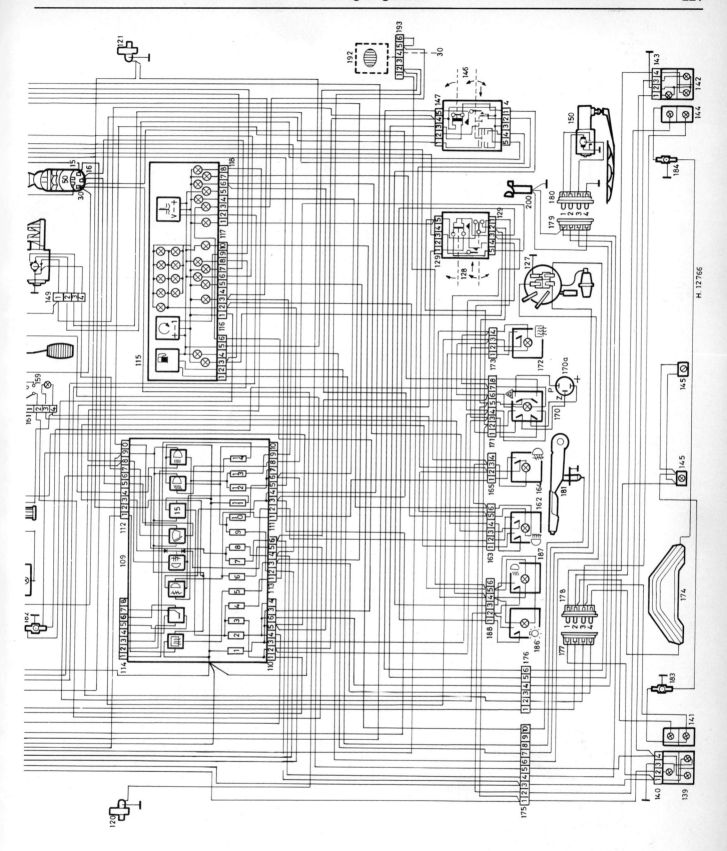

Wiring diagram – all models (continued)

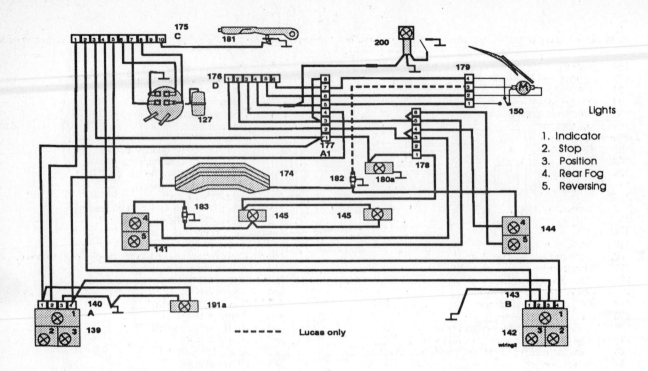

Lights

1. Indicator
2. Stop
3. Position
4. Rear Fog
5. Reversing

– – – – – Lucas only

Rear wiring loom diagram – Estate models

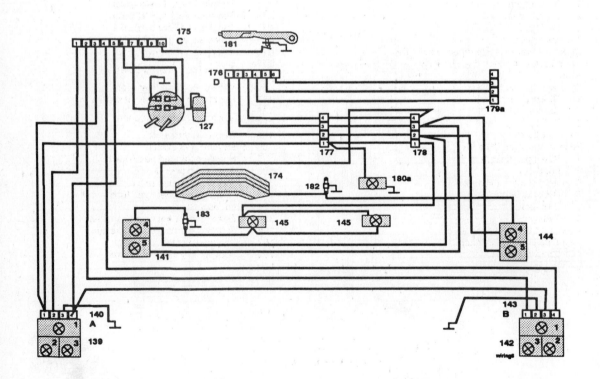

Rear wiring loom diagram – Freeway Van models

Note: *No wiring colour code is available from the manufacturers, and none is used on the wiring diagrams. Not all items are fitted to all models.*

100	Battery
101	Ignition switch connector
102	Alternator
103	Starter motor
104	Electronic ignition unit
105	Ignition coil
106	Ignition coil HT lead
107	Distributor
108	Spark plug HT leads
109	Fusebox
110 to 114	Terminal blocks
115	Instrument cluster
116 to 118	Terminal blocks
119	Inspection light socket
120	Door courtesy light switch, LH
121	Door courtesy light switch, RH
122	Courtesy light with manual switch
123	Radiator cooling fan switch
124	Radiator cooling fan motor
125	Oil pressure switch
126	Coolant temperature sender unit
127	Fuel gauge float – low fuel level warning
128	Direction indicator, horn and headlight dip switch
129	Terminal block
130	Headlight unit, LH
	1 Main beam
	2 Dipped beam
	3 Sidelight
131	Terminal block
132	Direction indicator side repeater light, LH
133	Terminal block
134	Headlight unit, RH
	1 Main beam
	2 Dipped beam
	3 Sidelight
135	Terminal block
136	Direction indicator side repeater light, RH
137	Terminal block
138	Horn
139	Rear light cluster, LH outer
	1 Direction indicator
	2 Stop-light
	3 Tail light
140	Terminal block
141	Rear light cluster, LH inner
	4 Reversing light
	5 Foglight
142	Rear light cluster, RH outer
	1 Direction indicator
	2 Stop-light
	3 Tail light
143	Terminal block
144	Rear light cluster, RH inner
	4 Reversing light
	5 Foglight

145	Number plate light
146	Windscreen/tailgate wash/wipe switch
147	Terminal block
148	Windscreen wiper motor
149	Terminal block
150	Tailgate wiper motor
151	Washer reservoir and washer pumps
	1 Windscreen washer pump
	2 Tailgate washer pump
	3 Headlight washer pump (151a)
152	Reversing light switch
153	Stop-light switch
154	Brake fluid level warning light switch
155	Automatic choke switch (not UK)
156	Carburettor
157	Automatic choke heating
158	Carburettor idle cut-off valve (anti-run-on solenoid)
159	Heater fan switch
160	Heater fan motor
161	Terminal block
162	Rear foglight switch
163	Terminal block
164	Front foglight switch
165	Terminal block
166	Front foglight, LH
167	Terminal block
168	Front foglight, RH
169	Terminal block
170	Hazard warning lights switch
170a	Direction indicator flasher unit
171	Terminal block
172	Heated rear window switch
173	Terminal block
174	Heated rear window element
175	Terminal block (LH 'A' pillar)
176	Terminal block (LH 'A' pillar)
177	Tailgate fixed contact, LH
178	Tailgate spring contact, LH
179	Tailgate fixed contact, RH
179a/ 180	Tailgate spring contact, RH
180a	Van interior light (rear roof)
181	Handbrake warning light switch
182 to 184	Terminal block/earth point
185	Radio/cassette unit
186	Exterior light switch
187	Headlight dipped beam switch
188	Terminal block
189	Headlight washer relay
190	Headlight washer relay fuse
191	Loudspeakers
191a	Estate interior light (LH rear side)
192	Seat belt warning system relay
193	Terminal block
200	Boot light/rechargeable torch

Index

A

About this manual – 5
Accelerator cable – 101
Accelerator pedal – 102
Acknowledgements – 2
Aerial – 219
Air cleaner assembly – 96
Air filter – 40
Alternator – 201, 202
    drivebelt – 48
Antifreeze – 39

B

Battery – 17, 47, 200
Bleeding (brake hydraulic system) – 142
Bodywork and fittings – 47, 180 *et seq*, 186
Bodywork repair – *see colour pages between pages 32 and 33*
Bonnet – 185
    lock and release mechanism – 185
Booster battery starting – 17
Brake
    caliper – 148
    drum – 151
    disc – 149
    fluid – 30, 44
    master cylinder – 143
    pads – 146
    pedal – 138
    pedal crossover linkage – 138
    shoes – 152
Braking system – 44, 135 *et seq*
Braking system warning lights and switches – 157
Bulbs (exterior lights) – 209
Bulbs (interior lights) – 210
Bumpers – 184

C

Cables
    throttle (accelerator) – 101
    clutch – 42, 118
    handbrake – 156
Caliper – 148
Camshaft and followers – 73
Capacities – 30
Carburettor – 102, 104, 105
Charging system – 201
Clutch – 42, 117 *et seq*, 119
Clutch cable – 42, 118
Clutch pedal – 119
Clutch release mechanism – 120
Coil (ignition) – 115
Compression test – 54
Conversion factors – 18
Coolant draining/changing – 38
Coolant level check – 37

Cooling, heating and ventilation systems – 37, 85 *et seq*
Cooling system electrical switches – 89
Cooling system hoses – 86
Crankshaft – 76, 79, 81
Crankshaft oil seals – 65
Cylinder block/crankcase – 76
Cylinder head – 57, 70, 71, 72

D

Dim-dip headlamp system – 213
Dimensions – 6
Distributor – 111
Door window glass and regulator – 191
Door lock and handle components – 189
Doors and hinges – 188
Drivebelt (alternator) – 48
Driveshaft overhaul – 133
Driveshaft rubber gaiters – 43, 132
Driveshafts – 43, 130 *et seq*, 131

E

Electrical fault-finding – 199
Electrical system – 197 *et seq*
Engine – 36, 50 *et seq*, 67, 70, 81, 84
Engine/transmission mounting rubbers – 66
Engine/transmission removal – 68
Exhaust manifold – 107
Exhaust system – 107
Exterior light units – 211

F

Facia – 196
Fault diagnosis – 19 *et seq*
    braking system – 22
    clutch – 21
    cooling system – 21
    driveshafts – 22
    electrical system – 23, 199
    engine – 20
    fuel and exhaust systems – 21
    suspension and steering – 22
    transmission – 21
Flasher unit – 205
Flywheel – 65
Front brake caliper – 44, 148
Front brake disc – 44, 149
Front brake disc shield – 150
Front brake pads – 44, 146
Front hub, carrier and bearing – 162
Front suspension lower arm, pivot bushes and balljoints – 165
Front suspension subframe – 166
Front suspension strut – 163
Front wings – 183
Front-end panel – 183

Fuel and exhaust systems – 39, 95 *et seq*
Fuel filter – 40
Fuel gauge sender unit – 99
Fuel pump – 97
Fuel tank – 100
Fuel tank filler components – 101
Fuses, relays and flasher unit – 205

G

Gearbox – *see* Transmission
Gearchange linkage – 123
Glovebox – 195

H

Handbrake adjustment – 44
Handbrake cables – 156
Handbrake lever – 155
Headlight beam alignment – 211
Headlight alignment control system – 212
Heated rear window – 215
Heater unit – 92
  controls – 94
  control valve – 91
  matrix – 91
Heater/fresh air blower motor – 94
  control switch – 94
Horn – 215
HT leads – 41
Hub (wheel) – 162, 166
Hydraulic pipes and hoses – 44, 143
Hydraulic system – 44, 142

I

Idle speed and mixture – 40
Ignition control unit – 114
Ignition HT coil – 115
Ignition switch – 172
Ignition system – 41, 110 *et seq*, 115
Ignition timing – 41
Inlet manifold – 106
Instrument panel – 213
Interior trim – 193
Introduction to the Skoda Favorit – 5

J

Jacking – 7
Jump starting – 17

L

Light units (exterior) – 211
Locks – 187, 189
Loudspeakers – 219
Lubricants and fluids – 30

M

Main and big-end bearings – 80
Maintenance procedures – 36
Maintenance schedule – 31
Major body damage – 183
Master cylinder – 143

Minor body damage – 181
Mirrors – 192
MOT test checks – 24
Mountings (engine/transmission) – 66

O

Oil
  change (engine) – 36
  change (transmission) – 43
  level check (engine) – 36
  level check (transmission) – 43
  type – 30
Oil cooler – 62
Oil filter – 36
Oil pump – 62
Oil seals – 65, 125

P

Pads (brake) – 146
Pedals – 119, 138
Piston/connecting rod assembly – 74, 78, 83
Piston rings – 81
Pressure-regulating valve (Pick-up) – 150
Pressure-regulating valves (except Pick-up) – 145

R

Radiator cooling fan – 89
Radiator, expansion tank and filler cap – 87
Radio aerial – 219
Radio/cassette unit – 218
Rear brake backplate – 155
Rear brake drum – 44, 151
Rear brake shoes – 44, 152
Rear hub and bearings – 46, 166
Rear stub axle – 167
Rear suspension torsion beam axle – 169
Rear suspension unit – 167
Rear wheel cylinder – 154
Rear window wiper motor – 217
Relays – 205
Repair procedures – 12
Reversing light switch – 126
Rocker cover – 56
Rocker gear – 56
Routine maintenance and servicing – 28 *et seq*
  bodywork and fittings – 47
  braking system – 44
  clutch – 42
  cooling, heating and ventilation systems – 37
  driveshafts – 43
  electrical system – 11
  engine – 36
  fuel, exhaust and emission control systems – 39
  ignition system – 41
  suspension and steering – 45
  transmission – 43

S

Safety first! – 10
  braking system – 137
  cooling system – 85
  electrical system – 198
  fuel system – 96
  ignition system – 110
Seat belt warning system – 215

Seat belts – 47, 193
Seats – 193
Spare parts – 9
Spark plugs – 41
Spark plug conditions – *see colour pages between pages 32 and 33*
Speakers – 219
Speedometer drive – 124
Speedometer drive cable – 214
Starter motor – 204
Starting system – 203
Steering column – 170, 172
Steering gear – 174
Steering gear rubber gaiters – 173
Steering lock/ignition switch – 172
Steering wheel – 170
Stop-light switch – 157
Sump – 64
Suspension and steering – 45, 158 *et seq*
Switches – 89, 94, 126, 157, 172, 207

T

Tailgate – 187
    lock components – 187
    support struts – 187
Thermostat – 88
Throttle cable – 101
Throttle pedal – 102
Timing cover, chain and sprockets – 59
Tools – 13
Top Dead Centre (TDC) for No 1 piston – 55
Towing – 7
Track rod balljoint – 177
Tracking – 177

Transmission – 43, 122 *et seq*, 127
Transmission overhaul – 129
Tyres – 46
Tyre pressures – 29, 46

U

Unleaded petrol – 102

V

Vacuum servo unit – 140, 141
Valve clearances – 36
Vehicle identification numbers – 9

W

Washer system components – 218
Water pump – 90
Weights – 6
Wheel alignment and steering angles – 177
Wheel changing – 7
Wheel cylinders – 44, 154
Wheels and tyres – 46
Windscreen, rear quarterlight and tailgate glass – 186
Windscreen wiper motor and linkage – 215
Wiper arms – 215
Wiring diagrams – 220 *et seq*
Working facilities – 13